OS X
El Capitan™
FOR
DUMMIES®
A Wiley Brand

by Bob "Dr. Mac" LeVitus

OS X El Capitan™ For Dummies®

Published by: **John Wiley & Sons, Inc.,** 111 River Street, Hoboken, NJ 07030-5774, www.wiley.com

Copyright © 2016 by John Wiley & Sons, Inc., Hoboken, New Jersey

Published simultaneously in Canada

For general information on our other products and services, please contact our Customer Care Department within the U.S. at 877-762-2974, outside the U.S. at 317-572-3993, or fax 317-572-4002. For technical support, please visit www.wiley.com/techsupport.

Wiley publishes in a variety of print and electronic formats and by print-on-demand. Some material included with standard print versions of this book may not be included in e-books or in print-on-demand. If this book refers to media such as a CD or DVD that is not included in the version you purchased, you may download this material at http://booksupport.wiley.com. For more information about Wiley products, visit www.wiley.com.

Library of Congress Control Number: 2015952267

ISBN 978-1-119-14961-3 (pbk); ISBN 978-1-119-14964-4 (ebk); ISBN 978-1-119-14963-7 (ebk)

Manufactured in the United States of America

10 9 8 7 6 5 4 3 2 1

Table of Contents

Introduction

*Y*ou made the right choice twice: OS X El Capitan (OS X 10.11) and this book. Take a deep breath and get ready to have a rollicking good time. That's right. This is a computer book, but it's fun. What a concept! Whether you're brand spanking new to the Mac or a grizzled Mac vet, I guarantee that reading this book to discover the ins and outs of OS X El Capitan will make everything easier. The publisher couldn't say as much on the cover if it weren't true!

About This Book

This book's roots lie with my international best seller *Macintosh System 7.5 For Dummies,* an award-winning book so good that long-deceased Mac clone-maker Power Computing gave away a copy with every Mac clone it sold. *OS X El Capitan For Dummies* is the latest revision and has been, once again, completely updated to include all the tasty OS X goodness in El Capitan. In other words, this edition combines all the old, familiar features of previous editions — but is once again updated to reflect the latest and greatest offering from Apple as well as feedback from readers.

Why write a *For Dummies* book about El Capitan? Well, El Capitan is a big, somewhat complicated personal-computer operating system. So I made *OS X El Capitan For Dummies* a not-so-big, not-too-complicated book that shows you what El Capitan is all about without boring you to tears, confusing you, or poking you with sharp objects.

In fact, I think you'll be so darned comfortable that I wanted the title to be *OS X El Capitan Made Easy,* but the publishers wouldn't let me. Apparently, we *For Dummies* authors have to follow some rules, and using *For Dummies* in this book's title is one of them.

And speaking of dummies — remember, that's just a word. I don't think you're a dummy at all — quite the opposite! My second choice for this book's title was *OS X El Capitan For People Smart Enough to Know They Need This Book,* but you can just imagine what Wiley thought of that. ("C'mon, that's the whole point of the name!" they insisted. "Besides, it's shorter our way.")

The book is chock-full of information and advice, explaining everything you need to know about OS X in language you can understand — along with time-saving tips, tricks, techniques, and step-by-step instructions, all served up in generous quantities.

Another rule we *For Dummies* authors must follow is that our books cannot exceed a certain number of pages. (Brevity is the soul of wit, and all that.) So I wish I could have included some things that didn't fit. Although I feel confident you'll find what you need to know about OS X El Capitan in this book, some things bear further looking into, including these:

- ✔ **Information about many of the applications (programs) that come with OS X El Capitan:** An installation of OS X El Capitan includes roughly 55 applications, mostly located in the Applications folder and the Utilities folder within it. I'd love to walk you through each one of them, but that would have required a book a whole lot bigger, heavier, and more expensive than this one.

  I brief you on the handful of bundled applications essential to using OS X El Capitan and keep the focus there — namely, Calendar, Contacts, Messages, Mail, Safari, TextEdit, and the like — as well as several important utilities you may need to know how to use someday.

- ✔ **Information about Microsoft Office, Apple lifestyle and productivity apps (iMovie, Numbers, Pages, and so on), Adobe Photoshop, Quicken, and other third-party applications:** Okay, if all the gory details of all the bundled (read: *free)* OS X El Capitan applications don't fit here, I think you'll understand why digging into third-party applications that cost extra was out of the question.

- ✔ **Information about programming for the Mac:** This book is about *using* OS X El Capitan, not writing code for it. Dozens of books — most of which are two or three times the size of this book — cover programming on the Mac; this one doesn't.

Conventions Used in This Book

To get the most out of this book, you need to know how I do things and why. Here are a few conventions I use in this book to make your life easier:

- ✔ When I want you to open an item in a menu, I write something like Choose File ➪ Open, which means, "Pull down the File menu and choose the Open command."

- ✔ Stuff you're supposed to type appears in bold type, **like this**.

- ✔ Web addresses and things that appear onscreen are shown in a special monofont typeface, `like this`. (If you're reading an e-book version of this book, web addresses are clickable links.)

- ✔ For keyboard shortcuts, I write something like ⌘+A, which means to hold down the ⌘ (Command) key and then press the A key on the keyboard.

Foolish Assumptions

Although I know what happens when you make assumptions, I've made a few anyway. First, I assume that you, gentle reader, know nothing about using OS X — beyond knowing what a Mac is, that you want to use OS X, that you want to understand OS X without having to digest an incomprehensible technical manual, and that you made the right choice by selecting this particular book. And so I do my best to explain each new concept in full and loving detail. Maybe that's foolish, but . . . that's how I roll.

Oh, and I also assume that you can read. If you can't, ignore this paragraph.

Beyond the Book

I have written a lot of extra content that you won't find in this book. Go online to find the following:

- **Cheat Sheet:** www.dummies.com/cheatsheet/osxelcapitan
- **Additional articles:** www.dummies.com/extras/osxelcapitan
- **Updates to this book, if any:** www.dummies.com/extras/osxelcapitan

Icons Used in This Book

Little round pictures (icons) appear off to the left side of the text throughout this book. Consider these icons miniature road signs, telling you a little something extra about the topic at hand. Here's what the different icons look like and what they all mean.

Look for Tip icons to find the juiciest morsels: shortcuts, tips, and undocumented secrets about El Capitan. Try them all; impress your friends!

When you see this icon, it means that this particular morsel is something that I think you should memorize (or at least write on your shirt cuff).

Put on your propeller-beanie hat and pocket protector; these parts include the truly geeky stuff. It's certainly not required reading, but it must be interesting or informative, or I wouldn't have wasted your time with it.

Read these notes very, very, very carefully. (Did I say *very?*) Warning icons flag important cautionary information. The author and publisher won't be responsible if your Mac explodes or spews flaming parts because you ignored a Warning icon. Just kidding. Macs don't explode or spew (with the exception of a few choice PowerBook 5300s, which won't run El Capitan anyway). But I got your attention, didn't I?

These icons represent my ranting or raving about something that either bugs me or makes me smile. When I'm ranting, imagine foam coming from my mouth. Rants and raves are required to be irreverent, irrelevant, or both. I try to keep them short, for your sake.

Well, now, what could this icon possibly be about? Named by famous editorial consultant Mr. Obvious, this icon highlights all things new and different in OS X El Capitan.

Where to Go from Here

The first few chapters of this book are where I describe the basic things that you need to understand to operate your Mac effectively. If you're new to Macs and OS X El Capitan, start there.

OS X El Capitan is only slightly different from previous Mac operating systems, and the first part of the book presents concepts so basic that if you've been using a Mac for long, you might think you know it all — and okay, you might know most of it. But remember that not-so-old-timers need a solid foundation, too. So here's my advice: Skim through stuff you already know and you'll get to the better stuff sooner.

I would love to hear how this book worked for you. So please send me your thoughts, platitudes, likes and dislikes, and any other comments. Did this book work for you? What did you like? What didn't you like? What questions were unanswered? Did you want to know more (or less) about something? Tell me! I have received more than 100 suggestions about previous editions, many of which are incorporated here. So please (please!) keep up the good work! Email me at ElCapitan4Dummies@boblevitus.com. I appreciate your feedback, and I *try* to respond to all reasonably polite email within a few days.

So what are you waiting for? Go! Enjoy the book!

Part I

Introducing OS X El Capitan: The Basics

getting started

with

OS X El Capitan

In this part . . .

- ✏ In the beginning: The most basic of basics including how to turn on your Mac

- ✏ A gentle introduction to the El Capitan Finder and its Desktop

- ✏ Your Dock: Making it work harder for you

- ✏ Everything you need to know about El Capitan's windows, icons, and menus (oh my)!

- ✏ All the bad puns and wisecracks you've come to expect

- ✏ A plethora of Finder tips and tricks to make life with El Capitan even easier (and more fulfilling)

OS X El Capitan 101 (Prerequisites: None)

In This Chapter

▶ Understanding what an operating system is and is not

▶ Turning on your Mac

▶ Getting to know the startup process

▶ Turning off your Mac

▶ Avoiding major Mac mistakes

▶ Pointing, clicking, dragging, and other uses for your mouse

▶ Getting help from your Mac

*C*ongratulate yourself on choosing OS X, which stands for (Mac) *Operating System X* — and that's the Roman numeral *ten,* not the letter *X* (pronounced *ten,* not *ex*). You made a smart move because you scored more than just an operating system (OS) upgrade. OS X El Capitan includes several new features that make using your Mac easier and dozens of improvements under the hood that help you do more work in less time.

In this chapter, I start at the very beginning and talk about OS X in mostly abstract terms; then I move on to explain what you need to know to use OS X El Capitan successfully.

If you've been using OS X for a while, most of the information in this chapter may seem hauntingly familiar; a number of features that I describe haven't changed from previous versions of OS X. But if you decide to skip this chapter because you think you have all the new stuff figured out, I assure you that you'll miss at least a couple of things that Apple didn't bother to tell you (as if you read every word in OS X Help — the only user manual Apple provides — anyway!).

Tantalized? Let's rock.

One last thing: If you're about to upgrade to El Capitan from an earlier version of OS X, you might want to peruse the article on installing and reinstalling El Capitan in full and loving detail, found at `www.dummies.com/extras/osxelcapitan`.

Gnawing to the Core of OS X

The operating system (that is, the *OS* in *OS X*) is what makes a Mac a Mac. Without it, your Mac is a pile of silicon and circuits — no smarter than a toaster.

"So what does an operating system do?" you ask. Good question. The short answer is that an OS controls the basic and most important functions of your computer. In the case of OS X and your Mac, the operating system

- Manages memory
- Controls how windows, icons, and menus work
- Keeps track of files
- Manages networking and security
- Does housekeeping (No kidding!)

Other forms of software, such as word processors and web browsers, rely on the OS to create and maintain the environment in which they work their magic. When you create a memo, for example, the word processor provides the tools for you to type and format the information and save it in a file. In the background, the OS is the muscle for the word processor, performing crucial functions such as the following:

- Providing the mechanism for drawing and moving the onscreen window in which you write the memo
- Keeping track of the file when you save it
- Helping the word processor create drop-down menus and dialogs for you to interact with
- Communicating with other programs
- And much, much more (stuff that only geeks could care about)

So, armed with a little background in operating systems, take a gander at the next section before you do anything else with your Mac.

One last thing: As I mention in this book's Introduction (I'm repeating it here only in case you normally don't read introductions), OS X El Capitan comes with more than 50 applications. Although I'd love to tell you all about each and every one, I have only so many pages at my disposal.

The Mac advantage

Most of the world's personal computers use Microsoft Windows (although more and more people are switching to the Mac). But you're among the lucky few to have a computer with an OS that's intuitive, easy to use, and (dare I say?) fun. If you don't believe me, try using Windows for a day or two. Go ahead. You probably won't suffer any permanent damage. In fact, you'll really begin to appreciate how good you have it. Feel free to hug your Mac. Or give it a peck on the disc drive slot (assuming that your Mac has one; most, including the MacBook, MacBook Air, and Mac mini at this writing, don't). Just try not to get your tongue caught.

As someone once told me, "Claiming that OS X is inferior to Windows because more people use Windows is like saying that all other restaurants serve food that's inferior to McDonald's."

We might be a minority, but Mac users have the best, most stable, most modern all-purpose operating system in the world, and here's why: Unix, on which OS X is based, is widely regarded as the best industrial-strength operating system on the planet. For now, just know that being based on Unix means that a Mac running OS X will crash less often than an older (pre-OS X) Mac or a Windows machine, which means less

downtime. Being Unix-based also means getting far fewer viruses and encounters with malicious software. But perhaps the biggest advantage OS X has is that when an application crashes, it doesn't crash your entire computer, and you don't have to restart the whole computer to continue working.

By the way, since the advent of Intel-powered Macs a few years ago, you can run Windows natively also on any Mac powered by an Intel processor, as I describe in Chapter 17. Note that the opposite isn't true: You can run Windows on your Mac if you like, but you can't run OS X on a Dell or HP (or any other computer not made by Apple) without serious hacking (which is technically illegal anyway).

And don't let that Unix or Windows stuff scare you. It's there if you want it, but if you don't want it or don't care (like most of us), you'll rarely even know it's there. In fact, you'll rarely (if ever) see the word *Unix* or *Windows* again in this book. As far as you're concerned, Unix under the hood means your Mac will just run and run and run without crashing and crashing and crashing. As for Windows, your Mac can run it if you need it; otherwise, it's just another checklist item on the list of reasons Macs are better.

A Safety Net for the Absolute Beginner (or Any User)

In the following sections, I deal with the stuff that OS X Help doesn't cover — or doesn't cover in nearly enough detail. If you're a first-time Macintosh user, please, *please* read this section of the book carefully; it could save your life. Okay, okay, perhaps I'm being overly dramatic. What I mean to say is that reading this section could save your Mac or your sanity. Even if you're an experienced Mac user, you may want to read this section. Chances are you'll see at least a few things you've forgotten that will come in handy now that you've been reminded of them.

Turning the dang thing on

Okay. This is the big moment — turning on your Mac! Gaze at it longingly first, and say something cheesy, such as, "You're the most awesome computer I've ever known." If that doesn't turn on your Mac (and it probably won't), keep reading.

Apple, in its infinite wisdom, has manufactured Macs with power buttons on every conceivable surface: on the front, side, and back of the computer itself, and even on the keyboard and monitor.

So if you don't know how to turn on your Mac, don't feel bad; just look in the manual or booklet that came with your Mac. It's at least one thing that the documentation *always* covers.

These days, most Macs have a Power button near the keyboard (notebooks) or the back (iMacs). It usually looks like the little circle thingy you see in the margin.

Don't bother choosing Help ⇨ Mac Help, which opens the Help Viewer program. It can't tell you where the switch is. Although the Help program is good for finding out a lot of things, the location of the power button isn't among them. If you haven't found the switch and turned on the Mac, of course, you can't access Help anyway. (D'oh!)

What you should see on startup

When you finally do turn on your Macintosh, you set in motion a sophisticated and complex series of events that culminates in the loading of OS X and the appearance of the OS X Desktop. After a small bit of whirring, buzzing, and flashing (meaning that the OS is loading), OS X first tests all your hardware — slots, ports, disks, random access memory (RAM), and so on. If everything passes, you hear a pleasing musical tone and see the tasteful whitish Apple logo in the middle of your screen, as shown in Figure 1-1.

Here are the things that might happen when you power-up your Mac:

✔ **Fine and dandy:** Next, you might or might not see the OS X login screen, where you enter your name and password. If you do, press Return after you type your name and password, of course, and away you go.

TIP

If you don't want to have to type your name and password every time you start or restart your Mac (or even if you do), check out Chapter 17 for the scoop on how to turn the login screen on or off.

Figure 1-1: This is what you'll see if everything is fine and dandy when you turn on your Mac.

Either way, the Desktop soon materializes before your eyes. If you haven't customized, configured, or tinkered with your Desktop, it should look pretty much like Figure 1-2. Now is a good time to take a moment for positive thoughts about the person who convinced you that you wanted a Mac. That person was right!

Figure 1-2: The OS X El Capitan Desktop after a brand-spanking-new installation of OS X.

✔ **Blue/black/gray screen of death:** If any of your hardware fails when it's tested, you may see a blue, black, or gray screen.

Some older Macs played the sound of a horrible car wreck instead of the chimes, complete with crying tires and busting glass. It was exceptionally unnerving, which might be why Apple doesn't use it anymore.

The fact that something went wrong is no reflection on your prowess as a Macintosh user. Something is broken, and your Mac may need repairs. If this is happening to you right now, check out Chapter 20 to try to get your Mac well again.

If your computer is under warranty, set up a Genius Bar appointment at your nearest Apple Store or dial 1-800-SOS-APPL, and a customer service person can tell you what to do. Before you do anything, though, skip ahead to Chapter 20. It's entirely possible that one of the suggestions there can get you back on track without your having to spend even a moment on hold.

✔ **Prohibitory sign (formerly known as the "flashing question mark on a disk"):** Most users eventually encounter the prohibitory sign shown in the left margin (which replaced the flashing question-mark-on-a-disk icon and flashing folder icon back in OS X Jaguar). This icon means that your Mac can't find a startup disk, hard drive, network server, or DVD-ROM containing a valid Macintosh operating system. See Chapter 20 for ways to ease your Mac's ills.

✔ **Kernel panic:** You shouldn't see this very often, but you may occasionally see a block of text in six languages, including English, as shown in Figure 1-3. This means that your Mac has experienced a *kernel panic,* the most severe type of system crash. If you restart your Mac and see this message again, look in Chapter 20 for a myriad of possible cures for all kinds of ailments, including this one.

Your computer restarted because of a problem. Press a key or wait a few seconds to continue starting up.

Votre ordinateur a redémarré en raison d'un problème. Pour poursuivre le redémarrage, appuyez sur une touche ou patientez quelques secondes.

El ordenador se ha reiniciado debido a un problema. Para continuar con el arranque, pulse cualquier tecla o espere unos segundos.

Ihr Computer wurde aufgrund eines Problems neu gestartet. Drücken Sie zum Fortfahren eine Taste oder warten Sie einige Sekunden.

問題が起きたためコンピュータを再起動しました。このまま起動する場合は、いずれかのキーを押すか、数秒間そのままお待ちください。

电脑因出现问题而重新启动。请按一下按键，或等几秒钟以继续启动。

Figure 1-3: If this is what you're seeing, things are definitely *not* fine and dandy.

How do you know which version of the Mac OS your computer has? Simple:

1. **Choose About This Mac from the menu (the menu with the symbol in the top-left corner of the menu bar).**

A window pops up on your screen, as shown in Figure 1-4. The version you're running appears just below *OS X El Capitan* near the top of the window. Version 10.11 is the release we know as *El Capitan*.

Figure 1-4: See which version of OS X you're running.

If you're curious or just want to impress your friends, OS X version 10.10 was known as Yosemite; 10.9 was known as Mavericks; 10.8 as Mountain Lion; 10.7 as Lion; 10.6 as Snow Leopard; 10.5 as Leopard; 10.4 as Tiger; 10.3 as Panther; 10.2 as Jaguar; 10.1 as Puma; and 10.0 as Cheetah.

2. **(Optional) Click the Overview, Displays, Storage, Support, or Service tabs to see additional information about your Mac and the version of OS X that it's running.**

3. **Click the System Report button to launch the System Information application and see even more details.**

   The System Information app shows you even more about your Mac including bus speed, number of processors, caches, installed memory, networking, storage devices, and much more. You can find more about this useful program in Chapter 19.

Shutting down properly

Turning off the power without shutting down your Mac properly is one of the worst things you can do to your poor Mac. Shutting down your Mac improperly can really screw up your hard or solid-state drive, scramble the contents of your most important files, or both.

If a thunderstorm is rumbling nearby, or you're unfortunate enough to have rolling blackouts where you live, you may really want to shut down your Mac and unplug it from the wall. (See the next section, where I briefly discuss lightning and your Mac.)

To turn off your Mac, always use the Shut Down command from the menu or shut down in one of these kind-and-gentle ways:

- Press the Power button for approximately two seconds and then click the Shut Down button in the Are You Sure You Want to Shut Down Your Computer Now? dialog.

- On keyboards that don't have a Power key, press Control+Eject instead, and then click the Shut Down button that appears in the Are You Sure You Want to Shut Down Your Computer Now? dialog.

You can use a handy keyboard shortcut when the Shut Down button (or any button, for that matter) is highlighted in blue and pulsating slightly. Pressing the Return key is almost always the same as clicking a high-lighted button.

The Are You Sure You Want to Shut Down Your Computer Now? dialog sports a check box option in OS X El Capitan: Reopen Windows When Logging Back In. If you select this check box, your Mac will start back up with the same windows (and applications) that were open when you shut down or restarted. I think that's pretty darn sweet, but you can clear this option if that's not what you want!

Eternally yours . . . now

OS X is designed so that you never have to shut it down. You can configure it to sleep after a specified period of inactivity. (See Chapter 17 for more info on the Energy Saver features of OS X.) If you do so, your Mac will consume very little electricity when it's sleeping and will usually be ready to use (when you press any key or click the mouse) in a few seconds. On the other hand, if you're not going to be using it for a few days, you might want to shut it down anyway.

Note: If you leave your Mac on constantly, and you're gone when a lightning storm or rolling blackout hits, your Mac might get hit by a power surge or worse. So be sure you have adequate protection — say, a decent surge protector

designed specifically for computers — if you decide to leave your Mac on and unattended for long periods. See the section "A few things you should definitely *not* do with your Mac," else-where in this chapter, for more info on lightning and your Mac. Often as not, I leave it on when I'm on the road so that I can access it from my laptop via remote screen sharing. So, because OS X is designed to run 24/7, I don't shut it down at night unless the night happens to be dark and stormy.

One last thing: If your Mac is a notebook and will be enclosed in a bag or briefcase for more than a few hours, turn it off. Otherwise, it could overheat — even in Sleep mode.

Most Mac users have been forced to shut down improperly more than once without anything horrible happening, of course — but don't be lulled into a false sense of security. Break the rules one time too many (or under the wrong circumstances), and your most important files *could* be toast. The *only* time you should turn off your Mac without shutting down properly is when your screen is completely frozen or when your system crashed due to a kernel panic and you've already tried everything else. (See Chapter 20 for what those "everything elses" are.) A really stubborn crash doesn't happen often — and less often under OS X than ever before — but when it does, forcing your Mac to turn off and then back on might be the only solution.

A few things you should definitely not do with your Mac

In this section, I cover the bad stuff that can happen to your computer if you do the wrong things with it. If something bad has already happened to you . . . . I know, I'm beginning to sound like a broken record, but see Chapter 20.

- **Don't unplug your Mac when it's turned on.** Very bad things can happen, such as having your OS break. See the preceding section, where I discuss shutting down your system properly.

  Note that this warning doesn't apply to laptops as long as their battery is at least partially charged. As long as there's enough juice in the battery to power your Mac, you can connect and disconnect its power adapter to your heart's content.

- **Don't use your Mac when lightning is near.** Here's a simple life equation for you: Mac + lightning = dead Mac. 'Nuff said. Oh, and don't place much faith in inexpensive surge protectors. A good jolt of lightning will fry the surge protector and your computer, as well as possibly frying your modem, printer, and anything else plugged into the surge protector. Some surge protectors can withstand most lightning strikes, but those warriors aren't the cheapies that you buy at your local computer emporium. Unplugging your Mac from the wall during electrical storms is safer and less expensive. (Don't forget to unplug your external modem, network hubs, printers, and other hardware that plugs into the wall as well; lightning can fry them, too.)

  For laptops, disconnect the power adapter and all other cables because whatever those cables are connected to could fry and fry your laptop right along with it. After you do that, you can use your laptop during a storm if you care to. Just make sure that it's 100 percent wireless and cableless if you do.

- **Don't jostle, bump, shake, kick, throw, dribble, or punt your Mac, especially while it's running.** Many Macs contain a hard drive that spins at 5,200 revolutions per minute (rpm) or more. A jolt to a hard drive while it's reading or writing a file can cause the head to crash into the disk, which can render many — or all — files on it unrecoverable. Ouch!

Don't think you're exempt if your Mac uses a solid-state drive with no moving parts. A good bump to your Mac could damage other components. Treat your Mac like it's a carton of eggs, and you'll never be sorry.

✔ **Don't forget to back up your data!** If the files on your hard drive mean anything to you, you must back up. Not maybe. *Must.* Even if your most important file is your last saved game of Bejeweled, you still need to back up your files. Fortunately, El Capitan includes an awesome backup utility called Time Machine. (Unfortunately, you need either an external hard drive or an Apple Time Capsule device to take advantage of it.) So I beg you: Please read Chapter 18 now, and find out how to back up before something horrible happens to your valuable data!

I *strongly* recommend that you read Chapter 18 sooner rather than later — preferably before you do any significant work on your Mac. Dr. Macintosh says, "There are only two kinds of Mac users: Those who have lost data and those who will." Which kind do you want to be?

✔ **Don't kiss your monitor while wearing stuff on your lips.** For obvious reasons! Use a clean, soft cloth and/or OmniCleanz display cleaning solution (I love the stuff, made by RadTech; www.radtech.us) to clean your display.

Don't use household window cleaners or paper towels. Either one can harm your display. Use a soft clean cloth (preferably microfiber), and if you're going to use a cleaner, make sure it's specifically designed not to harm computer displays. Finally, spray the cleaner on the *cloth,* not on the screen.

Point-and-click boot camp

Are you new to the Mac? Just figuring out how to move the mouse around? Now is a good time to go over some fundamental stuff that you need to know for just about everything you'll be doing on the Mac. Spend a few minutes reading this section, and soon you'll be clicking, double-clicking, pressing, and pointing all over the place. If you think you have the whole mousing thing pretty much figured out, feel free to skip this section. I'll catch you on the other side.

Still with me? Good. Now for some basic terminology:

✔ **Point:** Before you can click or press anything, you have to *point* to it. Place your hand on your mouse, and move it so that the cursor arrow is over the object you want — like on top of an icon or a button.

If you're using a trackpad, slide your finger lightly across the pad until the cursor arrow is over the object you want.

✔ **Click:** Also called *single click.* Use your index finger to push the mouse button all the way down and then let go so that the button (usually) produces a satisfying clicking sound. (If you have one of the optical Apple Pro mice, you push the whole thing down to click.) Use a single click to highlight an icon, press a button, or activate a check box or window.

In other words, first you point and then you click — *point and click,* in computer lingo.

If you're using a trackpad, press down on it to click.

✔ **Double-click:** *Click twice* in rapid succession. With a little practice, you can perfect this technique in no time. Use a double-click to open a folder or to launch a file or application.

Trackpad users: Press down on the pad two times in rapid succession.

✔ **Control-click:** Hold down the Control key while single-clicking. (Also called *secondary-click* or *right-click.*)

Trackpad users can either hold down the Control key while pressing down on the pad with one finger, or by tapping the trackpad with two fingers without holding down the Control key.

If tapping your trackpad with two fingers didn't bring up the little menu, check your Trackpad System Preferences pane (see Chapter 5).

Control-clicking — the same as right-clicking a Windows system — displays a menu (called a *contextual* or *shortcut menu*). In fact, if you're blessed with a two-or-more-button mouse (such as the Apple Magic Mouse), you can right-click and avoid having to hold down the Control key. (You may have to enable this feature in the Mouse System Preference pane.)

✔ **Drag:** *Dragging* something usually means you have to click it first and hold down the mouse or trackpad button. Then you move the mouse on your desk or mouse pad (or your finger on the trackpad) so that the cursor and whatever you select moves across the screen. The combination of holding down the button and dragging the mouse is usually referred to as *clicking and dragging.*

✔ **Wiggle (or jiggle):** This welcome improvement, introduced in El Capitan (and terrific if I do say so myself) is awesome when you lose track of the pointer on your screen. Just wiggle your mouse back and forth (or jiggle your finger back and forth on the trackpad) for a few seconds and the pointer will magically get much bigger, making it easier to see on the screen. And, of course, when you stop wiggling or jiggling, the pointer returns to its normal size.

✓ **Choosing an item from a menu:** To get to OS X menu commands, you must first open a menu and then choose the option you want. Point at the name of the menu you want with your cursor, press the mouse button, and then drag downward until you select the command you want. When the command is highlighted, finish selecting by letting go of the mouse button.

If you're a longtime Mac user, you probably hold down the mouse button the whole time between clicking the name of the menu and selecting the command you want. You can still do it that way, but you can also click the menu name to open it, release the mouse button, point at the item you want to select, *and then click again.* In other words, OS X menus stay open after you click their names, even if you're not holding down the mouse button. After you click a menu's name to open it, you can even type the first letter (or letters) of the item to select it and then execute that item by pressing the spacebar or the Return key. Furthermore, menus remain open until you click something else.

Go ahead and give it a try . . . I'll wait.

The terms given in the preceding list apply to all Mac laptop, desktop, and tower systems. If you use a MacBook, MacBook Pro, MacBook Air, or Apple Magic Trackpad, however, there are a few more terms — such as *tap, swipe, rotate, pinch,* and *spread* — you'll want to add to your lexicon. You can read all about them in full and loving detail in Chapter 4.

Not Just a Beatles Movie: Help and the Help Menu

One of the best features about all Macs is the excellent built-in help, and OS X El Capitan doesn't cheat you on that legacy: This system has online help in abundance. When you have a question about how to do something, the Help Center is the first place you should visit (after this book, of course).

Clicking the Help menu reveals the Search field at the top of the menu and the Mac Help and New to Mac items. Choosing Mac Help opens the Mac Help window, as shown in Figure 1-5; choosing New to Mac launches Safari and displays a tour of OS X El Capitan.

Though the keyboard shortcut for Help no long appears on the Help menu, the same shortcut as always, Shift+⌘+?, still opens Help.

You can browse Help by clicking a topic in the Table of Contents and then clicking a subtopic. If you don't see the Table of Contents, click the Table of Contents button as shown in Figure 1-5.

Table of Contents button

Figure 1-5: Mac Help is nothing if not helpful.

To search Mac Help, simply type a word or phrase in either Search field — the one in the Help menu itself or the one near the top of the Help window on the right side — and then press Return. In a few seconds, your Mac provides you one or more articles to read, which (theoretically) are related to your question. Usually. If you type **menus** and press Return, for example, you get 49 results, as shown in Figure 1-6.

As long as your Mac is connected to the Internet, search results include articles from the Apple online support database.

Although you don't have to be connected to the Internet to use Mac Help, you do need an Internet connection to get the most out of it. (Chapter 9 can help you set up an Internet connection, if you don't have one.) That's because OS X installs only certain help articles on your hard drive. If you ask a question that those articles don't answer, Mac Help connects to the Apple website and downloads the answer (assuming that you have an active Internet connection). These answers appear when you click See All Help Results near the bottom of Figure 1-6. Click one of these entries, and Help Viewer retrieves the text over the Internet. Although this can sometimes be inconvenient, it's also quite smart. This way, Apple can update the Help system at any time without requiring any action from you.

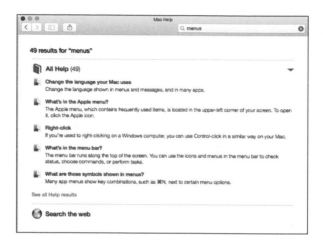

Figure 1-6: You have questions? Mac Help has answers.

Furthermore, after you ask a question and Mac Help has grabbed the answer from the Apple website, the answer remains on your hard drive forever. If you ask for it again — even at a later date — your computer won't have to download it from the Apple website again.

Click Search the Web (near the bottom of Figure 1-6) to launch Safari and perform a web search for the phrase you typed.

Here's a cool feature I like to call automatic visual help cues. Here's how they work:

1. **Type a word or phrase in the Help menu's Search field.**

2. **Select any item that has a menu icon to its left (such as the three items with *Trash* in their names in Figure 1-7).**

   The automatic visual cue — an arrow — appears, pointing at that command in the appropriate menu.

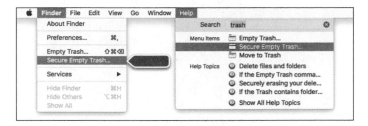

Figure 1-7: If you choose an item with a menu icon, an arrow points to that item in context.

Finally, don't forget that most apps have their own Help systems, so if you want general help with your Mac, you need to first click the Finder icon in the Dock to activate the Finder, and then choose Mac Help from the Finder's Help menu.

Finder   File   Finder   File   Finder   File
File   Preview   File   Preview   File   Preview   File
File   TextEdit   File   TextEdit   File   TextEdit   File

Finder   File   Finder   File   Finder   File   Finder   File
Preview   File   Preview   File   Preview   File   Preview   File
TextEdit   File   TextEdit   File   TextEdit   File   TextEdit   File

2

Desktop and Windows and Menus (Oh My!)

In This Chapter

▶ Understanding the Finder

▶ Checking out the parts of a window

▶ Dealing with dealie-boppers in windows

▶ Resizing, moving, and closing windows

▶ Getting comfortable with menu basics

*T*his chapter introduces important features of OS X, starting with the first things you see when you log in: the Finder and its Desktop. After a quick look around the Desktop, you get a look into two of its most useful features: windows and menus.

Windows are (and have always been) an integral part of Macintosh computing. Windows in the Finder (or, as a PC user would say, "on the Desktop") show you the contents of the hard drive, optical drive, flash (thumb) drive, network drive, disk image, and folder icons. Windows in applications do many things. The point is that windows are part of what makes your Mac a Mac; knowing how they work — and how to use them — is essential.

Menus are another quintessential part of the Macintosh experience. The latter part of this chapter starts you out with a few menu basics. As needed, I direct you to other parts of the book for greater detail. So relax and don't worry. By the end of this chapter, you'll be ready to work with windows and menus in any application that uses them (and most applications, games excluded, do).

Touring the Finder and Its Desktop

The *Finder* is the program that creates the Desktop, keeps track of your files and folders, and is always running. Just about everything you do on your Mac begins and ends with the Finder. It's where you manage files, store documents, launch programs, and much more. If you ever expect to master your Mac, the first step is to master the Finder and Desktop. (The default El Capitan Finder and Desktop appear in the preceding chapter, in Figure 1-2.)

The Finder is the center of your Mac OS experience, so before I go any further, here's a quick description of its most prominent features:

✔ **Desktop:** The Desktop is the area behind the windows and the Dock. In OS X 10.11, the default Desktop picture again honors its namesake, showing El Capitan National Park's spectacular granite wonder, Half Dome.

It's also where your hard drive icon (ordinarily) lives, although if you bought a new Mac with El Capitan preinstalled, there won't be any icons on it at all.

If you don't see your disk icon(s), and you're old-school like me and prefer to always see them on the Desktop, never fear — you'll learn how to enable this behavior in Chapter 4.

The Desktop isn't a window, yet it acts like one. Like a folder window or disk window, the Desktop can contain icons. But unlike most windows, which require a bit of navigation to get to, the Desktop is a great place for things you use a lot, such as oft-used folders, applications, or particular documents.

Some folks use the terms *Desktop* and *Finder* interchangeably to refer to the total Macintosh environment you see after you log in — the icons, windows, menus, and all that other cool stuff. Just to make things confusing, the background you see on your screen — the picture behind your hard drive icon and your open windows — is *also* called the Desktop. In this book, I refer to the application you use when the Desktop is showing as the *Finder*. When I say *Desktop,* I'm talking about the picture background behind your windows and the Dock, which you can use as a storage place for icons if you like.

To make things even more confusing, the Desktop is a full-screen representation of the icons in the Desktop folder inside your Home folder. Don't panic. This will become crystal clear in upcoming pages and chapters.

✔ **Dock:** The Dock is the Finder's main navigation shortcut tool. It makes getting to frequently used icons easy, even when you have a screen full of windows. Like the Desktop, the Dock is a great place for the folders, applications, and specific documents you use most. Besides putting your frequently used icons at your fingertips, it's extremely customizable; read more about it in Chapter 3.

✔ **Icons:** Icons are the little pictures you see in your windows and even on your Desktop. Icons represent the things you work with on your Mac, such as applications (programs), documents, folders, utilities, and more.

✔ **Windows:** Opening most icons (by double-clicking them) makes a window appear. Windows in the Finder show you the contents of hard drive and folder icons, and windows in applications usually show you the contents of your documents. In the sections that follow, you can find the full scoop on El Capitan windows, which, I might add, have undergone significant changes since OS X 10.9 Mavericks.

✔ **Menus:** Menus let you choose to do things, such as create new folders; duplicate files; cut, copy, or paste text; and so on. I introduce menu basics later in this chapter in the "Menu Basics" section; you find details about working with menus for specific tasks throughout this book.

Whereas this chapter offers a basic introduction to the Finder and Desktop, Chapter 6 explains in detail how to navigate and manage your files in the Finder. But before you start using the Finder, it helps to know the basics of working with windows and menus; if these Mac features are new to you, I suggest that you read this entire chapter and pay special attention to Chapter 6 later.

Anatomy of a Window

Windows are a ubiquitous part of using a Mac. When you open a folder, you see a window. When you write a letter, the document that you're working on appears in a window. When you browse the Internet, web pages appear in a window . . . and so on.

For the most part, windows are windows from program to program. You'll probably notice that some programs (Adobe Photoshop or Microsoft Word, for example) take liberties with windows by adding features such as custom toolbars or textual information (such as zoom percentage or file size) that may appear around the edges of the document window.

Don't let it bug you; that extra fluff is just window dressing (pun intended). Maintaining the window metaphor, many information windows display different kinds of information in different *panes,* or discrete sections within the window.

When you finish this chapter, which focuses exclusively on OS X Finder windows, you'll know how to use most windows in most applications.

And so, without further ado, the following list gives you a look at the main features of a typical Finder window (as shown in Figure 2-1). I discuss these features in greater detail in later sections of this chapter.

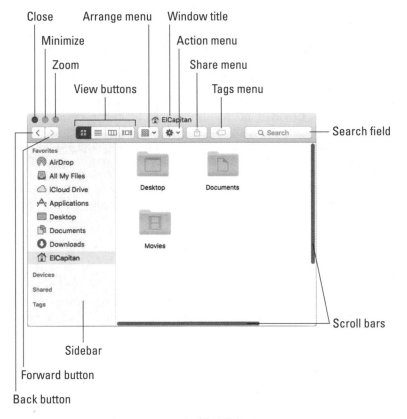

Figure 2-1: A typical Finder window in OS X El Capitan.

If your windows don't look exactly like the one shown in Figure 2-1, don't be concerned. You can make your windows look and feel any way you like. As I explain later in the "Working with Windows" section, moving and resizing windows are easy tasks.

Meanwhile, here's what you see on the toolbar: (clockwise from top left):

- **Close, Minimize, and Zoom buttons:** Shut 'em, shrink 'em, and grow 'em.

- **View buttons:** Choose among four exciting views of your window: Icon, List, Column, and Cover Flow. Find out more about views in Chapter 4.

- **Arrange menu:** Click this little doohickey to arrange this window's icons by Name, Kind, Application, Date Modified, Date Created, Date Last Opened, Date Added, Size, or Tags. Or, of course, by None, which is the default.

- **Action menu:** This button is really a pop-up menu of commands you can apply to currently selected items in the Finder window or on the Desktop. (These are generally the same commands you'd see in the Contextual menu if you right-clicked or Control-clicked the same items.)

- **Window title:** Shows the name of the window.

⌘-click the name of the window to see a pop-up menu with the complete path to this folder (try it). This tip applies to most windows you'll encounter, not just Finder windows. So ⌘-click a window's title, and you'll usually see the path to its enclosing folder on your disk.

You can also have the path displayed at the bottom of *every* Finder window by choosing View⇨Show Path Bar.

- **Share menu:** Another button that's actually a menu; click it to share selected files or folders via email, Messages, or AirDrop.

- **Tags menu:** Yet another button/menu; click it to assign a tag to the selected files or folders.

- **Search field:** Type a string of characters here, and OS X El Capitan digs into your system to find items that match by filename or document contents (yes, words within documents).

- **Scroll bars:** Use the scroll bars for moving around a window.

- **Sidebar:** Frequently used items live here.

- **Forward and Back buttons:** These buttons take you to the next or previous folder displayed in this particular window.

If you're familiar with web browsers, the Forward and Back buttons in the Finder work the same way. The first time you open a window, neither button is active. But as you navigate from folder to folder, these buttons remember your breadcrumb trail so you can quickly traverse backward or forward, window by window. You can even navigate this way from the keyboard by using the shortcuts ⌘+[for Back and ⌘+] for Forward.

The Forward and Back buttons remember only the other folders you've visited that appear in *that* open window. If you've set a Finder Preference so that a folder always opens in a new window — or if you forced a folder to open in a new window, which I describe in a bit — the Forward and Back buttons won't work. You have to use the modern, OS X–style window option, which uses a single window, or the buttons are useless.

Top o' the window to ya!

Take a gander at the top of a window — any window. You see three buttons in the top-left corner and the name of the window in the top center. The three buttons (called "gumdrop buttons" by some folks because they look like, well, gumdrops) are officially known as Close, Minimize, and Zoom, and their colors (red, yellow, and green, respectively unless you've switched to the Graphite appearance in the General System Preference pane as described in Chapter 5) pop off the screen. Here's what they do:

- **Close (red):** Click this button to close the window.
- **Minimize (yellow):** Click this button to minimize the window. Clicking Minimize appears to close the window, but instead of making it disappear, Minimize adds an icon for the window to the right side of the Dock.

See the section about minimizing windows into application icons in Chapter 3 if a document icon doesn't appear in your Dock when you minimize its window.

To view the window again, click the Dock icon for the window that you minimized. If the window happens to be a QuickTime movie, the movie audio continues to play and a tiny still image from the video appears as its icon in the Dock. (I discuss the Dock in detail in Chapter 3.)

- **Zoom (green):** Click a window's green Zoom button, and the window expands to cover the whole screen, including the menu bar.

If you prefer the old behavior, where a window zoomed to the largest size it could but didn't cover the full screen, hold down the Option key when you click the green button.

To shrink the window back to its previous dimensions, slide the cursor up to the very top of the screen, wait for the menu bar to appear, and then click the green Zoom button.

Another way to shrink a full-screen window, at least in the Finder, is to press the Esc key on your keyboard. Sadly, this trick doesn't work with many apps, though it's quite useful in the Finder.

If you prefer the old behavior, where a window zoomed to a larger size but didn't cover the full screen, hold down the Option key when you click the green button.

El Capitan introduces a new feature called Split View to the green gum-drop button. To see Split View in action, press the green button for a moment (that is, perform the first half of a click). Half the screen turns light blue. Without releasing the mouse button, drag to the left or right; the blue tint moves to the left or right side of the screen. Release the mouse button and the window fills the blue half of the screen. The other half of the screen displays miniature versions of all open windows. Hover the cursor over a miniature window to see its name; click a minia-ture window and it fills that half of the screen.

To work in Split View, click either window to activate it and do what you have to do. To activate the other window, click it. To exit Split View, do one of the following:

- Press Esc.

- Move the pointer to the top of the screen; when the buttons (for both windows) reappear, click any button.

- Quit either application.

My colleague at The Mac Observer, John Martellaro, called Split View silly, but I'm not so sure. I think I'll use it for certain tasks (assuming I can remember that it's hiding under the green gumdrop button).

A scroll new world

Yet another way to see more of what's in a window or pane is to scroll through it. Scroll bars appear at the bottom and right sides of any window or pane that contains more stuff — icons, text, pixels, or whatever — than you can see in the window. Figure 2-2, for example, shows two instances of the same window: Dragging the scroll bar on the right side of the smaller window would reveal the icons above and below the six that are currently visible. Dragging the scroll bar on the bottom of the smaller window would reveal items to the left and right of the six that are currently visible.

Scroll bars

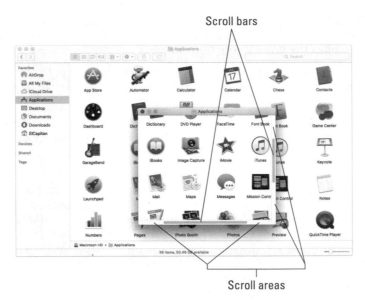

Scroll areas

Figure 2-2: The same window twice; in the front window, you use the scroll bars to see the hidden icons that are visible in the back window.

Simply click and drag a scroll bar to move it up or down or side to side.

If your scroll bars don't look exactly like the ones in Figure 2-2 or work as described in the following list, don't worry. These are System Preferences you can configure to your heart's desire, which you can discover in Chapter 5.

Here are some ways you can scroll in a window:

- **Click a scroll bar and drag.** The content of the window scrolls proportionally to how far you drag the scroll bar.

- **Click in the scroll bar area but don't click the scroll bar itself.** The window scrolls either one page up (if you click above the scroll bar) or down (if you click below the scroll bar). You can change a setting in your General System Preference pane to cause the window to scroll proportionally to where you click.

For what it's worth, the Page Up and Page Down keys on your keyboard function the same way as clicking the white scroll area (the vertical scroll bar only) in the Finder and many applications. These keys don't work in every program, though, so don't become too dependent on them. Also, if you purchased a mouse, trackball, or other pointing device that has a scroll wheel, you can scroll vertically in the active (front) window with the scroll wheel or press and hold down the Shift key to scroll horizontally. Alas, this horizontal scrolling-with-the-Shift-key works in Finder windows but not in all applications. For example, it works in the Apple TextEdit application, but not in Microsoft Word.

✔ **Use the keyboard.** In the Finder, first click an icon in the window and then use the arrow keys to move up, down, left, or right. Using an arrow key selects the next icon in the direction it indicates — and automatically scrolls the window, if necessary. In other programs, you might or might not be able to use the keyboard to scroll. The best advice I can give you is to try it — either it will work or it won't.

✔ **Use a two-finger swipe (on a trackpad).** If you have a notebook with a trackpad or use a Magic Trackpad or Magic Mouse, just move the arrow cursor over the window and then swipe the trackpad with two fingers to scroll.

(Hyper)active windows

To work within a window, the window must be active. The *active* window is always the frontmost window, and *inactive* windows always appear behind the active window. Only one window can be active at a time. To make a window active, click it anywhere — in the middle, on the title bar, or on a scroll bar. It doesn't matter where; just click anywhere to activate it.

The exceptions are the Close, Minimize, and Zoom buttons on inactive windows, which always do what they do, regardless of whether a window is active or inactive.

Look at Figure 2-3 for an example of an active window in front of an inactive window (the Applications window and the Utilities window, respectively).

Figure 2-3: An active window in front of an inactive window.

The following is a list of the major visual cues that distinguish active from inactive windows:

- **The active window's title bar:** By default, the Close, Minimize, and Zoom buttons are bright red, yellow, and green, respectively. If you chose the Graphite Appearance in the General System Preferences pane, they'll be dark gray; the inactive windows' buttons are light gray regardless of Appearance settings.

  This is a nice visual cue. Colored items are active, and gray ones are inactive. Better still, if you move your mouse over an inactive window's gumdrop buttons, they light up in their usual colors so you can close, minimize, or zoom an inactive window without first clicking it to making it active. Neat!

- **The active window's toolbar:** Toolbar buttons are darker and more distinctive; the inactive window's toolbar buttons are light gray and more subdued.

- **The active window's drop shadow:** Notice how the active window has a more prominent shadow? This tricks your eye into thinking the active window is in front of the inactive one.

One last thing: If you're wondering how to resize a window, just hover the cursor over a window's edge or corner or over the dividing line between two panes in the same window (such as the Sidebar and the main area of Finder windows). A helpful little arrow appears as a visual cue that you can now drag the edge, corner, or dividing line to resize the window or pane.

Dialog Dealie-Boppers

Dialogs are special windows that pop up over the active window. You generally see them when you select a menu item that ends in an ellipsis (. . .).

Dialogs can contain a number of standard Macintosh features (I call them *dealie-boppers*), such as radio buttons, pop-up menus, tabs, text entry fields, and check boxes. You see these features again and again in dialogs. Take a moment to look at each of these dealie-boppers in Figure 2-4.

- **Radio buttons:** *Radio buttons* are so named because, like the buttons on your car radio (if you have a very old car), only one at a time can be active. (When they're active, they appear to be pushed in, just like the old radio buttons.) Radio buttons always appear in a group of two or more; when you select one, all the others are automatically deselected.

Radio buttons   Tabs

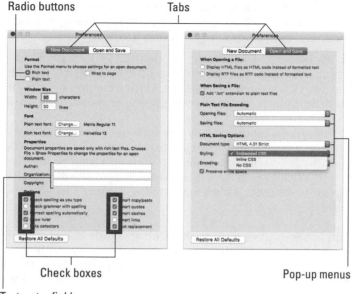

Check boxes   Pop-up menus

Text-entry fields

Figure 2-4: This window offers most dealie-boppers you're ever likely to encounter.

Here's a nifty and undocumented shortcut: You can usually select check boxes and radio buttons by clicking their names (instead of the buttons or boxes).

✔ **Tabs:** When a dialog contains more information than can fit in a single window, the info may be divided among panes denoted by tabs. In Figure 2-4, the New Document tab is selected on the left, and the Open and Save tab is selected on the right.

✔ **Pop-up menus:** These menus are appropriately named because that's what they do: They pop up when you click them. In Figure 2-4, the Styling menu has been clicked and is popped up; the other pop-up menus — Opening Files, Saving Files, Document Type, and Encoding (mostly obscured by the popped-up Styling menu) — are unclicked and unpopped.

You can always recognize a pop-up menu because it appears in a slightly rounded rectangle and has a double-ended arrow symbol (or a pair of triangles, if you like) on the right.

Have you figured out yet what radio buttons, tabs, and pop-up menus have in common? *Hint:* All three enable you to make a single selection from a group of options. (Well, okay, that was more of an answer than a hint.)

✔ **Text-entry fields:** In text entry fields, you type text (including numbers) from the keyboard. In Figure 2-4, the Width, Height, Author, Organization, and Copyright options are text-entry fields.

✔ **Check boxes:** The last dealie-bopper that you see frequently is the check box. In a group of check boxes, you can select as many options as you like. Check boxes are selected when they contain a check mark, and they're deselected when they're empty, as shown in Figure 2-4.

I couldn't find a dialog or window that included all of the aforementioned dealie-boppers as well as the one other dealie-bopper you should become familiar with, the disclosure triangle. If you see a triangle in a dialog box or sheet, try clicking it. If it's a disclosure triangle, it will reveal additional options (or its contents if it's a folder in the Finder's List view, as you'll see in Chapter 6).

Some applications have *tri-state* check boxes (and no, I'm not talking geography here). These special check boxes are empty when nothing in the group is selected, sport an X when everything in the group is selected, and sport a minus sign (–) when some items in the group are selected and some are not.

Working with Windows

In the following sections, I give you a closer look at windows themselves: how you move them, size them, and use them. And although El Capitan windows are similar to windows you've used in other versions of Mac OS (and even, dare I say it, Windows), you may just discover a new wrinkle or two.

If you're relatively new to the Mac, you may want to read this section while sitting at your computer, trying the techniques as you read them. You may find it easier to remember something you read if you actually do it. If you've been using your Mac for a while, you've probably figured out how windows work by now.

Opening and closing windows

To start peering into windows on your Mac, first you need to know how to open and close them. When you're working in the Finder, you can choose the following commands from the File menu. Note that you'll probably find similar commands on the File menu of programs other than the Finder.

You'll use many of these commands frequently, so it would behoove you to memorize the keyboard shortcuts. If you're not sure how keyboard shortcuts work, check out "Using keyboard shortcut commands," later in this chapter.

✓ **New Finder Window (⌘+N):** Opens a new Finder window. In other programs, ⌘+N might open a new document, project, or whatever that program helps you create.

✓ **Open (⌘+O):** Opens the selected item, be it an icon, a window, or a folder.

✓ **Close Window (⌘+W):** Closes the active window. If no windows are open or if no window is selected, the Close Window command is grayed out and can't be chosen. Or if you prefer, you can close a window by clicking the red Close button in the top-left corner.

If you hold down the Option key with the File menu open, the Close Window command changes to Close All. This very useful command enables you to close all open Finder windows. But it shows up only when you press the Option key or use its keyboard shortcut (⌘+Option+W); otherwise, it remains hidden.

Note that several other commands in the File menu transmogrify when you press the Option key. It would be off topic to get into them here, but here's a tip: Press the Option key, and browse all the Finder menus. At least a dozen useful commands appear only when the Option key is pressed. Press it early and often for hidden (often time-saving) commands.

Resizing windows and window panes

If you want to see more (or less) of what's in a window, just hover the pointer over any edge or corner and drag. When the cursor turns into a little double-headed arrow, as shown in Figure 2-5, click and drag to resize the window.

Display windows, like those in the Finder, frequently consist of multiple panes. If you look at Figure 2-5, the line divides the Sidebar to the left of it and the actual contents of the window to the right. When your mouse pointer hovers over the resizing area of this bar, the cursor changes to a vertical bar (or it could be horizontal if the panes are one above the other) with little arrows pointing out of both sides, as shown in the margin and Figure 2-5.

When you see this cursor, you can click and drag anywhere in the dividing line that separates the Sidebar from the rest of the window. Doing so resizes the two panes relative to each other; one gets larger and one gets smaller.

Moving windows

To move a window, click anywhere in a window's gray title bar or toolbar (except on a button, menu, or search field) and drag the window to wherever you want it. The window moves wherever you move the mouse, stopping dead in its tracks when you release the mouse button.

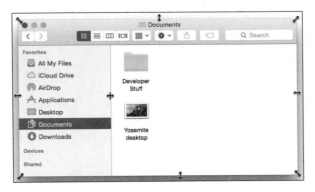

Figure 2-5: Hover the pointer over any corner or edge; when the double-headed arrow (resizer) cursor appears, click and drag to resize the window.

If you can't find the cursor on the screen, wiggle your finger on the trackpad or jiggle the mouse. In El Capitan, these movements magnify the pointer to make it easier to find onscreen.

Shuffling windows

I've already spent plenty of pages giving you the scoop on how to work with windows. But wait. There's more! The commands on the Window menu provide tools you can use to manage your windows.

Here is a brief look at each of the items on the Window menu (and if you're unfamiliar with menus and keyboard shortcuts, I explain how they work later in this chapter):

- **Minimize (⌘+M):** Use this command to minimize the active Finder window to the Dock and unclutter your Desktop. It's the same as clicking the yellow gumdrop button.

- **Zoom:** This command does the same thing as the green gumdrop button. If you've forgotten what the green gumdrop does already, just turn back a few pages to the "Top o' the window to ya!" section and read it again.

- **Cycle through Windows (⌘+`):** Each time you choose this command or use the keyboard shortcut for it, a different window becomes active. So if you have three windows — call 'em Window 1, Window 2, and Window 3 — and you're using Window 1, this command deactivates Window 1 and activates Window 2. If you choose it again, the command deactivates Window 2 and activates Window 3. Choose it one more time, and it deactivates Window 3 and reactivates Window 1.

The next four commands in the Window menu help you manage El Capitan Finder window tabs (which were introduced in OS X 10.9 Mavericks). If you're a fan of tabbed browsing (*à la* Safari), you'll love tabs in a Finder window.

Tabs let you view multiple folders and/or disks in a single window, with each folder or disk in its own tab, as shown in Figure 2-6.

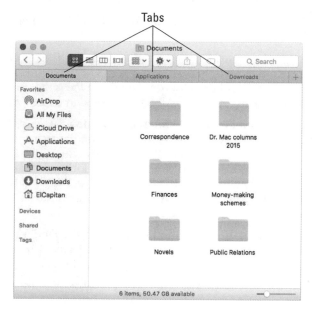

Figure 2-6: I can view the contents of my Downloads, Applications, or Documents folders by merely clicking the appropriate tab.

Tabbed windows are an ingenious way to cram a lot of information into a little space. I've tried a number of third-party utilities that purported to provide tabbed Finder windows, but I've never found one that's reliable and robust enough to continue using. This one, on the other hand, just works. The remaining commands in the Window menu are

✓ **Show Previous Tab (Control+Shift+Tab):** Each time you choose this command or use the keyboard shortcut for it, the previous tab — the one to its left, unless it's the leftmost tab — becomes active. For example, in Figure 2-6, Documents is the active tab. Use this command, and Applications becomes the active tab. Use it a third time, and Downloads becomes active. Because Downloads is the leftmost tab, if you use this command yet again, it wraps around and Documents becomes the active tab again.

- ✔ **Show Next Tab (Control+Tab):** Same as Show Previous Tab except in reverse. Instead of showing the previous tab (the one to the left), this command shows the next tab (the one to the right). Use this command three times in a row (refer to the order shown in Figure 2-6), and you see the Downloads, then the Applications, and finally the Documents tabs again.

- ✔ **Move Tab to New Window (no keyboard shortcut):** Does just what it says: Moves the active tab into a new window of its own.

- ✔ **Merge All Windows (no keyboard shortcut):** Combines all open windows and tabs in one window.

You can click a tab and drag it left or right to change the order. You can also drag and drop a tab from one Finder window to another. The trick is to click right on a tab and drag it *onto the tabs in the target window*. If you release it anywhere else, the tab will be displayed in a new window.

- ✔ **Bring All to Front (no keyboard shortcut):** Windows from different applications can interleave. For example, you can have (from front to back) a Finder window, a Microsoft Word window, an Adobe Photoshop window, another Microsoft Word window, and another Finder window. In this example, choosing Bring All to Front while the Finder is the active application enables you to have both of the Finder windows move in front of those belonging to Word and Photoshop.

If you want to bring all the windows belonging to the Finder (or any other program, for that matter) to the front at the same time, you can also click the appropriate Dock icon (the Finder, in this case).

If you hold down the Option key when you click the Window menu, Minimize Window changes to Minimize All, and the Zoom command changes to Zoom All.

- ✔ **Other items:** The remaining items on the Window menu are the names of all currently open Finder windows. Click a window's name to bring it to the front.

Menu Basics

Mac menus are often referred to as *pull-down menus*. To check out the OS X menus, click the Finder button on the Dock to activate the Finder and then look at the top of your screen. From left to right, you see the Apple menu (), the Finder menu, and six other menus. To use an OS X menu, click its name to make the menu appear and then pull (drag) down to select a menu item. Piece of cake!

Note that menus stay down after you click their names, and stay open until you either select an item or click outside the menu's boundaries.

The ever-changing menu bar

Before you start working with OS X menus, you really, really should know this: *Menu items can change unexpectedly.* Why? Well, the menus you see on the menu bar at the top of the screen always reflect the program that's active at the time. When you switch from the Finder to a particular program — or from one program to another — the menus change immediately to match whatever program you switched to.

Figure 2-7 shows the menu bars for the Finder, Preview, and TextEdit applications.

Figure 2-7: Menu bars change to reflect the active application.

An easy way to tell which program is active is to look at the application menu — it's the leftmost menu with a name, just to the right of the menu. When you're in the Finder, of course, the application menu reads *Finder*. But if you switch to another program (by clicking its icon on the Dock or by clicking any window associated with the program) or launch a new program, that menu changes to the name of the active program.

When you have an application open, the commands on the menu change, too — but just a little bit. What makes this cool is that you have access to some standard application menu items whether you're running Mail or Safari. For example, most (but not all) applications have Cut, Copy, and Paste commands in their Edit menus, and Open, Save, and Print commands in their File menus. You can find much more about commands for applications in Part III, which explains how applications that come with OS X El Capitan can help you get things done.

Contextual menus: They're sooo contextual!

Contextual menus (also called *shortcut menus*) list commands that apply only to the item that is currently selected. Contextual menus might be available in windows, on icons, and in most places on the Desktop.

To see whether a contextual menu is available, either hold down the Control key and click — which you can call a *Control-click* to sound cool to your Mac friends — or, for those with two or more buttons on their mice, *right-click*. Finally, most Mac laptops (as well as the Magic Trackpad and the Magic Mouse) let you click the trackpad using two fingers to simulate a right-click or Control-click.

If this doesn't work for you, launch System Preferences and click the Trackpad icon. Click the Point & Click tab and make sure that Click with Two Fingers is selected and also that the Secondary Click check box is enabled.

Another reason the contextual menu might not appear is that they are available only if any of their commands make sense for the item that you Control-click or right-click. That's why people call 'em *contextual!* They're specific to the current context, which is whatever is selected or Control-clicked.

Figure 2-8, left, shows the contextual menu that appears when you Control-click (or right-click) a document icon. Figure 2-8, right, shows the contextual menu you see when you Control-click the Desktop.

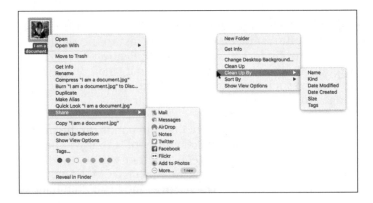

Figure 2-8: Only relevant items appear in a contextual menu.

Contextual menus are also available in most applications. Open your favorite app and try Control-clicking to find out whether those menus are there. In most cases, using a contextual menu is a quick way to avoid going to the menu bar to choose a command. In some programs — such as iMovie, iTunes, and many more — contextual menus are the *only* way to access some commands.

To make the Finder-related contextual menus available to users who didn't have the foresight to purchase this book, Apple added the Actions button to the toolbar. As a result, people who don't know about Control-clicking or right-clicking (or have only one free hand) can access most contextual menu commands by clicking the Actions button and displaying its context-sensitive menu of shortcuts. You, on the other hand, gentle reader, know how to get at these commands without having to run your mouse all the way up to the Action button in the toolbar. Plus, a handful of commands appear in the Control-click/right-click contextual menu but don't appear in the Actions button/menu.

I'm a big fan of multibutton mice, and contextual menus are a huge reason for this preference. Fortunately, Apple now includes a trackpad or a mouse that can discern between a left-click and a right-click (or a two-fingered tap) with all its computers except the Mac mini, which doesn't include a mouse, keyboard, or monitor.

Apple's current mouse doesn't have two physical buttons, but I consider it a multibutton mouse anyway.

If you have an older Mac with a single-button mouse, you may want to replace that mouse with one that offers you at least two buttons. With a multibutton mouse, you need only one hand to access these beautiful little contextual menus.

Get in the habit of Control-clicking (or right-clicking or two-finger clicking) items on your screen. Before you know it, using Contextual menus will become second nature to you.

Recognizing disabled options

Menu items that appear in black on a menu are currently available. Menu items that aren't currently available are grayed out, meaning that they're disabled for the time being. You can't select a disabled menu item.

In Figure 2-9, the File menu on the left is pulled down while nothing is selected in the Finder; this is why many of the menu items are disabled (in gray). These items are disabled because an item (such as a window or icon) must be selected for you to use one of these menu items. For example, the Show Original command is grayed out because it works only if the selected item is an alias. On the right side of Figure 2-9, I selected a document before I pulled down the menu; notice that many of the formerly disabled commands are enabled when an icon is selected. (The Show Original command is still grayed out because the selected icon *is not* an alias.)

Figure 2-9: File menu with nothing selected (left) and with a document icon selected (right); the disabled items are grayed out.

Finally, notice that items that end in an ellipsis (. . .), such as the Burn "I Am a Document" to Disc command in Figure 2-9, will open a dialog with additional options.

Navigating submenus

Some menu items have more menus attached to them, and these are called *submenus,* which are menus that are subordinate to a menu item. If a menu has a black triangle to the right of its name, it has a submenu.

To use a submenu, click a menu name once (to drop the menu down) and then slide your cursor down to any item with a black triangle. When the item is highlighted, move your mouse to the right just slightly. The submenu should pop out of the original menu's item, as shown in Figure 2-10.

Figure 2-10: The Apple menu Recent Items selection, with its submenu popped out.

Under the Apple menu tree

On the far-left side of the menu bar sits a little , which, if you click it, actually displays a menu. No matter what application is active, the menu is always available in the top-left corner of your menu bar.

The menu bar is always available, even with apps that hide it in full-screen mode. To make it reappear, move the pointer to the top of the screen, wait a second or two, and watch the menu bar magically reappear.

From top to bottom, the menu gives you a number of options, including the following:

- **About This Mac:** Choose this item to see what version of OS X you're running, what kind of Mac and processor you're using, how much memory your Mac has, the name of your Startup Disk, and much more. The window sports multiple tabs across the top of the window — Overview, Displays, Storage, and so on.

  Click System Report on the Overview tab to launch the Apple System Information utility; there, you can find out more than you'll probably ever want or need to know about your Mac's hardware and software.

  Click Software Update on the Overview tab to have your Mac check with the mothership (Apple) to see whether any updates are available for OS X; its included applications; third-party applications purchased at the Mac App Store; other Apple-branded applications, such as GarageBand, Final Cut Pro, Pages, or even Apple-branded peripheral devices, such as the iPod or iPhone.

- **System Preferences:** Choose this item to open the System Preferences window (which I discuss further in Chapter 5 and elsewhere).

- **App Store:** Choose this item to launch the Mac App Store.

- **Dock (submenu):** This lets you mess with options for the Dock. Scour Chapter 3 for more info on the Dock.

- **Recent Items:** This lets you quickly access applications, documents, and servers you've used recently, as shown earlier in Figure 2-10.

- **Force Quit:** Use this option only in emergencies. What's an emergency? Use it when an application becomes recalcitrant or otherwise misbehaves or refuses to quit when you say Quit.

Memorize the keyboard shortcut for Force Quit (⌘+Option+Esc). Sometimes a program gets so badly hosed that you can't click anywhere and other keyboard shortcuts won't do anything at all. It doesn't happen often, nor does it happen to everyone. If it should happen to you, calmly press the magic key combo you memorized (⌘+Option+Esc), and the Force Quit Applications dialog (usually) appears. Click the name of the program that's acting up and then click the Force Quit button or press the Return key to make the balky application stop balking.

The reason Force Quit should be used only in an emergency is that if you use it on an application that's working fine and have any unsaved documents, your work since the last time you saved the file will be blown away.

Or not. The Auto Save and Versions features, which first appeared in Lion, are still the default for Apple's own applications. You'll hear more about these features in Chapter 6; if the app you're using supports Auto Save features, you shouldn't lose any (or at least not much) of your work regardless of when you last saved.

✔ **Shut Down options:** These four commands do exactly what their names imply:

  • *Sleep:* Puts your Mac into an energy-efficient state of suspended animation. See the section about Energy Saver in Chapter 17 for details on the Energy Saver System Preference pane and sleeping.

  • *Restart:* Quits all open programs and restarts your Mac. It's quite polite about this task, asking if you want to save any unsaved changes in open documents before complying.

  • *Shut Down:* Turns off your Mac. Refer to Chapter 1 for details.

  • *Log Out:* Quits all open programs and logs you out. Again, your Mac will be ever so polite, asking if you want to save unsaved changes in open documents before complying. When it's done, the login screen appears.

Using keyboard shortcut commands

Most menu items, or at least the most common ones, have *keyboard shortcuts* to help you quickly navigate your Mac without having to haggle so much with the mouse. Using these key combinations activates menu items without using the mouse; to use them, you press the Command (⌘) key and then press another key (or keys) without releasing the ⌘ key. Memorize the shortcuts that you use often.

Learn how to change keyboard shortcuts and even how to create ones of your own in Chapter 5.

Some people refer to the Command key as the *Apple key.* That's because on many keyboards that key has both the pretzel-like Command key symbol (⌘) and an Apple logo (🍎) on it. To avoid confusion, I always refer to ⌘ as the Command key.

For additional information on keyboard shortcuts, visit www.dummies.com/cheatsheet/osxelcapitan.

What's Up, Dock?

In This Chapter

▶ Getting to know the Dock
▶ Discovering the default Dock icons
▶ Talkin' trash
▶ Checking out Dock icons and their menus
▶ Delving into Dock customization

*T*he Dock appears at the bottom of your screen by default, providing quick access to your most often-used applications, documents, and folders.

Many users prefer to have the Dock located on the left or right side of the screen instead of at the bottom. You see how to relocate your Dock (and more) in the coming pages.

Folder icons on the Dock are *stacks,* and they display a fan, grid, or list of their contents when clicked. Other icons on the Dock open an application or document with one click.

The Dock is your friend. It's a great place to put files, folders, and apps you use a lot so that they're always just a click away.

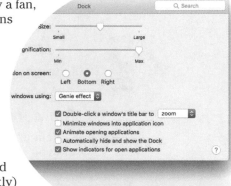

A Dock icon is merely a pointer (also known as an *alias* or *shortcut*) to applications, documents, and folders stored on your hard disk. So, you can add and remove icons from your Dock (as you discover shortly) without affecting the actual applications, documents, and folders. The point is that you don't need to be shy about adding or removing items from your Dock to make it more useful to you.

A Quick Introduction to Your Dock

Take a minute to look at the row of icons at the bottom of your display. That row, good friend, is the *Dock* (shown in Figure 3-1), and those individual pictures are known as *icons* (which I discuss in greater detail momentarily).

Figure 3-1: The Dock and all its default icons.

Icons in the Dock and Launchpad (see Chapter 7) are odd ducks; you activate them with a single click. Most other Finder icons are *selected* (highlighted) when you single-click and *opened* only when you double-click them. So Dock icons (and their Launchpad brethren) are kind of like links on a web page; you need only a single click to open them.

Here's the rundown on what happens when you click Dock icons:

- If it's **an application icon,** the application opens and becomes active. If the application is already open, it becomes active, which brings it and all its windows to the front.

- If it's **a document icon,** that document opens in its appropriate application, which becomes the active application. If that application is already open, it becomes the active application with this document in the front.

- If it's **a folder or disk icon,** a stack, fan, or grid with its contents appears so you can pick an item. If you choose Show in Finder from this menu, the folder's window opens in the Finder.

If the item is open already when you click its Dock icon, it becomes active.

The default icons of the Dock

By default, the Dock contains a number of commonly used OS X applications, and you can also store your own applications, files, or folders there. (I show you how to do that in the "Adding Dock icons" section, later in this chapter.)

But first, look at the items you find in a standard OS X El Capitan Dock. If they aren't familiar to you, they certainly will be as you get to know El Capitan.

I admit that I can't do justice to all the programs that come with OS X El Capitan that aren't, strictly speaking, part of the operating system (OS). Alas, some of the programs in the default Dock are ones you won't be seeing much more of. But I'd hate to leave you wondering what all those icons in the Dock are, so Table 3-1 gives you a brief description of each default Dock icon (moving from left to right onscreen). If additional coverage of an item appears elsewhere in the book, the table tells you where.

Table 3-1		Icons on the Dock	
Icon	*Name*	*What It Is*	*Go Here for More Information*
	Finder	The always-running application that manages the Desktop, files, folders, disks, and more	This chapter, and Chapters 4, 5, and 6
	Launchpad	See all your applications arranged on a grid that looks suspiciously like an iPad or iPhone	Chapter 7
	Safari	A web browser	Chapter 9
	Mail	An email program	Chapter 11
	Contacts	A contact manager application	Chapter 10
	Calendar	Apple calendar program	Chapter 8
	Notes	A program for making notes	Chapter 8
	Reminders	A to-do list and reminder application	Chapter 8
	Maps	Program with maps and driving directions	Chapter 10

(continued)

Table 3-1 *(continued)*

Icon	Name	What It Is	Go Here for More Information
	Photos	Program for managing and editing photographs	Chapter 14
	Messages	Program for sending and receiving text and multimedia messages as well as transferring files to and from and remotely controlling other Macs	Chapters 11 and 12
	FaceTime	A video chat program	Chapter 9
	iTunes	An audio and video player and iPod manager (part of the iLife package and the only one of its apps that's free)	Chapter 13
	iBooks	Where you buy and read books from Apple	Chapter 14
	Mac App Store	Where you buy Mac apps from Apple	Chapter 17
	System Preferences	An application to configure the way many aspects of your Mac work	Chapters 5, 12, and 17
	Divider	Line that separates apps (on the left) and documents or folders (on the right)	This chapter
	Downloads folder	This folder will contain files downloaded by Safari or Mail	Chapter 6
	Trash	Drag files and folders onto this icon to get rid of them or drag removable discs onto it to eject them	This chapter

To get a quick look at the name of a Dock icon, just move (hover) your pointer over any item in the Dock. Like magic, that item's name appears above it (like *Safari* on the left side of Figure 3-4 later in this chapter). And as I describe in the section "Resizing the Dock" (also later in this chapter), you can resize the Dock to make the icons smaller (which also makes them more difficult to see). Hovering the cursor to discover the name of a teeny icon makes this feature even more useful.

It's likely that your Dock won't look exactly like the one shown in Figure 3-1. If you added icons to your Dock before you upgraded to El Capitan, for example, you'll see those icons. If you have Apple apps such as iMovie, GarageBand, Pages, Numbers, or Keynote installed, or you get a new Mac with El Capitan preinstalled, you may see their icons in your Dock. And if you've ever deleted one of the default icons shown in Figure 3-1 from your Dock, it won't come back when you install El Capitan.

If you don't understand what I just said or want to make your Dock look exactly like the one shown in Figure 3-1, I have good news: You find out how to do that and much more before the end of this chapter.

Trash talkin'

The *Trash* is a special container where you put the icons you no longer want to hang around on your hard drive(s). Got four copies of a document named *Letter to the Editor re: Bird Waste Issue* on your hard drive? Drag three of them to the Trash. Tired of tripping over old PDF and DMG files you've down-loaded but no longer need? Drag them to the Trash, too.

To put something in the Trash, just drag its icon onto the Trash icon in the Dock and it will move into the Trash. As with other icons, you know that you've connected with the Trash while dragging when the Trash icon is high-lighted. And as with other Dock icons, the Trash icon's name appears when you move the cursor over the icon.

Two other ways to put items into the Trash are to select the items you want to dispose of and then choose File ⇨ Move to Trash or press ⌘+Delete (⌘+Backspace on some keyboards).

If you accidentally move something to the Trash and want it back right now, you can magically put it back where it came from — but only if the next thing you do is choose Edit ⇨ Undo or press ⌘+Z.

In El Capitan (as in Yosemite), the Finder usually remembers more than one action for Undo and can often undo the last *few* things you did in the Finder. That's the good news. The bad news is that it redoes things in reverse order, so don't wait too long. If you perform several other file-related activities in the Finder, you'll have to Undo all those actions before you can Undo your accidental Move to Trash.

In other words, as soon as you create or rename a folder, move a file from one place to another, drag a different file to the Trash, create an alias, or almost anything that affects a file or folder, choosing Edit ⇨ Undo or pressing ⌘+Z will undo *that* action first.

You'll find that some Finder actions — most of the items in the View menu, for example — don't affect Undo. So if you drag a file to the Trash and then switch views (see Chapter 4), Undo will still un-trash the file.

Even if you do something and can't use Undo, files you drag to the Trash aren't deleted immediately. You know how the garbage in the can on the street curb sits there until the sanitation engineers come by and pick it up each Thursday? El Capitan's Trash works the same way, but without the smell. Items sit in the Trash, waiting for a sanitation engineer (you) to come along and empty it.

So, if you miss the window of opportunity to use the Undo command, don't worry; you can still retrieve the file from the Trash:

- ✔ **To open the Trash and see what's in there,** just click its icon on the Dock. A Finder window called Trash opens, showing you the files it contains (namely, files and folders put in the Trash since the last time it was emptied).

- ✔ **To retrieve an item that's already in the Trash,** drag it back out, either onto the Desktop or back into the folder where it belongs.

  Or use the secret keyboard shortcut: Select the item(s) in the Trash that you want to retrieve and press ⌘+Delete. This technique has the added benefit of magically transporting the files or folders you select from the Trash back into the folder from which they came. And, unlike Undo, the secret keyboard shortcut will work on a file or folder at any time, or at least until the next time you empty the Trash. Try it — it's sweet. And if that doesn't work, you can right-click or Control-click a file and choose Put Back from the contextual menu.

- ✔ **To empty the Trash,** choose Finder ⇨ Empty Trash or press Shift+⌘+Delete. If the Trash window is open and files are in the Trash, you see an Empty button just below its toolbar on the right. Clicking the button, of course, also empties the Trash.

You can also empty the Trash from the Dock by positioning the pointer on the Trash icon and pressing and holding down the mouse button for a second or two, or right-clicking or Control-clicking the Trash icon. The Empty Trash menu item pops up like magic. Move the pointer over Empty Trash to select it and then release the mouse button.

Think twice before you invoke the Empty Trash command. After you empty the Trash, the files that it contained are pretty much gone forever, or at least gone from your hard disk. There is no Undo for Empty Trash. So my advice is: Before you get too bold, read Chapter 18, and back up your hard drive at least once (several times is better). After you get proficient at backups, chances improve greatly that even though the files are technically gone forever from your hard drive, you can get them back if you really want to (from your backups).

The Trash icon shows you when it has files waiting for you there; as in real life, Trash that contains files or folders looks like it's full of crumpled paper (see upcoming Figure 3-2). Conversely, when your Trash is empty, the Trash icon looks, well, empty (refer to Figure 3-1).

Finally, although you can't open a file that's in the Trash, you can select it and use Quick Look (shortcut: ⌘+Y) to see its contents before you decide to use Empty Trash and permanently delete it.

And that's pretty much all there is to know about the Trash.

Opening application menus on the Dock

Single-clicking an application icon on the Dock launches that application — or, if the application is already open, switches you to that application and brings forward all open windows in that application.

But application icons on the Dock — such as Calendar, Safari, iTunes, and others — also hide menus containing some handy commands. (Folder icons in the Dock have a different but no less handy menu, which I discuss in a moment.)

You can make menus for applications on the Dock appear in two ways:

- Press and continue to hold down the mouse button.
- Right-click or Control-click.

If you use a trackpad or a Magic Mouse, a two-finger tap should do the trick.

Do any of the above and you'll see the menu for the icon you clicked or tapped, as shown in Figure 3-2.

Figure 3-2: The Options menu for an application icon (Mac App Store) on the Dock.

From the top (in Figure 3-2):

- ✓ **Remove from Dock:** Removes that application's icon from the Dock (waiting until after you quit the application if it's running). If an application is running and its icon *isn't* already in the Dock, you'll see Add to Dock rather than Remove from Dock.

- ✓ **Open at Login:** Launches this application automatically every time you log in to this user account. This is handy for apps you want to keep running all the time, such as Mail or Safari.

- ✓ **Show in Finder:** Opens the enclosing folder (in this instance, that would be the Applications folder) and selects the application's icon.

The three Assign To items (All Desktops, This Desktop, and None) involve Mission Control, which you'll learn about in Chapter 7.

And finally, choosing Open launches the application.

So there you have it: That's the default Options menu, which is what you'll see for most applications when they aren't open.

There is one last thing: When you press and hold down or right-click/Control-click the Dock icon for an application that's currently running (look for the little dot below its icon), you may see different menus, like the ones shown in Figure 3-3 (clockwise from top left: Safari, Preview, System Preferences, TextEdit, and iTunes).

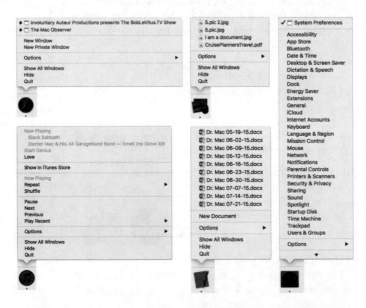

Figure 3-3: Press and hold down or right-click/Control-click an open application's Dock icon, and menus such as these appear.

As you can see, some open applications provide useful program-specific commands or options.

iTunes has one of my favorite Dock menus, letting me control my music from the Dock with options such as Play/Pause, Next or Previous Track, Repeat, and Shuffle.

Other programs, including Preview and Safari in Figure 3-3, offer you a list of open windows with a check mark to indicate the active window.

Finally, the items above the list of open windows for TextEdit (a bunch of Dr. Mac columns in Figure 3-3) are recently used documents.

Reading Dock icon body language

As you use the Dock or when you're just doing regular stuff on your Mac, the Dock icons like to communicate with you. They can't talk, so they have a few moves and symbols that indicate things you might want to know. Table 3-2 clarifies what's up with your Dock icons.

Table 3-2	What Dock Icons Are Telling You
Icon Movement or Symbol	*What It Means*
The icon moves up and out of its place in the Dock for a moment, as shown on the right of Figure 3-4.	You single-clicked a Dock icon, and it's letting you know that you activated it.
The icon does a little bouncy dance when that program is open but isn't *active* (that is, the menu bar isn't showing, and it isn't the frontmost program).	The program desires your attention; give its icon a click to find out what it wants.
A dot appears below its Dock icon, as shown below both Safari icons in Figure 3-4.	This application is open.
An icon that isn't ordinarily in the Dock magically appears.	You see a temporary Dock icon for every program that's currently open until you quit that application. The icon appears because you've opened something. When you quit, its icon magically disappears.

Opening files from the Dock

One useful function of the Dock is that you can use it to open icons easily. The following tips explain several handy ways to open what you need from the Dock:

Figure 3-4: The Safari Dock icon at rest (left) and caught doing the bouncy dance (right).

✔ **You can drag a document icon onto an application's Dock icon.** If the application knows how to handle that type of document, its Dock icon is highlighted, and the document opens in that application. If the application can't handle that particular type of document, the Dock icon isn't highlighted, and you can't drop the document onto it.

I'm getting ahead of myself here, but if the application can't handle a document, try opening the document this way: Select the document icon and choose File➪ Open With, or right-click/Control-click the document icon and use the Open With menu to choose the application you want to open the document with. And, if you hold down the Option key, the Open With command changes to Always Open With, which enables you to change the default application for this document permanently.

✔ **You can find the original icon of any item you see in the Dock by choosing Show in Finder from its Dock menu.** This trick opens the window containing the item's actual icon and thoughtfully selects that icon for you.

Customizing Your Dock

The Dock is a convenient way to get at oft-used icons. By default, the Dock comes stocked with icons that Apple thinks you'll need most frequently (refer to Table 3-1), but you can customize it to contain any icons that you choose, as you discover in the following sections. You also find out how to resize the Dock to fit your new set of icons and how to tell Dock icons what your preferences are.

Adding Dock icons

You can customize your Dock with favorite applications, a document you update daily, or maybe a folder containing your favorite recipes. Use the Dock for anything you need quick access to.

Adding an application, file, or folder to the Dock is as easy as 1-2-3:

1. **Open a Finder window that contains an application, a document file, or a folder you use frequently.**

   You can also drag an icon — including a hard drive icon — from the Desktop or any Finder window.

2. **Click the item you want to add to the Dock.**

   As shown in Figure 3-5, I chose the TextEdit application. (It's high-lighted.) I use TextEdit all the time to type and edit quick text notes, so having its icon on the Dock is very convenient for me.

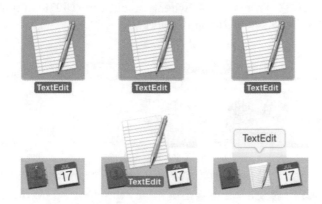

Figure 3-5: Adding an icon to the Dock is as easy as 1-2-3. Just drag the icon onto the Dock.

3. **Drag the icon out of the Finder window and onto the Dock.**

   The icons to the left and right of the new icon magically part to make room for it. Note that the Dock item isn't the actual item. That item remains wherever it was — in a window or on the Desktop. The icon you see in the Dock is a shortcut that opens the item. I briefly mentioned aliases (known as *shortcuts* in the Windows world) earlier, but the icon on the Dock is actually an alias of the icon you dragged onto the Dock.

   Furthermore, when you remove an icon from the Dock, as you find out how to do in a moment, you aren't removing the actual application, document, or folder. You're removing *only its shortcut* from the Dock.

   Folder, disk, document, and URL icons must sit on the right side of the divider line in the Dock; Application icons must sit on the left side of it. Why does the Dock force these rules upon you? I suppose that some-one at Apple thinks this is what's best for you. Who knows? But that's the rule: apps on the left; folders, disks, documents, and URLs on the right.

As long as you follow the rule, you can add several items to either side of the divider line at the same time by selecting them all and dragging the group to that side of the Dock. You can delete only one icon at a time from the Dock, however.

Adding a URL to the Dock works slightly differently. Here's a quick way to add a URL to the Dock:

1. **Open Safari, and go to the page with a URL that you want to save in the Dock.**

2. **Click the small icon that you find to the left of the URL in the address bar and drag it to the right side of the dividing line in the Dock.**

3. **Release the mouse button when the icon is right where you want it.**

   The icons in the Dock slide over and make room for your URL, as shown in Figure 3-6. From now on, when you click the URL icon that you moved to your Dock, Safari opens to that page.

Figure 3-6: Drag the icon from the address bar (top) to the right side of the Dock (middle). The URL appears as a Dock icon (bottom).

If you open an icon that normally doesn't appear in the Dock, and you want to keep its temporary icon in the Dock permanently, you have two ways to tell it to stick around after you quit the program:

- ✔ Control-click (or click and hold down) and choose Keep in Dock from the menu that pops up.

- ✔ Drag the icon (for an application that's currently open) off and then back to the Dock (or to a different position in the Dock) without letting go of the mouse button.

Removing an icon from the Dock

Removing an item from the Dock is as easy as 1-2-3 but without the 3:

1. **Drag its icon off the Dock and onto the Desktop.**

2. **When you see the Remove bubble (see Figure 3-7), release the icon (mouse button).**

3. **There is no Step 3.**

You can also choose Remove from Dock in the item's Dock menu to get it out of your Dock, but this way is way more fun.

Figure 3-7: To remove an icon, drag it off the Dock until it says Remove.

You can't remove the icon of a program that's currently running from the Dock by dragging it. Either wait until you quit the program or choose Remove from Dock in its Dock menu.

Also, note that by moving an icon off the Dock, you aren't moving, deleting, or copying the item itself; you're just removing its icon from the Dock. The item is unchanged. The icon is sort of like a library catalog card: Just because you remove the card from the card catalog doesn't mean that the book is gone from the library.

The Dock in OS X releases prior to Mountain Lion included icons for the Documents and Applications folders. The Dock in Mountain Lion, Yosemite, and El Capitan does not, at least not by default, show those folders. I mention it only because having those folders on the Dock is convenient, and you should consider adding them to your Dock if they aren't already there.

On the other hand, for those with Macs that once ran OS X 10.7 (Lion) or earlier versions and have since been upgraded to El Capitan, your Documents and Applications folders should still be on your El Capitan Dock unless you removed them at some point.

Resizing the Dock

If the default size of the Dock bugs you, you can make the Dock smaller and save yourself a lot of screen real estate. This space comes in especially handy when you add your own stuff to the Dock.

To shrink or enlarge the Dock (and its icons) without opening the Dock Preferences window, follow these steps:

1. **Make the Sizer appear by moving your cursor over the divider line that you find between apps and documents near the right side of the Dock.**

2. **Drag the Sizer down to make the Dock smaller, holding down the mouse button until you find the size you like.**

   The more you drag this control down, the smaller the Dock gets.

3. **To enlarge the Dock again, just drag the Sizer back up.**

   Bam! Big Dock! You can enlarge the Dock until it fills your screen from side to side.

What should you put on your Dock?

Put things on the Dock that you need quick access to and that you use often, or add items that aren't quickly available from menus or a Finder window's Sidebar. If you like using the Dock better than the Finder window's Sidebar (for example), add your Documents, Movies, Pictures, Music, or even your Home folder or hard drive to the Dock.

I suggest adding these items to your Dock:

- ✔ **A word-processing application:** Most people use word-processing software more than any other applications. Just drag the icon for yours to the left side of the Dock, and you're good to go.

  If you don't have a word processor like Microsoft Word or Apple Pages already, give TextEdit a try. It's in every OS X Applications folder, and it's more powerful than you expect from a freebie.

- ✔ **A project folder:** You know — the folder that contains all the documents for your thesis, or all the notes for the biggest project you have at work, or your massive recipe collection . . . whatever. If you add that folder to the Dock, you can access it much quicker than if you have to open several folders to find it.

- ✔ **A special utility or application:** The Preview application is an essential part of my work because I receive a lot of different image files every day. You may also want to add Internet-enabled programs you use (such as Skype, Spotify, Twitter, and so on), your favorite graphics applications (such as Adobe Photoshop or Photoshop Elements), or the game you play every afternoon when you think the boss isn't watching.

✏ **Your favorite URLs:** Save links to sites that you visit every day — the ones you use in your job, your favorite Mac news sites, or your personalized page from an Internet service provider (ISP). Sure, you can make one of these pages your browser's start page or bookmark it, but the Dock lets you add one or more additional URLs. (Refer to the "Adding Dock icons" section, earlier in this chapter, for details.)

You can add several URL icons to the Dock, but bear in mind that the Dock and its icons shrink to accommodate added icons, which makes them harder to see. Perhaps the best idea — if you want easy access to several URLs — is to create a folder full of URLs and put that folder on the Dock. Then you can just press and hold your cursor on the folder (or Control-click the folder) to pop up a menu with all your URLs.

Even though you can make the Dock smaller, you're still limited to one row of icons. The smaller you make the Dock, the larger the crowd of icons you can amass. You have to determine for yourself what's best for you: having lots of icons available in the Dock (even though they might be difficult to see because they're so tiny) or having less clutter but fewer icons on your Dock.

Figure 3-8 shows my Dock, customized to my liking.

Figure 3-8: I keep icons for the apps I use most in my Dock.

After you figure out which programs you use and don't use, it's a good idea to relieve overcrowding by removing the ones you never (or rarely) use from the Dock.

Setting your Dock preferences

You can change a few things about the Dock to make it look and behave just the way you want it to. First, I cover global preferences that apply to the Dock itself. After that, I discuss some preferences that apply only to folder and disk icons in the Dock.

Global Dock preferences

To change global Dock preferences, choose ⌘⇨System Preferences and then click the Dock icon. The System Preferences application opens to the Dock pane (see Figure 3-9).

You can open the Dock System Preferences pane also by right-clicking or Control-clicking the Dock Resizer and choosing Dock Preferences from the shortcut menu.

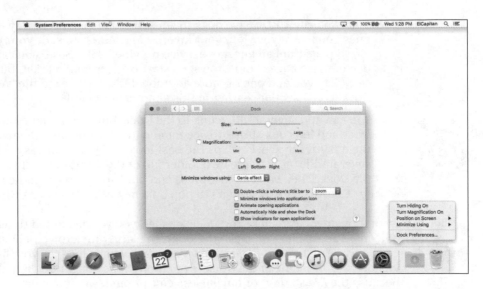

Figure 3-9: The Dock System Preferences pane (left) and the Dock Resizer shortcut menu (right).

Now you can adjust your Dock with the following preferences:

- ✔ **Size:** Note the slider bar here. Move this slider to the right (larger) or left (smaller) to adjust the size of the Dock in your Finder. As you move the slider, watch the Dock change size. (Now, *there's* a fun way to spend a Saturday afternoon!)

  As you add items to the Dock, the icons — and the Dock itself — shrink to accommodate the new ones.

- ✔ **Magnification:** This slider controls how big icons grow when you pass the arrow cursor over them. Or you can deselect this check box to turn off magnification entirely.

- ✔ **Position on Screen:** Choose one of these three radio buttons to attach the Dock to the left side, the right side, or the bottom of your screen (the default). Personally, I prefer it on the bottom, but you should probably try all three before you decide.

- ✔ **Minimize Windows Using:** From this handy pop-up menu (PC users would call it a *drop-down list,* but what the heck; there's no gravity in a computer screen anyway), choose the animation that you see when you click a window's Minimize (yellow by default) button. The Genie Effect is the default, but the Scale Effect seems a bit faster to me.

  Want to amaze your friends? Surreptitiously hold down the Shift key when you click the Minimize button or the Dock icon of a minimized window to make the animation effect play in super slow motion.

✔ **Double-Click a Window's Title Bar to Minimize (or Zoom):** If you select this option, double-clicking anywhere in a window's title bar minimizes (or zooms) the window.

This option achieves the exact same result as clicking the (usually) yellow button in a windows' upper-left corner. The difference is that the Minimize button is a tiny target and way over on the upper-left side of the window, whereas the title bar — the gray area with the window's title (Dock in Figure 3-9) — makes a huge target the width of the window.

✔ **Minimize Windows into Application Icon:** If you select this option, when you minimize a window by clicking its yellow gumdrop button, you won't see a separate Dock icon for that window.

If this option isn't selected, each window you minimize gets its own personal icon on the right side of your Dock.

✔ **Animate Opening Applications:** OS X animates *(bounces)* Dock icons when you click them to open an item. If you don't like the animation, deselect (that is, uncheck) this check box, and the bouncing ceases evermore.

✔ **Automatically Hide and Show the Dock:** Don't like the Dock? Maybe you want to free the screen real estate on your monitor? Then choose the Automatically Hide and Show the Dock check box; after that, the Dock displays itself only when you move the cursor to the bottom of the screen where the Dock would ordinarily appear. It's like magic! (Okay, it's like Windows that way, but I hate to admit it.)

If the Dock isn't visible, deselect the Automatically Hide and Show the Dock check box to bring back the Dock. The option remains turned off unless you change it by checking the Automatically Hide and Show the Dock check box. Choose ➪ Dock ➪ Turn Hiding On (or use its keyboard shortcut ⌘+Option+D).

The keyboard shortcut ⌘+Option+D is a toggle, so it reverses the state of this option each time you use it.

✔ **Show Indicators for Open Applications:** Select this option if you want all open applications to display a little black indicator dot below their Dock, like the Finder icon in Figure 3-1. This program is open, whereas the others — the ones without black dots — are not. If you disable this option (although I can't imagine why you'd ever want to), none of your Dock icons will ever display an indicator dot.

Folder and Disk Dock Icon menu preferences

If you click a folder or disk icon in the Dock, its contents are displayed in a Fan, Grid, or List menu, as shown in Figure 3-10.

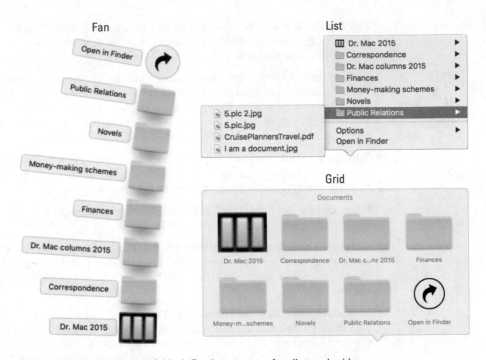

Figure 3-10: My Documents folder's Dock menu as a fan, list, and grid.

If you right-click or Control-click a folder or disk icon in the Dock, its Options menu appears, as shown in Figure 3-11.

Here are the choices on the Options menu:

- ✔ **Sort By** determines the order in which items in the folder or disk appear when you click its Dock icon.

- ✔ **Display As** determines what the Dock icon for a folder or disk looks like. If you choose Stack, the icon takes on the appearance of the last item moved into the folder or disk. If you choose Folder, the Dock icon looks like a folder, as does the Documents folder icon in Figure 3-11.

- ✔ **View Contents As** lets you choose Fan, Grid, or List as the menu type for the folder or disk.

Figure 3-11: The Options menu for my Documents folder.

The default is Automatic, which is to say that the Dock tries to pick the menu for you. I much prefer picking the menu I consider most appropriate for a particular folder or disk. I like List menus best, especially for folders or disks with a lot of subfolders. As you can see in Figure 3-10, the List menu is the only one that lets you see and access folders inside folders (and subfolders inside other subfolders). For folders with images, I like the Grid menu because it displays easily discernible icons for the folder or disk's contents. The Fan menu is fantastic (ha!) when the folder or disk contains only a few items.

✔ **The Options submenu** contains the following items:

 • *Remove from Dock* removes the icon from the Dock.

 • *Show in Finder* opens the window containing the item and selects the item. So, for example, in Figures 3-10 and 3-11, my Home folder would open, and the Documents folder inside it would be selected.

The Dock is your friend. Now that you know how it works, make it work the way you want it to. Put those programs and folders you use most in the Dock, and you'll save yourself a significant amount of time and effort.

4

Delving Deeper into the Finder and Its Desktop

*O*n your Mac, the Finder is your starting point — the centerpiece of your Mac experience, if you will — and it's always available. In Finder windows or the Desktop, you can double-click your way to your favorite application, your documents, or your folders. So in this chapter, I show you how to get the most from the OS X El Capitan Finder and its Desktop.

Introducing the Finder and Its Minions: The Desktop and Icons

The Finder is a special application unlike any other. Its most significant difference from other applications is that it launches automatically when you log in, is always running in the background, and doesn't include a Quit command. The Desktop is a special part of the Finder unlike any other. Finally, icons and windows are the units of currency used by the Finder and Desktop.

Before I tackle any deep thoughts — such as what the Finder does or what the Desktop is — I start with a quick overview of some of the icons you're likely to encounter as you get to know the Finder and Desktop.

Introducing the Desktop

The *Desktop* is the backdrop for the Finder — everything you see behind the Dock and any open windows. The Desktop is always available and is where you can usually find your hard drive icon(s).

This will be a whole lot easier with a picture for reference, so take a gander at Figure 4-1, which is a glorious depiction of a typical OS X El Capitan Finder.

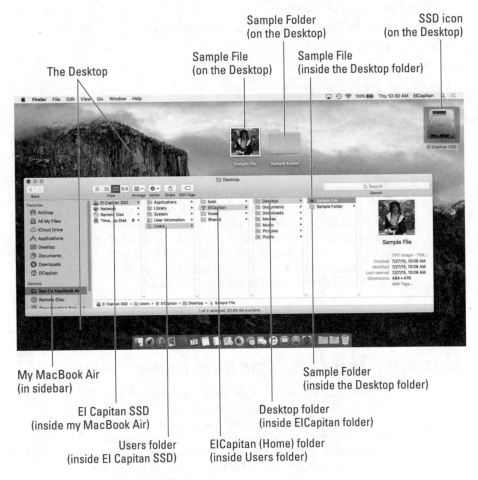

Figure 4-1: A typical Finder and Desktop.

If you're not familiar with the Finder and its Desktop, here are a few tips that will come in handy as you become familiar with the icons that hang out there:

- **Icons on the Desktop behave the same as icons in a window.** You move them and copy them just as you would icons in a window. The only difference is that icons on the Desktop aren't in a window. Because they're on the Desktop, they're more convenient to use.

- **The first icon you need to get to know is the icon for your startup disk (a hard disk or SSD; see Figure 4-2).** You used to be able to find it on the top-right side of the Desktop, as it is in Figure 4-1. Yours probably has the name Macintosh HD unless you've already renamed it. (I renamed my hard drive *El Capitan SSD* in Figure 4-2; see the section on renaming icons in Chapter 6 if you'd like to rename your own hard drive.) You can see how selected and deselected hard drive icons look in Figure 4-2, too.

Figure 4-2: Unselected (left) and selected (right) hard-drive icons.

  El Capitan does not display optical disc and hard drive icons on the Desktop by default. If you don't see your startup disk's icon on the Desktop and you'd like to, select the check box for hard drives in Finder Preferences as described in the "Setting Finder preferences" section, later in this chapter.

- **Other disc or hard drive icons appear on the Desktop by default.** When you insert a CD or DVD or connect an external hard drive, the disc or drive icon appears on the Desktop just below your startup hard-drive icon (space permitting). If it doesn't, open Finder Preferences and select its check box.

  You can find details about working with discs and drives by visiting www.dummies.com/extras/osxelcapitan.

- **You can move an item to the Desktop so you can find it right away.** Simply click its icon in any window and then, without releasing the mouse button, drag it out of the window and onto the Desktop. Then release the mouse button. This will move it from wherever it was to the Desktop.

If you drag an item from an external volume to the Desktop (or any location on your startup disk for that matter), the item is copied, not moved. Put another way, the item is moved if it's on the same disk or volume, or copied if it's on any other disk or volume.

Volume is the generic term for any storage container — a hard disk, solid-state drive, CD, DVD, disk image, or remote disk — that appears in the Sidebar's Devices section.

At the bottom of the Finder window in Figure 4-1 are two optional bars. The lower of the two is called the *status bar;* it tells you how many items are in each window and, if any are selected, how many you've selected out of the total, as well as how much space is available on the hard drive containing this window. And just above the status bar is the *path bar*, which shows the path from the top level of your hard drive to the selected folder (which is Sample File in Figure 4-1). You can show or hide the status bar by choosing View➪Hide/Show Status Bar and show or hide the path bar by choosing View➪Hide/Show Path Bar. Finally, when the toolbar is hidden (see the "Bellying up to the toolbar" section, later in this chapter), the status bar moves to the top of the window (the path bar remains at the bottom of the window no matter what).

Bellying up to the toolbar

In addition to the Sidebar (introduced in Chapter 2) and some good old-fashioned double-clicking, the OS X Finder window offers additional navigation aids on the toolbar — namely, the Back and Forward buttons, as well as the extra-helpful view buttons. You can find other handy features on the Go menu, discussed a little later in this chapter.

In case you didn't know, the toolbar is the light gray band (see Figure 4-3) at the top of the window, which (among other things) displays the window's name. On the toolbar you'll find buttons to navigate quickly and act on selected icons.

Figure 4-3: A Finder window's default toolbar.

To activate a toolbar button, click it once.

You say you don't want to see the toolbar at the top of the window? Okay! Just choose View➪Hide Toolbar or use its keyboard shortcut (⌘+Option+T), and it's gone. (If only life were always so easy!) Want it back? Choose View➪Show Toolbar or use the same keyboard shortcut: ⌘+Option+T.

Alas, hiding the toolbar also hides the useful Sidebar. If only you could choose to hide them independently. . . . I find this fact annoying because I use the Sidebar a lot but don't use the toolbar much. To make matters worse, View➪Hide Sidebar (shortcut: ⌘+Option+S) lets you hide the Sidebar without hiding the toolbar. It's been like this for a long time, and for whatever reason, you *still* can't hide the toolbar while keeping the Sidebar visible! Boo. Hiss.

When you hide the toolbar, opening a folder spawns a *new* Finder window. The default, which is probably what you're used to, is for folders to open in place, displaying their contents in the current window.

The toolbar's default buttons are shown in Figure 4-3.

One last thing: If you customized your toolbar by choosing View➪Customize Toolbar, yours won't look exactly like Figure 4-3.

Here is the lowdown on the toolbar's default buttons, from left to right:

✔ **Forward and Back buttons:** Clicking the Forward and Back buttons displays the folders that you've viewed in this window in sequential order. If you've used a web browser, it's a lot like that.

Here's an example of how the Back button works. Say you're in your Home folder; you click the Favorites button, and a split-second later, you realize that you actually need something in the Home folder. Just a quick click of the Back button and — *poof!* — you're back Home. As for the Forward button, well, it moves you in the opposite direction, through folders that you've visited in this window. Play around with them both; you'll find them invaluable. The keyboard shortcuts ⌘+[for Back and ⌘+] for Forward are even more useful (in my opinion) than the buttons.

✔ **View buttons:** The four view buttons change the way that the window displays its contents.

You have four ways to view a window: Icon, List, Column, and Cover Flow. Some people like columns, some like icons, and others love lists or flows. To each her own. Play with the four Finder views to see which one works best for you. For what it's worth, I usually prefer Column view with a dash of List view thrown in when I need a folder's contents sorted by creation date or size. And the Cover Flow view is great for folders with documents because you can see the contents of many document types right in the window, as I explain shortly.

Don't forget that each view also has a handy keyboard shortcut: ⌘+1 for Icon view, ⌘+2 for List view, ⌘+3 for Column view, and ⌘+4 for Cover Flow view. (Views are so useful you'll find an entire section devoted to them later in this chapter.)

✔ **Arrange:** Click this button to see a pop-up menu with options for displaying this window's contents, as shown in Figure 4-4, which also shows the View menu's Arrange By submenu. Note that unlike the pop-up version, it displays useful keyboard shortcuts next to most commands. I use them often, and you should, too! (Read more about Arrange By in the later section, "What's on the (View) menu?")

In Figure 4-4, I selected Date Last Opened, and my Documents folder reflects that choice.

One last thing: The Arrange By menu works in all four views.

Figure 4-4: The View menu and pop-up menu versions of Arrange By with my Documents folder arranged by Date Last Opened.

✔ **Action:** Click this button to see a pop-up menu of all the context-sensitive actions you can perform on selected icons, as shown in Figure 4-5.

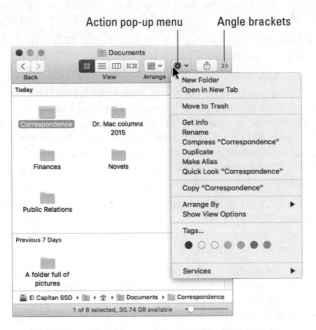

Figure 4-5: Use the Action pop-up menu to perform common actions on selected items.

If you see angle brackets (>>) at the right edge of the toolbar, as shown in Figure 4-5, at least one toolbar item is not visible (the Edit Tags button and the Search box in Figure 4-5). Click the angle brackets to select a hidden item. Or expand the window enough to display all the items in the toolbar.

✔ **Share:** Click here to share the selected items with others. A pop-up menu lets you choose to share via Mail, Messages, or AirDrop for all files and folders, with Facebook, Twitter, and Flickr also appearing if the selected item is an image (.jpeg, .jpg, .tiff, .tif, .png, and so on).

El Capitan's extensible architecture lets you add other services (such as Vimeo or LinkedIn) and apps (such as iPhoto and Aperture) to your Share menu. To manage these extensions, choose More from the Share pop-up menu. Alternatively, you can launch the System Preferences application, click the Extensions icon, and then click the Share Menu item on the left side of the window.

✔ **Tags:** Click here to assign one or more colored tags to selected items. You'll find out more about tags and tagging in the "Customizing Finder Windows" section later in this chapter.

✔ **Search:** The toolbar's Search box is a nifty way to search for files or folders. Just type a word (or even just a few letters), and in a few seconds, the window fills with a list of files that match. You can also start a search by choosing File⇨Find (shortcut: ⌘+F). You find out about Search in Chapter 7.

Figuring out what an icon is

What's an icon? Glad you asked. Each Finder icon represents an item or a container on your hard drive. *Containers* — hard disks, USB thumb drives, folders, CDs, DVDs, shared network volumes, and so on — can contain a virtually unlimited number of application files, document files, and folders.

Icons on the Dock and the Sidebar of Finder windows are not the same as the Finder icons I'll be discussing in this chapter. They're simply convenient pointers to actual Finder icons. Technically, Dock and Sidebar icons are aliases. (If you don't yet know what an alias is, you're going to find out long before the thrilling conclusion of this chapter.)

Anyway, working with icons is easy:

✔ Single-click to select.

✔ Double-click to open.

✔ Click and drag to move.

✔ Release mouse button to drop.

But enough talk. It's time to see what these puppies actually look like.

Identifying your Finder icons in the wild

Although icons all work the same, they come in different kinds, shapes, and sizes. When you've been around the Macintosh for a while, you develop a sixth sense about icons and can guess what an unfamiliar icon contains just by looking at it.

Here are the major icon types:

✔ **Application icons** are *programs* — the software you use to accomplish tasks on your Mac. Mail, Safari, and Calendar are applications. So are Microsoft Word and Adobe Photoshop.

Application icons come in a variety of shapes. For example, application icons are often square-ish, diamond-shaped, rectangular, or just oddly shaped. Figure 4-6 displays application icons of various shapes.

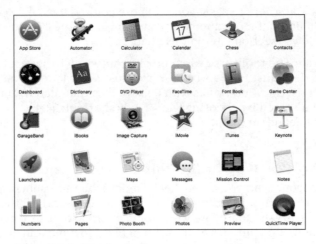

Figure 4-6: Application icons come in many shapes.

✔ **Document icons** are files created by applications. Letters created with TextEdit are documents. This chapter began life as a document created in Microsoft Word. And spreadsheet, PDF, video, image, and song files are all documents.

Document icons are often reminiscent of a piece of paper, as shown in Figure 4-7.

TIP

If your document icons are generic, like the six icons on top in Figure 4-7, but you'd prefer icons that reflect their contents, like the six icons on the bottom in Figure 4-7, open View Options or use the ⌘+J shortcut, and then select the Show Icon Preview check box (see Chapter 21 for additional details about View Options).

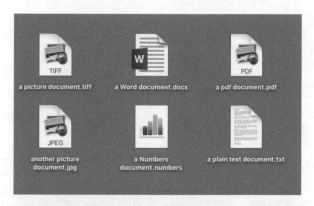

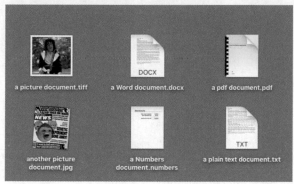

Figure 4-7: Typical document icons.

✔ **Folder and Disk icons** are the Mac's organizational containers. You can put icons — and the applications or documents they stand for — in folders or disks. You can put folders in disks or in other folders, but you can't put a disk inside another disk.

Folders look like, well, manila folders (what a concept) and can contain just about any other icon. You use folders to organize your files and applications on your hard drive. You can have as many folders as you want, so don't be afraid to create new ones. The thought behind the whole folders thing is pretty obvious: If your hard drive is a filing cabinet, folders are its drawers and folders (duh!). Figure 4-8 shows some typical folder icons.

Figure 4-8: The folders in my Home folder are typical folder icons.

And while disks behave pretty much like folders, their icons often look like disks, as shown in Figure 4-9.

✔ **Alias icons** are wonderful — no, make that *fabulous* — organizational tools. I like aliases so much, in fact, that they get a whole entire section to themselves.

Figure 4-9: Disk icons generally look a lot like, well, disks.

If you're looking for details about how to organize your icons in folders, move them around, delete them, and so on, hang in there. Chapter 6 is about organizing and managing files and folders.

Aliases Are Awesome!

An *alias* is a tiny file that automatically opens the file, folder, disk, or network volume that it represents. Although an alias is technically an icon, it's different from other icons; it actually does nothing but open a different icon when you double-click. Put another way, aliases are organizational tools that let you store an icon in more than one place without creating multiple copies of the file.

An alias is very different from a duplicated file. For example, the iTunes application uses around 340 megabytes (MB) of hard drive space. If I were to *duplicate* iTunes, I'd have two files on my hard disk, each requiring around 340MB of disk space.

An *alias* of iTunes, on the other hand, looks just like the original iTunes icon and opens iTunes when you double-click it but uses less than 2MB of hard disk space. So try placing aliases of programs and files you use most often in convenient places such as the Desktop or a folder in your Home folder.

In effect, Microsoft stole the alias feature from Apple. (If you've used Windows, you may know aliases as *shortcuts*.) But what else is new? And for what it's worth, the Mac's aliases don't usually break when you move or rename the original file; Windows shortcuts have been known to do so (although I hear it's less frequent in Windows 10 than in the last version I touched on purpose, which was Windows XP).

Why else do I think that aliases are so great? Well, they open any file or folder (or application) on any hard drive from anywhere else on any hard drive — which is a very good trick. But there are other reasons why I think aliases are awesome:

- ✔ **Convenience:** Aliases enable you to make items appear to be in more than one place, which on many occasions is exactly what you want to do. For example, keep an alias of your word-processor program on your Desktop and another in your Documents folder for quick access. Aliases enable you to open your word processor right away without having to navigate into the depths of your Applications folder every time you need it.

  While you're at it, you might want to put an icon for your word processor in both the Dock and the Sidebar to make it even easier to open your word processor without a lot of clicking.

- ✔ **Flexibility and organization:** You can create aliases and store them anywhere on your hard drive to represent the same document in several different folders. This is a great help when you need to file a document that can logically be stored in any of several folders. If you write a memo to Fred Smith about the Smythe Marketing Campaign to be executed in the fourth quarter, which folder does the document belong in? Smith? Smythe? Marketing? Memos? 4th Quarter? Correct answer: With aliases, it can go in every folder, if you like. Then you can find the memo wherever you look instead of guessing which folder you filed it in.

- ✔ **Integrity:** Some programs must remain in the same folder as their supporting files and folders. Some programs, for example, won't function properly unless they're in the same folder as their dictionaries, thesauruses, data files (for games), templates, and so on. Thus, you can't put the actual icon for such programs on the Desktop without impairing their functionality. An alias lets you access a program like that from anywhere on your hard drive. (And it's probably best to leave all your apps in the Applications folder, where they belong.)

I admit I'm somewhat old-school when it comes to organizing my files in the proper folders (see Chapter 6), but El Capitan's speedy Spotlight search mechanism along with tools like Launchpad and Mission Control (all, not coincidentally, discussed in Chapter 7), as well as the Sidebar's All My Files item, let you find pretty much any file on your disk in seconds.

Creating aliases

When you create an alias, its icon looks the same as the original icon it represents, but the suffix *alias* is tacked onto its name, and a tiny arrow called a *badge* (as shown in the margin) appears in the bottom-left corner of its icon. Figure 4-10 shows an alias and its *parent* icon — the icon that opens if you double-click the alias.

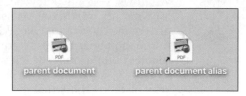

Figure 4-10: An alias (right) and its parent.

To create an alias for an icon, do one of the following:

- ✔ Click the parent icon and choose File➪Make Alias.
- ✔ Click the parent icon and press ⌘+L.
- ✔ Click the parent icon and use the Action menu's Make Alias command (in the Toolbar of all Finder windows).
- ✔ Click an icon while holding down the Control key (or right-click it or tap it with two fingers on a trackpad) and then choose the Make Alias command from the contextual menu that appears. (You can explore contextual menus — which are very cool — in Chapter 2.)
- ✔ Click any file or folder, press and hold down ⌘+Option, and then drag the file or folder while continuing to hold down ⌘+Option. Presto! An alias appears where you release the mouse button.

To organize or not . . .

These days, some users prefer to have all their files — every single one — in one folder, usually the Documents folder. There's nothing to prevent you from putting every file in one folder; OS X El Capitan could care less. That doesn't mean it's a good idea.

First, opening folders with thousands and thousands of files takes longer. And the more files there are, the longer it will be before you can use them. I don't know about you, but I don't like to wait, especially when I don't have to. Second, folders with thousands of files become a nightmare in applications' Open dialogs, like looking for a needle in a haystack.

The good news is that you find out how to tame the Open dialog, how to create and use subfolders, and how to organize your own stuff in Chapter 6. For those who choose to ignore this (good) advice, Chapter 7 introduces Spotlight, which makes it simple to find and open almost any file quickly, including files in the same folder as tens of thousands of other files. But I digress. . . .

When I first create a file, I save it in its proper folder inside the Documents folder in my Home folder. If it's a document that I plan to work on for more than a day or two (such as a magazine article or book chapter), I make an alias of the document (or folder) and plop it on my Desktop. After I finish the article or chapter and submit it to an editor, I trash the alias, leaving the original file safe and sound, filed away in its proper folder, and leaving my Desktop clean and uncluttered.

Deleting aliases

This is a short section because deleting an alias is such an easy chore. To delete an alias, simply drag it onto the Trash icon on the Dock. That's it! You can also Control-click it and choose Move to Trash from the contextual menu that appears (right-click or Control-click or two-finger tap), or select the icon and press ⌘+Delete.

Deleting an alias does *not* delete the parent item. (If you want to delete the parent item, you have to go hunt it down and kill it yourself.)

Hunting down an alias's parent

Suppose that you create an alias of a file, and later you want to delete both the alias and its parent file, but you can't find the parent file. What do you do? Well, you can use the Finder's Find function to find it (try saying that three times real fast), but here are four faster ways to find the parent icon of an alias:

- Select the alias icon and choose File ➪ Show Original.
- Select the alias icon and press ⌘+R.
- Select the alias icon and use the Action menu's Show Original command.
- Control-click (or right-click or two-fingered tap on a trackpad) the alias icon and choose Show Original from the contextual menu.

Any of these methods opens the window containing the parent document with its icon preselected for your convenience.

The View (s) from a Window

Views are part of what makes your Mac feel like *your* Mac. El Capitan offers four views so you can select the best one for any occasion. Some people like one view so much that they rarely (or never) use others. Other people, like me, memorize the keyboard shortcuts to switch views instantly without reaching for the mouse. Try 'em all, and use the one(s) you prefer.

Moving through folders fast in Column view

Column view is a darn handy way to quickly look through a lot of folders at once, and it's especially useful when those folders are filled with graphics files. The Column view is my favorite way to display windows in the Finder.

To display a window in Column view, shown in Figure 4-11, click the Column view button on the toolbar (as shown in the margin), choose View⇨As Columns from the Finder's menu bar, or press ⌘+3.

Preview column

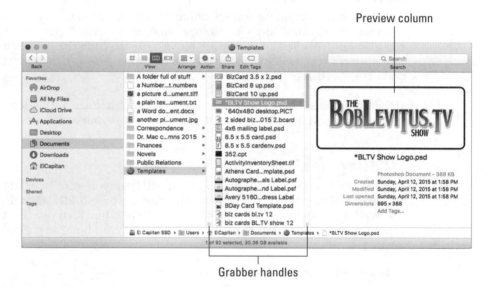

Grabber handles

Figure 4-11: A Finder window in Column view.

Here's how I clicked around in Column view to see the list of folders and files you see in Figure 4-11:

1. When I clicked the Documents icon in the Sidebar, its contents appeared in the column to the right.

2. When I clicked the Templates folder in this column, its contents appeared in the second column.

3. When I clicked *BLTV Show Logo.psd* in the third column, the contents of that file appeared in the fourth column along with information about the file (its size is 511K, it was created on June 9, 2014, and so on).

   The fourth column is displaying a Preview, a feature available in all views by choosing View⇨Show/Hide Preview.

Here are some helpful tips when you're poking around Column view:

- ✔ **You can have as many columns in a Column view window as your screen can handle.** Just drag any edge or corner of the window to enlarge it so new columns have room to open. You can also click the green Zoom (Maximize) button to make the window fill the screen. (*Hint:* To get out of full-screen mode, press Esc or move your cursor to the top of the screen and click the green Zoom button that appears near the top-left corner.)

  If you Option-click the green Zoom button, the window will expand just big enough to display all columns with content in them.

- ✔ **You can use the little grabber handles at the bottom of every column to resize the column width.**

  You'll see the grabber handles shown in Figure 4-11 only if you've selected Always Show Scroll Bars in the General System Preferences pane. If you select either of the other options, Automatically or When Scrolling, the grabber handles disappear. The funny thing is, everything works the same either way. So if you don't see the grabber handles and would like to, open System Preferences, select the General icon, and then select Always Show Scroll Bars. If you don't see grabber handles, click and drag the thin dividing line between the columns to achieve the same result.

  To be specific:

  - If you drag a handle left or right, the column to its left resizes.

  - If you hold down the Option key when you drag, *all* columns resize at the same time.

  - If you double-click one of these little handles, the column to its left expands to the Right Size, which is the width of the widest item in the column.

  - Right- or Control-click any grabber handle for a pop-up menu with three options: Right Size This Column, Right Size All Columns Individually, and Right Size All Columns Equally.

- ✔ **The preview column displays information about the highlighted item to its left, but only if that item isn't a folder or disk.** Why? Well, if it were a folder or disk, its contents would be in this column.

  For many items, the picture you see in the preview column is an enlarged view of the file's icon. You only see a preview (as shown in Figure 4-11) when the selected item is an image file saved in a format that Quick Look (which you'll discover in Chapter 7) can interpret (which is to say, most image file formats, including TIFF, JPEG, PNG, GIF, and PDF to name a few, as well as many other file formats, including Microsoft Word and Pages).

If you don't like having the preview displayed in Column view (but want it to remain in all other views), choose View➪Show View Options and deselect the check box for Show Preview Column. You can do the same for any other view, or turn the preview off in all views by choosing View➪Hide Preview.

Perusing in Icon view

Icon view is a free-form view that allows you to move your icons around within a window to your heart's content. Refer to Figure 4-6 to see the icons in my Applications folder in Icon view.

To display a window in Icon view, click the Icon view button in the toolbar (shown in the margin), choose View➪As Icons from the Finder's menu bar, or press ⌘+1.

The best part of Icon view, at least in my humble opinion, is the Icon Size slider in the lower-right corner of Icon view windows (or in the top-right corner if the Sidebar and toolbar are hidden).

Icon view: The ol' stick-in-the-mud view

In all fairness, I must say that many perfectly happy Macintosh users love Icon view and refuse to even consider anything else. Fine. But as the number of files on your hard drive increases (as it does for every Mac user), screen real estate becomes more and more valuable. In my humble opinion, the only real advantages that Icon view has over Column or List view are the ability to arrange the icons anywhere you like within the window and to put a background picture or color behind your icons. Big deal.

I offer this solution as a compromise: If you still want to see your files and folders in Icon view, make them smaller so that more of them fit in the same space onscreen. This is what I do with any icons I have on my Desktop (because the Desktop allows only Icon view).

To change the size of a window's icons, use the little slider in the bottom-right corner of the Finder window when the status bar is showing. If it's not, choose View➪Status Bar (or press ⌘+/).

Bigger icons make me crazy, but if you like them that way, your Mac can accommodate you. You can also alter the space between icons by dragging the Grid Spacing slider in the View Options window. *Note:* If you like Icon view, consider purchasing a larger monitor; monitors now come in sizes up to 35 inches, and you can even plug your Mac into a big-screen TV if you like things really big.

Listless? Try touring folders in List view

Now I come to my second-favorite view, List view (shown in Figure 4-12). I like it so much because of the little triangles to the left of each folder, known as *disclosure triangles,* which let you see the contents of a folder without actually opening it. This view also allows you to select items from multiple folders at once and move or copy items between folders in a single window. Finally, it's the view used to present Spotlight search results.

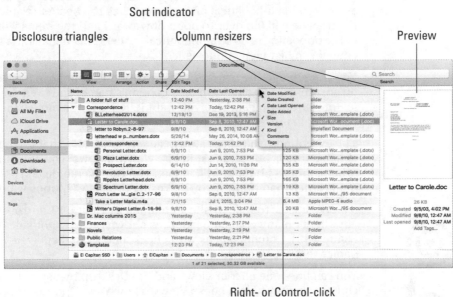

Figure 4-12: A window in List view.

 To display a window in List view, click the List view button on the toolbar (shown in the margin), choose View ⇨ As List from the Finder menu bar, or press ⌘+2.

When you're in List view, the following tips can help you breeze through your folders to find what you're looking for:

 ✔ **To disclose a folder's contents, click the triangle to its left or, if it's selected, press the right-arrow key.** Figure 4-12 shows the result of either clicking the triangle to the left of the Correspondence folder or selecting (highlighting) the Correspondence folder and pressing the right-arrow key.

I pressed Option+→ in Figure 4-12, so all of the Correspondence folder's subfolders (the Old Correspondence folder in this case) also expanded. And if the Old Correspondence folder (or any other folder in the Correspondence folder) had subfolders, they too would have been expanded.

✔ **Click the column header to sort items in List view.** Notice the little triangle at the right edge of the selected column (the Name column in Figure 4-12). That's the column's sorting indicator. If the triangle points upward, as it does in Figure 4-12, the items in the corresponding column are sorted in alphabetical order; if you click the header (Name) again, the triangle will flip over to point downward and the items will be listed in the opposite (reverse alphabetical) order. This behavior is true for all columns in List view windows.

✔ **You can change the order in which columns appear in a window.** To do so, press and hold down on a column's name, and then drag it to the left or right until it's where you want it. Release the mouse button, and the column moves.

The exception (isn't there always an exception?) is that the Name column always appears first in List view windows; you can move all other columns about at will. In fact, you can even hide and show columns other than Name if you like using the View Options window.

It's even easier to hide or show columns by right- or Control-clicking anywhere on any column header (as shown on the right side of Figure 4-12). Column names with check marks are displayed; column names that are unchecked are hidden.

You can fine-tune all four views and the Desktop by using the View Options window. Just choose View➪Show View Options or press ⌘+J. The options you see apply to the active window or the Desktop. Click the Use as Defaults button to apply these options to all windows in that view (that is, Icon, List, Column, or Cover Flow).

✔ **To widen or shrink a column, hover the cursor over the dividing line between that column and drag left or right.** When your cursor is over the dividing line in the header, it changes to a double-headed resizer, as shown in the margin.

You gotta go with the flow

If you're familiar with the Cover Flow feature in iTunes, you're already familiar with the Finder's Cover Flow view.

To display a window in Cover Flow view, click the Cover Flow view button on the toolbar (shown in the margin), choose View➪As Cover Flow from the Finder's menu bar, or press ⌘+4. Figure 4-13 shows Cover Flow view.

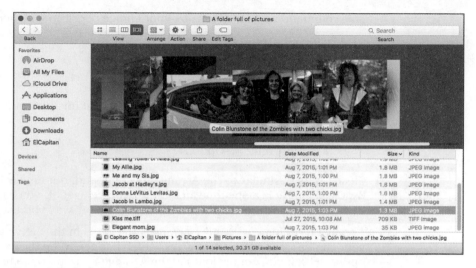

Figure 4-13: A window in Cover Flow mode.

Cover Flow view has two cool features:

✔ The item selected in the list (Zombies lead singer Colin Blunstone with my wife and her friend Kim in Figure 4-13) appears in a preview in the top part of the window.

✔ You can flip through the previews by clicking the images to the left or right of the current preview image or by sliding the scroll bar (above the Date Modified, Size, and Kind columns in Figure 4-13) to the left or right.

What's on the (View) menu?

The Finder View menu offers several commands that might help you peruse your icons more easily:

✔ **Clean Up:** Choose this command to align icons to an invisible grid; you use it to keep your windows and Desktop neat and tidy. (If you like this invisible grid, don't forget that you can turn it on or off for the Desktop and individual windows by using View Options.) Clean Up is available only in Icon view or when no windows are active. If no windows are active, the command instead cleans up your Desktop. (To deactivate all open windows, just click anywhere on the Desktop or close all open windows.)

If any icons are selected (highlighted) when you pull down the View menu, you see Clean Up Selection rather than Clean Up. If you choose this command, it moves only the icons that are currently selected.

✔ **Clean Up By:** This command combines the tidiness of the Clean Up command with the organizational yumminess of the Arrange By command, which I mention earlier in this chapter and discuss in more detail shortly.

This command sorts the icons by your choice of criteria, namely:

- Name (shortcut: ⌘+Option+1)

- Kind (shortcut: ⌘+Option+2)

- Date Modified (shortcut: ⌘+Option+5)

- Date Created (strangely, there's no shortcut for this command)

- Size (shortcut: ⌘+Option+6)

- Tags (shortcut: ⌘+Option+7)

Clean Up By is similar to the Arrange By command, but unlike Arrange By, Clean Up By is a one-time affair. After you've used it, you can once again move icons around and reorganize them any way you like.

✔ **Arrange By:** This command rearranges the icons in the active window in your choice from among nine ways, which happen to be the same nine options (10, if you count None) in the Arrange By pop-up menu (shown earlier in Figure 4-4).

Note that when the Desktop is active, this command is named Sort By; open a window in Icon view and it changes back to Arrange By. Seems weird, but it's true.

Unlike Clean Up By, which is a one-shot command, Arrange By is persistent and will continue to reorganize your icons automatically. In other words, you can't move icons around manually in an arranged window.

One last thing: The Clean Up and Clean Up By commands are available only for those windows viewed as icons. The Arrange By command is available in all four views and remains in effect if you switch to a different view or close the window. To stop the Finder from arranging icons in a window, choose None from either the View ⇨ Arrange By submenu or the toolbar's Arrange pop-up menu, or use the keyboard shortcut, ⌘+Control+0.

If you're like me, you've taken great pains to place icons carefully in specific places on your Desktop. If so, the Clean Up By and Arrange By/Sort By commands will mess up your perfectly arranged Desktop icons. And alas, cleaning up your Desktop is still not something OS X lets you undo.

Finder on the Menu

The Finder menu is packed with useful goodies, most of which are available in its menus. In the following sections, I look at those that pertain specifically to using the Finder.

The actual Finder menu

Here are a few of the main items you can find on the Finder menu:

✔ **About Finder:** Choose this command to find out which version of the Finder is running on your Mac. This menu item isn't particularly useful — or at least not for very long. But when a different application is running, the About Finder item becomes About *application name* and usually gives information about the program's version number, the developers, and any other tidbits that those developers decide to throw in. Sometimes these tidbits are useful, sometimes they're interesting, and sometimes they're both.

✔ **Preferences:** Use the choices here to control how the Finder looks and acts. Find out the details in the "Setting Finder preferences" section, later in this chapter.

✔ **Services:** One of the really cool features of OS X applications is the accessibility of Services. If nothing is selected in the Finder, the Services menu is empty, as shown in the top panel of Figure 4-14. When an icon or icons are selected, there are four Services you can choose, as shown in the middle panel of Figure 4-14. Finally, if a word or words are selected, you have five different options, as shown in bottom pane of Figure 4-14.

In other words, the items you see in the Services menu are context-sensitive, so what you see in yours will depend on what you have selected. If you look in the Services menu and don't find anything interesting, try selecting something else and looking again; you might be pleasantly surprised.

Choose the last item in the menu, Services Preferences, and you can enable dozens of useful Services that aren't available by default.

✔ **Hide Finder (⌘+H):** Use this command when you have Finder windows open, and they're distracting you. Choosing it makes the Finder inactive (another program becomes active) and hides any open Finder windows. To make the Finder visible again, either choose Show All from the application's self-named menu (the one that bears the name of the active application, such as Finder, TextEdit, System Preferences, and so on) or click the Finder icon, shown in the margin here, on the Dock.

The advantage to hiding the Finder — rather than closing or minimizing all your windows to get a clean screen — is that you don't have to open them all again when you're ready to get the windows back. Instead, just choose Show All (to see all windows in all apps) or click the Finder button on the Dock to see all Finder windows.

✔ **Hide Others (Option+⌘+H):** This command hides all windows associated with all running programs except the active program. It appears in most applications' self-named menu and is good for hiding distractions so you can focus on one thing: the unhidden application.

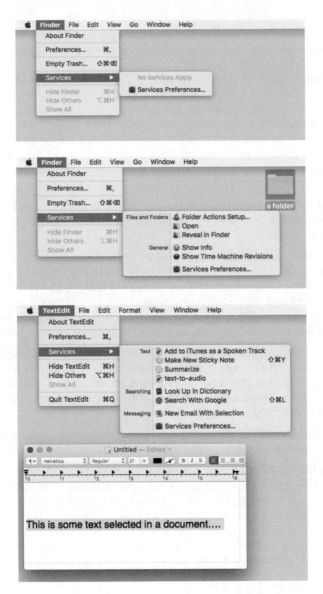

Figure 4-14: Services available with nothing selected (top), an icon selected (middle), and some text selected (bottom).

Another easy way to hide all open applications and windows while activating the Finder is to hold down the ⌘ and Option keys and click the Finder icon on the Dock. This technique works with whatever application is active, not just the Finder. So if you're surfing the web and decide you want to see only Safari's windows on your screen, ⌘+Option-click the Safari button on the Dock, and it will happen instantly.

✔ **Show All:** Use this command as the antidote to both of the Hide commands. Choose this, and nothing is hidden anymore.

Note that all three of these commands require that at least one application be running in addition to the Finder. Put another way, when the Finder is the only app running, these three commands are grayed out and unavailable.

You can achieve much the same effect as all this hide-and-show jazz with Mission Control, which I discuss in Chapter 7.

Finally, if you noticed that the Finder menu's Empty Trash command isn't mentioned here, that's because it gets detailed coverage in Chapter 6.

Like a road map: The current folder's pop-up menu

In the center of the window's title bar is the name of the folder that you're viewing in this window: the highlighted folder. You know that already. What you might not know is that it offers a hidden road map to this folder from the top level. The following steps explain how it works:

1. **⌘-click or Control-click the folder's name in the title bar.**

   A pop-up menu appears, with the current folder (Desktop in Figure 4-15) at the top.

Figure 4-15: Traverse folders from this convenient pop-up menu.

2. **Select any folder in the menu, and it becomes the highlighted folder in the current window. Release the mouse button, and that folder's contents are displayed.**

   As shown in Figure 4-15, the contents of the Desktop folder — seven files — are displayed in the window. If I release the mouse button, the contents of the highlighted folder (ElCapitan) will appear, replacing the contents of the Desktop folder.

3. **After jumping to a new folder, you can click the Back button.**

   Hey, you're right back where you were before you touched that pop-up menu!

Don't forget that you can display the path bar near the bottom of the window (it's showing in Figures 4-12, 4-13, and 4-15) by choosing View➪ Show Path Bar. Then you can double-click any folder displayed in the path bar to open it.

Last but not least, this trick doesn't just work on Finder windows. It also works with the title bar of most document windows (Word, Photoshop, and so on), showing you the path to the folder containing the document you're working on.

Going places with the Go menu

The Go menu is chock-full of shortcuts. The items on this menu take you to places on your Mac — many of the same places you can go with the Finder window toolbar — and a few other places.

The following list gives you a brief look at the items on the Go menu:

- **Back (⌘+[):** Use this menu option to return to the last Finder window that you had open. It's equivalent to the Back button on the Finder toolbar, in case you have the toolbar hidden.

- **Forward (⌘+]):** This command is the opposite of using the Back command, moving you forward through every folder you open. Remember that if you haven't gone back, you can't go forward.

- **Enclosing Folder (⌘+↑):** This command tells the Finder window to display the folder where the currently selected item is located.

- **All My Files (Shift+⌘+F):** This command shows you all your document files at once.

  This is a good time to use the Arrange pop-up menu to sort these files into some semblance of order.

- **Documents (Shift+⌘+O):** You'll probably use this command often because the Documents folder is a great place to save documents you create.

- **Desktop (Shift+⌘+D):** Use this command to display the Desktop folder, which contains the same icons as the Desktop you see behind open windows.

- **Downloads (Option+⌘+L):** This opens your Downloads folder, which is where files you download in Safari, save as attachments in Mail, or receive via AirDrop (explained shortly) are saved by default.

- **Home (Shift+⌘+H):** Use this command to have the Finder window display your Home folder (which is named with your short name).

- **Computer (Shift+⌘+C):** This command tells the Finder window to display the Computer level, showing your Network and all your disks.

- **AirDrop (Shift+⌘+R):** AirDrop lets you share files wirelessly with anyone around you. No setup or special settings are required. Just click the AirDrop icon in the Finder Sidebar, use this menu item, or use the keyboard shortcut, and your Mac automatically discovers other people nearby who are using AirDrop. Bear in mind that not all Macs capable of running El Capitan support AirDrop. ***Note:*** If your Mac is 2009 vintage (or older), AirDrop might not work.

AirDrop now works between Macs and late-model iDevices running iOS 8. Which late model devices, you ask? AirDrop in El Capitan supports file sharing with the iPhone 5 and later, fourth-gen and later iPads, all iPad Minis, and fifth-gen and later iPod Touches.

- ✔ **Network (Shift+⌘+K):** This command displays whatever is accessible on your network in the Finder window.

- ✔ **iCloud Drive (Shift+⌘+I):** This command is new in El Capitan; it opens a window that displays the contents of your iCloud Drive (which you'll hear more about in Chapter 6).

- ✔ **Applications (Shift+⌘+A):** This command displays your Applications folder, the usual storehouse for all the programs that came with your Mac (and the most likely place to find the programs you install).

- ✔ **Utilities (Shift+⌘+U):** This command gets you to the Utilities folder inside the Applications folder in one fell swoop. The Utilities folder is the repository of such useful items as Disk Utility (which lets you erase, format, verify, and repair disks) and Disk Copy (which you use to create and mount disk-image files). You find out more about these useful tools in Chapter 20.

- ✔ **Recent Folders:** Use this submenu to quickly go back to a folder that you recently visited. Every time you open a folder, OS X creates an alias to it and stores it in the Recent Folders folder. You can open any of these aliases from the Recent Folders command on the Go menu.

- ✔ **Go to Folder (Shift+⌘+G):** This command summons the Go to the Folder dialog, shown in Figure 4-16. Look at your Desktop. Maybe it's cluttered with lots of windows, or maybe it's completely empty. Either way, suppose you're several clicks away from a folder that you want to open. If you know the path from your hard drive to that folder, you can type the path to the folder in the Go to the Folder text box — separating folder names with forward slashes (/) — and then click Go to move (relatively) quickly to the folder you need.

The first character you type must also be a forward slash, as shown in Figure 4-16, unless you're going to a subfolder of the current window (Desktop in Figure 4-16).

This particular dialog is a tad clairvoyant in that it tries to guess which folder you mean by the first letter or two that you type. For example, in Figure 4-16, I typed the letter **A** and paused, and the window guessed that I wanted *Applications*. Then I pressed the right-arrow key to accept the guess and typed **/U**, and the window guessed the rest *(tilities)* and filled it in for me.

- ✔ **Connect to Server (⌘+K):** If your Mac is connected to a network or to the Internet, use this command to reach those remote resources.

Figure 4-16: Go to a folder by typing its path.

One last thing: If you're looking for the Library folder inside your Home folder, which used to appear in the Go menu (before OS X 10.7 Lion), it's now hidden for your protection (as I explain in Chapter 6). To reveal it, hold down the Option key and open the Go menu.

Customizing Finder Windows

The Finder is outrageously handy. It not only gives you convenient access to multiple windows, but also offers ways to tweak what you see until you get what works best for you. So whereas earlier sections in this chapter explain what the Finder is and how it works, the following sections ask, "How would you like it to be?"

Adding folders to the Sidebar

Adding whatever folder you like to the Sidebar is easy. All you need to do is select the item you want to add and choose File⇨Add to Sidebar from the menu bar (or press ⌘+Control+T). You can now reach the item by clicking it in any Finder window's Sidebar. And you can move files or folders into that folder by dragging them onto the Sidebar icon for the item.

You can also add folders (but not files) to the Sidebar by dragging them onto the Sidebar.

Be careful not to drag it onto another folder or it will be moved into that folder instead of being added to the Sidebar. You'll see a little line above or below existing folders in the Sidebar; that shows you where this folder will appear if you release the mouse button. If a folder in the Sidebar is highlighted and you don't see the little line, releasing the mouse button will not add the folder to the Sidebar, but will move it into the highlighted folder.

To remove an item from the Sidebar, right- or Control-click the item and choose Remove from Sidebar.

Setting Finder preferences

You can find Finder and Desktop preferences by choosing Finder⇨Preferences. In the Finder Preferences window that appears, click the icons in the toolbar to select one of the four Finder preference panes: General, Tags, Sidebar, and Advanced, all of which are shown in Figure 4-17.

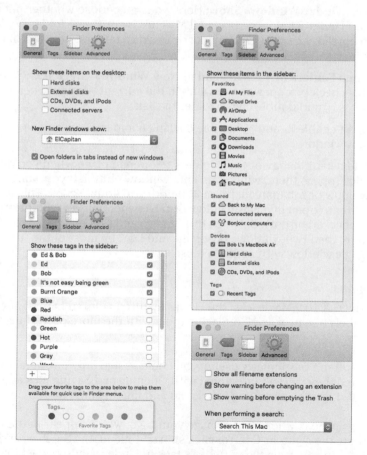

Figure 4-17: Set Finder preferences here.

General pane

In the General pane, you find the following options:

✔ **Show These Items on the Desktop check boxes:** Select or deselect these check boxes to choose whether icons for hard drives; external disks; CDs, DVDs, and iPods; and connected servers appear on the Desktop. OS X El Capitan deselects all four options by default. If you don't want disk icons cluttering your beautiful Desktop, deselect (clear) these check boxes as shown in Figure 4-17. When they're deselected, you can still work with hard drives, CDs, DVDs, and other types of disks. You just have to open a Finder window and select the disk or disc you want in the Sidebar.

✔ **New Finder Windows Show:** Here, you can choose whether opening a new Finder window displays All My Files, your Home folder (which is my preference), the Documents or Desktop folders, or any other disk or folder. (All My Files is the default.)

✔ **Open Folders in Tabs Instead of New Windows check box:** Selecting this check box spawns a new tab in the current window when you press ⌘ and double-click a folder or disk.

Don't enable it, and ⌘+double-clicking a folder or disk icon opens it in a new window.

The default behavior is for folders to open in place when you double-click (open) them, which prevents window clutter. If you want a new window or tab instead, press ⌘ before you double-click. This forces the folder to open in a new window or tab (depending on whether the box is checked or not). Between this feature and Column view, I rarely need more than two windows onscreen, and I get by most of the time with a single window with multiple tabs.

Tags pane

Prior to OS X 10.9 Mavericks, the Finder featured colored Labels; Mavericks took Labels to a new level, replacing them with the more powerful and versatile Tags.

Labels weren't particularly useful; you could assign only one label to a file or folder and they weren't integrated with Opening and Saving files at all. In a nutshell, Tags do everything Labels did and much, much more.

The Tags pane is where you manage your tags, which appear in the Finder's File menu, the right- or Control-click shortcut menu, the Sidebar, and the toolbar. You can see a file or folder's tags in Finder windows, Get Info windows and inspectors, and applications' Open and Save dialogs and sheets, and you can use them as criteria for searches and Smart Folders.

A sheet is nothing more than a dialog that's attached to a document window's title bar and can't be moved. Some apps use sheets, other apps use dialogs, but either way you'll see the same options.

✔ To rename a Tag, click its name and type a new one.

✔ To change a Tag's color, click the colored circle to the left of its name and choose a different color.

✔ Check the boxes for Tags you want to appear in the Sidebar and toolbar, as shown in Figure 4-18. (These are the selections made in the Finder Preference pane on the left in Figure 4-18.)

Figure 4-18: Selecting the check boxes for these five Tags displays then in the Sidebar and the toolbar's Tags button.

To see your unchecked Tags in the Sidebar or toolbar, click All Tags in (Sidebar) or Show All (toolbar).

Now, here's how to use 'em. To assign Tags to icons, select the icon(s) and then follow these steps:

1. **Choose File➪Tags and click one or more of the colored dots in the Tags section.**

2. **Right- or Control-click and click one or more of the colored dots in the Tags section of the shortcut menu.**

3. **Click the Tags button on the toolbar and click one or more of the Tags.**

Here are a few more handy tricks with Tags:

- **To create a custom Tag on the fly:** Right- or Control-click an item, choose Tags, type a label for the new tag, and then press Return.

- **To untag an item:** Right- or Control-click the item, choose Tags, select the tag you want to remove, and then press Delete.

- **To remove every instance of a Tag from every file and folder on your disk:** Right- or Control-click the Tag in the Tags pane of Finder Preferences, and then choose Delete Tag. Don't worry. Deleting a Tag won't delete the items; it just removes that Tag from every item.

Click the Tags in your Sidebar to see every file on all connected hard disks with that tag.

Sidebar pane

The Sidebar pane lets you choose which items are displayed in the Sidebar. Select the check box to display the item; deselect the check box to not display it.

Advanced pane

The Advanced pane is just big enough to offer the following check boxes and a pop-up menu:

- **Show All Filename Extensions check box:** Tells the Finder to display the little two-, three-, four-, or more character filename suffixes (such as .doc in summary.doc) that make your Mac's file lists look more like those of a Linux (or Windows) user. The Finder hides those from you by default, but if you want to be able to see them in the Finder when you open or save files, you need to turn on this option.

- **Show Warning Before Changing an Extension check box (on by default):** Allows you to turn off the nagging dialog that appears if you attempt to change the two-, three-, four-, or more character file extension.

- **Show Warning Before Emptying the Trash check box (on by default):** Allows you to turn off the nagging dialog telling you how many items are in the Trash and asking whether you really want to delete them.

- **When Performing a Search pop-up menu:** Lets you choose the default search location when you initiate a search as described earlier in this chapter. Your choices are Search This Mac, Search the Current Folder, and Use the Previous Search Scope.

Digging for Icon Data in the Info Window

Every icon has an Info window that gives you — big surprise! — information about that icon and enables you to choose which other users (if any) you want to have the privilege of using this icon. (I discuss sharing files and privileges in detail in Chapter 12.) The Info window is also where you can lock an icon so that it can't be renamed or dragged to the Trash.

To see an icon's Info window, click the icon and choose File⇨Get Info (or press ⌘+I). The Info window for that icon appears. Figure 4-19 shows the Info window for an image (a .tiff file named Kiss me).

Documents, folders, and disks each have slightly different Info windows. In this section, I give you highlights on the type of information and options that you can find.

The gray triangles reveal what information for an icon is available in this particular Info window. The sections that you see for most icons include the following:

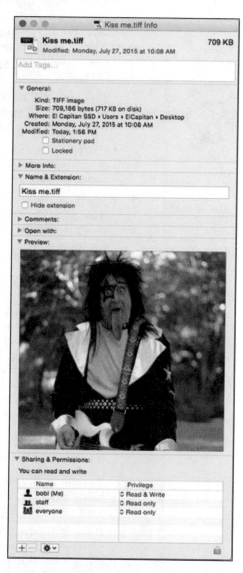

- ✔ **Add Tags:** Click in this field to add Tags to this item.

- ✔ **General:** For information of the general kind, such as

  - *Kind:* What kind of file this is — an application, document, disk, folder, and so on

  - *Size:* How much hard drive space this file uses

  - *Where:* The path to the folder that contains this file

  - *Created:* The date and time this file was created

  - *Modified:* The date and time this file was last modified (that is, saved)

Figure 4-19: A typical Info window for an image (a .tiff file named Kiss me).

Six other check boxes may or may not appear in the General section of a particular Info window. Here's the scoop on this quintet of optional options:

- *Version:* Copyright information and the file's version number

- *Open in 32-bit Mode* (check box): Most late-model Macs can take advantage of El Capitan's high-performance 64-bit processing mode. Some applications are designed to take advantage of El Capitan's faster 64-bit processing mode, but sometimes programs that should run in 64-bit mode don't run properly. If an application doesn't work properly — it often quits unexpectedly, freezes, or refuses to launch at all — try selecting this check box. It couldn't hurt.

  This option is available only for applications designed to run in both modes; if you don't see this check box, the program you're using can run in only one mode.

- *Shared Folder* (check box): Designates the folder as Shared, so other users are allowed to see and use its contents. You find out all about sharing in Chapter 12.

- *Stationery Pad* (check box): This one appears only in the Info window of document icons. If you select it, the file becomes a template. When you open a Stationery Pad document, a copy of its contents appears in a new Untitled document that you would typically save with a descriptive name.

- *Locked* (check box): If this box is checked, you receive a warning if you try to put the item in the Trash: *This Item Is Locked. Do You Want to Move It to the Trash Anyway?* Your options are Stop and Continue. If you continue, the item goes into the Trash as usual. Then, when you try to empty the Trash, you receive another warning: *There Are Some Locked Items in the Trash. Do You Want to Remove All the Items, Including the Locked Ones, or Just the Unlocked Ones?* Your choices this time are Cancel, Remove Unlocked Items, and Remove All Items. If you choose to Remove All Items, the locked item(s) is/are deleted. If you choose Remove Unlocked Items, the locked item(s) remain(s) in the Trash, and you receive the *There Are Some Locked Items* warning again the next time you try to empty it.

  To remove the locked item from the Trash, click the Trash icon in the Dock and drag the locked item out of the Trash and into a folder or onto the Desktop.

- *Prevent App Nap* (check box): OS X can tell when an app is completely hidden behind other windows. If an app isn't currently doing something — playing music, downloading files, or checking your email, for example — App Nap conserves valuable battery life on laptops by slowing the app down. As soon as you activate the app again, it shifts back to full speed instantly.

While App Nap can reduce CPU energy use by up to 23 percent, it may interfere with some programs' operation. If it does, try enabling this check box.

✔ **More Info:** When the file was created, modified, and last opened (documents only).

✔ **Name & Extension:** Tells the full name, including the (possibly hidden) extension.

✔ **Comments:** Provides a field in which you can type your own comments about this icon for Spotlight to use in its searches.

I talk about searching a little earlier in this chapter and discuss Spotlight searches in greater detail in Chapter 7.

✔ **Preview:** When you select a document icon, the menu offers a Preview option that you use to see a glimpse of what's in that document. You can also see this preview when you select a document icon in Column view; it magically appears in the rightmost column. If you select a QuickTime movie or sound, you can play your selection right there in the preview pane without launching a separate application. And when you select most pictures, you see a preview of the actual picture (Elvis in Figure 4-19).

✔ **Sharing & Permissions:** Governs which users have access to this icon and how much access they are allowed. (See Chapter 12 for more about access privileges.)

If you press the Option key before you pull down the Finder's File menu, the Get Info command changes to Show Inspector (alternatively, press ⌘+Option+I). The Get Info Inspector window looks and acts almost exactly like Get Info windows with two whopping exceptions:

✔ **The Inspector displays info only for the currently selected icon.** If you click a different icon, the Inspector instantly displays the info for the icon you clicked. That means you can Get Info on lots of icons in a row using the arrow keys or by pressing Tab or Shift+Tab. Try it — it's cool.

✔ **It displays cumulative info if multiple icons are selected.** In other words, if more than one icon is selected, the Inspector displays the total size for all the selected files and/or folders.

And that's about it for icons, which are among the most fundamental parts of what makes your Mac a Mac (and not a toaster or an Xbox).

Part II
Inside El Capitan
(or How Stuff Works)

Visit www.dummies.com/extras/osxelcapitan for more on how to burn a CD or DVD.

In this part . . .

- Making El Capitan work the way you want it to by customizing it to suit your style
- Organizing your El Capitan to save yourself time and heartache
- Understanding what goes where, and why
- Saving and opening files — two important things you need to know
- The secret to finding anything, anywhere, on any disk
- Mastering Mission Control — try saying that three times real fast
- Timesaving secrets of Quick Look and Launchpad

5

Have It Your Way

In This Chapter

▶ Making it just the way you like it with System Preferences

▶ Beautifying your El Capitan with a Desktop background and screen saver

▶ Working with those wonderful Dashboard widgets

▶ Customizing hardware and keyboard shortcuts

▶ Setting up for superb sound

*E*veryone works a bit differently, and everyone likes to use the Mac in a particular way. In this chapter, you find out how to tweak various options so everything is just the way you like it. The first things many people like to do are set their background and screen saver to something more interesting. You can begin with that stuff, but keep in mind that you can do much more.

You can change the colors in windows, the standard font, and more if you like. Your Mac lets you choose how onscreen elements behave and how your hardware — such as the keyboard, mouse, and any wireless Bluetooth gadgets — interacts with your Mac.

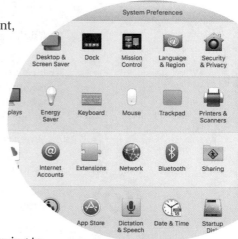

Introducing System Preferences

You should start by becoming familiar with System Preferences, which lives in the Applications folder and appears on the Apple (🍎) menu and in the Dock.

The following steps explain how to move around the System Preferences window, no matter what you're trying to tweak:

1. **Open the System Preferences window, shown in Figure 5-1.**

Figure 5-1: System Preferences is where you change many El Capitan options.

You can open System Preferences in at least four ways:

- Double-click the System Preferences icon in your Applications folder.

- Choose ➪ System Preferences.

- Click the System Preferences icon in Launchpad.

- Click the System Preferences icon on your Dock.

2. **Click any of the icons in the System Preferences window.**

   The contents of the window change to reflect the options for whichever icon you click. When this happens, I call the window a *pane.* So, for example, when you click the General icon in the System Preferences window, the icons disappear and are replaced by the General preference pane.

   When you finish working with System Preferences panes, you should (of course) quit by choosing System Preferences ➪ Quit System Preferences (shortcut: ⌘+Q).

   Not every app quits when you close its last open window, but System Preferences does, so closing its (only) window also quits the app.

3. **Click the Show All button in the toolbar to exit the pane and return to the icons in the System Preferences window.**

   You can accomplish the same thing by choosing View ➪ Show All Preferences, or by pressing ⌘+L; both return you to the window with icons for all of your System Preferences panes.

   Alternatively, you can choose a different preference pane right from the View menu or the Dock icon menu, both shown in Figure 5-2.

Figure 5-2: The View menu (left), the System Preferences window organized alphabetically (center), and the Dock icon menu (right).

If you right- or Control-click the System Preferences icon on the Dock (or just press and hold down for a couple of seconds), a menu pops up listing all available preference panes. The cool part is that this works even if the System Preferences window isn't open. When you know which pane you need, this shortcut is often the fastest way to get to it.

Last but not least, notice that you can navigate to the next or previous pane you've viewed with the Back and Forward buttons beside the red and yellow gumdrops (shortcuts ⌘+[and ⌘+], respectively). Back and Forward commands also appear on the View menu.

One last general tip before you work with an actual preference pane: You can get rid of the categories altogether and display the icons in alphabetical order. As a bonus, it makes the System Preferences window roughly 25 percent smaller onscreen. To switch to alphabetical view, choose View⇨Organize Alphabetically. The categories disappear, the window shrinks, and the icons are alphabetized, as shown in Figure 5-2. To switch from alphabetical view back to category view, choose View⇨Organize by Categories.

El Capitan lets you hide little-used System Preferences pane icons. To manage icons, choose View⇨Customize, and a little check box appears next to each icon. Uncheck the box if you want to hide the icon; recheck the box to make the icon reappear.

Click Done when you're finished checking and unchecking.

Putting a Picture on the Desktop

Figure 5-3 shows my Desktop with a portrait of my dog Zeke painted by talented artist Jeanne Illenye. (Refer to the default Desktop background in Figure 5-2.)

Image well

Figure 5-3: My beautified Desktop.

Here's how you can change your Desktop picture:

1. **From the Desktop, choose ⇨ System Preferences.**

   Or right- or Control-click the Desktop, choose Change Desktop Background from the contextual menu, and skip to Step 3.

   The System Preferences window appears.

2. **Click the Desktop & Screen Saver icon.**

   When the Desktop & Screen Saver pane appears, click the Desktop tab (if it's not selected already, as it is in Figure 5-3).

3. **Click a folder in the column on the left and then click a picture in the area on the right.**

   In Figure 5-3, I clicked a picture called Zeke Vizsla, one of the items in the Pictures folder inside my Home folder.

You have at least three other ways to change your Desktop picture:

- Drag a picture file from the Finder onto the *image well* (the little rectangular picture to the left of the picture's name).

- Click the Desktop tab in the Desktop & Screen Saver System Preferences pane and then click the + button at the bottom of the list on the left. Choose a folder in the standard Open File sheet and that folder appears in the list; you can use any picture files it contains for your Desktop picture.

✔ Click the disclosure triangle next to Photos in the column on the left side of the Desktop & Screen Saver preference pane and choose from pictures stored in your Photos (or iPhoto or Aperture) libraries.

Although I love having a beautiful Desktop picture, I use a light gray or white Desktop (click Solid Colors in the list, and then click the light gray or white color swatch) for most of the figures in this book so you can see fine details.

If you need a color other than the 16 hues displayed in the Desktop & Screen Saver System Preferences pane, click the Custom Color button. When the Color Picker window appears, either click a color to choose it or click the eyedropper icon and then click any color displayed on your screen to select and use that color.

Setting Up a Screen Saver

OS X comes with several screen-saver modules, and many more are available for free (search for *OS X Screen Saver*). To set up your screen saver, follow these steps:

1. **Open System Preferences, click the Desktop & Screen Saver icon, and then click the Screen Saver tab to see the options shown in Figure 5-4.**

Figure 5-4: The Screen Saver tab (foreground) with a preview of the Shuffling Tiles screen saver (background).

2. **In the Screen Savers column on the left side of the pane, choose a screen saver that interests you.**

   Scroll down to see all the available Slideshows and Screen Savers.

If you can't decide, scroll to the bottom of the screen savers list and choose Random to have your Mac choose a different screen saver at random each time the screen saver kicks in.

3. **(Optional) To see what the chosen module looks like in action, click the Preview image on the right.**

    A little Preview button (shown in Figure 5-4) appears on the image when you hover your cursor over it to remind you how to see a preview. Nice touch!

    Press any key or click anywhere to end the test.

4. **After you choose a screen saver, select the number of minutes you want the Mac to wait before activating the screen saver from the Start After pop-up menu.**

5. **Select the Show with Clock check box to display a digital clock along with the screen saver.**

6. **(Optional) Click the Hot Corners button to choose which corner of your screen activates the screen saver and which disables it.**

    If you enable this option, when you move your cursor to the chosen corner of the screen, you activate or disable the screen saver until you move the cursor elsewhere. Note that hot corners are optional and are turned off by default.

7. **When you're done, close the Desktop & Screen Saver pane.**

You can require a password to wake your Mac from sleep or a screen saver. To do so, follow these steps:

1. **Click the Security & Privacy icon, and then click the General tab in the Security & Privacy System Preferences pane.**

2. **Select the Require Password after Sleep or Screen Saver Begins check box.**

3. **Choose a length of time from the pop-up menu between the words *Password* and *After,* which contains options such as Immediately, 15 minutes, and 1 hour.**

    From now on, you must supply the user account password to wake up your computer. (I discuss user accounts and passwords in Chapter 12 and in the installation article found at www.dummies.com/extras/elcapitan.)

Putting Widgets on the Dashboard

Dashboard offers a way-cool set of *widgets,* Apple's name for the mini-applications that live inside the Dashboard layer. You see, Dashboard takes over your screen when you invoke it (as shown in Figure 5-5) by opening it (it's in the Applications folder) or pressing its keyboard shortcut: F12 (or Fn+F12). In Figure 5-5, Dashboard is shown with just a few of its default widgets: Calculator, Weather, World Clock, and Calendar.

Little "i" (click to configure this widget)

Minus button   Close Dashboard button

Plus button

Figure 5-5: Dashboard lives in its own gray overlay layer.

Plus Widgets are small, single-function applications that work only within Dashboard. Some widgets, such as Contacts and Calendar, talk to applications on your hard drive. Other widgets — such as Flight Tracker, Stocks, Movies, and Weather — gather information for you via the Internet.

The following tips can help you work with widgets:

- **Each time you invoke Dashboard,** widgets that were open the last time you used it will be on your screen.

- **To close an open widget,** click the minus sign in a circle in the lower-left corner of the screen and then click the encircled X in the top-left corner of the widget you want to close. Alternatively, you can press the Option key and hover the cursor over a widget to reveal its encircled X; click the X to close the widget.

- **To configure most widgets,** move your cursor over the bottom-right corner of a widget and click the little *i* that appears (as it does with the Weather widget in Figure 5-5). The widget then flips around so you can see its backside, where the configuration options reside. For example, the Weather widget gives you choices that include your City, State, or Zip Code, Fahrenheit or Celsius, and whether to include lows in the six-day forecast (as shown in Figure 5-5), and the Clock widget allows you to choose your region and city. When you finish configuring a widget, click the Done button, which is usually (but not always) in the bottom-right corner; doing so flips the widget around again.

Not all widgets can be configured. For example, the Calendar and Calculator widgets have no options to configure. If a little *i* doesn't appear when you hover the pointer over the bottom-right corner of a widget with your cursor (or hover while pressing the Option key), that widget has no options to configure.

✓ **To move a widget around on your screen,** click almost anywhere on the widget and then drag it to the appropriate location.

✓ **To access widgets other than the four on your screen by default,** click the Open button (the large encircled plus sign shown earlier in the bottom-left corner of Figure 5-5) to open the Widget Selection Screen, which displays your currently available widgets, as shown in Figure 5-6.

Figure 5-6: The Widget Selection Screen with the default selection of widgets.

Widget Selection Screen may sound like a mouthful, but its former moniker, The Widget Bar, made it sound like some trendy watering hole downtown.

✓ **To add a widget from the Widget Selection Screen to your Dashboard,** click the widget on the Widget Selection Screen.

✔ **To manage your widgets on the Widget Selection Screen,** click the Manage Widgets button (the large encircled minus sign visible in the bottom-left corner of Figures 5-5 and 5-6), and all your widgets will begin to wiggle on the screen. If you have an iPhone, iPad, or iPod touch, you'll recognize this wiggling as the rearrange-the-icons dance.

✔ **To download additional widgets,** click the More Widgets (at the bottom of the Widget Selection Screen) to launch your web browser and show you additional widgets you can download from the Apple website.

✔ **To close the Widget Selection Screen,** click anywhere on the gray background or click the Open button again.

✔ **To uninstall a third-party widget that you no longer want,** merely open the Widget Selection Screen and click the red minus sign next to its name. Your Mac politely asks whether you want to move this widget to the trash. You do.

Finally, to close your Dashboard (if you're not displaying widgets as overlays), press the same key you pressed to open Dashboard (F12 or fn+F12), press the Esc key, or click the Close Dashboard button (the encircled angle bracket at the bottom-right corner of the screen).

Think of your Dashboard widgets as being handy-yet-potent mini-programs available at any time with a keystroke or click. Widgets are just so danged cool that I want to give you a quick look at a couple I consider particularly useful. Read on for details.

Translation

The Translation widget could be a lifesaver. You've been able to do this trick on the web for a while, but you can also do it right on your Dashboard. This widget translates words from one language to another. It offers more than a dozen language choices — including French, German, Spanish, Russian, Dutch, Chinese, and more — and can translate in either direction. I love the Translation widget, shown in Figure 5-7, so much that sometimes it hurts.

Figure 5-7: The Translation widget is incredibly useful when you travel abroad.

It's fun at parties, too. Try this: Type a paragraph or two of your purplest prose into Translation. Now translate back and forth to any language a few times. Howl when prose written as "It was a dark and stormy night when our heroine met her untimely demise" turns into something like "It was one night dark and stormy where our heroin met an ugly transfer." It doesn't get much better than this, folks. Alternatively, you could use iTranslate or Google Translate, both free translation apps, on your iPhone or iPad.

Flight Tracker

Flight Tracker, shown in Figure 5-8, can find flights on most airlines and report the flight's status in real time — a terrific timesaver when you have to meet a flight.

Figure 5-8: Finding a flight (top) and viewing its status (bottom).

When you have to meet someone's flight, this widget can be a lifesaver. Just open Dashboard every few minutes, and you know exactly what the flight's status is at that moment.

This is a really good tip for harried air travelers: You can open more than one instance of a widget. So if you're trying to track *more than one flight,* or you want to know the weather or time in *more than one city,* just click the appropriate widget on the Widget Selection Screen, and another instance of it appears.

Giving Buttons, Menus, and Windows a Makeover

 Computers don't care about appearances, but if you want your Mac to look a bit more festive (or, for that matter, businesslike), you have options in the General pane (see Figure 5-9) at your disposal. To open this pane, choose System Preferences, and then click the General icon.

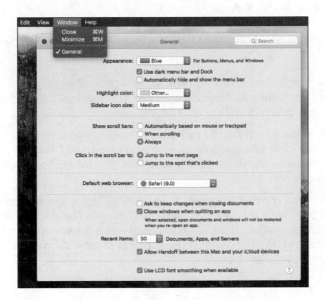

Figure 5-9: The General pane.

First up are the general appearance options:

- **Appearance pop-up menu:** Use this menu to choose different appearances and change the overall look of buttons, such as the three Close, Minimize, and Zoom buttons in the top-left corner of most windows.

  Apple, however, in its infinite wisdom, provides only two choices: Blue or Graphite.

- **Use Dark Menu Bar and Dock check box:** This option will darken your menu bar and Dock as shown in Figure 5-9.

- **Automatically Hide and Show the Menu Bar check box:** This new option will show and hide the menu bar automatically; to make it reappear, move your cursor to the top of the screen (just as you would if the app were in full-screen mode).

✔ **Highlight Color pop-up menu:** From here, you can choose the color that text is surrounded by when you choose it in a document or select an icon. This time, Apple isn't so restrictive: You have eight highlight colors you can choose, plus Other, which brings up a color picker from which you can choose almost any color.

I'm partial to Yellow, which makes selections look like they've been run over by a yellow highlighter.

✔ **Sidebar Icon Size pop-up menu:** Choose Small, Medium, or Large for icons in your Finder Sidebar.

The next area in the General pane enables you to set the behavior of scroll bars and title bars:

✔ The Show Scroll Bars radio buttons let you choose when you want to see scroll bars on windows. Your choices are Automatically Based on Mouse or Trackpad, When Scrolling, or Always.

✔ The Click in the Scroll Bar To radio buttons give you the option of moving your view of a window up or down by a page (the default) or to the position in the document roughly proportionate to where you clicked in the scroll bar.

An easy way to try these options is to open a Finder window and place it side by side with the General pane, as shown in Figure 5-10, reducing the size of the window if necessary to make scroll bars appear. Select an option, observe the behavior of the scroll bars, and then select a different option and observe again.

Scroll bars

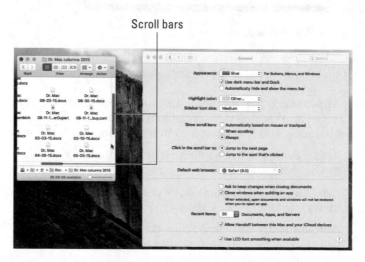

Figure 5-10: Here's how I try different scroll bar settings.

Choose the Jump to the Spot That's Clicked radio button if you often work with long (multipage) documents. It's quite handy for navigating long documents. And don't forget — the Page Down key does the same thing as choosing the Jump to the Next Page choice, so you lose nothing by choosing Jump to the Spot That's Clicked.

It would be even nicer if all third-party apps supported this feature, but some — including Microsoft Office 2011 (but not Office 2016, which finally behaves properly with respect to your scroll bar setting) — don't behave properly no matter what you choose for this setting.

Use the Default Web Browser drop-down menu to choose (what else?) your default browser. Unless you've installed another web browser, such as Chrome or Firefox, Safari will be the only option.

The first two items in the next section are a pair of check boxes:

- **Ask to Keep Changes when Closing Documents:** El Capitan can save versions of your documents automatically and without any action on your part. So when you quit an application or close a document, your changes can be saved automatically. If you want to be able to close documents without having to manually save your changes, enable this option.

- **Close Windows when Quitting an Application:** Your Mac's default behavior is to reopen documents and windows that were open when you quit that app. When you launch the app again, all the windows and documents magically reappear right where you left them. So enable this option to have your apps open to a clean slate, without reopening documents or windows from the previous session.

These last two items may not work as expected with older third-party applications. As a rule, the longer it's been since a program's last update, the more likely it is that the app will ignore these two settings.

The next item in this section of the General pane is Recent Items. It controls the number of recent items that are remembered and displayed in your ⌘⇨ Recent Items submenu. The default is ten, but I like having access to more than ten applications and documents in my Recent Items submenu, so I crank mine up to 30, as shown in Figure 5-10.

The final area offers a single option for how fonts look: The Use LCD Font Smoothing when Available check box, which makes text look better on most flat-screen displays. Unless your monitor is a very old tube-type (CRT) display or you're a photographer or artist who insists on a CRT for its color accuracy, you probably want to select this check box.

Adjusting the Keyboard, Mouse, Trackpad, and Other Hardware

No one uses the keyboard, mouse, or trackpad in the same way. Some folks don't use a mouse at all. (You might not even use the keyboard if you use voice-recognition software or other devices, as I explain in Chapter 17.) If you're using OS X on a notebook, you have a *trackpad,* that little surface where you move your finger around to control the cursor. Or perhaps you have a Bluetooth-enabled keyboard and mouse so you can hook them up wirelessly. Regardless of what you have, you should give some thought to customizing the way it works so it feels just right for you.

The Keyboard, Mouse, and Trackpad System Preference panes offer several tabs to do just that: enable you to modify the behavior of your keyboard, mouse, and trackpad so it feels just right for you. The first thing to do is open the Keyboard Preference pane by choosing ⇨ System Preferences and clicking the Keyboard icon.

Keyboard

The Keyboard System Preference pane has four tabs: Keyboard, Text, Shortcuts, and Input Sources.

Keyboard tab

On the Keyboard tab, you can adjust your settings in the following ways:

- Drag the Key Repeat slider to set how fast a key repeats when you hold it down. This feature comes into play when (for example) you hold down the hyphen (-) key to make a line or the asterisk (*) key to make a divider.

- Drag the Delay Until Repeat slider to set how long you have to hold down a key before it starts repeating.

If you have a notebook Mac (such as a MacBook, MacBook Pro, or MacBook Air), you also see one or more of these additional features:

- **Use All F1, F2 Keys as Standard Function Keys:** If this check box is selected, the F keys at the top of your keyboard control the active software application.

  To use the special hardware features printed on each F key (display brightness, screen mirroring, sound volume, mute, and so on), you have to press the Fn (Function) key before pressing the F key. If the check box is left deselected, you have to press the Fn key if you want to use the F keys with a software application. Got it? Good.

  Finally, these keys may not work if you use a third-party keyboard (one not manufactured by Apple).

- **Adjust Keyboard Brightness in Low Light:** This check box turns your laptop's ambient keyboard lighting on and off.

- **Turn Off When Computer Is Not Used For:** This slide control lets you determine how long the ambient keyboard lighting remains on when your computer isn't in use.

  Of course, if your MacBook doesn't *have* ambient keyboard lighting, as many don't, you don't see the last two items.

  Ambient keyboard lighting is a cool feature, but it reduces battery life. My recommendation is to use it only when you really need it.

- **Show Keyboard, Emoji & Symbol Viewers in the Menu Bar:** This check box adds a new menu for opening either of these useful windows, as shown in Figure 5-11.

Figure 5-11: (Clockwise) Keyboard tab, Character Viewer window (Characters), Keyboard and Character Viewer menu, and Keyboard Viewer window (U.S.) in all their glory.

Click any character (smiley faces in Figure 5-11) to insert it in your document; click the little icons at the bottom of the window to view additional screens full of characters.

Some people prefer the look the Character Viewer had prior to Mavericks (OS X 10.9). While both looks offer the same old characters you know and love, the presentation has changed. Never fear. If you prefer the old look and feel, scroll to the top of the window and click the little Character Viewer icon to the right of the search field (shown in the margin). This transforms the Character Viewer back to its pre-Mavericks look, as shown in Figure 5-12.

Little character viewer icon

Figure 5-12: The little Character Viewer icon toggles the look of the Character Viewer window between the old look shown here and the new look (smiley faces in Figure 5-11).

To return the window to its other state, just click the little icon again.

Click the Action menu (the little gear near the upper-left corner) and choose Customize List to enable additional character categories, including Braille Patterns, Dingbats, Musical Symbols, Sign/Standard Symbols, and many more.

✔ **Set Up Bluetooth Keyboard button:** Launches the Bluetooth assistant and walks you through pairing and setup as described in Chapter 12.

✔ **Modifier Keys button:** Lets you change the action performed by the Caps Lock, Control, Option, and Command keys. It's particularly useful if you use a non-Apple keyboard, although it works just fine on Apple keyboards, too.

I'm always engaging the Caps Lock key accidentally with my overactive left pinky, so I set *my* Caps Lock key to perform No Action. Now I never type half a sentence in ALL CAPS BECAUSE I ACCIDENTALLY PRESSED THE CAPS LOCK KEY.

Text tab

This is one of my favorite features in all of Macdom 'cause it saves me countless keystrokes every day. Not because it's the tab with the Correct Spelling Automatically check box. Enable it (if it's not already enabled) and be done. Spelling correction is good, but the reason I love the Text tab so much is because it lets me create shortcuts to replace short phrases with longer ones.

When I type:	*My Mac replaces it with:*
btw	by the way . . .
vty	Very truly yours,
	Bob "Dr. Mac" LeVitus
	Writer, Raconteur, and Troublemaker
blc	boblevitus@boblevitus.com

It's a very handy trick, indeed. Plus, a preview pops up just below your typing so you can accept the replacement by pressing the spacebar or reject it by clicking the little X or pressing Esc.

To create your own shortcuts, click the little plus sign near the bottom-left corner of the window. Type the short phrase in the Replace field, click in the With field or press Tab, and then type the replacement phrase. You can see what happens when I type **blc** in the TextEdit window in the foreground of Figure 5-13.

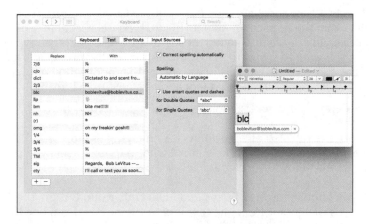

Figure 5-13: The Text tab of the Keyboard System Preference pane (background) and what I see when I type **blc** in a TextEdit document (foreground).

Although it's not obvious, you can create multiline substitutions. Just hold down Option and press Return to start a new line of text.

Shortcuts tab

If you really hate to use your mouse or if your mouse is broken, keyboard shortcuts can be really handy. I tend to use them more on my laptop because I really don't like using the built-in-touch-mouse thing (technically, it's a *trackpad,* and I talk more about it in the next section).

I introduce some commonly used keyboard shortcuts in Chapter 2. You probably don't want to mess with those, but you can assign other commands you use often to just about any key combination you like. By creating your own keyboard shortcuts, you can have whatever commands you need literally at your fingertips.

Not only can you add, delete, or change keyboard shortcuts for many operating system functions (such as taking a picture of the screen or using the keyboard to choose menu and Dock items), but you can also add, delete, or change keyboard shortcuts for your applications.

To begin, choose the Shortcuts tab in the Keyboard System Preference pane. Now you can do any or all of the following:

- **To change a shortcut,** first click the appropriate application, preference, or feature in the left column. Next, double-click the shortcut you want to change on the right side of the right column (for example, F3 or ⌘+G). The old shortcut becomes highlighted; when it does, press the new shortcut keys you want to use.

- **To add a new shortcut,** click the + button. Choose the appropriate application from the Application pop-up menu, type the exact name of the menu command you want to add in the Menu Title field, and then type the shortcut you want to assign to that command in the Keyboard Shortcut field. If the shortcut you press is in use by another application or preference, a yellow triangular caution symbol appears next to it. It really is that simple.

- **To delete a shortcut,** choose it and then click the – button.

The Shortcuts tab also offers options for changing the tab order. The Full Keyboard Access radio buttons control what happens when you press the Tab key in a window or dialog:

- If you choose the Text Boxes and Lists Only radio button, the Tab key moves the cursor from one text box to the next or from one list item to the next item (usually alphabetically).

- If you choose the All Controls radio button, you can avoid using the mouse for the most part, if that's your preference.

  When All Controls is selected, the Tab key moves the focus from one item to the next in a window or dialog. So (for example) every time you press the Tab key in an Open File dialog or sheet, the focus moves — say, from the Sidebar to the file list to the Cancel button to the icon view button, and so on. Each item is highlighted to show it's selected, and you can activate the highlighted item from the keyboard by pressing the spacebar.

  You can toggle this setting by pressing Control+F7. And if you don't care for Control+F7 as its shortcut, you can change it by clicking Keyboard in the left column, double-clicking the Change the Way Tab Moves Focus item in the right column, and then pressing the new shortcut.

Input Sources tab

The Input Sources tab is where you can choose to display one or more foreign language keyboards in the Input menu.

The Input menu and the Keyboard and Character Viewer menu are one and the same. If you add one or more foreign keyboards, the icon in your menu bar changes from the rather tame icon shown in Figure 5-12 to the flag of the selected keyboard, as shown in the margin (that's the Dutch flag, by the way).

Mouse

The Mouse System Preference pane is where you set your mouse tracking speed, scrolling speed, and double-click delays.

If you use a notebook Mac, you won't see a Mouse icon in the System Preferences application unless you have a mouse connected, or have at some time in your Mac's life connected a USB or Bluetooth mouse.

Don't be sad. If you use a notebook or an Apple Magic Trackpad, you have something that most iMac, Mac mini, and Mac Pro users don't have — namely, the System Preference pane named Trackpad, which I tell you about in the upcoming section, "Trackpad (Notebooks and desktops with a Magic Trackpad)."

The first item in this pane is a check box: Scroll Direction: Natural. If scrolling or navigating in windows feels backward to you, try unchecking this box.

Moving right along, here are the features you'll find in the Mouse System Preference pane (if you have a mouse connected):

- ✔ Move the Tracking Speed slider to change the relationship between hand movement of the mouse and cursor movement onscreen. This slider works just like the slider for trackpads, as I explain in the upcoming section on trackpads.

- ✔ The Double-Click Speed setting determines how close together two clicks must be for the Mac to interpret them as a double-click and not as two separate clicks. Move the slider arrow to the leftmost setting, Very Slow, for the slowest. The rightmost position, Fast, is the fastest setting. I prefer the setting one tick shy of Fast.

- ✔ If your mouse has a scroll ball or scroll wheel, you also see a Scrolling Speed slider, which lets you adjust how fast the contents of a window scroll when you use the scroll wheel or ball.

- ✔ If your mouse has more than one button, you see a pair of Primary Mouse Button radio buttons. These let you choose which button — left or right — you use to make your primary (regular) click. Conversely, the other mouse button (the one you didn't choose) becomes your secondary (Control or right) click.

This is a setting many lefties like to change. Set the primary button as the right button, and you can click with the index finger of your left hand.

Being right-handed, I've chosen the defaults in Figure 5-14, so the left button is the primary click and the right button is the secondary (right or Control) click.

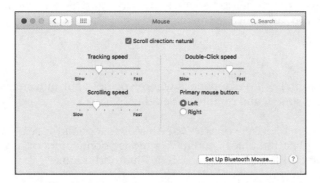

Figure 5-14: The Mouse System Preference pane set up for a right-hander.

Changes in the Mouse System Preference pane take place immediately, so you should definitely play around a little and see what settings feel best for you.

Bluetooth

Bluetooth is a technology that lets you make wireless connections between your Mac and devices such as Bluetooth mice and phones. You can see a Bluetooth tab in the Mouse System Preference pane if you're using a Bluetooth mouse. Most Macs manufactured in the past few years have Bluetooth built in; some older models don't.

You configure Bluetooth devices you want to use with your Mac elsewhere in the Bluetooth System Preference pane (as I describe in Chapter 12 and Chapter 17).

If your Mac has Bluetooth built in, the Bluetooth tab shows you the battery level of your Bluetooth mouse or keyboard. It also offers a check box to add a Bluetooth status menu to your menu bar and a check box to let Bluetooth devices wake your computer from sleep.

Trackpad (notebooks and desktops with a Magic Trackpad)

If you use a notebook Mac — a MacBook, MacBook Air, and MacBook Pro — or a desktop Mac with a Magic Trackpad, you'll have an additional System Preferences pane called Trackpad. This pane lets you configure tracking and clicking speed as well as the gesturing behavior of your Mac's built-in trackpad.

If you're looking for a replacement for your mouse, consider Apple's $69 Magic Trackpad. This nifty wireless device can be used with any Mac or PC that has Bluetooth. It's also the biggest glass Multi-Touch trackpad yet, nearly 80 percent larger than the MacBook Pro built-in trackpad. Yes, you can use the Magic Trackpad with your MacBook Pro, and yes, that does mean you have dual trackpads.

I have become more of a trackpad believer and love using iPhone-like gestures on my Mac. I have a Magic Trackpad and a mouse and grab whichever is appropriate at the moment.

The Trackpad System Preference pane has three tabs — Point & Click, Scroll & Zoom, and More Gestures — as shown in Figure 5-15.

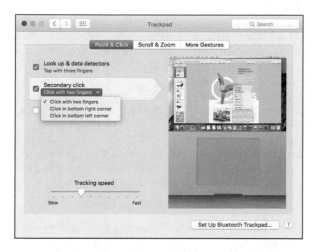

Figure 5-15: The Trackpad System Preference pane offers controls for one-finger and multi-finger gestures.

If you have an older notebook with the older-style trackpad, you may not see all the controls in Figure 5-15.

All three tabs work the same way as the Point & Click tab shown in Figure 5-15. To enable or disable a feature, click its check box. To see how a feature works, just move your cursor over it (you don't even have to click), and a movie demonstrates that gesture on the right side of the window. In Figure 5-15, I'm pointing to the Secondary Click feature on the left; how it works is demonstrated in the movie playing on the right. Pretty cool, don't you think?

You need to know a couple of other things about the Trackpad System Preference pane before you move on:

✔ If you see a little v to the right of a feature's description (Click with Two Fingers in Figure 5-15), a drop-down menu is available; click near the v to display the options for that feature.

✔ The Tracking Speed slider lets you change the relationship between finger movement on the trackpad and cursor movement onscreen. A faster tracking-speed setting (moving the slider to the right) sends your cursor flying across the screen with a mere flick of the finger; slower tracking-speed settings (moving the slider to the left) make the cursor crawl across in seemingly slow motion, even when your finger is flying. Set this setting as fast as you can stand it — I like the fastest speed. Try it: You might like it.

Styling Your Sound

Out of the box, OS X El Capitan comes with a preset collection of beeps and controls. From the Sound Preference pane, however, you can change the way your Mac plays and records sound by changing settings on each of its three tabs: Sound Effects, Output, and Input.

Three items appear at the bottom of the Sound pane, no matter which of the three tabs is active:

✔ To make your Mac's volume louder or softer, use the Output Volume slider. You can also change or mute the volume with the designated volume and mute keys found on most Apple keyboards.

✔ Select the Mute check box to turn off all sound.

✔ Click the Show Volume in Menu Bar check box to add a volume control menu to your menu bar.

A shortcut to the Sound System Preference pane is to press Option while pressing any of the volume keys (usually the F11 and F12 keys on newer laptops and keyboards and F4 and F5 keys on older ones).

Changing sound effects

On the Sound Effects tab, choose an alert (beep) sound by clicking its name; set its volume by using the Alert Volume slider control.

You can also specify the output device through which sound effects play (if you have more than one device) by choosing it from the Play Sound Effects Through pop-up menu.

The Play User Interface Sound Effects check box turns on sound effects for actions, such as dragging a file to the Trash. The Play Feedback when Volume Is Changed check box tells your Mac to beep once for each key press to increase or decrease volume.

Choosing output and input options

If you have more than one sound-output device (in addition to the built-in speakers), you can choose it here. The Balance slider makes one stereo speaker — left or right — louder than the other.

If you have more than one sound-input device (in addition to the built-in microphone on many Macs or an iSight camera, which contains its own mic), you can choose it here. The Input Volume slider controls the Input Level (how loud input from that device will be), which is displayed as a row of blue dots. If the dots light up all the way to the right side, your input volume is too loud. Ideally, the input level should light up with about three-fourths of the little blue dots — and no more.

Some input sources (microphones) don't let you adjust their level in the Sound System Preference pane.

6

The Care and Feeding of Files and Folders

*T*his could be the most important chapter in this book. If you don't understand how to open and save files by using the Open dialog and Save sheets or how to use the file and folder system, you'll have a heck of a time getting the hang of your Mac.

A sheet is nothing more than a dialog that's attached to a document window's title bar and can't be moved. Some apps use sheets, other apps use dialogs, but either way you'll see the same options.

This chapter is a tonic for finding the file or folder you want. Knowing where your files are is something every Mac user should *grok* (fully understand). Hang with me and pay attention; everything will soon become crystal clear.

Later in the chapter, I look at using Open dialogs and Save sheets within applications to find files and folders. You see them only *after* you launch a program and use that program's File menu to open or save a file. (For more on launching applications, read the parts of Chapter 4 about icons; for more on creating and opening documents, see the documentation or Help file for the program that you're using.)

A Quick Primer on Finding Files

Before we even look at organizing your files, let's look at the problem organizing files and folders can solve. Ask any longtime Mac user; the old lament is pretty common: "Well, I saved the file, but I don't know where I saved it." It happens all the time with new users (and occasionally with long-time users like my wife). If they don't master these essential techniques, they often become confused about where files are located on their hard drives. Sure, the Sidebar has an item called All My Files that displays all your files, and Spotlight can find files in milliseconds — but if you have thousands or tens of thousands of files, both can be more of a curse than a blessing.

All My Files (in the Sidebar of Finder windows) is a fast and easy way to find a file or folder (although the sheer number of files it displays may overwhelm you, no matter how you sort or arrange them).

All My Files is especially handy when you know you either created or worked on the file recently. Just use List view sorted or arranged by Date Last Opened and the most recently used files will be at or near the top of the list.

And Chapter 7 is chock-full of tools and tips for finding files and folders when you misplace them. Furthermore, although you can often find files or folders by using Spotlight, you have to remember enough details about the file or its contents for Spotlight to find it.

At the end of the day, all the aforementioned techniques are useful and good to know, but take it from me: It's often faster and easier if you know exactly where a file or folder is than to hunt for it.

Spotlight (which you discover in Chapter 7) is OS X's built-in search mechanism. It's available just about everywhere you look in El Capitan: The magnifying glass on the menu bar, the toolbar of Finder windows, and Open dialogs and Save sheets. The point is, if you can't find a file or folder manually as described in the rest of this chapter, try Spotlight.

Understanding the OS X Folder Structure

Start by looking at the folder structure of a typical OS X installation. Open a Finder window and click the icon for your hard drive (typically called Macintosh HD) in the Sidebar. You should now see at least four folders: Applications, Library, System, and Users. Within the Users folder, each user with an account on this Mac (see Chapter 12 for the skinny on Users and Accounts) has his or her own set of folders containing documents, preferences, and other information that belongs to that user and account.

If you're the sole person who accesses your Mac, you probably have only one user. Regardless, the folder structure that OS X uses is the same whether you have one user or dozens.

Within the Users folder, you find your personal Home folder (which bears your Account Name), along with a Shared folder, where you can put files you want to share with other users. All these files are stored in a nested folder structure that's a bit tricky to understand at first. This structure makes more sense after you spend a little time with it and figure out some basic concepts.

If you display the path bar (at the bottom of your windows; choose View⇨Show Path Bar), it'll start to make sense much sooner.

Take a look at Figure 6-1; you can see how these main folders are related to one another. In the sections that follow, you look at each of these folders in more depth and find out more about what's nested inside each one.

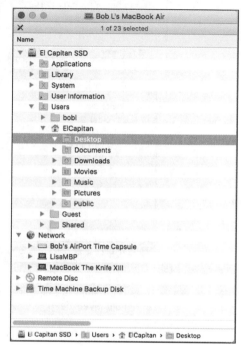

Figure 6-1: A bird's-eye view of key folders on your Mac.

Understanding nested folders

Folders within other folders are often called *nested folders*. To get a feel for the way nested folders work in OS X, check out the example of nested folders on my Desktop in Figure 6-2.

You can see the following in Figure 6-2:

- The Desktop is the top-level folder in this example; all the other folders and files you see reside within the Desktop folder.
- Folder 1 is inside the Desktop folder, which is one level deep.
- Folder 2 is inside Folder 1, which is one level deeper than Folder 1, or two levels deep.
- Folder 3 is inside Folder 2 and is three levels deep.
- The two files inside Folder 3 are four levels deep.

Folder 1 (in Desktop folder):
One level deep

Folder 2 (in Folder 1):
Two levels deep

Folder 3 (in Folder 2):
Three levels deep

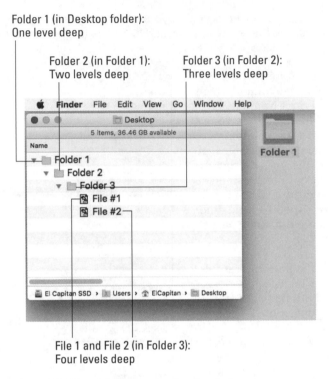

File 1 and File 2 (in Folder 3):
Four levels deep

Figure 6-2: Nested folders, going four levels deep.

If the preceding list makes sense to you, you're golden. What's important here is that you can visualize the path to Folder 3. That is, to get to files inside Folder 3, you open Folder 1 and then open Folder 2 to be able to open Folder 3. Understanding this concept is important to understanding the relationships between files and folders. Keep reviewing this section, and eventually, the concept will click. You'll slap yourself in the head and say, "Now I get it!"

From the top: The Computer folder

I start with the Computer folder, which is the top level of the folder hierarchy. The Computer folder shows all the storage devices (hard drives, CD- or DVD-ROM, USB flash drive, and so forth) that are connected to your Mac. The following steps show how you can start at the Computer folder and drill down through the folder structure:

1. **Choose Go⇨Computer or press Shift+⌘+C.**

   Now you are at the Computer folder. In Figure 6-1, the Computer folder is called Bob L's MacBook Air (look in the title bar), and it contains a solid-state drive icon (El Capitan SSD), an external hard disk icon (Time Machine Backup Disk), a Remote Disk icon (because my wife has DVD or CD Sharing enabled in the Sharing System Preferences pane), and a Network icon, from which you can access servers or other computers on your local network.

If that seems mysterious, read Chapter 12 for the scoop on sharing files (and more) with other users.

You might have more or fewer icons in your Computer folder than you see in Figure 6-1, depending on how many disks you have mounted.

You might also find a Computer icon in your Sidebar. If not and you'd like to have Computer in your Sidebar, choose Finder➪Preferences, click the Sidebar tab at the top, and then select the check box for your computer.

You can change a Mac's name (Bob L's MacBook Air in Figure 6-1) by opening the Sharing System Preferences pane (see Chapter 12) and changing the computer's name in the Computer Name field.

2. **Double-click the icon that holds your OS X stuff.**

   Technically, this drive is called your *boot drive*. In Figure 6-1, that hard drive is called El Capitan SSD. I have no idea what yours is called, of course; if you haven't changed it, it's probably called Macintosh HD.

3. **Check out the folders you find there.**

   You should see at least four folders, unless you've added some. (If you installed the Xcode programming tools, for example, you have more.) In the next few sections, I walk you through what you can find in each one.

Peeking into the Applications folder

You can access the Applications folder, located at the root level of your boot drive (the one with OS X installed on it), by clicking the Applications icon in the Sidebar, by choosing it in the Go menu, or by pressing Shift+⌘+A. In this folder, you find applications and utilities that Apple includes with OS X. Most users of a Mac have access to all the items in the Applications folder, with the exception of managed accounts or accounts with Parental Controls, as discussed in Chapter 12.

Visiting the Library folders

The Library folder, at the root level of your OS X hard drive, is like a public library; it stores items available to everyone who logs into any account on this Mac.

There are actually three or more Library folders on your hard drive:

- ✔ At the root level of your OS X disk
- ✔ In the root-level System folder
- ✔ In each user's Home folder

In El Capitan, your Home Library folder is hidden from view to protect you from yourself. Never fear: You'll discover the secret to making it visible if you need it in the "Your personal Library card" section later in this chapter.

Now, here's the scoop on your various Library folders:

- ✔ **Public Library:** You find a bunch of folders inside the Library folder at root level (the public Library folder). Most of them contain files that you never need to open, move, or delete.

  By and large, the public Library subfolder that gets the most use is the Fonts folder, which houses many of the fonts installed on the Mac.

- ✔ **System Library:** This is the nerve center of your Mac. In other words, you should never have to touch this particular Library folder.

  Leave the /System/Library folder alone. Don't move, remove, or rename it, or do anything within it.

- ✔ **Library in each user's Home folder:** This is where OS X stores configuration and preferences files for each user account.

The locations of all these libraries are illustrated in Figure 6-3.

If your Mac is set up for multiple users, only users with administrator (admin) privileges can put stuff in the public (root-level) Library folder. (For more information on admin privileges, check out Chapter 12.)

Let it be: The System folder

The System folder contains the files that OS X needs to start up and keep working.

Leave the System folder alone. Don't move, remove, or rename it or anything within it. It's part of the nerve center of your Mac.

So now you can forget everything outside your Home folder because with few exceptions, that's where all of your stuff will reside.

There's no place like Home

Your Home folder is inside the Users folder. When the user logs on to this Mac, the contents of her Home folder appear whenever she clicks the Home icon in the Sidebar, chooses Go⇨Home, or uses the keyboard shortcut Shift+⌘+H.

Your Home folder is the most important folder for you as a user — or at least the one where you stash most of your files. I strongly recommend that you store all the files you create in subfolders within your Home folder — preferably, in

Hard disk/System/Library

Hard disk/Library (Public Library)

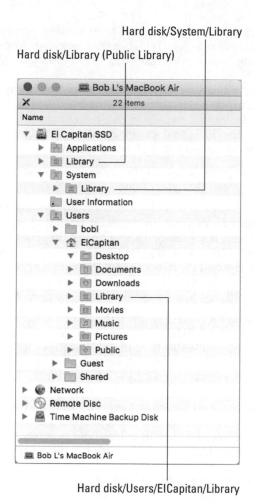

Hard disk/Users/ElCapitan/Library

Figure 6-3: A guide to which Library is which.

subfolders in your Home/Documents folder. The advantage of doing so is that your Home/Documents folder is easy to find, and many programs use it as the default folder for opening or saving a file.

When you open your Home folder, you see a Finder window with a little house icon and your short username in the title bar. Seeing your short username in the title bar tells you that you're in *your* Home folder. Every user has a Home folder named after his or her short username (as specified in the Users & Groups System Preferences pane). If you refer to Figure 6-1, you'll see that my Home folder contains seven subfolders — Desktop, Documents, Downloads, Movies, Music, Pictures, and Public — and that my Home folder is named ElCapitan — the short name I used when I first set up my Mac.

If your Mac has more than one user, you can see their Home folders in the Users folder (for example, bobl in Figure 6-1), but OS X prevents you from opening files from or saving files to other users' Home folders.

By default, your Home folder has several folders inside it created by OS X. The following four are the most important:

- ✔ **Desktop:** If you put items (files, folders, applications, or aliases) on the Desktop, they're actually stored in the Desktop folder.

- ✔ **Documents:** This is the place to put all the documents (letters, spreadsheets, recipes, and novels) that you create.

- ✔ **Library:** As I mention earlier in this chapter, this Library folder is invisible in OS X El Capitan; I show you how to deal with that shortly. Rest assured that even though it's hidden, it's still one of the most important folders in your Home folder, containing Preferences (files containing the settings you create in System Preferences and individual applications' preferences), fonts available only to you (as described earlier in this chapter), and other stuff that you — and only you — expect to use.

- ✔ **Public:** If others on your local area network (LAN) use file sharing to connect with your Mac, they can't see or use the files or folders in your Home folder (unless you explicitly share them), but they can share files you store in your Home folder's Public folder. (Read more about file sharing and Public folders in Chapter 12.)

You can create more folders, if you like. In fact, every folder that you *ever* create (at least every one you create on this particular hard drive or volume) *should* be within your Home folder. I explain more about creating folders and subfolders and organizing your stuff inside them later in this chapter.

The following are a few more tidbits to keep in mind as you dig around your Home folder:

- ✔ If you decide that you don't want an item on the Desktop anymore, delete it by dragging its icon from the Desktop folder to the Trash or by dragging its icon from the Desktop itself to the Trash. Both techniques yield the same effect: The file is in the Trash, where it remains until you empty the Trash. Or if you don't want it on the Desktop anymore but don't want to get rid of it either, you can drag it from the Desktop into any other folder you like.

- ✔ The other four folders that you should see in your Home folder are Downloads, Movies, Music, and Pictures. All these folders are empty until you (or a program such as iTunes, GarageBand, Photos, or iMovie, which create files inside these folders automatically the first time you launch them) put something in them.

Your personal Library card

The invisible Library subfolder of your Home folder is the repository of everything that OS X needs to customize *your* Mac to *your* tastes. If you want to add something to a Library folder, it's usually best to add it to your Home/ Library folder. You won't spend much time (if any) adding things to the Library folder or moving them around within it, and that's probably why it's now hidden from sight. Still, I think it's a good idea for you to know what's in your Home/Library.

Earlier in this chapter I mention the public Library folder (refer to Figure 6-3), which is used to specify preferences for all users on this Mac. *This* Library folder, however, is all about you and your stuff.

Be cautious with all Library folders. OS X is very persnickety about how the folders and files within it are organized. As I discuss earlier in the chapter, you can add items to and remove items safely from most public or Home Library folders, but *leave the folders themselves alone.* If you remove or rename the wrong folder, you could render OS X inoperable. It's like the old joke about the guy who said to the doctor, "It hurts when I do that," and the doctor replies, "Then don't do that."

To find your hidden Home/Library folder, do this:

1. **Hold down the Option key on your keyboard.**

2. **Click the Go menu.**

   The (formerly) invisible Library folder appears in the Go menu as long as the Option key is pressed, as shown in Figure 6-4.

3. **Select Library and release the mouse button.**

You should see several folders in the Home/Library folder; the exact number depends on the software that you install on your Mac. You probably have folders called Mail, Safari, Logs, and Preferences, for example.

If you don't want to have to do this dance every time you want to open your Home/Library, select your Home folder in the Finder and choose View ⇨ Show View Options (or press ⌘+J). Enable the Show Library Folder check box and your Home Library will be visible evermore (or at least until you deselect the check box).

Some of the most important standard folders in the Library folder include the following:

   ✓ **Application Support:** Some applications store their support files here; others store theirs in the main (root-level) public Library folder.

Go	Window	Help		Go	Window	Help	
Back		⌘[		Back		⌘[	
Forward		⌘]		Forward		⌘]	
Enclosing Folder		⌘↑		Enclosing Folder		⌥⌘↑	
🗐 All My Files		⇧⌘F		🗐 All My Files		⇧⌘F	
🗐 Documents		⇧⌘O		🗐 Documents		⇧⌘O	
🖥 Desktop		⇧⌘D		🖥 Desktop		⇧⌘D	
⊙ Downloads		⌥⌘L		⊙ Downloads		⌥⌘L	
🏠 Home		⇧⌘H		🏠 Home		⇧⌘H	
🖥 Computer		⇧⌘C		📁 Library			
⊚ AirDrop		⇧⌘R		🖥 Computer		⇧⌘C	
🌐 Network		⇧⌘K		⊚ AirDrop		⇧⌘R	
☁ iCloud Drive		⇧⌘I		🌐 Network		⇧⌘K	
𝖠 Applications		⇧⌘A		☁ iCloud Drive		⇧⌘I	
✂ Utilities		⇧⌘U		𝖠 Applications		⇧⌘A	
				✂ Utilities		⇧⌘U	
Recent Folders		▶		Recent Folders		▶	
Go to Folder...		⇧⌘G		Go to Folder...		⇧⌘G	
Connect to Server...		⌘K		Connect to Server...		⌘K	

Figure 6-4: A normal Go menu (left) and a Go menu with the Option key pressed (right).

✓ **Fonts:** This folder is empty until you install your own fonts here. The easiest way to install a font is to double-click its icon and let the Font Book utility handle it for you, as described in Chapter 15. But I'd be remiss if I didn't also mention how to install a font manually:

   • *To install a font that only you can use:* Drag the font file's icon to the Fonts folder in your Home/Library. The font is available only to this user account (because other users can't use fonts stored in *your* Home/Library folder).

   • *To install a font for all users of this Mac:* Drag the font file's icon into the Fonts folder in the public Library folder — the one at root level that you see when you open your hard drive's icon.

It might not be a great idea to add too many fonts for all users because the Fonts menu will become long and unwieldy.

✓ **Preferences:** The files here hold the information about whichever things you customize in OS X or in the applications you run. Whenever you change a system or application preference, that info is saved to a file in the Preferences folder.

Don't mess with the Preferences folder! You should never need to open or use this folder unless something bad happens — say, you suspect that a particular preferences file has become *corrupted* (that is, damaged). My advice is to just forget that you know about this folder and let it do its job. If you don't know why you're doing something to a folder (other than the Fonts folder) in your Home/Library, *don't do it.* There must be some good reasons why Apple decided to hide the Home/Library folder in OS X El Capitan, and I'm sure that one of them is to keep you (or me) from accidentally screwing something up.

Saving Your Document Before It's Too Late

If you have a feel for the OS X folder structure, you can get down to the important stuff — namely, how to save documents and where to save them. You can create as many documents as you want, using one program or dozens of 'em, but all could be lost if you don't save the files (or versions of the files) to a storage device such as your startup drive, external hard disks, USB thumb drives (aka USB flash drives), or solid-state drives (SSDs). Another option is to save documents in iCloud, so they're available on all of your Apple devices all the time without syncing or doing much of anything beyond saving the file.

When you *save* a file, you're committing a copy to a disk, whether it's a disk connected directly to your Mac, one available over a local area network, a removable disk such as a USB thumb drive or portable hard or solid-state disk, or even to a disk on a cloud-based server somewhere else (such as iCloud).

Speaking of iCloud, you'll be hearing a lot more about it — and especially the iCloud Drive feature introduced in Yosemite — later in this chapter after you get the hang of saving and opening files from disks.

OS X's Resume feature automatically reopens all windows that were onscreen when you quit the app. So, when you launch the app again, all the windows are reopened in the same position onscreen as when you quit. Best of all, Resume seems to work with *most* (but not all) third-party apps.

Individual programs have offered Auto Save before, but it's baked into OS X. Auto Save automatically saves versions (which you'll learn more about shortly) of your work as you work, when you pause, and every five minutes, whether you need it or not.

Versions are awesome. Every time you Save or Auto Save, a new version of the document is created. For as long as we've had Macs, we've saved unique versions of our files, creating and managing them with the Save As command or by duplicating and renaming them in the Finder. Now OS X takes over version control for you by automatically saving versions as described in the preceding paragraph.

The big advantage is that rather than ending up with a separate file on your hard disk each time you Save As or duplicate and rename a file, Versions saves them all in the same document icon. To access a previous version, click the Choose File ⇨ Revert To ⇨ Browse All Versions or choose Enter Time Machine from the Time Machine icon on the menu bar while the document is active onscreen (see Chapter 18 for more on Time Machine).

That's the good news, but there's also bad news. Although Auto Save and Versions are baked right into OS X, third-party apps require a software update before they can take advantage of these features. So please don't get too comfortable with Auto Save and Versions until you're sure that your applications take advantage of these features. Even four plus years after the debut of these features in OS X, many third-party apps still rely on the good old Save and Save As commands for versioning. And if these features aren't in a third-party app by now, I wouldn't hold my breath.

The bottom line is that if the app you're using doesn't have Auto Save and Versioning, OS X takes no responsibility for saving files and saving versions of files; it's all up to you.

In the following sections, I show you how to save your masterpieces. Prevent unnecessary pain in your life by developing good saving habits. I recommend that you save your work (or save a version in apps that support versions)

- ✔ Every few minutes
- ✔ Before you switch to another program
- ✔ Before you print a document
- ✔ Before you stand up

The keyboard shortcut for Save in almost every Mac program is ⌘+S. Memorize it. See it in your dreams. Train your finger muscles to do it unconsciously. Use it (the keyboard shortcut) or lose it (your unsaved work).

If you don't heed this advice — and then the program that you're using crashes while switching programs, printing, or sitting idle (the three likeliest times for a crash) — you may lose everything you did since your last save or saved version. The fact that a program crash doesn't bring down the entire system or force a restart is small consolation when you've lost everything you've typed, drawn, copied, pasted, or whatever since the last time you saved or saved a version.

Stepping through a basic Save

This section walks you through the steps you use the first time you save a document. The process is the same whether your app supports Auto Save and Versions or not. It's only after the initial save that Auto Save and Versions come into play.

Does it have Auto Save and Versions or not?

It can be hard to discern at a glance whether an app uses the Auto Save and Versions features introduced with OS X Lion. In Mavericks, the Save a Version command went back to its original (and less-confusing) moniker, which is plain ol' Save. Fortunately, there are other ways to determine whether a program supports Auto Save and Versions.

The first is whether the app has a Save As or Duplicate command in its File menu. Programs with a Save As command are old-school and don't support the new Auto Save and Versions features. Programs with a Duplicate command have usually been updated with support for Auto Save and Versions. (Interestingly, the shortcut for Duplicate and Save As is almost always the same: ⌘+Shift+S.)

The next is whether the app has Rename and Move To commands in its File menu. If it doesn't, it's old-school; if it does, it's Auto Save- and Versions-savvy.

The easiest way to tell, however, is to look at the title bar of a document. If it displays a little V to the right of the document's name when you hover your cursor over it (as shown on top of the figure here) and a pop-up window appears if you click the triangle (as shown on the bottom of the following figure), it means that the app supports Auto Save and Versions. (You read more about the options in the pop-up window later in this chapter.)

One last thing: Everything I've just said so far in this chapter applies to every app that saves files, with or without Auto Save and Versions. But I'd be remiss if I didn't reiterate that saving a file with Auto Save and Versions has one additional effect: It creates a new version of the file that you can access with Time Machine. To obtain that kind of functionality in apps without Auto Save and Versions, you'll need to use Save As to create a new version of the file periodically.

Click the little "v"

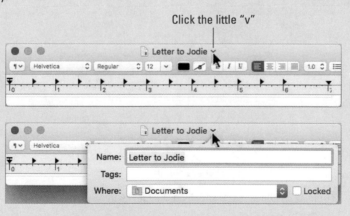

In a few sections of this book, I ask you not only to read the instructions while sitting in front of your Mac but also to perform each step of the instructions as described. This section is one of them. If you read it and follow along, I can pretty much guarantee that it'll make sense. If you read it somewhere other than at your Mac, it could be a mite confusing.

Saving a file works pretty much the same way in any application you use to create documents. For this example, I use the OS X word processing application, TextEdit, but the process will be very similar in Microsoft Word, Adobe Photoshop, Apple Keynote, or any other application.

If you're going to follow along as I recommend, please launch the TextEdit program now (it's in your Applications folder), click the New Document button or choose File➪New, and type a few words on the Untitled page that appears after you launch it.

Now that we're both on the same page (literally and figuratively), here's how saving a file works. When you choose to save a file for the first time (choose File➪Save or press ⌘+S), a Save sheet appears in front of the document that you're saving, as shown in Figure 6-5. I call this a *basic* Save sheet (as opposed to an *expanded* Save sheet, which I get to in a moment):

1. **In the Save As field, type a name for your file.**

   When a Save sheet appears for the first time, the Save As field is active and displays the name of the document. The document name (usually, Untitled) is selected; when you begin typing, the name disappears and is replaced by the name you type.

Disclosure button

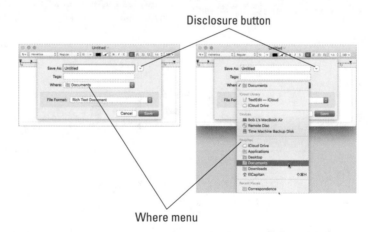

Where menu

Figure 6-5: A basic Save sheet looks a lot like this.

2. **If the Where pop-up menu lists the location where you want to save your file, choose that location and proceed to Step 5; if not, click the disclosure button (the one with the little V on the right of the *Save As* field in Figure 6-5).**

   You can choose from a short list of folders and volumes listed in the basic Save sheet's Where pop-up menu (which are the same devices and favorites you see in the Sidebar of Finder windows). Or, if you click the disclosure button on the right of the Save As field, the sheet expands so that you can navigate folders just as you do in the Finder: by opening them to see their contents.

If you click the Save button shown on the left in Figure 6-5, your file will be saved to Cloud Drive, Apple's free online storage service (which you discover later in this chapter). Or you can choose another location from the Where menu, as shown on the right in Figure 6-5.

If you switch to expanded view by clicking the disclosure button (the one with the little down-pointing V on the right of the *Save As* field in Figure 6-5), a standard Save sheet appears so you can save your file in any folder you like.

Note that the Where menu in the expanded Save sheet on the right in Figure 6-6 doesn't have Favorites, but instead displays the path to the folder the file will be saved in (Documents). I think that the Where menu should be the same in both basic and expanded Save sheets, as it was before OS X 10.5 Leopard. It seems more confusing to have the contents of this menu change based on whether the Save sheet is expanded or not. I've called it to your attention so it won't confuse you.

Figure 6-6: An expanded Save sheet looks similar to this one (shown in List view).

For what it's worth, Favorites are still available in an expanded Save sheet, but instead of being in the Where menu, they're in the Sidebar.

Switch between the basic and expanded Save sheets a few times by clicking the disclosure button. Make sure that you see and understand the difference between what you see in the Where menu in a basic Save sheet and what you see in the Where menu in an expanded Save sheet. All the steps that follow assume you're using the expanded Save sheet:

3. **To make it easier to find the folder you want to save your file into, choose among views by clicking the Icon, List, or Column view button.**

   The buttons look like their counterparts in Finder windows. In Icon view, you double-click a folder to open it. List view offers disclosure triangles for folders and disks, so single-click the disclosure triangles of folders to see their contents. In Column view, you click an item on the left to see its contents on the right, just as you do in a column-view Finder window.

   You can also use the Forward and Back buttons or the Sidebar, both available only in an expanded Save dialog, to conveniently navigate your disk. Many of these navigation aids work just like the ones in the Finder; see Chapter 4 for more details. You can enlarge the Save sheet to see more the same way you enlarge a Finder window: Drag an edge or corner of the sheet.

   If you can't find the folder in which you want to save your document, type the folder name in the Search box. It works just like the Search box in a Finder window, as described in Chapters 4 and 7. You don't even have to press Return; the Save sheet updates itself to show you only items that match the characters as you typed them.

4. **Select the folder where you want to save your file in the Where pop-up menu or Sidebar.**

5. **If you want to create a new subfolder of the selected folder to save your file in, click the New Folder button, give the new folder a name, and then save your file in it.**

   In Figure 6-7, I selected an existing folder named Novels. You can tell that it's selected because its name is displayed in the Where menu and highlighted below that in the first column.

   The selected folder is where your file will be saved.

   The keyboard shortcut for New Folder is Shift+⌘+N, regardless of whether you're in a Save sheet or the Finder. If I want to create a new folder inside the Novels folder in Figure 6-7, I could click the New Folder button or press the shortcut.

6. **In the File Format pop-up menu (hidden in Figure 6-5), make sure the format selected is the one you want.**

7. **If you want to turn off the display of file extensions (such as .rtf, .pdf, and .txt) in Save sheets, select the Hide Extension check box.**

   Note that this option isn't available in the Basic save sheet; it's only available when the Save sheet is expanded.

8. **Double-check the Where pop-up menu one last time to make sure that the correct folder is selected; then click the Save button to save the file to the active folder.**

Where menu

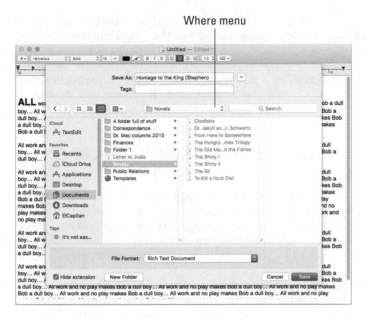

Figure 6-7: Saving a file in the Novels folder (which is in the Documents folder).

If you click Save, the file appears in the folder you selected. If you change your mind about saving this file, clicking Cancel dismisses the Save sheet without saving anything anywhere. In other words, the Cancel button returns things to the way they were before you displayed the Save sheet.

After you save a file for the first time, choosing File⇨Save or pressing ⌘+S won't bring up a Save sheet. Instead, what happens next depends on whether the app supports El Capitan's Auto Save and Versions. If the app *doesn't* support Auto Save and Versions, Save and its shortcut (⌘+S), merely resave your document in the same location and with the same name. If you want to save a unique version with a different name you choose the Save As command and save the file under a new name. If the app *does* support Auto Save and Versions, however, the upcoming section, "Save As versus Duplicate: Different names for the same result," explains how things work.

When you use apps that don't support Auto Save and Versions, I beg you to get into the habit of pressing ⌘+S often. It can't hurt — and just might save your bacon someday.

One last thing: In Figures 6-5, 6-6, and 6-7, I used the Save sheet for TextEdit as an example. In programs other than TextEdit, the Save sheet might contain additional options, fewer options, or different options, and therefore may look slightly different. The File Format menu, for example, is a feature specific to TextEdit; it might not appear in other applications' Save sheets. Don't worry. The Save sheet always *works* the same way, no matter what options it offers.

Save As versus Duplicate: Different names for the same result

The two commands File ⇨ Duplicate and File ⇨ Save As serve the same purpose and achieve the same result. The difference is that you'll find File ⇨ Duplicate in apps that support Versions and Auto Save, and File ⇨ Save As in apps that don't. They're different names for achieving the same result: Saving a file that's already been saved with a different name.

Before I get into the details, you may be wondering *why* you would want to save an existing file with a different name. So here's a good (albeit kind of rude) example: Suppose that you have two cousins, Kate and Nancy. You write Kate a long, chatty letter and save this document with the name Letter to Kate. Later, you decide that you want to send almost the same letter to Nancy, but you want to change a few things. So you change the part about your date last night and replace all references to Kate's husband, Kevin, with references to Nancy's husband, Norman. (Aren't computers grand?)

So you make all these changes in Letter to Kate, but you haven't resaved this document yet — and although the document on your screen is actually a letter to Nancy, its filename is still Letter to Kate. Think of what would happen if you were to save it now without using the Save As feature: Letter to Kate reflects the changes that you just made. (The stuff in the letter meant for Kate is blown away, replaced by the stuff that you just wrote to Nancy.) Thus the filename Letter to Kate is inaccurate. Even worse, you might no longer have a copy of the original letter you sent to Kate! The solution? Just use Save As or Duplicate to rename this file Letter to Nancy by choosing File ⇨ Save As or File ⇨ Duplicate.

If you opt for Save As: A Save sheet appears, in which you can type a different filename in the Save As field. You can also navigate to another folder, if you like, and save the newly named version of the file there. Now you have two distinct files: Letter to Kate and Letter to Nancy. Both contain the stuff they should, but both started life from the same file.

If you choose Duplicate: The title bar of the document becomes editable so you can change its name without even seeing a Save sheet. (Refer to the figure in the earlier sidebar, "Does it have Auto Save and Versions or not?") Press Return, and the renamed file will be saved in the same folder as the original. Or, if you want to save the newly renamed file in a different location, choose File⇨Move To or click the little triangle to the right of the document's name, choose Move To in its pop-up menu, and then from the pop-up menu, select a folder in which to save the file.

Now that you understand what Save As or Duplicate are all about, here's an easier way to get the same result: Before you start, duplicate the document in the Finder (choose File⇨Duplicate or press ⌘+D). Rename the copy and open it. This way, when you're done making changes, you don't have to remember to choose Save As; you can just perform your habitual Save. This approach also protects you from accidentally saving part of the letter to Nancy without changing the file's name first (which you're likely to do if you're following my advice about saving often). So when you decide that you're going to reuse a document, choose Save As (or duplicate and rename the file) *before* you begin working on it, just to be safe.

For those who, like yours truly, prefer to use Save As, just press the Option key before you click the File menu and Duplicate magically transmogrifies into Save As. Sweet!

Versions gives you the benefits of Save As without any action on your part, but many programs still lack support for Auto Save and Versions as of this writing. And, in fact, some Apple apps, as well as most third-party apps, still use the Save As technique, and I expect that to be the status quo for quite some time. But because some of Apple's offerings (most notably TextEdit and the iWork apps) use Auto Save and Versions, I'd be remiss if I glossed over the newer way of doing things.

One last thing: If the app you're using supports Versions, it creates a snapshot called a Version automatically as you work, when you pause, every five minutes, and every time you choose File⇨Save (⌘+S). Choose File⇨Revert To⇨Browse All Versions or click the Time Machine icon in the Dock while the document is active onscreen (see Chapter 18 for more on Time Machine). Either way, Time Machine displays versions of the document side-by-side, as shown in Figure 6-8.

Just so you know, Figure 6-8 is the Time Machine backup utility displaying the various Versions.

The Tab key is useful for navigating the Save or Save As sheet. See www.dummies.com/cheatsheet/osxelcapitan for details.

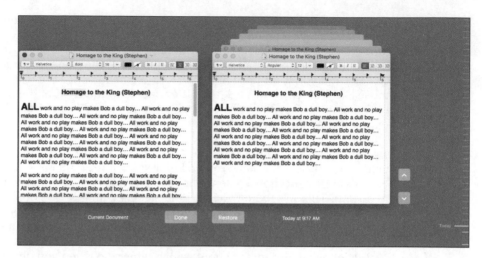

Figure 6-8: Browse All Versions lets you compare all versions and revert to an earlier version.

Open, Sez Me

You can open any icon in the Finder — whether it's a file or a folder — in at least six ways. (Okay, there are at least *seven* ways, but one of them belongs to aliases, which I discuss in great detail back in Chapter 4.) Anyway, here are the ways:

- Click the icon once to select it and choose File➪Open.
- Double-click the icon.

  If the icon doesn't open, you double-clicked too slowly. You can test (and adjust) your mouse's sensitivity to double-click speed in the Mouse (or Trackpad) System Preference pane, which you can access by launching the System Preferences application (from the Applications folder, the Dock, or the menu) and then clicking the Mouse (or Trackpad) icon.

- Select the icon and then press either ⌘+O or ⌘+↓.
- Right-click or Control-click it and then choose Open from the contextual menu.
- If the icon is a document, drag it onto the application icon (or the Dock icon of an application) that can open that type of document.
- If the icon is a document, right-click or Control-click it and choose an application from the Open With submenu of the contextual menu.

You can also open any document icon from within an application, of course. Here's how that works:

1. **Just launch your favorite program, and choose File ⇨ Open (or press ⌘+O, which works in most Mac programs).**

   An Open dialog appears, like the one shown in Figure 6-9.

iBooks Author application
(gray; can't be opened)

Figure 6-9: The Open dialog using Column view.

When you use a program's Open dialog, only files that the program knows how to open appear enabled (in black rather than light gray) in the file list. In effect, the program filters out the files it can't open, so you barely see them in the Open dialog. This method of selectively displaying certain items in Open dialogs is a feature of most applications. Therefore, when you're using TextEdit, its Open dialog dims all files it can't open, like the iBooks Author application in the Novels folder in Figure 6-9. Pretty neat, eh?

For what it's worth, TextEdit can open text, Rich Text Format, Microsoft Word, Microsoft Excel, and some picture files.

2. **In the dialog, simply navigate to the file you want to open (using the same techniques you use in a Save sheet).**

   Click a favorite folder in the Sidebar or use Spotlight (see Chapter 7) if you can't remember where the file resides.

3. **Select your file and click the Open button.**

For what it's worth, some applications allow you to select multiple files in their Open dialogs by holding down either Shift (for contiguous selections) or ⌘ (for noncontiguous selections). If you need to open several files, it's worth a try; the worst thing that could happen is that it won't work and you'll have to open the items one at a time.

Some programs, including Microsoft Word and Adobe Photoshop, have a Show or Format menu in their Open dialogs. This menu lets you specify the type(s) of files you want to see as available in the Open dialog. You can often open a file that appears dimmed by choosing All Documents from the Show or Format menu (in those applications with Open dialogs that offer such a menu).

With drag-and-drop

Macintosh drag-and-drop is usually all about dragging text and graphics from one place to another. But there's another angle to drag-and-drop — one that has to do with files and icons.

You can open a document by dragging its icon onto the icon of the proper application. You can open a document created with Microsoft Word, for example, by dragging the document icon onto the Microsoft Word application icon. The Word icon highlights, and the document launches. Usually, of course, it's easier to double-click a document's icon to open it; the proper application opens automatically when you do — or at least, it does most of the time. Which reminds me. . . .

With a Quick Look

The Quick Look window, shown in Figure 6-10, shows you the contents of many types of files.

Figure 6-10: The Quick Look window showing the contents of an image file.

To use the Quick Look command to peek at the contents of most files in Open dialogs, right-click or Control-click the file and choose Quick Look, or use its easy-to-remember shortcut: Press the spacebar or ⌘+Y. Whichever way, you'll soon see the contents of that file in a floating window without launching another application.

Chapter 7 contains more information about Quick Look.

When your Mac can't open a file

If you try to open a file, but OS X can't find a program to open that file, OS X prompts you with an alert window. I tried to open a very old (1993) file created on a long-defunct Psion Series 3 handheld PDA (a file so old that most of you have probably never seen the .wrd file extension), shown in Figure 6-11.

Figure 6-11: Oops! OS X helps you find the correct application.

Click Cancel to abort the attempt to open the file, or click the Choose Application or Search App Store button to select another application to open this file.

If you click the Choose Application button, a dialog appears (conveniently opened to your Applications folder). Applications that OS X doesn't think can be used to open the file are dimmed. For a wider choice of applications, choose All Applications (instead of Recommended Applications) from the Enable pop-up menu.

You can't open every file with every program. If you try to open an MP3 (audio) file with Microsoft Excel (a spreadsheet), for example, it just won't work; you get an error message or a screen full of gibberish. Sometimes, you just have to keep trying until you find the right program; at other times, you don't have a program that can open the file.

TIP

When in doubt, use a search engine to read about the file extension. You'll usually find out more than you need to know about what application(s) create files with that extension.

With the application of your choice

I don't know about you, but people send me files all the time that were created by applications I don't use . . . or at least that I don't use for that document type. OS X lets you specify the application in which you want to open a document in the future when you double-click it. More than that, you can specify that you want all documents of that type to open with the specified application. "Where is this magic bullet hidden?" you ask. Right there in the file's Info window.

Assigning a file type to an application

Suppose that you want all .jpg files that usually open in Preview to open instead in Pixelmator, a more capable third-party image-editing program. Here's what to do:

1. **Click one of the files in the Finder.**

2. **Choose File⇨Get Info (⌘+I).**

   Or right-click, Control-click, or tap with two fingers on the file and then select Get Info from the contextual shortcut menu.

3. **In the Info window, click the gray triangle to disclose the Open With pane.**

4. **From the pop-up menu, choose an application that OS X believes will open this document type.**

   In Figure 6-12, I'm choosing Pixelmator. Now Pixelmator opens when I open this file (instead of the default application, Preview).

5. **(Optional) If you click the Change All button at the bottom of the Open With pane, as shown in Figure 6-12, you make Pixelmator the new default application for all .jpg files that would otherwise be opened in Preview.**

Figure 6-12: Changing the application that opens this document.

Notice the handy alert that appears when you click the Change All button and how nicely it explains what will happen if you click Continue.

Opening a file with an application other than the default

Here's one more technique that works great when you want to open a document with a program other than its default. Just drag the file onto the application's icon or alias icon or Dock icon, and presto — the file opens in the application.

If I were to double-click an MP3 file, for example, the file usually would open in iTunes (and, by default, would be copied into my iTunes Library). But I frequently want to audition (listen to) MP3 files with QuickTime Player, so they're not automatically added to my iTunes music library. Dragging the MP3 file onto QuickTime Player's icon in the Applications folder or its Dock icon (if it's on the Dock) solves this conundrum quickly and easily.

If the icon doesn't highlight and you release the mouse button anyway, the file ends up in the same folder as the application with the icon that didn't highlight. If that happens, just choose Edit➪Undo (or press ⌘+Z), and the mislaid file magically returns to where it was before you dropped it. Just remember — don't do anything else after you drop the file, or Undo might not work. If Undo doesn't work, you must move the file back to its original location manually.

Only applications that *might* be able to open the file should highlight when you drag the file on them. That doesn't mean the document will be usable — just that the application can *open* it. Suffice it to say that OS X is usually smart enough to figure out which applications on your hard drive can open what documents — and to offer you a choice.

One last thing: If all you want to do is open a file with an application other than its default (and not change anything for the future), the techniques I just described work fine, but an even easier way is to right-click the file and choose another app from the contextual menu, as shown in Figure 6-13.

You can also change the default application to open this file by pressing Option after you right-click the file, and the Open With command will magically transform into Always Open With. Alas, you can't change the default application for *all* files of this type (.jpg in Figures 6-12 and 6-13); for that, you'll have to visit the Info window.

Figure 6-13: To open a file with an app other than its default, right-click and choose the app you desire.

Organizing Your Stuff in Folders

I won't pretend to be able to organize your Mac for you. Organizing your files is as personal as your taste in music; you develop your own style with the Mac. But after you know how to open and save documents when you're using applications, these sections provide food for thought — some ideas about how I organize things — and some suggestions that can make organization easier for you, regardless of how you choose to do it.

The upcoming sections look at the difference between a file and a folder; show you how to set up nested folders; and cover how some special folder features work. After you have a good handle on these things, you'll almost certainly be a savvier — and better organized — OS X user.

Files versus folders

When I speak of a *file,* I'm talking about what's connected to any icon except a folder or disk icon. A file can be a document, an application, an alias of a file or an application, a dictionary, a font, or any other icon that *isn't* a folder or disk. The main distinction is that you can't put something *in* most file icons.

The exceptions are icons that represent OS X packages. A *package* is an icon that acts like a file but isn't. Examples of icons that are really packages include many software installers and applications, as well as documents saved by some programs (such as Keynote, GarageBand, Pages, or TextEdit files saved in its .rtfd format). When you open an icon that represents a package in the usual way (double-click, choose File⇨Open, press ⌘+O, and so on), the program or document opens. If you want to see the contents of an icon that represents a package, right-click or Control-click the icon and choose Show Package Contents from the contextual menu. If you see an item by that name, you know that the icon is a package; if you don't see Show Package Contents on the contextual menu, the icon represents a file, not a package.

When I talk about *folders,* I'm talking about things that work like manila folders in the real world. Their icons look like folders, like the one in the margin to the left; they can contain files or other folders, called *subfolders.* You can put any icon — any file or folder — inside a folder.

Here's an exception: If you try to put a disk icon in a folder, all you get is an alias to the disk *unless* you hold down the Option key. Remember that you can't put a disk icon in a folder that exists on the disk itself. In other words, you can copy a disk icon only to a *different disk;* you can never copy a disk icon to a folder that resides on that disk. For more about aliases, flip to Chapter 4.

File icons can look like practically anything. If the icon doesn't look like a folder, package, or one of the numerous disk icons, you can be pretty sure that it's a file.

Organizing your stuff with subfolders

As I mention earlier in this chapter, you can put folders inside other folders to organize your icons. A folder nested inside another folder is a *subfolder*.

You can create subfolders according to whatever system makes sense to you — but why reinvent the wheel? Here are some organizational topic ideas and naming examples for subfolders:

- **By type of document:** Word-Processing Documents, Spreadsheet Documents, Graphics Documents
- **By date:** Documents May–June, Documents Spring '12
- **By content:** Memos, Outgoing Letters, Expense Reports
- **By project:** Project X, Project Y, Project Z

When you notice your folders swelling and starting to get messy (that is, filling with tons of files), subdivide them again by using a combination of these methods that makes sense to you. Suppose that you start by subdividing your Documents folder into multiple subfolders. Later, when those folders begin to get full, you can subdivide them even further, as shown in Figure 6-14.

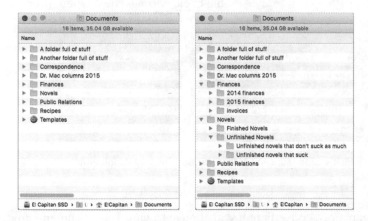

Figure 6-14: Before (left) and after (right) organizing the Novels and Finances folders with subfolders.

My point (yes, I do have one!): Allow your folder structure to be organic, growing as you need it to grow. Let it happen. Don't let any single folder get so full that it's a hassle to deal with. Create new subfolders when things start to get crowded. (I explain how to create folders in the next section.)

How do you know when a folder is too full and you should start creating subfolders? See www.dummies.com/cheatsheet/osxelcapitan for details.

If you want to monkey around with some subfolders, a good place to start is the Documents folder, which is inside your Home folder (that is, the Documents folder is a *subfolder* of your Home folder).

If you use a particular folder a great deal, put it in your Dock, or make an alias of it and move the alias from the Documents folder to your Home folder or to your Desktop (for more info on aliases, see Chapter 4) to make the folder easier to access. Or drag the folder (or its alias) to the Sidebar, so it's always available, including in Open dialogs and Save sheets. If you write a lot of letters, keep an alias to your Correspondence folder in your Home folder, on the Dock, on your Desktop, or in the Sidebar for quick access. (By the way, there's no reason why you can't have a folder appear in all four places, if you like. That's what aliases are for, right?)

If you create your own subfolders in the Documents folder, you can click that folder on the Dock to reveal them, as shown in Figure 6-15. I show you how to customize the Dock in Chapter 3.

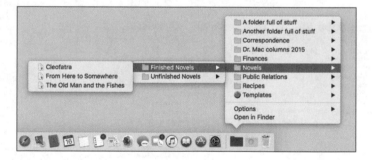

Figure 6-15: It's super-convenient to have your Documents folder on the Dock.

It's even more convenient if you choose to view the Documents folder as a list, as described in Chapter 3 and shown in Figure 6-15.

Creating new folders

So you think that Apple has already given you enough folders? Can't imagine why you'd need more? Think of creating new folders the same way you'd think of labeling a new folder at work for a specific project. New folders help you keep your files organized, enabling you to reorganize them just the way you want. Creating folders is really quite simple.

To create a new folder, just follow these steps:

1. **Decide which window you want the new folder to appear in — and then make sure that window is active.**

   If you want to create a new folder right on the Desktop, make sure that *no* window is active or that you're working in your Home/Desktop folder window. You can make a window active by clicking it, and you can make the Desktop active if you have windows onscreen by clicking the Desktop itself.

2. **Choose File ⇨ New Folder (or press Shift+⌘+N).**

   A new, untitled folder appears in the active window with its name box already highlighted, ready for you to type a new name for it.

3. **Type a name for your folder.**

   If you accidentally click anywhere before you type a name for the folder, the name box is no longer highlighted. To highlight it again, select the icon (single-click it) and press Return once. Now you can type its new name.

Give your folders relevant names. Folders with nebulous titles like sfdghb or Stuff or Untitled won't make it any easier to find something six months from now.

For folders and files that you might share with users of non-Macintosh computers, here's the rule for maximum compatibility: Use no punctuation and no Option-key characters in the folder name. Periods, slashes, backslashes, and colons in particular can be reserved for use by other operating systems. When I say Option-key characters, I'm talking about special-purpose ones, such as ™ (Option+2), ® (Option+R), ¢ (Option+4), and even © (Option+G).

Navigating with spring-loaded folders

A *spring-loaded folder* pops open when you drag something onto it without releasing the mouse button. Spring-loaded folders work with all folder or disk icons in all views and in the Sidebar. Because you just got the short course on folders, subfolders, and various ways to organize your stuff, you're ready for your introduction to one of my favorite ways to get around my disks, folders, and subfolders.

Here's how spring-loaded folders work:

1. **Select any icon except a disk icon.**

   The folder highlights to indicate that it's selected.

2. **Drag the selected icon onto any folder or disk icon — but don't release the mouse button.**

   I call this *hovering* because you're doing just that: hovering the cursor over a folder or disk icon without releasing the button.

   In a second or two, the highlighted folder or disk flashes twice and then springs open, right under the cursor.

   Press the spacebar to make the folder spring open immediately.

3. **After the folder springs open, perform any of these handy operations:**

   - Continue to traverse your folder structure this way. Subfolders continue to pop open until you release the mouse button.

   - If you release the mouse button, the icon you've been dragging is dropped into the active folder at the time. That window remains open — but all the windows you traversed clean up after themselves by closing automatically, leaving your window clean and uncluttered.

   - If you want to cancel a spring-loaded folder, drag the cursor away from the folder icon or outside the boundaries of the sprung window. The folder pops shut.

After you get used to spring-loaded folders, you'll wonder how you ever got along without them. They work in all four views, and they work with icons in the Sidebar or Dock. Give 'em a try, and you'll be hooked.

In previous versions of OS X you could toggle spring-loaded folders on or off in the Finder's Preferences window, which also offered a setting for how long the Finder waits before it springs the folders open. Both the on/off switch and the length of time slider are missing in El Capitan. Perhaps their demise was because no one ever used them, or it could be an oversight on Apple's part and they'll return in a future version of OS X.

Smart folders

As the late Steve Jobs was fond of saying near the end of his keynotes, "There is one more thing," and when it comes to folders, that one last thing is the smart folder.

A *smart folder* lets you save search criteria and have them work in the background to display the results in real time. In other words, a smart folder is updated continuously, so it displays all the files on your computer that match the search criteria at the moment.

So, for example, I create a smart folder that gathers all files with Dr. Mac in their name that were created after 1/1/2015, as shown in Figure 6-16. Or you can create a smart folder that displays graphics files, but only the ones bigger (or smaller) than a specified file size. Then all those files appear in one convenient smart folder.

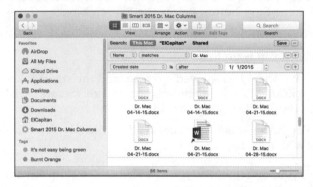

Figure 6-16: A smart folder that displays files that meet certain criteria.

The possibilities are endless. Because smart folders use alias-like technology to display items, the actual files reside in only one location: the folder where you originally put them. True to their name, smart folders don't gather the files themselves in a separate place; rather, they gather *aliases* of files, leaving the originals right where you stashed them. Neat!

Also, because Spotlight (discussed in Chapter 7) is built deep into the bowels of the OS X file system and kernel, smart folders are updated in real time and so are always current, even after you add or delete files on your hard drive since creating the smart folder.

Smart folders are so useful that Apple provides five ways to create one. The following steps show you how:

1. **Start your smart folder by using any of the following methods:**

   • Choose File ⇨ New Smart Folder.

   • Press ⌘+Option+N.

- Choose File➪Find.

- Press ⌘+F.

- Type at least one character in the Search box of a Finder window.

If you have All My Files selected in the Sidebar, you can't use the last method, because All My Files is a smart folder itself — one with a weird icon, but a smart folder nonetheless.

2. **Refine the criteria for your search by clicking the + button to add a criterion or the – button to delete one.**

3. **When you're satisfied and ready to gather your criteria into a smart folder, click the Save button below the Search box.**

   A sheet drops down.

4. **Choose where you want to save your folder.**

   While the Save sheet is displayed, you can add the smart folder to the Sidebar by clicking the Add to Sidebar check box (Smart 2015 Dr. Mac Columns in the Sidebar in Figure 6-16).

5. **When you're finished editing criteria, click the Save button to save the folder with its criteria.**

After you create your smart folder, you can save it anywhere on any hard drive and use it like any other folder.

If you want to *change* the criteria for a smart folder you created, right-click or Control-click the smart folder in the Sidebar and choose Show Search Criteria.

When you're finished changing the criteria, click the Save button to resave your folder. Don't worry — if you try to close a smart folder that you modify without saving your changes, OS X politely asks whether you want to save this smart folder and warns that if you don't save, the changes you made will be lost. You may be asked whether you want to replace the previous smart folder of the same name; usually, you do.

Smart folders (with the exception of the Sidebar's All My Files, which has its own weird little icon) display a little gear in their center, making them easy to tell apart from regular folders.

Smart folders can save you a lot of time and effort, so if you haven't played with them much (or at all) yet, be sure to give 'em a try.

Shuffling Files and Folders

Sometimes, keeping files and folders organized means moving them from one place to another. At other times, you want to copy them, rename them, or compress them to send to a friend. These sections explain all those things and more.

All the techniques that I discuss in the following sections work at least as well for windows that use List, Column, or Cover Flow view as they do for windows that use Icon view. I use Icon view in the figures in this section only because it's the best view for pictures to show you what's going on. For what it's worth, I find moving and copying files much easier in windows that use List or Column view.

Moving files and folders

You can move files and folders around within a window to your heart's content — *as long as that window is set to Icon view.* Just click and drag any icon to its new location in the window. If the icons won't move, make sure View⇨Arrange By is set to None.

Some people spend hours arranging icons in a window until they're just so. But because using Icon view wastes so much screen space, I avoid using icons in a window.

You can't move icons around in a window that is displayed in List, Column, or Cover Flow view, which makes total sense when you think about it. (Well, you can move them to put them in a different folder in List, Column, or Cover Flow view, but that's not moving them around, really.) And you can't move icons around in a window under the spell of the Arrange By command.

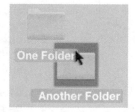

As you probably expect from Apple by now, you have choices for how you move one file or folder into another folder. You can use these techniques to move any icon (folder, document, alias, or program icon) into folders or onto other disks.

  ✓ **Drag an icon onto a folder icon.** Drag the icon for one folder (or file) onto the icon for another folder (or disk) and then release when the second icon is highlighted, as shown in Figure 6-17, top. The first folder will then be inside the second folder. Put another way, the first folder is now a subfolder of the second folder. This technique works regardless of whether the second folder's window is open.

Figure 6-17: Two ways of putting one folder into another.

✔ **Drag an icon into an open folder's window.** Drag the icon for one folder (or file) into the open window for a second folder (or disk), and then release it when the second folder's window is highlighted in yellow, as shown in Figure 6-17 (bottom).

If you want to move an item from one *disk* to another disk, you can't use the preceding tricks. Your item is copied, not moved. If you want to *move* a file or folder from one disk to another, you have to hold down the ⌘ key when you drag an icon from one disk to another. The little Copying Files window even changes to read *Moving* Files. Nice touch, eh?

Selecting multiple icons

Sometimes you want to move or copy several items into a single folder. The process is pretty much the same as it is when you copy one file or folder: that is, you just drag the icon to where you want it and drop it there. But you need to select all the items you want before you can drag them en masse to their destination.

If you want to move all the files in a particular folder, simply choose Edit⇨Select All or press ⌘+A. This command selects all icons in the active window, regardless of whether you can see them onscreen. If no window is active, choosing Select All selects every icon on the Desktop.

But what if you want to select only some of the files in the active window or on the Desktop? Here's the most convenient method:

1. **To select more than one icon in a folder, do one of the following:**

   • *Click once within the folder window (don't click any one icon), and drag your mouse (or keypad) while continuing to hold down the mouse button.* You see an outline of a box around the icons while you drag, and all icons within or touching the box become highlighted (see Figure 6-18).

   • *Click one icon and hold down the Shift key while you click others.* As long as you hold down the Shift key, each new icon that you click is added to the selection. To deselect an icon, click it a second time while still holding down the Shift key.

   • *Click one icon and hold down the ⌘ key while you click others.* The difference between using the Shift and ⌘ keys is that the ⌘ key doesn't select everything between it and the first item selected when your window is in List, Cover Flow, or Column view. In Icon view, it really doesn't make much difference.

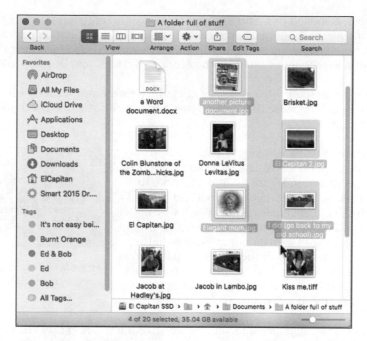

Figure 6-18: Select more than one icon by clicking and dragging with your mouse (or trackpad).

To deselect an icon, click it while holding down the ⌘ key.

2. **After you select the icons, click one of them (clicking anywhere else deselects the icons) and drag them to the location where you want to move them (or Option-drag to copy them).**

Be careful with multiple selections, especially when you drag icons to the Trash. You can easily — and accidentally — select more than one icon, so watch out that you don't accidentally put the wrong icon in the Trash by not paying close attention. (I detail how the Trash icon works later in this chapter.)

Playing the icon name game: Renaming icons

Icon, icon, bo-bicon, banana-fanna fo-ficon. Betcha can change the name of any old icon! Well, that's not entirely true. . . .

If an icon is locked or busy (the application is currently open), or if you don't have the owner's permission to rename that icon (see Chapter 12 for details about permissions), you can't rename it. Similarly, you should never rename certain reserved icons (such as the Library, System, and Desktop folders).

To rename an icon, you can either click the icon's name directly (don't click the icon itself because that selects the icon) or click the icon and press Return once.

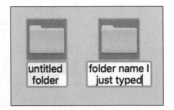

Figure 6-19: Change an icon's name by typing over the old one.

Either way, the icon's name is selected and surrounded with a box, and you can type a new name, as shown in Figure 6-19. In addition, the cursor changes from a pointer to a text-editing I-beam. An I-beam cursor is the Mac's way of telling you that you can type now. At this point, if you click the I-beam cursor anywhere in the name box, you can edit the icon's original name. If you don't click the I-beam cursor in the name box but just begin typing, the icon's original name is replaced by what you type.

If you've never changed an icon's name, give it a try. And don't forget: If you click the icon itself, the icon is selected, and you won't be able to change its name. If you do accidentally select the icon, just press Return once to edit the name of the icon. Yosemite was the first version of OS X to allow you to rename more than one file at a time, and El Capitan continues the tradition. To rename a group of files, first select them all, and then right-click anywhere in your selection and choose Rename *x* Items (where *x* is the number of files selected) from the pop-up menu. A sheet appears with options for adding or replacing text in the existing filename, or creating a custom format with indexes, counters, and dates before or after whatever new filename you choose.

I use a more powerful third-party app called Better Rename ($19.99 in the Mac App Store), primarily because I've been using it for years and it has useful options that El Capitan's new batch-renaming feature doesn't offer. On the other hand, El Capitan's new batch-renaming feature is pretty good and all that many people will ever need. For those who wish it were a little more robust or powerful, Better Rename is just what the doctor ordered.

One last thing: If you have two or more icons you want to move to a new folder, select the items and choose File⇨New Folder with Selection, press ⌘+Control+N, or right-click or Control-click one of the selected items and choose New Folder with Selection. All three techniques will create a new folder, move the selected icons into it, and select the name of the new folder (which will be New Folder with Items) so you can type its new name immediately.

Comprehending the Clipboard

Before you start copying files, let me introduce you to the Clipboard. The *Clipboard* is a holding area for the last thing that you cut or copied. That copied item can be text, a picture, a portion of a picture, an object in a drawing program, a column of numbers in a spreadsheet, any icon (except a disk), or just about anything else that can be selected. In other words, the Clipboard is the Mac's temporary storage area.

Most of the time, the Clipboard works quietly in the background, but you can ask the Clipboard to reveal itself by choosing Edit⇨Show Clipboard. This command summons the Clipboard window, which lists the type of item (such as text, picture, or sound) on the Clipboard — and a message letting you know whether the item on the Clipboard can be displayed.

As a storage area, the Clipboard's contents are temporary. *Very* temporary. When you cut or copy an item, that item remains on the Clipboard only until you cut or copy something else, logout, or restart. When you do cut or copy something else, the new item replaces the Clipboard's contents, and the newcomer remains on the Clipboard until you cut or copy something else. And so it goes.

Whatever is on the Clipboard heads straight for oblivion if you crash, lose power, log out, or shut down your Mac, so don't count on it too heavily or for too long.

The Clipboard commands on the Edit menu are enabled only when they can actually be used. If the selected item can be cut or copied, the Cut and Copy commands in the Edit menu are enabled. If the selected item can't be cut or copied, the commands are unavailable and are dimmed (gray). If the Clipboard is empty or the current document can't accept what's on the Clipboard, the Paste command is dimmed. Finally, when nothing is selected, the Cut, Copy, and Clear commands are dimmed.

Icons can't be cut; they can only be copied or pasted. So when an icon is selected, the Cut command is always gray.

Copying files and folders

One way to copy icons from one place to another is to use the Clipboard. When a file or folder icon is selected, choose Edit⇨Copy (or use its shortcut, ⌘+C) to copy the selected icon to the Clipboard. Note that this doesn't delete the selected item; it just makes a copy of it on the Clipboard.

To paste the copied icon in another location, choose Edit ⇨ Paste (or use its shortcut, ⌘+V).

Other methods of copying icons from one place to another include these:

- **Drag an icon from one folder icon onto another folder icon while holding down the Option key.** Release the mouse button when the second folder is highlighted. This technique works regardless of whether the second folder's window is open. If you don't hold down the Option key, you move the icon to a new location rather than copy it, as I explain a little later in this section.

  When you copy something by dragging and dropping it with the Option key held down, the cursor changes to include a little plus sign (+) next to the arrow, as shown in the margin. Neat!

- **Drag an icon into an open window for another folder while holding down the Option key.** Drag the icon for the file or folder that you want to copy into the open window for a second folder (or other hard disk or removable media, such as a USB flash drive).

- **Choose File ⇨ Duplicate (⌘+D) or right-click or Control-click the file or folder that you want to duplicate; then choose Duplicate from the contextual menu that appears.** This makes a copy of the selected icon, adds the word *copy* to its name, and then places the copy in the same window as the original icon. You can use the Duplicate command on any icon except a disk icon.

  You can't duplicate an entire disk onto itself. But you can copy an entire disk (call it Disk 1) to any other actual, physical, separate disk (call it Disk 2) as long as Disk 2 has enough space available. Just hold down Option and drag Disk 1 onto Disk 2's icon. The contents of Disk 1 are copied to Disk 2 and appear on Disk 2 in a folder named Disk 1.

You can cut an icon's name, but you can't cut the icon itself; you may only copy an icon. To achieve the effect of cutting an icon, select the icon, copy it to the Clipboard, paste it in its new location, and then move the original icon to the Trash.

If you're wondering why anyone would ever want to copy a file, trust me: Someday, you will. Suppose that you have a file called Long Letter to Mom in a folder called Old Correspondence. You figure that Mom has forgotten that letter by now, and you want to send it again. But before you do, you want to change the date and delete the reference to Clarence, her pit bull, who passed away last year. So now you need to put a copy of Long Letter to Mom in your Current Correspondence folder. This technique yields the same result as making a copy of a file by using Save As, which I describe earlier in this chapter.

When you copy a file, it's wise to change the name of the copied file. Having more than one file on your hard drive with exactly the same name isn't a good idea, even if the files are in different folders. Trust me that having 12 files called Expense Report or 15 files named Doctor Mac Consulting Invoice can be confusing, no matter how well organized your folder structure is. Add distinguishing words or dates to file and folder names so that they're named something more explicit, such as Expense Report Q3 2010 or Doctor Mac Consulting Invoice 4-4-2011.

You can have lots of files with the same name *on the same disk* (although, as I mention earlier, it's probably not a good idea). But your Mac won't let you have more than one file with the same name and extension (.txt, .jpg, .doc) *in the same folder.*

Pasting from the Clipboard

As I mention earlier in this chapter, to place the icon that's on the Clipboard someplace new, click where you want the item to go, and choose Edit ➪ Paste or use the keyboard shortcut ⌘+V to paste what you've copied or cut.

Pasting doesn't purge the contents of the Clipboard. In fact, an item stays on the Clipboard until you cut, copy, restart, shut down, log out, or crash. This means that you can paste the same item over and over and over again, which can come in pretty handy at times.

Almost all programs have an Edit menu and use the Macintosh Clipboard, which means you can usually cut or copy something from a document in one program and paste it into a document in another program. Usually.

Compressing files

If you're going to send files as an email enclosure, creating a compressed archive of the files first and sending the archive instead of the originals usually saves you time sending the files and saves the recipient time downloading them. To create this compressed archive, simply select the file(s) or folder(s) and then choose File ➪ Compress. The name of the document or folder you're compressing appears after the word Compress in the menu, so if you were compressing a file called *Foo.doc*, the File menu command would read Compress Foo.doc. This creates a compressed .zip file out of your selection. The compressed file is smaller than the original — sometimes by quite a bit. Double-click a compressed (.zip) file to decompress it.

Getting rid of icons

To get rid of an icon — any icon — merely drag it onto the Trash icon in your Dock.

Trashing an alias gets rid of only the alias, not the parent file. But trashing a document, folder, or application icon puts it in the Trash, where it *will* be deleted permanently the next time you empty the Trash. The Finder menu offers a couple of commands that help you manage the Trash:

  ✔ **Finder ➪ Empty Trash:** This command deletes all items in the Trash from your hard drive, period.

I'll probably say this more than once: *Use this command with a modicum of caution.* After a file is dragged into the Trash and the Trash is emptied, the file is gone, gone, gone unless you have a Time Machine or other backup. (Okay, maybe ProSoft Engineering's Data Rescue or some other third-party utility can bring it back, but I wouldn't bet the farm on it.)

If you put something in the Trash by accident, you can almost always return it from whence it came: Just invoke the magical Undo command. Choose Edit ➪ Undo or press ⌘+Z. The accidentally trashed file returns to its original location. Usually. Unfortunately, Undo doesn't work every time — and it remembers only the very last action that you performed when it does work — so don't rely on it too much.

The Incredible New iCloud Drive

iCloud has been around in various forms for years, but iCloud Drive is the current incarnation for taking advantage of Apple's remote storage service.

iCloud Drive stores files of any type in iCloud. It's built into El Capitan and works like any other folder on your Mac. In other words, you can drag documents of any type into it, organize them with folders and tags (Chapter 4) if you care to, and find them with Spotlight (Chapter 7).

The best part is that the files are not only available on your Mac, but on your iPhone, iPad, or Windows PC as well. That's the good news. The bad news is that if you need more than 5GB of storage space, it's going to cost you. You get up to 5GB at no cost; if you need more it's 99 cents per month for 50GB, $2.99 per month for 200GB, or $9.99 per month for 1TB.

Before El Capitan, iCloud was much more expensive: $40 per year for 25GB, or $100 per year for 55GB. Compare that to the current pricing of $12 per year for 50GB or $24 per year for 200GB. Kudos to Apple for making iCloud Drive not just convenient but also (more) affordable.

Although iCloud Drive should be enabled by default, if yours isn't (you don't see it in the Sidebar), launch System Preferences (🍎 ➪ System Preferences), click the iCloud icon, and then enable the check box for iCloud Drive.

If you still don't see it in your Sidebar, open Finder Preferences (Finder ➪ Finder Preferences), click the Sidebar icon, and then enable the check box to Show iCloud Drive in the Sidebar.

One last thing for iDevice users only: iCloud-savvy apps on your Mac save files in an eponymous folder on iCloud Drive by default (for example, Pages saves files in an iCloud folder named Pages). The thing is, apps on iDevices can only see files in this iCloud Drive folder. If you save a Pages file to an iCloud Drive folder other than the Pages folder, you won't be able to use it on your iDevices.

Four Terrific Timesaving Tools

- -

In This Chapter

▶ Taking a quick look inside files with Quick Look

▶ Finding your files and folders, fast

▶ Taking charge with Mission Control

▶ Learning to love the El Capitan Launchpad

- -

*I*n this chapter, I show you the ins and outs of four terrific timesaving tools: Quick Look, Spotlight, Mission Control, and Launchpad. Each is designed to let you use your Mac better, faster, and more elegantly. Yes, you can use your mouse and click your way to any file or folder on any disk, but these features are built into El Capitan for your convenience.

At the risk of repeating myself, Apple frequently provides more than one way to accomplish a task in OS X, so there's duplication and overlap among and between the tools in this chapter and tools I discuss elsewhere in this book. Don't worry. Take what you need, and leave the rest. Most users love Quick Look, but some never use it. Some people love Spotlight; others rarely invoke it. Mission Control is amazingly helpful, especially on laptops with small screens, but quite a few users don't care for it at all.

My advice: Try all the tools and techniques in this chapter at least a few times before you decide whether you want or need them.

With a Quick Look

The Quick Look command displays the contents of the selected file in a floating window. The key point is that you can see what's in a file without double-clicking (to open) it and without launching any application. This is quite handy when you want to peek at the contents of a file without having to open it.

To take a Quick Look yourself, select an icon and do any of the following:

- ✔ Choose File➪Quick Look.
- ✔ Right-click or Control-click the file's icon and choose Quick Look from its contextual menu.
- ✔ Choose Quick Look from the Action button/menu on the toolbar.
- ✔ Use one of its two keyboard shortcuts: ⌘+Y or the easiest shortcut ever, spacebar.

One of my favorite ways to use Quick Look is with a folder full of images, such as the one shown in in Figure 7-1.

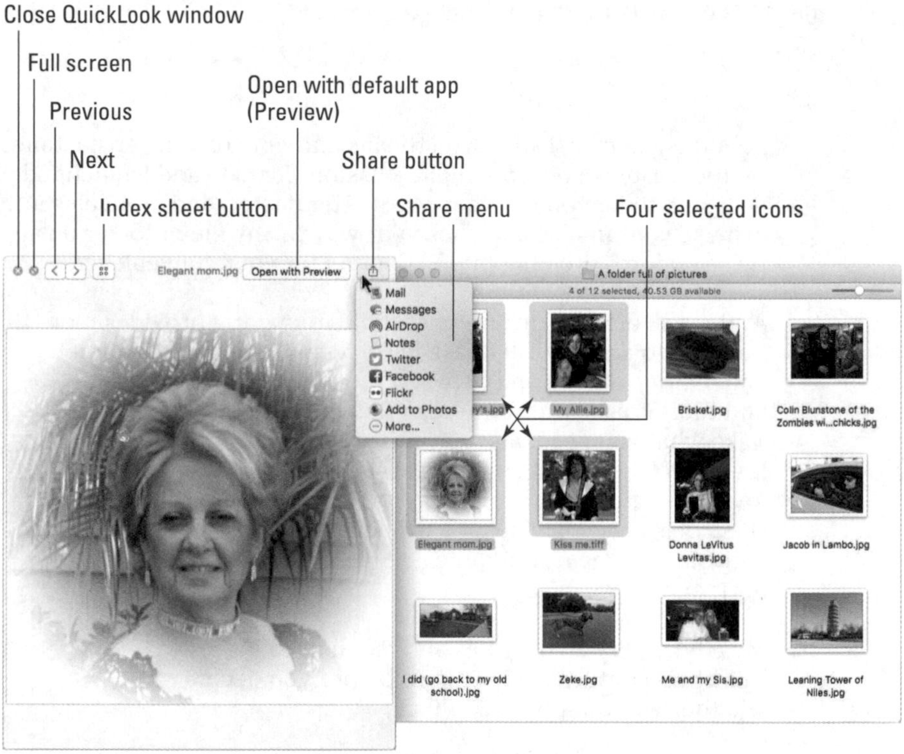

Close QuickLook window

Full screen

Previous

Open with default app
(Preview)

Next

Share button

Index sheet button

Share menu

Four selected icons

Figure 7-1: The Quick Look window (left) displaying an image from one of the selected icons in a folder full of pictures.

The cool part is that while the Quick Look window is open, you can select different icons in the Finder window and very quickly peek at their contents in the Quick Look window.

The bad news is that although Quick Look works with many types of files — Microsoft Office, Apple iWork, plain-text, PDF, TIFF, GIF, JPEG, PNG, and most types of audio and video — it doesn't work with *all* files. You'll know it doesn't work if Quick Look shows you a big document, folder, or application icon instead of the contents of that file.

If you select multiple items before you invoke Quick Look, as I did in Figure 7-1, three buttons appear at the top of the Quick Look window near the left side: the Next, Previous, and Index Sheet buttons. With these controls, you can view all of the selected items at the same time as an *index sheet,* as shown in Figure 7-2, or view them one at a time by clicking the Next or Previous buttons.

Figure 7-2: Four selected files displayed as a Quick Look index sheet.

The blue outline around the image at the bottom on the right indicates that the pointer is hovering over that image; if I were to click, that image would fill the window, and the icons shown at the top of the Quick Look window in Figure 7-1 would reappear.

Share and share alike with the Share menu

If you use an Apple iDevice, you're surely familiar with the rectangular button with an arrow escaping from it, as shown in the margin and in Figure 7-1. That's the Share menu, and it has as many as seven options (depending upon the type of file you selected):

- **E-mail:** Launches the Mail app and attaches the selected file to a blank message, ready for you to address and send.
- **Message:** Launches the Messages app and puts the selected file in an outgoing message, ready for you to address and send.

  You become well acquainted with the Messages app in Chapter 11.

- **AirDrop:** Sends the selected file to other Mac users or iDevice users. As long as you're on the same Wi-Fi network, your file transfer takes but a single click (or a single tap on iDevices).

  Note that the next three options appear only when you select an image file. If you *don't* see them when you click your Share button, you probably selected a PDF or other type of file that can't be uploaded to Twitter, Facebook, or Flickr.

- **Twitter:** Tweets the selected file to your Twitter account.
- **Facebook:** Posts the selected file to your Facebook account.
- **Flickr:** Posts the selected file to Flickr, a popular photo-sharing site.
- **More:** El Capitan's extensible architecture lets you add other services (such as Vimeo or LinkedIn) and apps (such as iPhoto and Aperture) to your Share menu. To manage these extensions, choose More from the Share menu. Alternatively, you can launch the System Preferences application, click the Extensions icon, and then click the Share Menu item on the left side of the window.

Slide into Slideshow (full-screen) mode

Quick Look really shines in its Slideshow (full-screen) mode, which you can start with any of these techniques:

- Hold down Option and choose File⇨Slideshow.
- Press ⌘+Option+Y.

✔ If your file is already open in the Quick Look window, click the full-screen button, as noted in Figure 7-1 and shown here in the margin.

When you're in Slideshow mode, a completely different set of controls appears onscreen automatically, as shown in Figure 7-3.

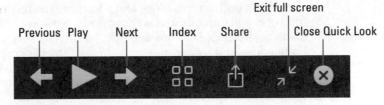

Figure 7-3: The Slideshow controls appear automatically in the full-screen Slideshow mode.

The Slideshow controls disappear after a few seconds of inactivity; if you don't see them when you need them, just move the pointer, and they'll magically reappear.

To exit Slideshow (full screen) mode, press Esc or click the Exit Full Screen button to return to the Quick Look window or the Close Quick Look button to both exit Slideshow mode and quit Quick Look.

When you're finished with the Quick Look window, click the X button in the top-left corner (refer to Figure 7-1). If you're in full-screen mode, click the X button in the control bar, as shown in Figure 7-3, or press ⌘+Y, which works in either mode.

Spotlight on Finding Files and Folders Faster

Even if you follow every single bit of advice provided in this chapter, a time will come when you won't be able to find a file or folder even though you know for certain that it's right there on your hard drive. Somewhere. Fortunately, El Capitan includes a fabulous technology called Spotlight that can help you find almost anything on any mounted disk in seconds. Spotlight can search for

✔ Files

✔ Folders

✔ Text inside documents

✔ Files and folders by their *metadata* (creation date, modification date, kind, size, and so on)

Spotlight finds what you're looking for and then organizes its results logically, all in the blink of an eye (on most Macs).

Spotlight is both a technology and a feature. The technology is pervasive throughout El Capitan, and is the underlying power behind the search boxes in many Apple applications and utilities such as Mail, Contacts, System Preferences, and Finder. You can also use it by clicking the Spotlight menu — the little magnifying glass at the right end of the menu bar. Finally, you can reuse Spotlight searches in the future by turning them into smart folders (which I explain in Chapter 6).

Finding files and folders has never been faster or easier than it is in El Capitan. So in the following sections, I look at the two separate but related ways that Spotlight helps you find files, folders, and even text inside document files and on the web: the Search box in the toolbar of Finder windows, and the main Spotlight menu.

Using the Search box in Finder windows

With its power provided by Spotlight, this definitely isn't your father's Search box.

The following steps walk you through all the features:

1. **Choose File⇨Find or press ⌘+F to move the pointer to the search box of the active window.**

   If there's a specific folder you want to search, open that folder before pressing ⌘+F.

   If no windows are open, the Desktop window will open with the pointer in its search box.

2. **Type a single character in the Search box.**

   I typed the letter *a,* and the window starts displaying the results, as shown in Figure 7-4.

   At the same time, a menu drops down below your pointer to offer search suggestions, such as Filenames and Kinds as shown in Figure 7-4, as well as others such as Dates, Sent By, or Downloaded From (not shown). Select an item from the menu to narrow the scope of your search. Or, type additional characters: The more you type, the fewer matches and suggestions you'll see.

   Spotlight's default behavior is to search files' contents if it can (and it can search the text inside files created by many popular applications).

Figure 7-4: Type one character in the Search box, and the magic begins.

Third-party Spotlight plug-ins are available that let you search the contents of file types not supported by El Capitan, including old WordPerfect and QuarkXPress files and many others. Search the Internet for *Spotlight plug-ins,* and you'll find them for dozens of popular apps.

If you know all or part of the file's name, you can limit your search to filenames (that is, exclude text in files and search only for files by name). Just choose Name Matches: (it's *a* in Figure 7-4) from the drop-down menu.

3. **When you find the file or folder, you can open any item in the window by double-clicking it.**

Keep these points in mind when you perform a search:

✔ You have a choice of where to search. This Mac is selected in Figure 7-5.

✔ You can choose additional search criteria — such as the kind of file (jpeg image in Figure 7-5) and the date the file was created (Within Last 60 Days in Figure 7-5) — as well as other attributes, including Modification Date, Creation Date, Keywords, Label, File Contents, and File Size.

✔ To add another criterion, simply click the + button on the right side of the window.

✔ To save a search for reuse in the future, click the Save button on the right side of the window.

Add criteria

Delete criteria

Save button

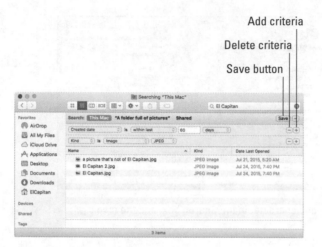

Figure 7-5: Search your whole Mac or a specific folder (and its subfolders) and then narrow your search using one or more criteria.

TIP

Try choosing different options from the window's Arrange menu — Application, Date Last Opened, and so on — to see the search results presented in different ways.

So there you have it — fast searches made easy in the Finder. But there are many ways to access the power of Spotlight, and the Search box in the toolbar of Finder windows is merely one of them.

Using the Spotlight menu and window

Another way to search for files and folders is to use the Spotlight menu itself — the magnifying-glass icon at the far-right end of your menu bar. Click the icon to open the Spotlight Search box, and then type a character, word, or series of words in the Search box to find an item, as shown in Figure 7-6.

Spotlight floats elegantly in the middle of your screen, as shown in Figure 7-6.

Check out the scrollable previews, and how they're culled not only from your hard disk, but also from Wikipedia, Bing, Maps, and other sources.

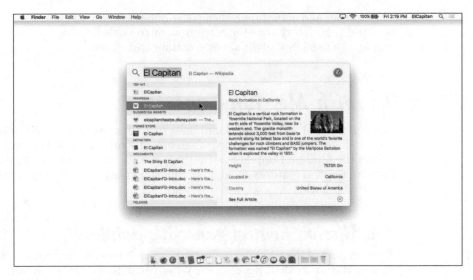

Figure 7-6: The new and improved Spotlight in El Capitan.

Also notice that a preview appears on the right of the selected item (the Wikipedia entry for *El Capitan* in Figure 7-6), a nice touch.

Memorize and use the super-convenient and easy-to-remember keyboard shortcut for opening the Spotlight Search box, which is ⌘+spacebar by default. If you don't find ⌘+spacebar appealing as a shortcut, you can change it to whatever you like in the Spotlight System Preference pane.

Spotlight is more than just a menu and Search box; it also uses a technology that's pervasive throughout OS X and apps including (but certainly not limited to) Mail, Contacts, and many, many more. The reason why it's so spectacularly speedy is that it indexes your files when your Mac is idle. The upshot is that Spotlight knows file locations and contents soon after a file is created or modified.

For more information on finding files by other attributes, visit www. dummies.com/extras/osxelcapitan.

One last thing: The Search field in Finder windows finds items only on your hard disk. To include results from the Internet, you have to use the Spotlight floating window via its menu icon or keyboard shortcut.

The bottom line is that regardless of which method you choose to invoke it — the Search box in a Finder window or the new floating Spotlight window — using Spotlight saves you time and effort.

Blast Off with Mission Control

Mission Control shows you thumbnails of all open windows and full-screen apps in a unified view. Before you see how it works, look at Figure 7-7, which shows the Mission Control System Preferences pane, where you turn specific Mission Control features on and off and assign keyboard or mouse shortcuts to them.

The Mission Control pane: It's painless

The top part of the pane contains four check boxes: Automatically Rearrange Spaces Based on Most Recent Use; When Switching to an Application, Switch to a Space with Open Windows for the Application; Group Windows By Application; and Displays Have Separate Spaces. If you've read Chapter 5, you know what Dashboard is all about, but because I haven't introduced you to Spaces yet (but will shortly), these check boxes will make sense to you only after you read the sections that follow. Suffice it to say that they do what you think they'll do. You should experiment with the settings, turning them on and off, to see which way you prefer them.

You can choose to display Dashboard as an overlay (the default, as shown in Chapter 5) or as a Space (which you'll understand shortly). You can also choose Off if you never want to see Dashboard.

Moving right along, most of this pane handles keyboard and mouse shortcuts for Mission Control. The eight pop-up menus — four each for keyboard and mouse shortcuts — let you specify the trigger for each of the four Mission Control features with a keystroke or mouse button. The default keyboard shortcuts appear in upcoming text, but yours may differ; to change them, click the appropriate pop-up menu and make a new selection.

Hold down the ⌘, Option, Control, and/or Shift keys when you choose an item from any of the eight shortcut menus to add modifier keys to the shortcuts you create. So, for example, if you were to hold down ⌘+Shift when you select F11 from a pop-up menu, the keyboard shortcut for that feature would be ⌘+Shift+F11. Or, if you were to hold down Shift when you select Middle Mouse Button from a pop-up menu, you'd have to hold down Shift and click the middle mouse button to invoke the command.

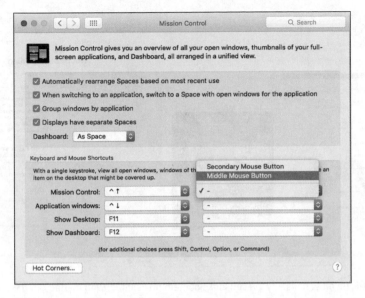

Figure 7-7: The Mission Control System Preferences pane.

Finally, most Apple keyboards made since April 2007 also include dedicated Mission Control and Dashboard shortcut keys (F3 and F4, respectively). If you see a tiny picture that looks like the Mission Control icon (shown in the margin) on your F3 key or that looks like the Dashboard icon on your F4 key, you can use them in addition to the other shortcuts discussed in this section.

A picture is worth a thousand words, so check out Figures 7-8, 7-9, and 7-10 as you read about each feature.

- Figure 7-8 shows a typical jumble of windows from a variety of applications strewn all over my screen.

- To see Mission Control, which displays all open windows in all open applications, as shown in Figure 7-9, press Control+↑ (up arrow).

- To see all open windows belonging to the current application (TextEdit in Figure 7-10), press Control+↓ (down arrow).

If you hover your cursor over a window on a Mission Control screen, a blue border appears around the item you're hovering over (a TextEdit document in Figure 7-9 and Chapter 16 in Figure 7-10). If you then press the spacebar, you'll see a preview of the window's contents, which is especially helpful when a window is partially obscured by another window.

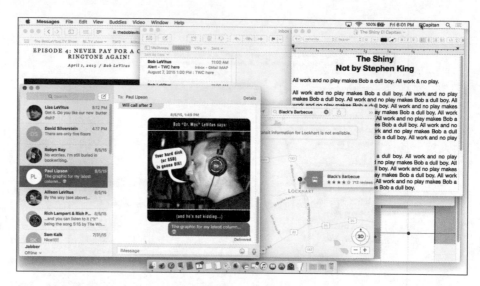

Figure 7-8: On most days, my screen looks something like this, with myriad open windows from numerous apps obscuring one another.

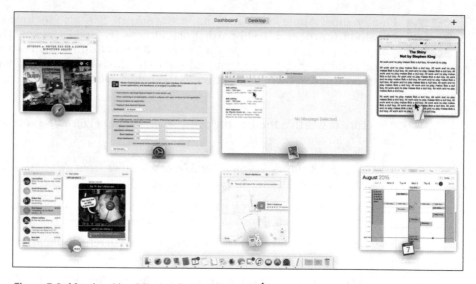

Figure 7-9: After invoking Mission Control (Control+↑).

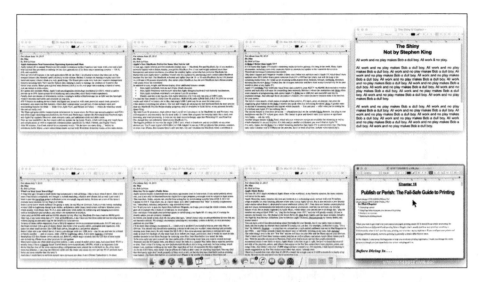

Figure 7-10: After invoking Application Windows (Control+↓) when TextEdit was active.

- To hide all open windows and display the Desktop, press F11 or Fn+F11.

- To summon forth the Dashboard (which displays your widgets, as I explain in Chapter 5), press F12 (or Fn+F12). Or, if your F4 key has a Dashboard icon printed on it, press F4.

Notice that when you're using Mission Control, windows appear as reduced-size thumbnails. Identifying information — either the program or window name — appears below the mini-window, making it easier to discern what each item contains. When you click any of these small windows, Mission Control deactivates, and the window you clicked becomes the active window.

One last thing: If you use a trackpad, check out the More Gestures tab in the Trackpad System Preferences pane, where you can enable a three- or four-fingered swipe upwards to invoke Mission Control.

Hot corners!

In the bottom-left corner of the Mission Control System Preferences pane is a Hot Corners button, which lets you designate any or all of the corners of your screen as hot spots to trigger Mission Control, Dashboard, Launchpad, Screen Saver, or Display Sleep. Click the menu for a corner, and select the feature you want associated with that corner. Then, whenever you move your pointer onto that corner and leave it there for a second or two, the feature executes.

Hot corners have been part of Mac OS since time immemorial and are still as useful as ever. I like to set the top-right corner to start my screen saver and the bottom-right corner to disable it, for example.

Mission Control is enabled by default, but you can disable any or all of its features by turning off its trigger: Just choose the minus sign from a pop-up menu instead of a keyboard or mouse-button shortcut. In Figure 7-7, the Mission Control mouse trigger is currently disabled, but I'm changing it to Middle Mouse Button.

Spaces from 30,000 feet (an overview)

If Mission Control lets you manage your windows in real time, its spaces let you manage windows by organizing them in groups called *spaces* and switch from space to space with a keystroke or gesture.

When you use spaces, only two kinds of windows are shown: windows from applications associated with the active space and windows from applications launched while that space is active.

If you find yourself spending too much time moving and resizing windows onscreen, consider setting up spaces for specific tasks. You might have one space dedicated to a specific project, another for web surfing, and a third for email, each with all its windows arranged just the way you like them.

Think of a space as being a single screen, set up just the way you like it, with its windows arranged just the way you like them. Take, for example, the three spaces shown in Figures 7-11, 7-12, and 7-13. I have one for web surfing (Figure 7-11), one for Mail (Figure 7-12), and one for working in the Finder (Figure 7-13), each one with its windows arranged exactly as I like 'em.

Moving right along, you manage your spaces with Mission Control, which provides an overview of what's running on your Mac, including all your spaces, the Dashboard, and all open windows. In a nutshell, this dynamic duo makes it easier than ever to manage and maintain the mélange of Finder and application windows that conspire to clutter and eventually consume your screen.

To see it in action, press the Mission Control key (Control+↑ by default). If you have a trackpad, you can also swipe upward using three fingers to see Mission Control, which will look something like Figure 7-14 based on the three spaces shown in Figures 7-11 through 7-13.

Figure 7-11: My web-surfing space, with three Safari windows all arranged the way I like 'em.

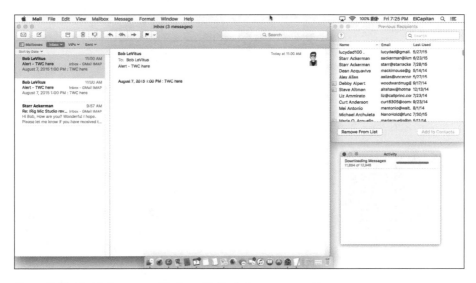

Figure 7-12: My Mail space, with three Mail windows arranged just so.

Note that you won't see a Dashboard Space in Mission Control unless you've selected As Space from the Dashboard pop-up menu in the Mission Control System Preferences pane. And if you don't see the thumbnail pictures above the names *Dashboard* and *Desktop,* hover your cursor over them and the thumbnails will appear like magic.

Figure 7-13: My Finder space, with two windows in list view plus a third window in Icon view.

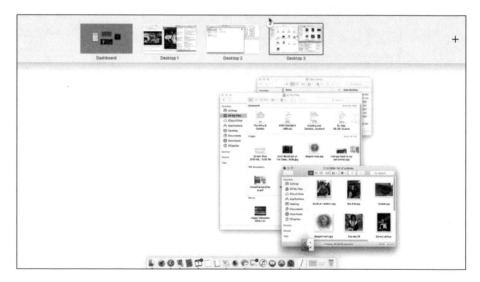

Figure 7-14: Mission Control showing off Dashboard and three spaces (Desktops 1, 2, and 3).

In earlier versions of OS X, these desktops were called *spaces*. Mission Control, improbably, uses the words *spaces* and *desktop* interchangeably, so as you see in Figure 7-14, my three spaces are named Desktop 1, Desktop 2, and Desktop 3. I think it's dumb, and I'm going to continue to call a space a space regardless of what Mission Control labels them (because calling them desktops would be even more confusing).

By the way, apps running in full-screen mode are automatically considered a space, which bears the name of the app rather than Desktop X.

To add a new space, first enter Mission Control; then move the pointer to the top-right corner of the screen and click the Add (+) button. Note that if you have your Dock on the right side of the screen, you have to move your pointer to the top-left corner for the + to appear.

You can use this technique to add as many spaces as you like. When you're finished using Mission Control, you can

 ✔ Click a space at the top of the screen to switch to it.

 or

 ✔ Press the Mission Control key, press the Esc key, or swipe upward with three or four fingers to return to the space you were using when you entered Mission Control.

The three-finger gesture requires a Magic Mouse, Magic Trackpad, or laptop with a new style (buttonless) trackpad.

If you're using a notebook Mac, I implore you to learn to use gestures with Mission Control. Visit the Trackpad System Preferences pane's More Gestures tab and make sure you've enabled three- or four-finger swipes. I love swiping between Mission Control spaces like the ones in Figures 7-11, 7-12, and 7-13. Swipe, and I've got Mail; swipe again, and I've got Safari; swipe again, and I have the Finder. Try it — I think you'll like swiping to switch spaces (desktops) as much as I do.

One last thing: OS X El Capitan takes full advantage of multiple displays no matter how many displays are connected to your Mac. So, for example, you can work in the Finder's Desktop on one display and use a full screen app on another. And finally, each display has its own exclusive set of Mission Control spaces associated with it.

You can drag and drop spaces from one display to another. Try it — it's way cool!

Getting around in space(s)

The previous section shows you one way to move from one space to another — enter Mission Control, and click the space you want to use. You can also navigate spaces in the following ways:

- ✔ Press the Control key and ← (left-arrow key) or → (right-arrow key) to move to the previous or next space.

- ✔ Swipe left or right with three fingers to move to the next or previous space.

    You can enable or disable these keyboard shortcuts in the Keyboard Shortcuts tab of the Keyboard System Preferences pane.

There will be times when you want to move a window from one space to another. To do so:

- ✔ Drag a window to the left or right edge of the screen, and pause. After a short delay, the window pops into the space on the left or right of the current space.

- ✔ Press and hold down the mouse button on the window you want to move while pressing the Control key and the

    - • Left-arrow key (←) to move the window to the space on the left of the current space

    - • Right-arrow key (→) to move the window to the space on the right of the current space

    or

- ✔ Start in the space that has the window you want to move. Enter Mission Control, drag the window from the middle part of the screen onto the space you want to move it to at the top of the screen, and then release the mouse button.

It's often useful to assign a specific application to a specific space. To do so, first launch the application in question; then press and hold down its Dock icon, and choose Options, as shown in Figure 7-15.

Here's the rundown on those options:

- ✔ **To have the application open in every space, choose All Desktops.**

    When the application is running, it will appear in every space.

Figure 7-15: Press and hold down (or right-click) an application's Dock icon to assign the application to a specific space (Desktop).

✔ **To have the application open only in the current space, choose This Desktop.**

The application opens in this space. If you're working in a different space and switch to this application, its assigned space scrolls into view.

✔ **To have the application open in whatever space you're using, choose None.**

Finally, should you want to delete one or more spaces, simply enter Mission Control, and move the pointer over the space. A Delete button — an X that should look familiar if you use an iPhone, iPad, or iPod touch, or the Dashboard — appears in its top-left corner, as shown in Figure 7-16. Click it to delete that space.

Deleting a space doesn't delete or quit any applications or close any documents. Applications and win-

Figure 7-16: Hover the pointer over a space, and a Delete button (X) appears.

dows in a deleted space move to the space called Desktop (the one *without* a numeric suffix).

The bottom line is that spaces can be particularly useful for those with a smaller display. And it can be even more useful for users with more than one display.

Using Mission Control can be an acquired taste, so even if you have a small screen or multiple screens, you may not care for it at first. My advice: Try it for a while, and if you decide that you hate it, turn its triggers off (by selecting the minus sign) and be done with it.

Launchpad: The Place for Applications

Launchpad presents all the applications in your Applications folder in a view that looks like the home screen of any iOS device (that is, iPhone, iPad, or iPod touch). In fact, if you use one of these devices, I suspect that you could skip everything that follows about Launchpad, because it works almost exactly like the home screen on an iPhone or other iDevice.

Click the Launchpad Dock icon (shown in the margin). It fills your screen with big, beautiful application icons, as shown in Figure 7-17.

Figure 7-17: Launchpad, in all its glory.

I changed my Desktop picture from plain white to the default El Capitan picture for Figure 7-17. The photo is actually in focus; the nifty blur effect happens only when Launchpad is active. Sure, it's just eye candy, but it's *elegant* eye candy.

If your Launchpad has more than one page of apps, you can press ⌘+ left-arrow (←) or right-arrow (→) to move to the previous or next page. Trackpad users can also use a three-finger swipe left or right to move from page to page.

To launch an app, just click its icon. In a heartbeat, Launchpad disappears, and the app replaces it on your screen.

Customizing Your Launchpad

Launchpad is configurable, just like home screens on iDevices. As you're about to see, you can rearrange app icons on a page, move them from one page to another, organize them in folders, and delete them. Say it all together now: "Just like on iDevices."

For those who are unfamiliar with iOS or devices that run it, here's how these things work on your Mac:

- **To find an app:** Type the first few characters of its name in the search box at the top of the screen.
- **To rearrange app icons:** Click and drag the app to its new location.

✔ **To move apps to the next or previous page:** Click and drag the app to the left or right edge of the screen. When the next page of apps appears, drag the app to its new location on that page.

✔ **To add an app to your Dock:** Click and drag the app onto the left side of the Dock.

✔ **To create a folder for apps:** Drag one app's icon on top of another app's icon to create a folder.

✔ **To add an app to a folder:** Drag the app onto that folder to add it.

✔ **To move an app out of a folder:** Click the folder to open it and drag the app out of the folder.

✔ **To change a folder's name:** Click to open the folder, click the current name, and then type a new name.

✔ **To uninstall apps:** Click an app's icon, but don't release the mouse button until all the icons begin to wiggle. Apps that can be uninstalled display a Delete button (X); click to uninstall the app.

✔ **To stop the wiggling:** Press Esc.

If an icon doesn't have a Delete button, it's installed with OS X El Capitan and can't be uninstalled.

And last but not least, some items in the Applications and Utilities folders on your startup disk will be found in a folder named Other in Launchpad. Why? Which apps and for what reason? Who knows?

Part III
Getting Things Done in El Capitan

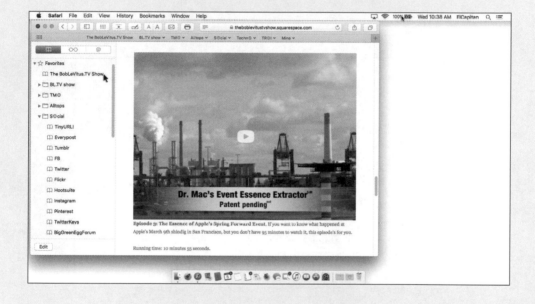

Visit www.dummies.com/extras/osxelcapitan for more on setting up speech recognition in El Capitan.

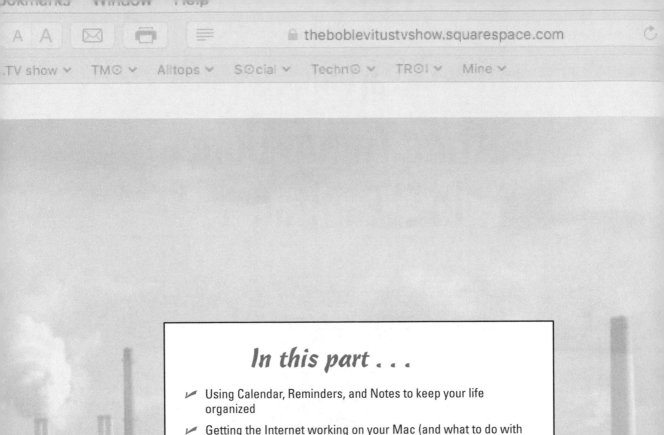

In this part . . .

- ✔ Using Calendar, Reminders, and Notes to keep your life organized
- ✔ Getting the Internet working on your Mac (and what to do with it after that)
- ✔ Surfin' Safari: How to surf the Internet with Safari
- ✔ Making imaginatively named apps such as Mail, Contacts, Messages, and Maps work for you
- ✔ Sharing files and more (and liking it)

Dr. Mac's Event Essence Extractor[SM]
Patent pending[not]

isode 3: The Essence of Apple's Spring Forward Event. If you want to know what happened
e's March 9th shindig in San Francisco, but you don't have 95 minutes to watch it, this episode's f

ning time: 10 minutes 55 seconds.

8

Organizing Your Life

In This Chapter

▶ Introducing Calendar

▶ Creating and using Calendar calendars

▶ Creating and organizing Calendar events

▶ Remembering events with Reminders and Notification Center

▶ Taking notes with Notes

*W*hen you buy OS X El Capitan, the folks at Apple generously include applications that can help simplify and organize your everyday affairs — Calendar, Reminders, and Notes (to name three you discover in this chapter).

In fact, OS X comes with a whole folder full of applications — software you can use to do everything from surfing the Internet to capturing an image of your Mac's screen to playing QuickTime movies to numeric calculations. Technically, most of these applications aren't even part of OS X. Rather, the vast majority of them are what are known as *bundled* apps — programs that come with the operating system but are unrelated to its function. Readers (bless them) tend to complain when I skip bundled applications, so I mention almost all of them in this book.

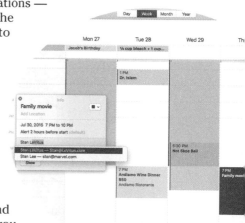

But in this chapter, you get a look at only the applications that help you organize your everyday life: your appointments, to-do items, notes to yourself, and how to keep them in sync with the various iDevices you may attach to and detach from your Mac.

The applications discussed in this chapter are stored in (where else?) the Applications folder, which you can get to in four ways:

✔ Click the Applications folder in the Sidebar of any Finder window.

✔ Choose Go ➪ Applications from the Finder.

✔ Press ⌘+Shift+A in the Finder.

✔ Click the Launchpad icon on the Dock to see all the applications installed on this Mac (refer to Chapter 7).

Other bundled apps you might be especially interested in include Safari (Chapter 9), Contacts (Chapter 10), Mail (Chapter 11), iTunes (Chapter 13), a whole handful of multimedia applications that enable you to play video and more on your Mac including Preview, which lets you view and annotate PDF and other image files (Chapter 14), and TextEdit (Chapter 15).

Keeping Track with Calendar

Calendar is a wonderful program that provides multiple appointment calendars with alerts. More precisely, you can have multiple color-coded calendars; several types of visual, audible, and emailed alerts; repeating events; and more. You can publish your calendar(s) on the web for others to view (which requires an iCloud account or other WebDAV server), and you can subscribe to calendars published by other Calendar users.

I love Calendar and keep it open most of the time on my Macs. In the sections that follow, I share some of the features I find most useful.

Navigating Calendar views

Calendar lets you display the main Calendar window just the way you like it:

✔ **You can view your calendar by the day, week, month, or year.** Figure 8-1 shows a weekly view. To select a view, click the Day, Week, Month, or Year button at the top.

✔ **To move back or forward,** click the arrow buttons on either side of the Today button (upper right). You see the previous or next week in Week view, yesterday or tomorrow in day view, and so on.

✔ **To go to today's date,** click the Today button.

✔ **To add a new calendar,** click the New Calendar (+) button.

You can find all these items, most of which have shortcuts, in the Calendar application's View menu, as shown in Figure 8-2. This menu offers almost total control of what you see and how you navigate.

If you want to master Calendar, it would behoove you to spend some time experimenting with these views and with their navigation commands and options.

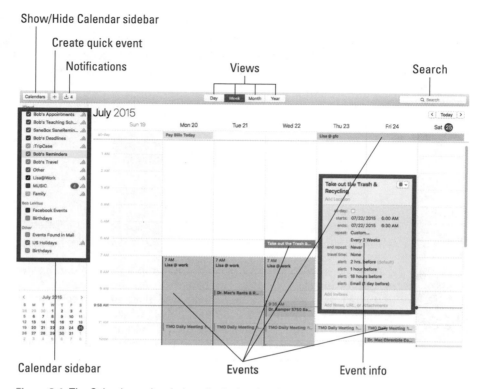

Show/Hide Calendar sidebar

Create quick event

Notifications

Views

Search

Calendar sidebar

Events

Event info

Figure 8-1: The Calendar main window displaying the view I prefer: Week view.

Creating calendars

If you refer to Figure 8-1, you see a list of my calendars in the top-left corner: Bob's Appointments, Bob's Teaching Schedule, Bob's Deadlines, Bob's Reminders, and so on. The check boxes turn the visibility of a calendar on (checked) and off (unchecked).

To create a new calendar in Calendar, follow these steps:

1. **Choose File⇨New Calendar⇨iCloud (or other account you enabled in the Internet Accounts System Preferences pane).**

   A new calendar named Untitled is created and added to the appropriate calendar list.

Figure 8-2: The Calendar application's View menu.

2. **To give your calendar a name, select Untitled and type a new name.**

3. **(Optional) To color-code the entries for this calendar, first select the calendar (click it); choose Edit⇨Get Info or press ⌘+I; and then select a color by clicking and holding down on the color swatch.**

In my humble opinion, Other is the coolest choice because it lets you select from thousands of colors — including the lovely shade of fuchsia I use for my Bob's Appointments calendar.

(Optional) Before you click OK to dismiss the Get Info sheet, feel free to add a short description of your calendar in the space provided. I never do, but you can if you care to.

4. **Click OK.**

Now, events created while this calendar is selected in the Calendar list on the left will appear in the appropriate color on the calendar.

If you have an iCloud account, you can publish your calendars and invite others to subscribe to them by right- or Control-clicking the iCloud calendar in the list and choosing Share Calendar. The invitees receive an email asking them to subscribe to your calendar. This is what my family does. Each of us maintains and publishes his or her own calendar and subscribes to everyone else's. That way, we can all see at a glance who's doing what and when they're doing it. This is by far the slickest solution we've found.

Deleting a calendar

To delete a calendar, select it in the list and choose Edit⇨Delete or press ⌘+Delete. If the calendar has events on it, you see an alert asking whether you're sure you want to delete that calendar; if not, the calendar will be deleted as soon as you choose Edit⇨Delete or press ⌘+Delete.

When you delete a calendar, all the events and reminder items in that calendar are also deleted. Although you *can* undo a deleted calendar (choose Edit⇨Undo or press ⌘+Z), you must do so before you quit Calendar. If you quit Calendar without undoing a calendar deletion, everything on that calendar (or calendars) will be gone forever (unless, of course, you have Time Machine or another backup, as I explain in Chapter 18).

If you sync your calendars with iCloud and/or other cloud-based services, the calendar will be deleted from all of your devices.

Creating and managing events

The heart of Calendar is the event. To create a new one, follow these steps:

1. **Choose File➪New Event, press ⌘+N, double-click a date on the calendar in any view, or drag up or down anywhere on a date in Week or Day view.**

   If you double-click or click and drag on the day of the event, you can skip Step 2, and you don't need to specify the date in Step 3.

   Alternatively, try the Create Quick Event (+) button. It's smart enough to interpret commands like "Family Movie 7–10PM Thursday" and create a new event on the proper day and time, as shown in Figure 8-3.

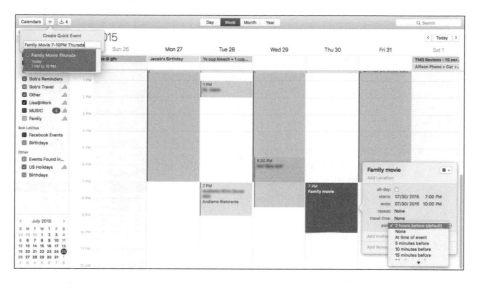

Figure 8-3: Creating a Quick Event (upper left) and the resulting event bubble (lower right) for this three-hour event on my Appointment calendar.

2. **If the event doesn't appear in the proper place, just click it and drag it wherever you like.**

3. **To edit an event, select it and choose Edit➪Edit Event, press ⌘+E, or double-click it to open its event bubble, as shown in Figure 8-3.**

   All the items can be edited. For example, click on the date or time to change it. The other items — *Repeat, Travel Time,* and *Alerts* — are pop-up menus. The *Alert* menu is popped up in Figure 8-3. The fuchsia square in the upper-right corner of the event bubble is also a pop-up menu, which lets you select a different calendar for this event.

   Travel Time, introduced in Mavericks, lets you include travel time to and from an event (and blocks out that time on your calendar), while preserving the event's actual start and end times.

4. **When you're satisfied with all of the event's items, press Return or click anywhere outside the event bubble.**

If you prefer working in a little window rather than the event bubble, check out the Edit⇨Show Inspector command (⌘+Option+I), which displays the selected event in a window. Click a different event, and its info instantly fills the Inspector window. Try it; you might like it.

The difference between Get Info and the Inspector is that the Inspector window changes contextually and displays information about the currently selected event. Get Info windows, on the other hand, display info for a specific event. Put another way, a Get Info window displays the info for a specific event, and you can have as many Get Info windows on the screen as you like. There's only one Inspector window, though, and it displays info for whichever event is currently selected.

Inviting others to attend an event

To invite other people to your event, open Contacts or the Calendar Address Panel (Window⇨Address Panel or ⌘+Option+A) and drag the contacts onto the event in Calendar. Alternatively, you can type the first few letters of the name in the Invitees field, and names that match magically appear. In Figure 8-4, I typed the letters *Stan L,* and Calendar offered me a choice of my two contacts with names that start with *Stan L* — Stan LeVitus and Stan Lee. Sweet! (If you're unfamiliar with Contacts, flip to Chapter 11 for details.)

Figure 8-4: Invite people to your event.

After you add one or more invitees, click the Send button to invite them to the event. If the invitees have a compatible calendar application (Calendar, its predecessor iCal, Microsoft Outlook, and most calendar programs on most platforms), they can open the enclosure (which is included with your invitation email), which adds the event to Calendar with Accept, Decline, and Maybe buttons. All they have to do is click the appropriate button, and you receive an email informing you of their decision along with an enclosure that adds their response to the event in Calendar. Nice, eh?

Note that if the recipient is using certain third-party mail clients, such as Mailsmith or Thunderbird to name a few, they may not send a reply. But the majority of people you know are more likely to use Apple Mail or Microsoft Outlook, which both do the right thing with Calendar invitations.

If the invitee doesn't have a compatible calendar app (or doesn't open the enclosure that was included with the email invitation), he or she has to respond the old-fashioned way: by replying to your email or calling you on the telephone.

Setting an alert

What's the point of putting an event on your calendar if you forget it? If you set an alert, Calendar won't let you forget. To set an alert, click the word *None* (just to the right of the word *alert)* in the Event info window or Inspector, as I did in Figure 8-3. A menu appears. Choose the type of alert you want from the menu and change its values to suit your needs. I find the Message with Sound and Email alerts so useful that I use both for almost every event I create.

You can have as many alerts as you like for each event. When you add the first alert to an event, a +-in-a-circle will appear to its right when you hover the cursor over the alert pop-up menu; click the + to create a second (or third or fifteenth) alert.

To remove an alert, click the pop-up menu to the right of the word *alert* and choose None from the pop-up menu.

You can choose separate default alerts for Events, All Day Events, and Birthdays in Calendar Preferences. Choose Calendar ⇨ Preferences or press ⌘+, (comma), and then click the Alerts tab at the top of the window.

All the features mentioned so far are wonderful, but my very favorite Calendar feature has to be alerts. I rarely miss an important event anymore; Calendar reminds me of them with time to spare. Better still, I sync events and alerts among my Mac and iPhone and iPad. I can create an event or alert, and within a few minutes — through the magic of iCloud — it appears on the other devices, as shown in Figure 8-5.

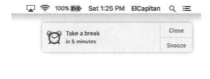

Figure 8-5: Alerts on my Mac (left) and iPhone (right).

Reminders: Protection Against Forgetting

Reminders will be familiar to anyone with an iDevice because it bears more than a passing resemblance to the iOS Reminders app.

Reminders help you stay organized. Unlike an event, a Reminder item isn't necessarily associated with a particular day or time (although it can be). Furthermore, reminders can be location-based, which is handier on an iDevice than a Mac, but a great feature if you have such a device. Finally, Reminders can have a priority level of Low, Medium, High, or None.

If you have an iDevice and sync with iCloud, or Microsoft Exchange or Office 365, your Reminders will appear on all your Apple devices — other Macs, iPhones, iPads, and iPod touches — simultaneously, which means you should never miss a reminder. Just set a reminder on your Mac or any iDevice, and you'll never forget anything.

Getting started with Reminders

Before you create or manage your own reminders, there are a couple of things you should know, starting with the concept of lists. Reminders includes a list called Reminders by default. You can delete or rename it if you like, and you can create additional lists if you care to by choosing File⇨New List, pressing ⌘+L, or clicking the plus button at the bottom of the window.

I like to have a bunch of lists with names like Next Actions; Talk To; Projects; Someday Maybe; and so on. And Reminders creates a section for completed items at the top of the list when you click the circle before each reminder's name to indicate a task is done, like *a completed action* and *a completed reminder* in Figure 8-6.

Figure 8-6: Nine lists (left) and all the reminders on the Next Actions list (right).

In other words, when you check the box for an item, the item is moved from whichever list it's on to the Completed List.

Here are more helpful techniques for working with lists:

- **To rename a list:** Right- or Control-click the list, choose Rename from the contextual menu, type the new name, and press Return when you're done. Or select the list, press Return, type the new name, and then press Return again when you're done.

- **To display a list in a separate window:** Double-click the list name; right- or Control-click the list, and choose Open List in New Window from the contextual menu; choose Window ➪ Open in New Window; or press ⌘+Return.

- **To show or hide the little calendar:** Choose View ➪ Show/Hide Calendar or press ⌘+Option+K.

- **To show or hide the List Sidebar:** Choose View ➪ Show/Hide Sidebar or press ⌘+Option+S.

You don't have to have more than one list. You don't even have to change the default list name (Reminders). That being said, I like having Reminders organized into separate To-Do Lists. The point is that you can make a bunch of lists or dump everything into a single list; just use lists to organize your reminders so they make sense to you.

To do or not to do: Setting reminders

The preceding sections tell you pretty much everything about Reminders except how to create one, so it's time to find out how to create a reminder. It couldn't be easier: Just choose File ➪ New Reminder; press ⌘+N; click the Plus button in the top-right corner of the Reminders window; or click the first blank line in any list and begin typing.

Ah, but there's much more to a Reminder. Reminders can

- Remind you at a specific time on a specific date.

- Repeatedly remind you at a specified interval.

- Remind you at a specific location (great for iPhone and cellular iPad owners).

And reminders can also have a priority and notes. To access these features, you need to Show Info for the reminder by choosing View ➪ Show Info; pressing ⌘+I; clicking the little *i* that appears on the right side of the reminder (hover your cursor over the right side of the reminder if you don't see it); or double-click a blank spot on the reminder.

Show Info for my Get Ice Cream reminder is shown in Figure 8-7.

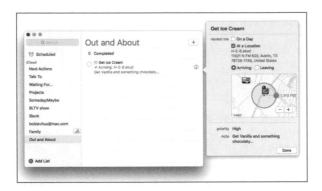

Figure 8-7: Reminders are indeed handy.

The first time you try to use At a Location, your Mac will present a dialog asking whether you want to Enable Location Services to Allow "Reminders" to Use Your Current Location. If you agree, you're done. If you disagree and don't want to enable Location Services for the Reminder app, just click the Cancel button. Finally, if you wish to enable Location Services at a later date, open the Security & Privacy System Preferences pane and click the Privacy tab. Click the lock and provide your password if necessary, then click Location Services in the list on the left, make sure the Enable Location Services check box is enabled, and then enable the check box for Reminders. Close the System Preferences app and you're done.

If you have an iPhone, location-based reminders are awesome. Give them a try, and I'm sure you'll be as hooked as I am.

Finally, to reorder reminders in a list, click a blank spot on any reminder, drag it up or down, and drop it into its new position.

Everything You Need to Know about the Notification Center

The item on the right in Figure 8-8 should look familiar to those of you who use an iPhone, iPad, or iPod touch. It's the Mac Notification Center, which was introduced in Mountain Lion but was included in iOS before that.

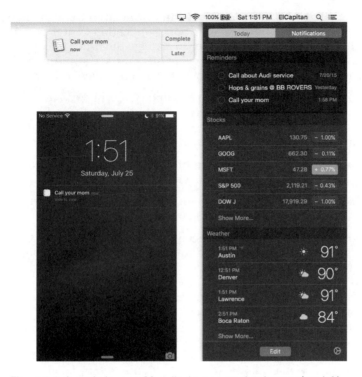

Figure 8-8: A reminder on a Mac displays as an alert banner (top left) or in the Notification Center's Today tab (right), and on an iPhone lock screen (bottom left).

 Notification Center manages and displays alerts from apps that support it. You can make it appear regardless of what application is currently active by clicking its menu bar icon (shown in the margin) or swiping from the very right edge of the trackpad to the left with two fingers.

You manage notifications in the Notifications System Preferences pane. Choose ➪ System Preferences, click the System Preferences Dock icon, or click the little gear near the bottom of Notification Center, which is a shortcut that opens the Notifications Preferences pane. On the left are all the apps on your hard disk that support the Notification Center protocol. To specify settings for an app, click it in the list. After you select an app, here's what you can do:

✔ **To have an app's notifications not appear in Notification Center:** Deselect the Show in Notification Center check box, or drag the app down to the Not in Notification Center section of the list.

- **To change how apps are sorted in Notification Center:** Choose Manually or By Time from the Sort Notification Center pop-up menu. Choose Manually if you prefer to arrange the order the apps appear in Notification Center by dragging them up or down (my preference); choose By Time to sort them with the most recent ones at the top.

- **To specify the alert style for the app:** Your choices are Banners, Alerts, or None. Alerts stay onscreen until you dismiss them; Banners appear in the upper-right corner of the screen below the Notification Center icon and fade away a few seconds after they appear.

- **To see the number of new notifications for the app on its Dock icon:** Select the Badge App Icon check box.

- **To hear a sound when receiving notifications:** Select the Play Sound when Receiving Notifications check box.

- **To specify the number of recent items that Notification Center displays for the app:** Click the Show in Notification Center pop-up menu and choose 1, 5, 10, or 20 recent items.

There's one more item in the Notifications System Preferences pane worth mentioning: the Do Not Disturb button, at the top of the list of apps. Click it to temporarily silence alerts and banners during the specified hours. Or temporarily enable Do Not Disturb: Option-click the Notification Center icon on the menu bar, which will turn gray to indicate that alerts and banners are suspended. Option-click the Notification Center icon again to disable Do Not Disturb.

The Today tab (refer to Figure 8-8, right) is sweet, offering a helpful list of upcoming events, reminders, weather, stock prices, and other information you may find useful.

To manage what you see in the Today tab, click the Edit button at the very bottom. The Today panel slides to the left to reveal a list of additional items that you can add to your Today panel, as shown in Figure 8-9. While these items are visible, you can change the order of items in the Today tab by dragging them up or down in the list.

Before you leave Edit mode, you might want to check out third-party items (widgets) for your Notification Center by clicking the App Store button at the bottom.

When you're happy with your Today tab, click the Done button.

Figure 8-9: Click the green + buttons to add Calculator, Social, World Clock, or iTunes to the Today tab of Notification Center.

Now, here's a quick rundown of ways you can use Notification Center:

- ✓ **To respond to a notification:** Click the banner or alert before it disappears. Or, open Notification Center, click the Notifications tab, and then click the notification to launch its app.

  If you hover the pointer over banners, you may see additional options such as the ability to reply to an email or message without launching Mail or Messages. Give it a try!

- ✓ **To repeat a notification in nine minutes:** Click its Snooze button.

- ✓ **To close all notifications for an app:** Hover the pointer over the right side of the app's name in the Notifications tab (iTunes in Figure 8-10) and click the little x when it appears.

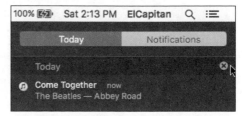

Figure 8-10: Click the x to close all notifications for the app.

Use Notes for Making Notes

 Notes is an electronic notepad for your Mac. A note is a convenient place to jot quick notes, recipes, phone numbers, or whatever. Some notes are shown in Figure 8-11.

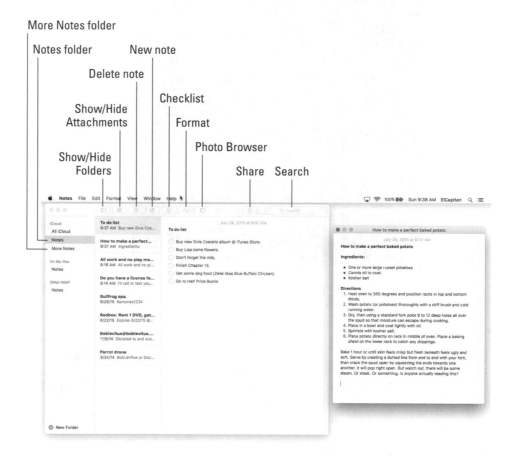

Figure 8-11: Notes is for making notes on your Mac.

To create a new note, choose File➪New Note; press ⌘+N; or click the button with the little square and pencil in the toolbar.

Notes is supremely flexible; here are just a few things you can do:

✔ **Double-click a note to open it in its own window** so you can drag it around onscreen by its title bar.

After opening a note in its own window, if you want the note to float in front of other windows so it's always visible, choose Window⇨Float on Top.

✔ **Change text** to any font, color, size, and style by selecting it and using the myriad of tools in the Format menu.

✔ **Search for a word or phrase** in any note by typing your query in the Search box.

✔ **Create bulleted, numbered, or dashed lists** by selecting the text and choosing Format⇨Font⇨Lists. (Ingredients is a bulleted list, and Directions is a numbered list in Figure 8-11.)

✔ **Create folders** (Notes and More Notes in Figure 8-11) to organize your notes by choosing File⇨New Folder, pressing ⌘+Shift+N, or clicking the New Folder button at the bottom of the Folder list.

The Notes window must be selected to create a new folder. If a note in a window is active, the New Folder command will be unavailable. So click the main Notes window if the New Folder command is grayed out.

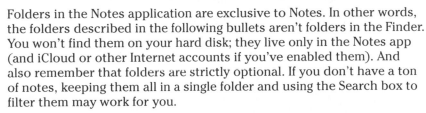

Folders in the Notes application are exclusive to Notes. In other words, the folders described in the following bullets aren't folders in the Finder. You won't find them on your hard disk; they live only in the Notes app (and iCloud or other Internet accounts if you've enabled them). And also remember that folders are strictly optional. If you don't have a ton of notes, keeping them all in a single folder and using the Search box to filter them may work for you.

✔ **Show or hide the Folders list** by choosing View⇨Show/Hide Folders or clicking the Show/Hide Folders button in the toolbar.

✔ **Show only Notes in a folder** by clicking the folder name in the Folders list, or click All iCloud to see all your notes.

✔ **Automatically sync notes with your iDevice by using iCloud or other Internet Accounts** by choosing Notes⇨Accounts, which will open the Internet Accounts System Preferences pane; then click the appropriate Internet account and enable its check box to sync Notes.

✔ **Send the contents of a Note via the Mail or Messages apps** by choosing File⇨Share or clicking the Share icon.

✔ **Print a note** by choosing File⇨Print or pressing ⌘+P.

Whatever you type in a note is saved automatically as you type it, so Notes has no Save, Save As, or Duplicate commands.

Other Notes goodies include a spell checker, spoken notes, text substitutions (such as Smart Quotes and Smart Dashes), and transformations (such as Make Upper or Lowercase). You can find all these options on the Edit menu.

Finally, El Capitan introduces four new features in Notes:

- ✔ You can drag and drop photos, PDFs, videos, and other files into a note, something that's never been possible in Notes before.

- ✔ The new Attachments browser displays every external file you've dragged into every note in a single place, making it easier to find things. Click the Attachments button in the toolbar to see this feature in action; click the Attachments button again to go back to your notes.

- ✔ Use the Share menu in apps such as Safari and Maps to add content to Notes.

- ✔ You can add checklists (in addition to bulleted, numbered, and dashed lists), as shown in the to-do list in the middle of Figure 8-11, by clicking the Checklist button in the toolbar, by choosing Format ⇨ Checklist, or by using the shortcut ⌘+Shift+L.

You now know everything you need to know to use and enjoy El Capitan's new, beefed-up Notes app!

(Inter)Networking

*T*hese days, networking online is easier than finding a log to fall off: You simply use the Internet to connect your Mac to a wealth of information residing on computers around the world. Luckily for you, OS X El Capitan has the best and most comprehensive Internet tools ever shipped with a Mac operating system.

OS X offers built-in Internet connectivity right out of the box. OS X El Capitan comes with

- Apple's Safari web browser, which you use to navigate the web, download remote files, and more

- The FaceTime app for video chats with other Mac or iDevice users

- The Messages app, used for instant messaging and live online chatting (text). Messages works with other Messages users and people using AOL Instant Messaging (AIM) clients, Jabber (an open-source chatting protocol), Google Talk, or Bonjour (which discovers other users on your local area network). It also includes audio and video chatting, screen sharing, and file transfers.

- The Mail application (for email)

In this chapter and the two that follow, I cover the top things most people use the Internet for: the World Wide Web (that's the www. you see so often in Internet addresses), and video and audio chatting. You discover Safari and FaceTime in this chapter, Contacts and Maps in Chapter 10, and Mail and Messages in Chapter 11.

But before I can talk about any of those things, I first have to walk you through configuring your Internet connection, given that none of them work very well without it. The good news is that after you finish making the connection, you can play with your Internet-enabled applications to your heart's content.

Getting Connected to the Internet

Before you can use (or surf) the Internet, you need to connect to it. If you're a typical home user, you need three things to surf the Internet:

- ✓ **A connection to the Internet,** such as a cable modem, digital subscriber line (DSL) modem, or a satellite Internet service (referred to generically as your Internet Box

  If you use technology other than DSL, cable, or satellite to connect your computer to the Internet, your network administrator (the person you run to at work when something goes wrong with your computer) or ISP might have to help you set up your Mac because setting up those other configurations is (sigh) beyond the scope of this book.

- ✓ **An account with an ISP** (Internet service provider), such as AT&T, Comcast, or RoadRunner

  The technical reviewer for previous editions of this book reminded me that these days, that's not necessarily true. All you really need is free Wi-Fi, which is available almost everywhere — in stores, restaurants, parks, libraries, and other places — and a free email account from Apple's iCloud, Microsoft's Outlook.com, Google's Gmail, or Yahoo! Mail.

- ✓ **A Mac,** preferably one running OS X 10.11 El Capitan

  You might need to tweak a few settings, as I explain in the upcoming section "Plugging in your Internet-connection settings."

After you set up each of these components, you can launch and use Safari, Mail, Messages, and any other Internet applications.

Your Internet service provider and you

You may have to select a company to provide you access to the Internet: an ISP. The prices and services that ISPs offer vary, often from minute to minute. Keep the following in mind when choosing an ISP:

✓ **If your connection comes from a cable or telephone company, your
ISP is probably that company.** In effect, the choice of ISP is pretty much
made for you when you decide on cable or DSL service.

✓ **Broadband access to the Internet starts at around $25 or $30 per
month.** If your service provider asks for considerably more than that,
find out why. Higher-throughput packages for cable and DSL connections
might run you twice that. For example, as of this writing, the highest-
speed DSL package from AT&T is around $60 per month. Check with
your ISP for details.

Because most Mac users like things to be easy, OS X includes a cool feature
in its Setup Assistant to help you find and configure an account with an ISP.
When you installed OS X El Capitan (assuming that you did and that it didn't
come preinstalled on your Mac), the Setup Assistant may have asked you a
bunch of questions about your Internet connection and set up everything
for you. (Installing OS X is detailed on this book's companion website at
www.dummies.com/extras/osxelcapitan.)

If you didn't have an Internet connection (an ISP) at that time, you may need
to configure the Network System Preferences pane yourself. Chances are you'll
be good to go as soon as you connect the cable, but in the event it doesn't just
work, these settings could be something you'll have to hash out with your ISP.

That being said, if you have questions or problems not answered by this
book, your ISP should be able to assist you. And if your ISP can't help, it's
probably time to try a different ISP.

Setting up your modem

If you have an Internet box — or are thinking about getting one — you can
use one with your Mac. In most cases, you merely connect your Mac to the
Internet via a cable plugged into the Ethernet port of your Mac and into an
external Internet box — which is connected to a coaxial or optical TV cable
or plugged into a telephone outlet, depending on what kind of access you
have to the Internet.

For a wireless connection, the setup is the same, but rather than plug the
Internet box's cable into the Ethernet port on your Mac, you plug it into
a wireless router such as Apple's AirPort or Time Capsule base station.
After this device is connected to the Internet box supplied by your ISP,
any Wi-Fi–equipped Mac (or PC) within range can connect to the Internet
wirelessly on your network.

Your cable or DSL installer should have set everything up for you before leaving your home or office. If you still cannot connect to the Internet, you should
call that service provider and give them heck. Troubleshooting a high-speed
connection is pretty abstruse (which puts it beyond the purview of this book).

Plugging in your Internet-connection settings

If you didn't set up your Internet connection when you installed OS X, you need to open System Preferences (from the Applications folder, the Dock, Launchpad, or the menu) and click the Network icon. The Network pane offers options for connecting your Mac to the Internet or to a network. Setting up your Internet connection manually in the Network System Preferences pane is beyond the purview of this book. The easiest way to use it is to click the Assist Me button at the bottom and let your Mac do the heavy lifting.

If you're part of a large office network, check with your system administrator before you change anything in this pane. If you ignore this advice, you run the risk of losing your network connection completely.

If your Mac asks you a question you can't answer during setup, ask your ISP or network administrator for the answer. I can't possibly tell you how in this book because there are just too many possible configurations, and each depends on your particular ISP and service.

That said, here's a brief rundown on the most common things you may need to know in order to set up a network connection:

- **TCP/IP:** TCP/IP is the language of the Internet. You may be asked to specify things such as your IP address, domain name servers, and search domains.

- **PPP or PPPoE:** These acronyms stand for *Point-to-Point Protocol* and *Point-to-Point Protocol over Ethernet.* Which one you see depends on what service you're using to connect. All analog modems use PPP; some cable and DSL modems use PPPoE.

- **Proxies:** If you're on a large network or your Mac is behind a firewall, you may need to specify one or more proxy servers. If so, your network administrator or ISP can help you with configuration. (Most home users will never need to touch this tab.) Some ISPs require you to specify proxy servers; if you need to do so, ask your ISP what to do.

If you use your Mac in more than one place, you can set up a separate configuration for each location and choose it from the Location menu. A *location,* in this context, consists of all settings in all items in the Network System Preferences pane.

My technical editor reminds me that you probably don't need to create separate locations these days. My MacBook Pro just works. I may have to choose a Wi-Fi network and provide a password the first time I visit a hotel, café, or office; after that, my Mac remembers everything so the next time I'm at that hotel, café, or office, it just works.

After you have this entire pane configured the way that you like, follow these steps to create separate locations:

1. **Pull down the Location menu and choose Edit Locations.**

2. **Click the + button at the bottom of the Locations list.**

   A new, untitled Location appears in the list.

3. **Type a descriptive name for the new location, such as** AirPort at Starbucks **or** Ethernet at Joe's Office.

4. **Click Done, and then click Apply.**

   From now on, you can change all your network settings at the same time by choosing the appropriate location from the Location pop-up menu.

If, on the other hand, your Mac has a single network or Internet connection (as most home users have), just leave the Location menu set to Automatic and be done with it.

Using the Network Setup Assistant (click the Assist Me button at the bottom of the Network System Preferences pane, and then click the Assistant button) to create a network connection usually makes it unnecessary for you to have to deal with most of these items. Still, I thought you should at least know the basics.

And while this may be beyond the purview of this book, I'd like to remind you to use only wireless networks that you know and trust, especially in public places such as hotels and airports.

Browsing the Web with Safari

With your Internet connection set up, you're ready to browse the web. In the following sections, I concentrate on browsing the web with Safari because it's the web browser installed with OS X El Capitan.

If you don't care for Safari, check out Firefox or Chrome, which are both free browsers and have features you won't find in Safari. It never hurts to have a spare in case Safari has issues with a particular website.

To begin, just open your web browser. No problem. As usual, there's more than one way. You can launch Safari by any of these methods:

✔ Single-clicking the Safari icon on the Dock or Launchpad (look for the big blue compass that looks like a stopwatch, as shown in the margin)

✔ Double-clicking the Safari icon in your Applications folder

- Single-clicking a URL link in an email or other document
- Double-clicking a URL link document (a .webloc file) in the Finder

When you first launch Safari, it displays the default Top Sites page (see Figure 9-1). In the sections that follow, I cover the highlights of using Safari, starting at the top of the screen.

Figure 9-1: Safari first displays the Top Sites page.

Owning your toolbar

The Safari toolbar consists of a narrow row of buttons and the Search or Enter Website Name field at the top of every Safari window, and they do pretty much what their names imply. From left to right, these buttons are

- **Back/Forward:** When you open a page and move to a second page (or third or fourth), the Back button takes you to a previously visited page. Remember that you need to go back before the Forward button will work.

- **Show/Hide Sidebar:** Click this button to see your Favorites, Reading List, and Links in the Sidebar, and then click it again to hide the Sidebar.
- **Search or Enter Website Name:** This field, to the right of the Show Sidebar button, is where you type web addresses, or URLs (Uniform Resource Locators) that you want to visit. Just type one, and press Return to surf to that site.

  To the right of the Search or Enter Website Name field are two more buttons. Keep reading.

- ✔ **Share:** When you find a page of interest or a page you know you'll want to remember, click this button (which is actually a drop-down menu) to tell Safari to remember it for you in El Capitan's cool Reading List or as a bookmark — two topics I explore further a little later in this chapter. Or send a link to it via Mail or Messages, both covered in Chapter 11, or post it on Facebook or tweet it on Twitter.

- ✔ **Show/Hide All Tabs:** Click the Show/Hide All Tabs button to see previews of all your open tabs (which you'll learn about shortly). If you have other Macs or iDevices, you'll also see the open tabs in this copy of Safari on other devices that have Safari enabled in iCloud.

This feature is so handy you can also find it in the View menu, where you'll also spy its handy keyboard shortcut, ⌘+Shift+\.

El Capitan introduces the concept of pinned tabs, which persist in the tab bar until you unpin them. To pin a tab, choose Window⇨Pin Tab or right- or Control-click the tab and choose Pin Tab from the contextual menu. To unpin a tab you've pinned previously, reverse the process and choose Window⇨ Unpin Tab or right- or Control-click the pinned tab and choose Unpin Tab.

But wait — there's more. To add other useful buttons to your toolbar, choose View⇨Customize Toolbar (or right-click anywhere on the toolbar and choose Customize Toolbar from the contextual menu). The Customize Toolbar sheet drops down, and you can drag items into or out of the toolbar to create your own custom set of buttons. In Figure 9-2, for example, I added six new buttons to my toolbar (left to right): Top Sites, Favorites Bar, AutoFill, Zoom In/Out, Mail, and Print to my toolbar.

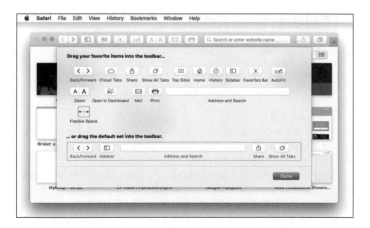

Figure 9-2: The Customize Toolbar sheet and my customized toolbar.

Web addresses almost always begin with http://www. But Safari has a cool trick: If you just type a name, you usually get to the appropriate website that way without typing http, ://, or www. If you type **apple** in the Search or Enter Website Name field and press Return, for example, you go to www.apple.com. Or if you type **boblevitus**, you're taken to www.boblevitus.com. Try it — it's pretty slick.

Below the Search or Enter Website Name field is the Favorites bar, already populated with some buttons of web pages Apple thinks you might enjoy, including Apple, Yahoo!, Google Maps, YouTube, and Wikipedia.

If you don't see your Favorites bar, choose View⇨Show Favorites Bar or press ⌘+Shift+B.

All buttons on my Safari toolbar are actually *drop-down menus*, as denoted by the little chevron after their names, as shown in Figure 9-3.

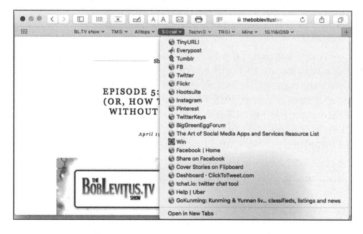

Figure 9-3: All the buttons in my Favorites bar are actually drop-down menus.

You can delete these bookmarks and/or add your own bookmarks to the Favorites bar (and Sidebar), as described in the next section.

One last thing: Favorites and bookmarks are not exactly the same in El Capitan. Favorites are a folder of bookmarks that appear in both the Favorites bar and in the Favorites view (if you click Favorites in the Show All Tabs view). You can see your Favorites folder at the top of the Bookmarks list in the Sidebar. And, perhaps to confuse matters, you can change what displays in the Favorites view (but not the Favorites bar) via a setting in Preferences' General pane. It can be a trifle confusing at first, but you'll get used to it.

Using the Safari Sidebar

Click the Sidebar button on the toolbar to show or hide the Safari Sidebar, which has three tabs — Favorites, Reading List, and Shared Links — which I explore in this section.

Bookmarking your favorite pages

When you find a web page you want to remember and return to, you *bookmark* it.

Here's how it works:

1. **Choose Bookmarks⇨Add Bookmark, press ⌘+D, or click the Share button and choose Add Bookmark.**

2. **Choose where to store the bookmark from the pop-up menu, as shown in Figure 9-4.**

   By default, Safari puts them in the Favorites folder.

3. **Rename the bookmark or use the name provided by Safari.**

   I accepted the name Safari suggested, so now this page will appear in the Favorites bar as The BobLeVitus.TV Show.

4. **Click the Add button to save the bookmark.**

Figure 9-4: Creating a bookmark.

Finding your bookmarks in the Sidebar

To return to a bookmarked page, click it in the Favorites bar, choose Bookmarks⇨Show Bookmarks, press ⌘+Option+B, or click the Show Sidebar button (shown in margin) to see all your bookmarks in the Sidebar, as shown in Figure 9-5.

If you add the Bookmark to the Favorites folder (as shown), it automatically appears in the Favorites bar; if you add the bookmark outside the Favorites folder in the Sidebar, it will not appear in the Favorites bar but will be available at the bottom of the Bookmarks menu and in the Bookmarks Sidebar.

Open bookmarked pages in the Sidebar by clicking them. View the contents of folders (such as Favorites, BL.TV show, Techno, TMO, Alltops, and Social in Figure 9-5) by single-clicking their name in the list. Figure 9-5 shows, in particular, the contents of the Favorites bar folder with the contents of the Social subfolder expanded.

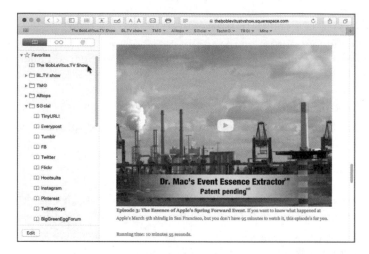

Figure 9-5: The Sidebar in all its glory.

To organize your Bookmarks window or place bookmarks on the toolbar or Bookmarks menu, move bookmarks by dragging them. You can place bookmarks and folders of bookmarks on the Safari Favorites bar or in the Bookmarks menu by dragging them to the appropriate folder. If you drag a folder of bookmarks to the Favorites folder (or directly onto the Favorites bar itself), the result is a drop-down menu, as shown in Figure 9-3, earlier in this chapter.

To delete a bookmark, right- or Control+click it and choose Delete.

⌘+click a folder in the Bookmarks window or Favorites bar to simultaneously open all the bookmarks it contains.

While we're on the subject of Favorites, you've probably noticed this handy behavior by now, but it's worth mentioning: When you click in the empty Search or Enter Website Name field, a sheet drops down displaying your Favorites. The sheet is replaced by a list of search results and suggestions as soon as you type the first character. Understandably, the sheet doesn't appear if the current page is Favorites or Top Sites. But it's a convenient feature I'd be remiss not to mention.

Last but not least, Safari gained a fabulous new feature in El Capitan — a little blue speaker icon that appears on the right side of the Search or Enter Website Name field if audio is playing on any page. Click the speaker and Safari will go silent even if the audio is coming from an inactive tab or a hidden window.

Thanks, Apple; we needed that.

What's on your Reading List?

The *Reading List* serves as a repository for pages or links you want to read but don't want to read right now. It's a lot like a bookmark but easier to create on the fly, which makes the Reading List perfect for sites or links you don't need to keep forever (that's what bookmarks are for).

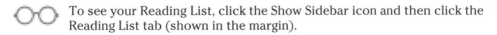

To see your Reading List, click the Show Sidebar icon and then click the Reading List tab (shown in the margin).

To add the page you're viewing to your Reading List, hover your cursor over the left side of the Search or Enter Website Name field and then click the + that appears, as shown in Figure 9-6. (You can also use the keyboard shortcut ⌘+Shift+D or click the Share button and choose Add to Reading List from its menu.)

Hover cursor here and then click the x to delete this page from your Reading List.

Hover cursor here and then click to add the page to your reading list.

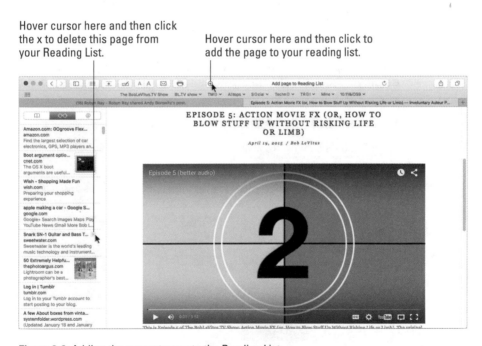

Figure 9-6: Adding the current page to the Reading List.

To add a link to your Reading List without actually visiting the page, just press the Shift key before you click a link. It's fast and easy, and it works even if the Sidebar is closed. Or you can right- or Control-click the link and choose Add to Reading List from the contextual menu.

To delete an item from the Reading List, hover the cursor over it and then click the little x that appears in its upper-right corner (as shown for the Snark SN-1 item in Figure 9-6), or right- or Control-click the item and then choose Remove Item.

If you have other Macs or iDevices, you can sync your Reading List among your devices by enabling Safari in the iCloud System Preferences pane.

What the heck is a shared link?

Shared Links is a cool feature that aggregates links shared by your friends on Twitter, Facebook, and other social media sites you've enabled in Internet Accounts or Extensions System Preferences panes as well as RSS feeds you've enabled by clicking the Subscriptions button at the bottom of the Sidebar. Then Shared Links displays them in a chronological list. And that, my friends, is what Shared Links is all about.

Using the terrific Top Sites page

The Top Sites page has quickly become one of my favorite Safari features. It displays a selection of sites you visit frequently, as shown in Figure 9-7.

Top Sites button in Favorites Bar

Top Sites button in Toolbar   Favorites

Pin

Delete site

Figure 9-7: Top Sites displays your favorite sites.

To see Top Sites, choose Bookmarks ⟹ Show Top Sites, or click the Top Sites button (shown in the margin), which is on the left edge of my Favorites bar (View ⟹ Show Favorites Bar) and also on my customized toolbar (both shown in Figure 9-7).

As you surf the web, Safari learns your favorite sites and replaces the sites on the Top Sites page with the ones you visit most.

Here are a few more things you can do with Top Sites:

- **Delete a site you don't want on your Top Sites page.** Click the little X in its top-left corner (see Figure 9-7).

- **Pin a site to your Top Sites page to make it remain one of your Top Sites, even if you don't visit that page for a while.** Click the pushpin in its top-left corner so it turns blue, as shown in Figure 9-7.

- **Change the number and size of the sites shown.** Choose Safari ⟹ Preferences, click the General tab at the top, and then choose 12 sites (shown in Figure 9-7), or 6 or 24 (not shown) from the Top Sites Shows pop-up menu.

Searching with Google

Looking for something on the Internet? Check out Google, the fantastic search engine that's totally integrated with Safari to help you hunt down just about anything on the Internet in no time.

Don't care for Google? Choose Safari ⟹ Preferences, click the Search tab, and choose a different one, as long as you prefer Yahoo!, Bing, or DuckDuckGo (a privacy-friendly search engine that unlike Google doesn't track your searches or collect information about your search habits).

In this section, you discover how to use Google to search the Internet and find almost anything, as well as how to get help with Google when all else fails.

To search the Internet with Google, follow these steps:

1. **Type the beginning of a word or phrase in the Search or Enter Website Name field.**

   As you type, Safari offers a list of suggestions and recent searches, as shown in Figure 9-8. Note that I had typed only *vizsla pi* when Safari offered this list.

2. **Click one of the list items; finish typing the word or phrase, or use the arrow keys to select a list item; and then press Return to start the search.**

   Google almost immediately offers your search results, as shown in Figure 9-8.

Figure 9-8: A Google search for pictures of Vizsla dogs.

3. **Click one of the result links.**

   Links appear in blue and are underlined. You're taken instantly to that particular page.

If the fish you catch on your first try aren't what you want, use different bait:

- **If a particular result isn't just what you're looking for:** Click the Back button, and try another result link.

- **If Google offers too many results that aren't just right:**

   a. *Click the gear button near the top of the results page and choose Advanced Search.*

   Advanced searches refine your search with a multitude of options, some of which are shown in Figure 9-9. I am refining my search for pictures of Vizsla dogs that are cute or puppies and not ugly, senior, or old.

   b. *Click the Advanced Search button (not visible in Figure 9-9).*

   A refined results page quickly appears. As before, click a result link to visit that page. If it's not just what you're looking for, click the Back button, and try a different result link.

By the way, the little double-chevron icons on the right side of the toolbar and Favorites bar in Figures 9-9 (and shown in the margin) indicate that the window is too narrow to display all the tools or bookmarks. Click the chevron, and a menu shows you the previously hidden choices, as shown in Figure 9-9. In this figure, the tool-bar overflow menu (not shown) would show the five hidden toolbar icons; the Favorites bar overflow menu (shown) shows the five hidden bookmark folders.

That's pretty much all you need to know to have a great time searching the web with Google.

Figure 9-9: Running a Google advanced search.

Checking out Help Center

Safari has a lot more features, and I could write an entire chapter about using Safari, but one of the rules we *For Dummies* authors must follow is that our books can't run 1,000 pages long.

So I'm going to give you the next best thing: Open the Help Center (by choosing Help⇨Safari Help). A special Safari Help window appears; you can search for any Safari-related topic or solution to any Safari-related problem right there.

Audio and Video Calls with FaceTime

In the beginning, FaceTime brought video calling to the iPhone 4. It was iPhone 4-to-iPhone 4 only and required Wi-Fi (not cellular 3G or 4G). Still, it was pretty cool and worked quite well. Not surprisingly, it soon spread to the second- and later-generation iPads, the iPod touch, and in OS X Snow Leopard on the Mac as well.

If you haven't read about Messages yet (Chapter 11), one of its features is video chat. Alas, Messages can video chat only with folks on Macs or PCs, but FaceTime lets you do video chat with other Mac users as well as users of iPhone 4 or later, as well as iPad and iPod touch users.

In addition to its aforementioned video-chat-with-iDevices prowess, FaceTime works beautifully for Mac-to-Mac video calls. And, because it's a single-purpose application, many users (including my mom) find it easier and less intimidating to set up and use than Messages or Skype.

By the way, there's no Windows version of FaceTime at the moment, so you'll have to use Messages (or third-party software like Skype) to have cross-platform video chats.

A feature introduced in Yosemite lets you use your Mac to make and receive phone calls on your iPhone with the FaceTime app. You find details on this feature and other Continuity features (Handoff, SMS, and Instant Hot Spot) by visiting www.dummies.com/cheatsheet/osxelcapitan.

For now, to get started, launch FaceTime from your Applications folder, Launchpad, or Dock. The main (only) FaceTime window appears, as shown in Figure 9-10.

Figure 9-10: The FaceTime window, ready to make a call.

The right side of the window shows what your Mac's camera is seeing (which happens to be me in Figure 9-10).

I clicked the camera icon next to my wife's name to initiate a call from my Mac to my wife's iPhone (or Mac). She was in the yard, so she answered on her iPhone; what we each saw is shown in Figure 9-11.

Figure 9-11: A FaceTime call: what the caller sees on a Mac screen
(left) and what the call receiver sees on an iPhone screen (right).

FaceTime uses Contacts (covered in Chapter 11), so if you have friends or
family who have an iPhone 4 or later, iPad 2 or later, iPad mini, iPod touch
(fourth generation or later), or a Mac, just type their name in the field in the
top-left corner, and then right- or Control-click on their name in the results
list, as shown for Lisa LeVitus in Figure 9-10.

10

Finding People and Places

In This Chapter

▶ Managing contacts with Contacts

▶ Finding places with Maps

*I*n this chapter and the next, you discover a quartet of programs that work beautifully together and make managing your contacts, email, maps, and messages (chats) a breeze. You're about to find out how these eponymous programs — Contacts and Maps in this chapter, and Mail and Messages in Chapter 11 — work, and how to use them individually and as a team.

I cover a lot of material in not a lot of space in these two chapters, so if there's something you want to find out about Contacts, Maps, Mail, or Messages that I don't cover, don't forget about the capable assistance you can find in Help➪Contacts Help (or Maps Help, Mail Help, or Messages Help).

Collecting Your Contacts

Contacts stores and manages information about your family, friends, companies, and any other entity you want to keep in touch with. It works seamlessly with the Mail, Messages, and Maps applications, enabling you to quickly look up phone numbers or email addresses when you're ready to communicate with someone.

In fact, Contacts works with several applications, both on and beyond your Mac, including the following:

✔ Use it with FaceTime (covered in Chapter 9) to video chat with friends and family.

✔ Use it with Calendar (covered in Chapter 8) to display your contacts by choosing Window⇨Address Panel or pressing ⌘+Option+A. You can then drag any person in your Contacts from the Address Panel to any date and time on the calendar, and a special Meeting event is created automatically by Calendar. The event even has a Send Invitation button; if you click it, it launches Mail and sends the person an invitation to this meeting. Very cool stuff.

✔ The Contacts application can also work with any other application whose programmers choose to make the connection or with any device that's compatible with Contacts. For example, BusyContacts ($49.99 in the Mac App Store) exchanges data with Contacts seamlessly, so changes made in Contacts appear in BusyContacts (and vice versa) almost immediately.

✔ It's also available in most programs that have a Share button or menu so you can share with your contacts via whichever method is appropriate, usually their phone number, email, or iCloud.com or Me.com address (for an iMessage).

✔ If you use iCloud, you can choose to sync contacts with devices that include (but are not limited to) other Macs, iPhones, iPads, and iPod touches. And you can also sync contacts via Google, Microsoft Exchange, or Microsoft Office 365, or any combination.

In the following sections, you find out the best ways to fill Contacts with your own contacts and how to keep those contacts organized.

Adding contacts

Follow these steps to create a new entry in the Contacts:

1. **Launch the Contacts application by double-clicking its icon in the Applications folder, clicking its Dock icon, or clicking its Launchpad icon.**

   The Contacts window appears. The first time that you open Contacts, you see two cards: Apple Computer, and the one with whatever personal identification information you supplied when you created your account.

2. **To create a new entry, click the + button at the bottom of the Contact card and choose New Contact from the drop-down menu.**

   An untitled address card appears. The First name text field is initially selected. (It's highlighted in Figure 10-1.)

3. **Type the person's first name in the First text field.**

   Here, I type **Bob**.

Figure 10-1: A new address card in Contacts.

4. **Press Tab.**

   Your cursor should now be in the Last text field.

   You can always move from one field to the next by pressing Tab. In fact, this shortcut works in almost all Mac programs with fields. (Move to the previous field by pressing Shift+Tab.)

5. **Type the last name for the person you're adding to your Contacts.**

   Here, I type **LeVitus**. Continue this process, filling in the rest of the fields shown in Figure 10-2.

6. **When you're done entering information, click the Done button to exit the editing mode.**

   The contact I created with this step appears in Figure 10-2.

   The little triangles (actually up and down arrows) between the labels and their contents fields in Figure 10-2 are pop-up menus that offer alternative labels for the field. For example, if you were to click the arrows next to the word *Child,* you would be able to choose Father, Parent, Brother, Sister, and so on to replace the label *Child.*

   To add more info about any Contacts entry, click the name in the list on the left (Bob LeVitus in Figure 10-2). You can tell when a name is selected because it's highlighted (Bob LeVitus in Figure 10-2). Click the Edit button at the bottom of the Contacts window, and make your changes.

   Repeat these steps for everyone you want to keep in touch with.

Pop-up menus

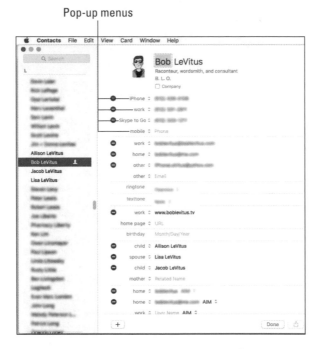

Figure 10-2: My address card displayed in the Contacts window.

Importing contacts from other programs

If your contacts are on another Mac, iDevice, or stored by Google, or Microsoft, you won't need to import your contacts. Just enable the appropriate account in the Internet Accounts System Preferences pane, and enable syncing for contacts.

Those who have contacts in another program (such as FileMaker Pro or ACT) might be able to import them into Contacts. Contacts can import contacts in vCard, LDIF, or text file format.

The first thing is to export the data from the other program in one of these formats.

I always export the file to the Desktop, so it's easy to find in the next step.

Choose File⇨Import, select the exported data file in the Open File dialog, and then click the Open button.

Creating a basic group

Now let me explain how to organize your contacts into groups. Why would you want to organize your contacts into groups? The main reason, at least for me, is practical: I can send email with a single click to everyone in a group that I've defined. For example, when it's time to send out a press release, I can simply send it to my Press/PR group, shooting the email off to all 50 people I have in that group. And when I want to send an email to all the parents of kids on my son's indoor football team, I merely address it to my Flag Football Parents group, and all 12 families in that group receive it.

Here's how to create a group and add contacts to it:

1. **Launch the Contacts application by double-clicking its icon in the Applications folder or clicking its Dock icon.**

2. **Create the new group by choosing File⇨New Group, pressing ⌘+Shift+N, or clicking the + button at the bottom of the window.**

   An untitled Group appears in the Group column with Untitled Group highlighted.

3. **Type a descriptive name for this group and then press Return.**

   I named mine **Family**.

4. **Click All Contacts on the left side of the window to show all your contacts on the right side.**

5. **Click the contacts you want in the group from the contacts list.**

   Hold down the ⌘ key as you select contacts if you want to select more than one contact.

   You can use the Search field (the magnifying glass icon) at the top of the window to find a contact or contacts, and then drag them onto the group to add them, which is what I did in Figure 10-3.

6. **Drag the selected contact names onto the group, as shown in Figure 10-3.**

   Contacts considerately displays the number of contacts you're dragging, which happens to be five in this instance.

Another way to create a group is to select contacts by clicking, ⌘-clicking, and/or Shift-clicking contacts and then choosing File⇨New Group from Selection.

Setting up a smart group (based on contact criteria)

A second type of group — a smart group — might be even more useful to you because it gathers contacts in your Contacts based on criteria you specify.

Drag to here   Select items and then drag from here

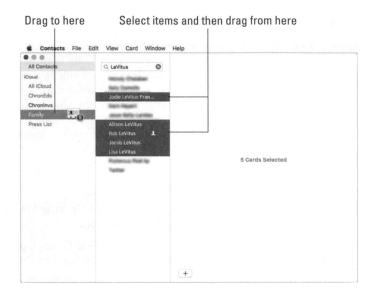

Figure 10-3: Adding five contacts to the Family group.

So, for example, say I create a group that automatically selects Apple staff members that have email addresses that end in @apple.com.

The big advantage of using a smart group instead of a regular group is that when I add, say, a new Apple contact, that contact automatically becomes a member of the Apple Smart Group with no further action on my part. And if you delete a card or modify it so the contact no longer matches the smart group criteria, the contact is removed from the group automatically.

To create a smart group, follow these steps:

1. **Choose File ⇨ New Smart Group or press ⌘+Option+N.**

   A Smart Group sheet appears in front of the Contacts window, as shown in Figure 10-4.

2. **Give the Smart Group a name.**

   I named mine **@Apple.com**.

3. **Select the appropriate items from the menus: Any, Company, Contains, Email, and so on.**

   In Figure 10-4, I created a smart group that includes any contact that contains *Apple* in the Company field or *@apple.com* in any email field.

4. **When you're happy with the criteria specified, click OK.**

Figure 10-4: Creating a new smart group.

Deleting a group or smart group

To delete a group or a smart group from your Contacts, click to select it, and then press Delete or choose Edit➪Delete Group.

The view is lovely

The Contacts View menu has but two options:

- **Show/Hide Groups (⌘+1):** Choose Show/Hide Groups to hide or show the leftmost column (where you see iCloud and Smart Groups in Figure 10-3).

  Note that you'll see On My Mac in this column (instead of iCloud) if you haven't enabled iCloud syncing.

- **Show/Hide Last Import (⌘+Option+L):** Choose Show/Hide Last Import to show or hide the Last Import Smart Group that Apple kindly provided for you.

- **Enter Full Screen (⌘+Control+F):** Does just what you'd expect, filling your screen with the Contacts window. To exit Full Screen, press ⌘+Control+F again, press the Esc key, or move the pointer to the top of the screen and click the red gumdrop button.

Sync + Contacts = Your contacts everywhere

If you're not syncing contacts with iCloud, Google, or Microsoft Exchange/Office 360 (I discuss syncing calendars and reminders with iCloud in Chapter 8; you're on your own with Google or Microsoft), your contacts will be stored locally on your hard disk. iCloud/Google/Microsoft users, on the other hand, can choose to store their contacts either locally or in iCloud,

Google's cloud, or Microsoft's cloud. The difference is if you store your contacts in the cloud, you can sync all your devices so they all display the same information. In other words, if you add a contact to your iPhone, you'll see it on your Mac in the Contacts app within a few minutes. Conversely, if you add a contact on your Mac, within a few minutes, it magically appears in the Contacts app on your iDevice.

Here is how to enable iCloud for Contacts:

1. **Choose Contacts⇨Preferences or press ⌘+, (comma).**

    The Contacts Preferences window appears.

2. **Click the Accounts icon at the top of the window.**

    The Accounts pane appears.

3. **Click the + button near the bottom of the window.**

    The Choose a Contacts Account to Add sheet appears.

4. **Click the iCloud (or Exchange or Google or other) button and then click Continue.**

5. **Type the name you want to use for this account, your username, and your password, and then click the Sign In (iCloud) or Set Up (other services) button.**

    The Use With sheet appears for the selected service with the Contacts check box already selected.

6. **Click Add Account.**

If you previously enabled iCloud for Contacts, re-enabling it is even easier: Choose Contacts⇨Preferences (⌘+,), click the Accounts icon at the top of the window, Click iCloud in the list on the left, and then select the Enable This Account check box.

To enable syncing with Google, Microsoft, Yahoo!, and other services the same way, click the + button at the bottom of the column on the left, click the service name (Google, Microsoft, and so on) on the right. Then, just provide your username and password, and click Set Up. Piece of cake.

If you've enabled any accounts in the Internet Accounts System Preferences pane, they appear in the list on the left in Contacts.

If you use iCloud, there's no reason to store contacts locally: that is, On My Mac. And, in fact, if you use iCloud, you won't even see an On My Mac section in the Groups list. My advice is that if you do see both sections (On My Mac and iCloud) in the Groups list, copy the contacts stored in On My Mac to iCloud by clicking All on My Mac in the Groups list and selecting all its contacts (Edit⇨Select All or ⌘+A) and dragging them onto the iCloud group. Now click the iCloud group and confirm that the contacts you just dragged are visible, and then delete the contacts in the On My Mac group (select all contacts and then choose Edit⇨Delete Cards). Finally, click iCloud and look for duplicate contacts by choosing Card⇨Look for Duplicates. If any duplicates are found, you're invited to either delete one (if they're the same) or merge them (if one is different).

Maps Are Where It's At

The Maps application should look familiar to anyone who uses an iOS device, which have sported a Maps app since time immemorial. If you know how to use the Maps app on your iPhone, iPad, or iPod touch, you already know most of what you need to know to use Maps on your Mac.

As for the rest of you — the ones without iOS devices — I'll have you up to speed RealSoonNow.

Finding your current location with Maps

I'll start with something supremely simple yet extremely useful: determining your current location. At the risk of sounding like a self-help guru, here's how to find yourself. Launch the Maps application from the Dock, Launchpad, or Applications folder, and then click the Current Location button, which is a little black arrowhead (shown in the margin) and found on the left of the Search or Enter an Address field.

Your location is indicated by a blue dot. I clicked the arrowhead in the toolbar, and the blue dot shows my location, as shown in Figure 10-5.

If you tap or drag the map, your Mac continues to update your location but won't re-center the blue marker — meaning that the blue dot can scroll (or zoom) off the screen. If that happens, click the Current Location button again to center the map on your current location again.

Finding a person, place, or thing

To find a person, place, or thing with Maps, choose Edit⇨Find, press ⌘+F, or click in the Search field in the center of the toolbar, and then type what you're looking for. You can search for addresses, ZIP codes, intersections, towns, landmarks, and businesses by category and by name, or combinations, such as *New York, NY 10022, pizza 60645,* or *Texas State Capitol.*

Current location button   Current location

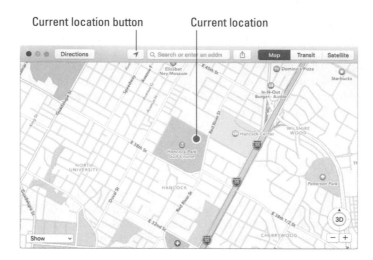

Figure 10-5: You are here.

If the letters you type match names stored in your Mac (or iDevice) Contacts app, the matching contacts appear in a list below the Search field. Click a name to see a map of that contact's location. The Maps app is smart about it, too, displaying only the names of contacts that have a street address.

If you don't find a match in the list, press Return, and with any luck, within a few seconds, a map will appear. If you search for a single location, it's marked with a single pushpin. If you search for a category (*BBQ Lockhart TX,* for example), you see multiple pushpins, one for each matching location (BBQ joints in Lockhart, TX), as shown in Figure 10-6.

Figure 10-6: Pushpins indicate matching locations.

You can search for all sorts of things, including intersections, neighborhoods, landmarks, restaurants, and businesses. Furthermore, you can combine several items, such as pizza and a ZIP code. The Maps app is quite adept at interpreting search terms and finding the right place. After you use the app a few times, you'll be as addicted as I am.

To find out more, click a name in the list below the Search field or click a pin. A little flag with the name of the location (Black's Barbecue in Figure 10-6) appears. Click the *i* on the right side of a flag, and a window with information about the location appears, as shown in Figure 10-7.

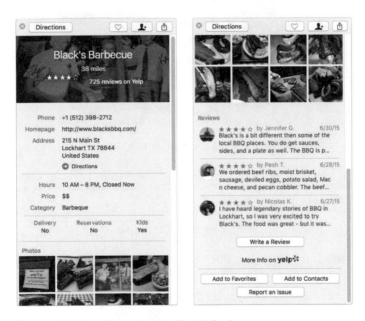

Figure 10-7: The Info window for Black's Barbecue.

This handy little info window sometimes contains reviews and/or photos (the one in Figure 10-7 has both), so you may have to scroll down to read reviews or see photos (as shown on the right). I'll get to the four buttons at the bottom of the window shortly, but first take a look at how to navigate your Maps.

Views, zooms, and pans

The preceding section talks about how to find just about anything with Maps, and the following section shows ways to use what you find. But before doing that, I want to take a little detour and explore how you can work with Maps.

Two views are available — map or satellite — and both are available in 3D. You can choose a view by clicking one of the two tabs on the toolbar. Refer to Figure 10-5 for map view and Figure 10-6 for a satellite view. Finally, check out Figure 10-8 for a satellite map in 3D.

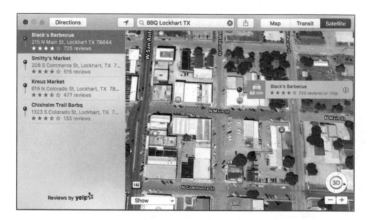

Figure 10-8: A 3D satellite map of Black's BBQ in Lockhart.

3D maps aren't available in every area. It appears that the more populated the area, the more likely it is available in 3D.

Speaking of which, here's the scoop on 3D maps:

- **To switch to a 3D map:** Click the 3D button (shown in the margin), choose View ⇨ 3D Map, or press ⌘+0.

  You may have to zoom in for the map to appear in 3D.

- **To zoom in:** Choose View ⇨ Zoom in or press ⌘++ (plus sign). If you have a trackpad, you can also expand (spread two fingers) to zoom out (just like on an iPhone).

  To zoom out: Choose View ⇨ Zoom Out or press ⌘+– (minus sign). If you have a trackpad, you can also pinch to zoom out (just like on an iPhone).

  If you have a scroll-wheel mouse, you can use the wheel to zoom in and out.

- **To scroll:** Hold down the mouse or trackpad button and drag left, right, up, or down. If you have a trackpad, you can drag using two fingers.

  If you click and then fling your mouse in any direction (or flick with two fingers on a trackpad), you'll "fly over" the ground below. It's not particularly useful, but it looks cool.

 ✔ **To adjust the camera angle or rotate the map:** Press the Option key before you click and drag on the map.

 ✔ **To scroll:** Click and drag up, down, left, or right. If you have a trackpad, you can also drag two fingers in any direction to scroll.

Maps and Contacts

Maps and Contacts go together like peanut butter and jelly. For example, if you want to see a map of a contact's street address, type a few letters of the contact's name in the Search field and click her name in the list that automatically appears.

If you're in the Contacts app, it's even easier: Hover your pointer over a street address and click the little blue icon that appears, as shown in Figure 10-9. Maps will then open with a pin at the address.

Click here to see this address in Maps

After you find a location by typing an address in Maps, you can add that location to one of your contacts. Or you can create a new contact with a location you've found. To do either, click the location's pushpin on the map and then click the little *i* to the right of the location's name (Black's Barbecue in Figure 10-6) to display its Info sheet, as shown in Figure 10-7.

Figure 10-9: Click the little blue icon to see this address in Maps.

Now click the Add to Contacts button on the Info sheet.

You can also get driving directions from most locations, including a contact's address, to most other locations, including another contact's address. You see how to do that in the "Smart map tricks" section, later in the chapter.

Finally, if you click in the Search field and then click Favorites in the drop-down menu that appears, you'll see your contacts and groups on the left. Click All Contacts or a group to see your contacts.

Timesaving map tools: Favorites, Recents, and Contacts

The Maps app offers three tools that can save you from having to type the same locations over and over. All three are in the Favorites sheet, which appears when you click in the Search field and then click Favorites in the drop-down list.

On the left side of the Favorites window is a list offering Favorites, Recents, and Contacts; the following sections give you the lowdown on these useful options.

Apple is inconsistent. In Mavericks, Favorites were called Bookmarks; in Yosemite and El Capitan, Favorites are called Favorites most of the time and bookmarks some of the time. Bottom line: A favorite is a bookmark, and a bookmark is a favorite. I'm going to go with Favorites for the remainder of the chapter, but remember that a favorite is the same as a bookmark as far as Maps is concerned.

Favorites

Favorites in the Maps app, like Favorites in Safari, lets you return to a location without typing a single character. To bookmark a location, click the little chevron-in-a-blue circle to the right of the location's name or description to display the Info screen for that location. Then click the Add to Favorites button on the Info sheet. (You may have to scroll down the Info screen to see the Add to Favorites button.)

You can also drop a *pin* (a kind of temporary favorite) anywhere on the map by clicking and holding down the mouse button for a couple of seconds. Or right-click and choose Drop Pin from the menu.

After you drop a pin, you can click and drag it anywhere on the map. When the pin is where you want it, lift your finger off the mouse button or trackpad to drop the pin. To bookmark this location, click the little *i* to the right of the banner on the pin to open the Info sheet; click the Add to Favorites button to add the bookmark.

After you add a favorite, you can recall it at any time. To do so, click in the Search field, and then click Favorites at the top of the sheet that appears. Then, click the desired item in the list that appears.

The first things you should add as favorites are your home and work address. You use these addresses all the time with Maps, so you might as well add them now to avoid typing them over and over.

To manage your favorites, first click the Edit button in the lower-right corner of the Favorites sheet. Then you can do the following:

✔ **To move a favorite up or down in the Favorites list:** Click and drag the bookmark upward to move it higher in the list or downward to move it lower in the list.

✔ **To delete a favorite from the Favorites list:** Click the tiny x-in-a-circle to the right of its name.

When you're finished using the Favorites list, click anywhere on the map or type in the Search field to dismiss it.

Recents

The Maps app automatically remembers every location you've searched for in its Recents list (unless you've cleared it, as described next). Click in the Search field, and then click Favorites in the sheet that appears below it. Click Recents to see your recent searches; click the item's name to see it on the map.

To clear the Recents list, click the Clear Recents button at the bottom of the list. Sadly, removing a single entry is not possible; clearing the Recents list is an all-or-nothing deal.

When you're finished using the Recents list, click anywhere on the map or type in the Search field to dismiss it.

Contacts

To see a map of a contact's location, click in the Search field and then click Favorites in the sheet that appears below it. Click All Contacts (or any group name) and then click the contact's name to see it on the map.

When you're finished using the Favorites list, click anywhere on the map or type in the Search field to dismiss it.

Smart map tricks

The Maps app has more tricks up its sleeve. This section lists a few nifty features you may find useful.

Get route maps and driving directions

You can get route maps and driving directions to any location from any other location in a couple of ways:

✔ **If a pushpin is already on the screen:** Click the little *i* to the right of the item's name to display the item's Info sheet, and then click its Directions button (upper-left) to open the Directions sidebar.

✔ **When you're looking at a map screen:** Click the Directions button on the toolbar. The Directions sidebar appears with Start and End fields at the top. Type the start and end points or select them from your Favorites, Recents, or Contacts if you prefer (by typing the first few letters and choosing it from the list that appears). If you want to swap the starting and ending locations, click the little swirly arrow button to the right of the Start and End fields.

If you need to change the start or end location, click the little x-in-a-circle to the right of its name and try again.

When the start and end locations are correct, press Return or Tab, and step-by-step directions appear in the sidebar on the left side of the Maps window, as shown in Figure 10-10.

Figure 10-10: Routes from the Texas State Capitol in Austin and Black's Barbecue in Lockhart, TX.

Maps will often suggest several routes. The number of suggestions appears at the top of the list of directions (it's 2 of 3 in Figure 10-10), and the alternate routes are shown on the map in lighter blue and cartoon balloons that tell you how long it will take. Click a cartoon balloon or light blue alternate route to see step-by-step directions for it, or cycle through the options using the left or right arrow key.

The selected route appears in dark blue; alternate routes appear in a lighter shade of blue.

Click a blue line or cartoon balloon to select a route, as in Figure 10-10, where Route 2 is selected.

You can print your directions (File⇨Print or ⌘+P); Export them as a PDF (File⇨Export as PDF); or share them (File⇨Share).

When you're finished with the step-by-step directions, click the Directions button to close the Directions sidebar.

Get walking directions

For step-by-step directions for walking, click the Walk button below the Start and End fields. Walking directions generally look a lot like driving directions except for your travel time.

Get directions for public transportation

El Capitan's Maps app is the first that offers directions for using public transportation. That's the good news. The bad news is that unless you live in New York, the San Francisco Bay Area, London, or Toronto, it may be a while (and quite possibly a long while, depending on the size of your city) before directions are available for your home town.

As far as I can tell, public transit directions work the same as driving directions; specify your start and end points and Maps suggests several routes via public transit.

If you zoom in far enough you can see the entrances to transportation facilities such as train stations, as shown in Figure 10-11.

Get traffic info in real time

You can find out the traffic conditions for whatever map you're viewing by choosing View⇨Show Traffic or clicking the Show drop-down menu lower-left on the map and choosing Show Traffic. When you do this, major roadways are color-coded to inform you of the current traffic speed, as shown in Figure 10-12.

Reverse this process to hide traffic.

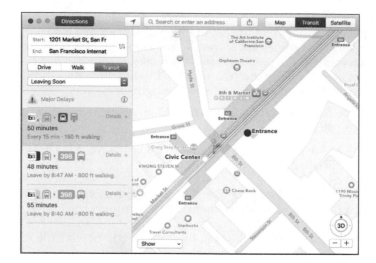

Figure 10-11: Zoom in far enough and you can even see the entrances.

Orange dots

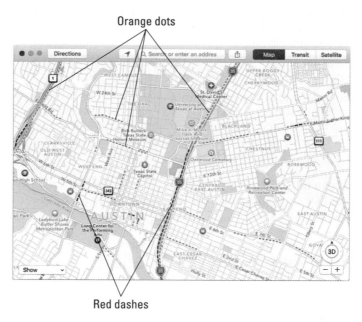

Red dashes

Figure 10-12: See whether traffic is moving very slowly (red dashes), kind of slowly (orange dots), or nice and fast (no color, dashes, or dots).

Here's the key to those colors:

- ✏ **Orange dots:** 25 to 50 miles per hour
- ✏ **Red dashes:** Under 25 miles per hour
- ✏ **No color:** No data available at this time

Traffic info isn't available in every location, but the only way to find out is to give it a try. If no color codes appear at all, assume that traffic information doesn't work for that particular location.

They may be too tiny to discern in Figure 10-12, but there are tiny blue arrows on most one-way streets to indicate the direction of traffic flow.

Do more on the Info sheet

If a location has a little *i* to the right of its name, you can click it to see the location's Info screen.

As I explain earlier in this chapter, you can get directions to or from that location, add the location to your favorites or contacts, or create a new contact from it. But you can do three more things with a location from its Info screen:

- ✏ Click the phone number to call it.
- ✏ Click the email address to launch the Mail app and send an email to it.
- ✏ Click the URL to launch Safari and view its website.

And that, my friends, should be all you need to know to get where you want to go with Maps.

11

Communicating with Mail and Messages

*I*n Chapter 10, you can see how to use Contacts and Maps to find people and places. In this chapter, I take a look at two more terrific programs — Mail and Messages — that work with Contacts to make managing your email and messages (chats) a breeze.

Sending and Receiving Email with Mail

I cover a lot of material in not a lot of space in this chapter, so if there's something you want to find out about Mail or Messages that I don't cover, don't forget about the wonderful assistance you can find in Help➪Mail Help (or Messages Help).

Mail is a program for sending, receiving, and organizing your email. Mail is fast and easy to use, too. Click the Mail icon on the Dock or Launchpad or double-click the Mail icon in the Applications folder to launch Mail. The Mail icon looks like a canceled postage stamp, as shown in the margin.

I'm a dork. I like dorky st

You can use other applications to read email. Mozilla (Thunderbird) and AOL, for example, have their own mail readers, as does Microsoft Office (Entourage or Outlook). And services such as Google's Gmail and Apple's iCloud (to name a couple) offer a web-based interface you can use in a pinch. But for Macs, the easiest and best mail reader around (meaning the best one on your hard drive by default) is almost certainly Mail. And of course, you can't beat the price; it's free!

The following sections, in some cases, offer you starting points. Even so, you should find everything perfectly straightforward. If you run into a question that the following sections don't answer, remember that you can always call upon the assistance of Help (Help ➪ Mail Help).

Setting up Mail

If this is your first time launching Mail, you need to set up your email account(s) before you can proceed. A set of New Account screens appears automatically. Just fill in the blanks on each screen and click the Continue button until you're finished.

If you don't know what to type in one or more of these fields, contact your ISP (Internet service provider) or mail provider for assistance.

After you set up one or more email accounts, you see a Welcome message asking whether you'd like to see what's new in Mail. If you click Yes, Help Viewer launches and shows you the What's New in Mail page; the Mail main window, which looks like Figure 11-1, appears in the background. Or if you click No, the Mail main window appears as the active window immediately.

Show/Hide Mailbox pane

Favorites bar   Toolbar   Smart Suggestion

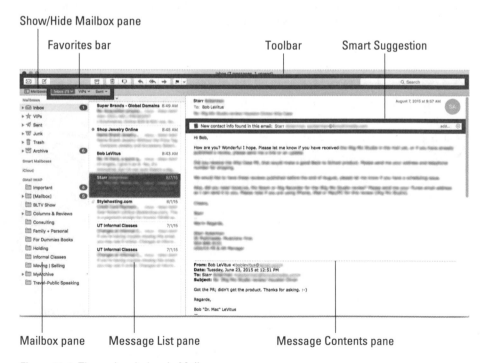

Mailbox pane   Message List pane   Message Contents pane

Figure 11-1: The main window in Mail.

The Mail main window is actually called a *viewer window* or *message viewer window*. You can have more than one of them on your screen, if you like; just choose File➪New Viewer Window or press ⌘+Option+N.

A quick overview of the toolbar

Before you go any further, look at Figure 11-2, which shows the nine handy buttons and a Search field on the viewer window's toolbar by default.

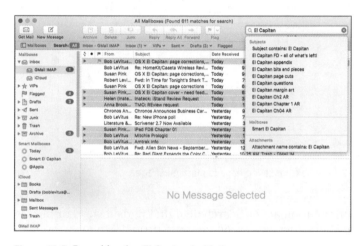

Figure 11-2: Searching for *El Capitan* in Mail.

✔ **Get Mail:** Checks for new email.

✔ **New Message:** Creates a new, blank email message.

✔ **Archive:** Archives selected message or messages.

✔ **Delete:** Deletes selected message or messages.

> To select more than one message in the list, hold down the ⌘ key when you click the second and subsequent messages.

✔ **Junk:** Marks the selected message or messages as junk mail. Mail has built-in junk mail filtering that can be enabled or disabled in Mail Preferences. (Choose Mail➪Preferences and click the Junk Mail icon on the toolbar.) If you receive a piece of *spam* (junk mail), select it and click this button to help train the Mail junk-mail filter. If a selected message has been marked as junk mail, the button changes to read Not Junk.

> For more info on junk mail filtering, click the question mark button in the Junk Mail pane of the Mail Preferences window.

✔ **Reply:** Creates a reply to the sender only.

✔ **Reply All:** Creates a reply to the sender and everyone who was sent the original message.

✔ **Forward:** Creates a copy of this message you can send to someone other than the sender or other recipients.

✔ **Flag/Unflag:** From this drop-down menu, you can mark or unmark one or more messages with any of seven colored flags. The selected message in Figure 11-3, for example, is flagged in green.

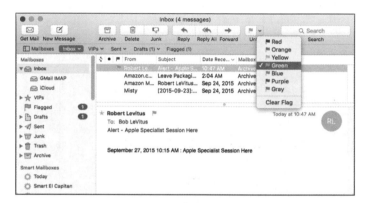

Figure 11-3: Choose from seven flags to mark messages.

Finally, on the toolbar is a Search field that finds a word or phrase in any item stored in Mail. When you begin typing, a drop-down menu appears, as shown in Figure 11-3, so you can narrow the search to people or subjects matching your search phrase. I searched for items with *El Capitan* in all mailboxes, which reveals 611 items. You can also click the buttons on the Favorites bar to limit your search to specific mailboxes — All, Inbox — Gmail IMAP, Inbox (1), VIPs, Sent and Drafts (3) in Figure 11-3.

The little numbers next to the mailbox buttons on the Favorites bar indicate the number of unread messages in that mailbox. A message is considered read after you click it.

Searching in Mail should be familiar to you; it works the same way as searching in the Finder. So, for example, if you want to save a search as a smart mailbox (Mail's version of a smart folder in the Finder), you click the Save button (hidden by the drop-down menu in Figure 11-3).

Mail populates the Favorites bar with mailboxes it expects you to use often, namely Inbox, VIPs, and Sent, as shown in Figure 11-3. Add your own mailboxes by dragging them from the Mailbox pane to the Favorites bar.

One last thing: My *Mavericks For Dummies* tech editor, the late Dennis Cohen, urged me to at least mention Classic layout, which puts the message list above the content as shown in Figure 11-3 instead of next to the content as shown in Figure 11-1.

If you prefer the old-school view, here's how to make the change:

1. **Choose Mail ⇨ Preferences.**
2. **Click the Viewing tab (icon) at the top of the window.**
3. **Select the Use Classic Layout check box.**
4. **Click the Close button (the red gumdrop) or press ⌘+W to close the Preferences window.**

If you decide you liked it better the other way, just go back and clear the Use Classic Layout check box.

Composing a new message

Here's how to create an email message:

1. **Choose File ⇨ New Message, click the New button on the toolbar (as shown in the margin), or press ⌘+N.**

   A new window appears. This is where you compose your email message, as shown in Figure 11-4.

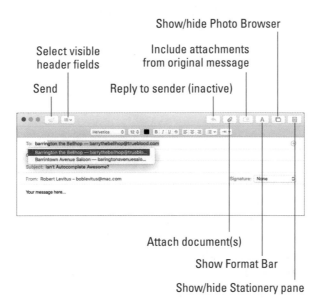

Figure 11-4: Composing an email message.

2. Click in the To field, and type someone's email address.

Use my address (ElCapitan4Dummies@boblevitus.com) if you don't know anyone else to send mail to.

If the recipient is in your Contacts (as Barrington the Bellhop and Barrintown Avenue Saloon are in mine), just type a few letters, and Mail's intelligent autocomplete function matches it up with Contacts. So, for example, in Figure 11-4, I typed the letters *b-a-r-r-i-n,* and a list of people in my Contacts with *barrin* in their names — namely, Barrintown Avenue Saloon and Barrington the Bellhop — appeared. I can select a name by clicking it and typing an additional letter or letters to narrow the search (typing a **g** would leave only Barrington the Bellhop; typing a **t** would leave only Barrintown Avenue Saloon), or by using the arrow keys and pressing Return.

3. Press the Tab key twice and type a subject for this message in the Subject text field.

I typed **Isn't Autocomplete Awesome?** in Figure 11-4.

4. Click in the main message portion of the window, and type your message there.

I typed **Your message here . . .** in Figure 11-4.

5. When you're finished writing your message, click the Send button to send the email immediately, or close it to save it in the Drafts mailbox so you can work on it later.

If you save your message to the Drafts mailbox (perhaps so you can write more later on), you can send it when you're ready by opening the Drafts mailbox, double-clicking the message, and then clicking the Send button.

Just for the record, here's what the buttons in the toolbar in Figure 11-4 are all about:

- ✔ **Send:** D'oh. Sends the message.
- ✔ **Header Fields:** This drop-down menu lets you add header fields — BCC, Reply-To, and Priority — to this message.

  If you want a BCC or Reply-To field in every new message you create, choose View➪BCC Address Field or View➪Reply-To Field (or use their keyboard shortcuts: ⌘+Option+B and ⌘+Option+R, respectively).

- ✔ **Reply to Sender:** Lets you reply to the sender directly from the message window. It's inactive in Figure 11-4 because this is a new message and there is no sender to reply to.
- ✔ **Attach:** Opens a standard Open File sheet so you can pick a file or files to enclose with this message. To enclose multiple files, hold down the ⌘ key while you click each file you want to enclose.

If the recipients of this message use Windows, you probably want to click the Options button and select the Send Windows-Friendly Attachments check box that appears at the bottom of the Open File sheet.

I recommend you select it even if you don't think you have Windows-using recipients. There is no downside for Mac or iOS users, just a benefit for Windows users.

✔ **Include Attachments from Original Message:** This button includes any files that were attached to the message you're replying to. It's inactive in Figure 11-3 because this is a new message, not a reply.

✔ **Format Toolbar:** Shows or hides the Format toolbar, which is showing (between the toolbar and the To field) in Figure 11-4.

✔ **Photo Browser:** Opens the Photo Browser panel, which displays the images in your photo library and lets you drag and drop them into a mail message.

✔ **Show/Hide Stationery:** Opens a sheet with a selection of stationery you can use for your email message. (You find out more about this feature in the upcoming section, "Working with stationery.")

Sending email from the Contacts app

You don't even have to open the Contacts app to send an email to a contact or group contained in your Contacts. In the previous section, you saw how Mail finds contacts (or groups) for you without launching Contacts. But if you already have Contacts open, this technique for sending email to a contact or group is probably most convenient.

To create a blank email message to a contact, click and hold down on the field label next to the desired email address, and choose Send Email from the pop-up menu that appears, as shown for the Other label in Figure 11-5. Or move the pointer over an email address and then click the blue envelope icon that appears to the right of its name, as shown for my Home address in Figure 11-5.

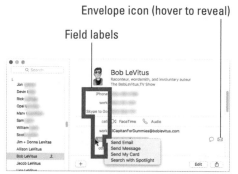

Envelope icon (hover to reveal)

Field labels

Figure 11-5: Sending email to a contact is as easy as clicking.

The Mail program becomes active, and a blank email message addressed to the selected contact appears on your screen. Just type your email as you normally would.

As you can see in Figure 11-5, in addition to sending an email, the pop-up menu next to email addresses lets you:

- ✏ Send an email.
- ✏ Send an iMessage (see the "Communicating with Messages" section, later in this chapter).
- ✏ Send your vCard (see the following Tip) to this email address.
- ✏ Search for this email address in documents on your Mac using Spotlight (see Chapter 7).

The information for each contact can be sent to others in an industry-standard file format known as a *vCard* (virtual business card). Choosing Send My Card works the same as Send Email, but instead of starting with a totally blank email message, the message starts with your vCard enclosed. When the recipient opens the vCard file, all your contact information will be added to his or her Contacts (or other contact manager in Windows).

Working with stationery

I personally find stationery for email dorky, but if you think it's the greatest thing since sliced kittens, here are some tips for working with it. First, to use it, click the Show Stationery button in a New Message window (refer to Figure 11-4).

I'm a Luddite when it comes to email. When I started using email a long, long time ago, it was considered bad form to add anything but text to an email message. It was generally agreed that email messages should include only what was necessary to convey the information and nothing more. That's why all these froufrou flowers and borders irritate me and why I find them a waste of bandwidth. So please do me a favor: If you decide to send me an email message, please don't use goofy stationery. End rant.

Here are some tips to help you have more fun with stationery:

- ✏ **Adding favorites:** If you find you're using a particular Stationery template a lot, you can add it to the Favorites category to make it easier to use. To do so, merely click the appropriate category in the list on the left (Birthday, Announcements, Photos, Stationery, and Sentiments in Figure 11-6); then click the stationery you want to make a favorite and drag it onto the word *Favorites* in the list on the left. When *Favorites* highlights, drop the stationery, and presto — that piece of stationery will appear when you click Favorites evermore.

Figure 11-6: Drag and drop your own pictures in stationery.

✔ **Replacing pictures:** You can replace any picture in any stationery with a picture of your own. Just drag a picture — from the Photo Browser (Window⇨Photo Browser) or the Finder — onto any picture in any piece of stationery. I've replaced the boilerplate text and all three of the dorky pictures in the Air Mail stationery, as shown in Figure 11-6.

✔ **Greeking out:** You can change the Greek/pseudo-Latin text that appears in all the stationery by selecting it, deleting it, and typing whatever text you want to appear. You have to do it only once; the text you type in any stationery appears in all other stationeries. That also means that once you add pictures and/or text to any stationery, you can click any other stationery to see how it looks with that text and pictures.

✔ **Removing stationery:** If you decide you don't want to use stationery with a message after you've applied it, click the Stationery category and choose the Original stationery, which changes your message back to an unadorned page with just the text and images you added.

Checking your mail

How do you check and open your mail? Easy. Just click the Get Mail button at the top of the main Mail window (refer to Figure 11-2) or press ⌘+Shift+N.

✔ **To read a new message,** select it. Its contents appear in the Message Content pane.

✔ **To delete a selected message,** click the Delete button on the toolbar or press Delete (or Backspace) on your keyboard.

El Capitan adds a new way to delete a message, but it's limited to those with a trackpad. Swipe with two fingers from right to left a little bit and the new Trash button appears, as shown in Figure 11-7. Now you can click the Trash button or continue your swipe to the left a bit farther. Either way, the message will disappear into Mail's Trash folder.

Figure 11-7: Swipe right-to-left with two fingers to reveal the Trash button; continue swiping or click the Trash button to delete the message.

✔ **To retrieve a message you accidentally deleted,** click Trash on the left and drag the message into the Inbox or other mailbox.

✔ **To configure Mail to send and check for your mail every *X* minutes,** choose Mail ⟹ Preferences and click the General icon at the top of the window. Click the Check for New Mail pop-up menu and make a selection — every 1, 5, 15, 30, or 60 minutes. The default is to automatically check for new mail every 5 minutes, so if you don't want Mail to check automatically, choose Manually instead.

✔ **To add a sender to Contacts:** When someone who isn't already in your Contacts sends you an email message, simply choose Message ⟹ Add Sender to Contacts.

Adding a sender to your Contacts has an additional benefit: It guards messages from that person against being mistaken for junk mail. In other words, your Contacts is a white list for the spam filter. See the next section in this chapter for how to deal with spam. If specific senders appear in your Contacts, their messages will never be mistakenly marked as junk mail.

When you receive an email containing details for an event, such as a flight or a dinner reservation, or even an invitation that says something like, *Let's have a beer at 6,* a Smart Suggestion appears between the message's header and body, so you can add the event to Calendar with just a click if you so desire. And, if you exchange email with people who are not in your Contacts,

Mail lets you add them with a single click, and even lets you know when the email address for one of your contacts has changed, as it has for the sender of the message shown in Figure 11-1.

Dealing with spam

Speaking of junk mail. . . . Although email is a wonderful thing, some people out there try to spoil it. They are *spammers,* and they're lowlifes who share their lists among themselves — and before you know it, your email inbox is flooded with get-rich-quick schemes, advertisements for pornographic web-sites and chat rooms, pills and powders that claim to perform miracles, and plenty of the more traditional buy-this-now junk mail.

Fortunately, Mail comes with a pretty darn good Junk Mail filter that analyzes incoming message subjects, senders, and contents to determine which ones are likely to contain bulk or junk mail. When you open Mail for the first time, it's running in its training mode, which is how Mail learns to differentiate between what it considers junk mail and what you consider junk mail; all it needs is your input. Mail identifies messages it thinks are junk, but if you disagree with its decisions, here's what you do:

- Click the Not Junk button in the brown bar for any message that *isn't* junk mail.

- Conversely, if a piece of junk mail slips past Mail's filters and ends up in the Inbox, select the message and click the Junk button on the Mail window toolbar.

After a few days (or weeks, depending upon your mail volume), Mail should be getting it right almost all the time. When you reach that point, choose Move It to the Junk Mailbox on the Junk Mail tab of Mail's Preferences dialog. Now Mail starts moving junk mail automatically out of your Inbox and into a Junk mailbox, where you can scan the items quickly and trash them when you're ready.

If you prefer to use your email provider or third-party spam filters, you can turn off junk mail processing in Mail by disabling it on the Junk Mail tab of Mail's Preferences dialog.

Mailboxes smart and plain

After reading mail, you can either delete it or file it in a mailbox. The follow-ing sections take a closer look at the two types of mailboxes you have at your disposal — plain and smart.

Plain old mailboxes

Plain mailboxes are just like folders in the Finder; you create them and name them, and they're empty until you put something in them. They even look like folders in the Mailboxes Sidebar in Mail. You use mailboxes to organize any messages you want to save.

Here are several ways to create a plain mailbox:

- Choose Mailbox ⇨ New Mailbox.
- Right-click or Control-click in the Mailboxes Sidebar and choose New Mailbox from the shortcut menu.

Whichever way you choose, the next thing that happens is that a sheet drops down with a Location pop-up menu and a field for you to type the name you want to give this mailbox. Choose On My Mac from the Location menu to store your filed messages locally, on your hard drive; or choose iCloud or another email provider to store filed messages remotely, on the mail server.

Choosing iCloud or your email provider means messages you move to that mailbox will be stored remotely. If you access your email from more than one device, I recommend you create all your mailboxes on the email server so they'll be available to you no matter where you are or what device you're using to check your mail.

Finally, name the mailbox anything you like and click OK, and the mailbox is created in the Mailboxes Sidebar.

If you right- or Control-click a mailbox and choose New Mailbox, the Location menu in the sheet will show the name of the mailbox you clicked. So, if you were to click OK now, the new mailbox would be a sub-mailbox of the mailbox you clicked. *Sub-mailboxes* — mailboxes inside other mailboxes — are a useful feature if you care to further subdivide your message storage system.

In Figure 11-8, the MyArchive mailbox has four sub-mailboxes: Geek Cruises, Old Consulting, Old Travel, and Other.

Note how the top of the window tells you that two mailboxes are selected, with 211 messages displayed. That happens to be the total number of messages in the highlighted mailboxes. Coincidence? I think not.

You can also drag and drop a mailbox or mailboxes from the top level of the list (Moving|Selling, Informal Classes, Holding, For Dummies Books, and so on in Figure 11-8) into another mailbox to make them sub-mailboxes. If you drag a mailbox into a sub-mailbox, it becomes a sub-sub-mailbox. And so on.

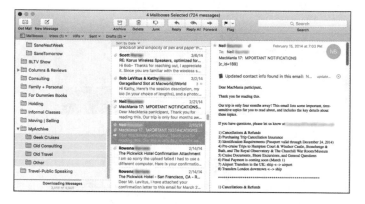

Figure 11-8: This mailbox is divided into four sub-mailboxes.

To delete a mailbox, click it to select it and then do one of the following:

- ↙ Choose Mailbox ➪ Delete Mailbox.
- ↙ Right-click or Control-click the mailbox and choose Delete Mailbox.

Intelligent smart mailboxes

A smart mailbox is Mail's version of the Finder's smart folder. In a nutshell, *smart mailboxes* are mailboxes that display the results of a search. The messages you see in a smart mailbox are *virtual;* they aren't really in the smart mailbox itself. Instead, the smart mailbox displays a list of messages stored in other mailboxes that match whatever criteria you defined for that smart mailbox. Like smart folders in the Finder, smart mailboxes update automatically when new messages that meet the criteria are received.

To create a smart mailbox:

- ↙ Choose Mailbox ➪ New Smart Mailbox.
- ↙ Click the +-in-a-circle on the right side of the Smart Mailboxes header in the Mailboxes Sidebar (visible in Figure 11-9).

Whichever method you choose, a sheet drops down with a field for the smart mailbox's name, plus some pop-up menus, buttons, and check boxes, as shown in Figure 11-9. This smart mailbox gathers messages with the word *ElCapitan* in the body or subject.

Name your smart mailbox, determine its criteria (by using the pop-up menus, plus and minus buttons, and check boxes), and then click OK. The smart mailbox appears in the Mailboxes Sidebar with a little gear to denote that it's smart. You can see the Smart ElCapitan smart mailbox highlighted on the left in Figure 11-9. Note that it has a gear to its left (plain mailboxes don't).

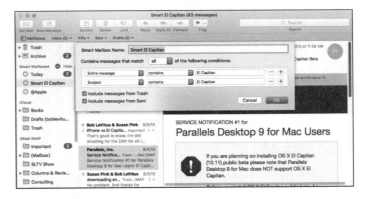

Figure 11-9: Set criteria for a smart mailbox.

I use a Smart Mailbox to have every mail message to or from my wife and children in one place. And I use another to see all my Dummies email in a single place. Since they don't use up any additional disk space, Smart Mailboxes are a great way to organize mail, automatically making it easier to find a message with no effort on your part (after you set them up).

Changing your preferences

Mail's preferences (Mail⇨Preferences or ⌘+,) are more than you might expect from the name. This window is the control center for Mail, where you can

- Create and delete email accounts
- Determine which fonts and colors are used for your messages
- Decide whether to download and save attachments (such as pictures)
- Decide whether to send formatted mail or plain text
- Decide whether to turn on the spell checker

  The default is to check spelling as you type, which many people (myself included) find annoying.

- Decide whether to have an automatic signature appended to your messages
- Establish rules to process mail that you receive

The first five items are up to you to decide; here's what you need to know about the last two — the two most important features of the Preferences window, namely automatically adding your signature(s) to outgoing messages and inbound mail processing rules.

Sign here, please

If you're like me, you'd rather not type your entire signature every time you send an email message, and you don't have to with Mail. If you create canned signatures, you can use them in outgoing messages without typing a single character.

Here's how it works:

1. **Choose Mail ⇨ Preferences or press ⌘+, (comma).**

2. **In the Preferences dialog's toolbar, click the Signatures icon.**

3. **In the left column, click the name of the mail account for which you want to create this signature.**

   I clicked iCloud in Figure 11-10.

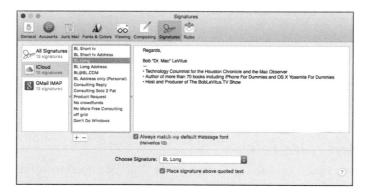

Figure 11-10: My newly created BL Long signature.

4. **To create a new, blank signature, click the little + sign at the bottom of the middle column.**

5. **Type a descriptive name for this signature to replace the default name Signature #1.**

   The default name in Figure 11-10 is BL Long.

6. **Type the signature exactly as you want it to appear in outgoing messages in the right column.**

   I typed *Regards, Bob "Dr. Mac" LeVitus – Houston Chronicle,* and so on in Figure 11-10.

7. **Drag the name you assigned this signature (BL Long in Figure 11-10) to the mail account you're using it with (iCloud in Figure 11-10).**

If you have more than one signature, you can select the one you want to use as the default: Choose the account in the column on the left, and then choose the signature from the Choose Signature pop-up menu.

If you have more than one signature, another cool thing happens: The Signature menu appears in new messages, as shown in Figure 11-11, so you can choose a signature other than the one you chose from the pop-up menu as the default.

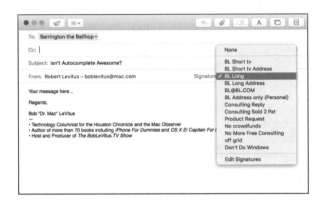

Figure 11-11: This menu shows all your signatures.

Mail rules rule

If you really want to tap the power of Mail, you need to set *rules.* With some cool rules, you can automatically tag messages with a color; file them in a specific mailbox; reply to/forward/redirect the messages automatically (handy when you're going to be away for a while); automatically reply to messages; and *kill-file* messages (just delete them without even bothering to look at them — what better fate for mail from people you hate?).

There's no way I can do rules justice in a page or so, but here's a quick look at how to create one. In broad terms, you create a condition and then an action. In this example, I create a filter named Message from LeVitus, with the action to sound a blow alert, as shown in Figure 11-12.

Here are the steps:

1. **Choose Mail ⇨ Preferences.**
2. **Click the Rules icon on the toolbar of the Preferences dialog.**
3. **Click the Add Rule button.**

Figure 11-12: Setting a rule.

4. **Type a description in the Description field.**

   I typed *Message from LeVitus.*

5. **Click the first pop-up menu (which says Any in Figure 11-12) to determine when to apply this rule.**

   The options are Any or All. I chose Any, which is the default.

   Note that my choice in this menu didn't matter for this rule, which only has one condition.

6. **Click the first pop-up menu in the Conditions section (From in Figure 11-12) to define the condition.**

   I chose From in Figure 11-12 but there are myriad other options including Date sent, Date received, Sender is or isn't in my Contacts, Sender is or isn't a member of a group, plus dozens more. I implore you to explore them at your leisure.

7. **Click the second pop-up menu in the Conditions section (Contains in Figure 11-12) and make a selection.**

   Your choices are Contains, Does Not Contain, Begins With, Ends With, or Is Equal To.

8. **Type a word or phrase in the field on the right side of the Conditions section.**

   I typed **LeVitus**, so my condition reads: From Contains LeVitus.

9. **Click the first pop-up menu in the Action section (Play Sound in Figure 11-12).**

   Look at your options in this pop-up menu (too numerous to mention) and pick one.

10. **Click the second pop-up menu in the Action section (Blow in Figure 11-12) to specify the sound you'll hear when this action is triggered.**

11. **Click OK.**

    Mail asks whether you want to apply your rule(s) to the selected mailboxes.

12. **Choose Apply if you want Mail to run this rule on the selected mailboxes, or choose Don't Apply if you don't.**

    And that's how you build a rule. From this point forward, every time you get a message from someone named LeVitus, you hear the Blow sound.

Notice the little + (plus) and – (minus) buttons to the right of each condition and action. Use the + button to add more conditions or actions and the – button to delete a condition or action. If you have multiple conditions, you can choose Any or All from the pop-up menu above them, which executes this rule when either any of the conditions or all of the conditions are met. Either way, all the actions you create are always executed when this rule is triggered.

Take a (Quick) look and (Slide) show me some photos

One last cool feature, and you're finished with Mail. That cool feature is Quick Look, which includes a slick Slideshow option. If you press and hold down on the button with the paper clip (shown in the margin and in Figure 11-13) and choose Quick Look from the resulting drop-down menu, a new window appears showing one of the enclosed pictures, as shown lower right in Figure 11-13.

Figure 11-13: Using Quick Look.

If you don't see a paperclip, hover your cursor over the line between the message header and the message body and the paper clip will magically appear. Or, click the image in the message body so it is highlighted, and then press Spacebar.

To close the Quick Look window, click the little X in its top-left corner or press Spacebar.

Relative Newcomers: Markup and Mail Drop

Last but not by any means least, two Mail features that were introduced in Yosemite: Markup and Mail Drop.

Markup

Markup lets you annotate images or PDF documents. When you're composing a message that has an image or PDF you've attached or dragged in, hover the pointer over the picture and a little chevron V appears in its upper-right corner. Click it and choose Markup, as shown in Figure 11-14.

Figure 11-14: Open the image in the Markup editor.

The image opens in a window in front of the message, as shown in Figure 11-15.

Figure 11-15: The Markup editor and some markup (the text and circle).

The tools at the top of the Markup editor are, from left to right: freehand pen, shapes, text, line thickness, line color, fill color, and text formatting. Click the one you want to use and draw or type your annotations. When you're done, click Done.

Note that your annotations are saved in a copy of the image, not the original.

Markup strikes me as a solution looking for a problem to solve. I don't get it. If I want to annotate an image or PDF, I fire up Preview (see Chapter 14) and use its annotation tools. The Markup editor is some weird kind of window that has no scroll bars and no way to resize it. Try it — you can move the whole window around, but that's about it. Worse, there's no way to zoom in or out. Preview, on the other hand, has the same tool set and much more, in a resizable window with zoom in and out commands at my fingertips. Needless to say, I don't think much of Markup and don't use it very much.

Mail Drop

Mail Drop, on the other hand, is an elegant solution for large email attachments. If you enclose files or a folder full of files in a message and Mail thinks the enclosure(s) might be too big to send via email, an alert appears when you try to send the message. A picture is worth a thousand words, so check out my alert in Figure 11-16.

Figure 11-16: Choose Mail Drop in the alert box (left), and your recipient sees this (right).

If you opt for Try Sending In Email, Mail will go ahead and try to send my message even though it has a total file size of 86MB. Chances are pretty good, though, that the mail server I send the message through will bounce it back to me for being too large. But if I choose Use Mail Drop, which uses iCloud, my message weight can be larger, and the message won't bounce. If I go this route, the recipient will receive a link to download the files from iCloud, as shown on the right in Figure 11-16.

Mail Drop should be enabled by default. If it's not, choose Mail ➪ Preferences and click the Accounts icon at the top of the window. Then click the Advanced tab and enable the Send Large Attachments Mail Drop check box.

Communicating with Messages

Instant messaging (IM) and chat rooms enable interactive communication among users all over the world. If you're into instant messaging, Messages gives you immediate access to all the other users of AIM, Jabber, Google Talk, and iCloud. All you need are their screen names, and you're set to go. You can even join any AOL chat room just by choosing File ➪ Go to Chat Room. To get started, launch Messages from either your Applications folder, Launchpad, or Dock.

What the heck is an iMessage?

iMessage is Apple's inter-device messaging protocol. That means you can send unlimited iMessages to anyone with an iPhone, iPad, or iPod touch running iOS 5 (or later) or a Mac running Mountain Lion (OS X 10.8) or later.

Think of it as MMS messaging, similar to what you find on smartphones, but you can send and receive messages from your Mac. Better still, an iMessage can include photos, audio recordings, videos, locations, and contacts in addition, of course, to text. And if you have more than one iOS device or Mac, iMessage keeps all your conversations going across all of them. You can also get delivery receipts letting you know your messages went through. You'll know it's been read, too, if your friend has enabled read receipts.

If you have an iPhone 4 or newer, the Continuity feature allows all SMS and MMS text messages you send and receive on your iPhone via your wireless carrier's messaging system to also appear in the Messages app on your Mac, iPad, and iPod touch almost simultaneously — even if the person you're messaging doesn't have an iPhone. Better yet, you can reply from whichever device is closest to you, regardless of what kind of cellphone the person has. You can also start a new iMessage by clicking a phone number in Safari, Contacts, or Calendar.

You can find details on this feature and other Continuity features for iDevices (Handoff, SMS, and Instant Hot Spot) at `www.dummies.com/cheatsheet/osxelcapitan`.

Chit-chatting with Messages

Your chats can be one to one, or they can be group bull sessions. Messages is integrated with Contacts, so you don't have to enter your buddies' information twice. It also communicates directly with the Mail application. Here's all the essential info you need to get started:

✔ **To start a text chat,** open Messages, select a buddy in your buddy list, and choose Buddies ➪ Start New Chat. If you don't see your Buddies List, choose Window ➪ Buddies or press ⌘+1.

In Figure 11-17, I sent the first message to my wife from Messages on my Mac. She replied from her iPhone. In a chat, each participant's text appears in a different color; my words are in blue bubbles with white text; hers are in gray bubbles with black text.

Figure 11-17: A chat between me and my wife.

- **To start a group text chat,** hold down the ⌘ key, click each person in your buddy list that you want to include, and then click the A button at the bottom of the buddy list. Or, type multiple names in the To field. In a group text chat, everyone sees every message from every participant.

  Click Details at the top right, and you can use your iPhone (if it's nearby) to call someone by clicking the phone icon next to the person's name. You can also choose Do Not Disturb for this conversation to mute notifications for this conversation only, which is great if one or more participants is a serial texter. Finally, click Leave This Conversation if you want to, well, leave this conversation permanently.

- **To attach a picture to a person in your Contacts** (as I have for myself on both Macs), copy a picture of the person to the Clipboard in your favorite graphics application (Preview, for example). Now open Contacts, and display the card for the person you want to add a picture to. Click the empty picture box at the top of the card, and paste the picture from the Clipboard. You should now see that picture on the Contacts card and also when you chat in Messages with the person. Neat!

  If you already attached a picture to a contact in Contacts, that picture will appear automatically when you chat.

- **To transfer a file or files,** just drag the icon(s) to the text field (where you type your messages), and then press Return. The file zips across the ether. This is a very convenient way to share photos or documents without resorting to file sharing or email.

  When you drag an image file onto the Messages window's message box, you see an oversize semitransparent preview, letting you know you're sure you're sending them the right image and not something totally embarrassing. Way to go, OS X ElCapitan.

  You could also choose Buddies⇨Send File or press ⌘+Option+F and then select the file(s) from a standard Open File sheet, but the drag-and-drop method is faster and easier.

- **To send a voice message,** click the microphone icon on the right of the text field where you type your messages and begin talking. When you're finished, click the red Record button and then click Cancel or Send.

- **To send an email from Messages,** just select a buddy in the Messages buddy list and choose Buddies⇨Send Email (or press ⌘+Option+E). Mail launches (if it's not already open) and addresses a new message to the selected buddy, ready for you to begin typing.

12

Sharing Your Mac and Liking It

In This Chapter

▶ Comprehending networks and file sharing

▶ Setting up file sharing

▶ Finding out about users

▶ Understanding access and permissions

▶ Sharing files, folders, and disks with other users

▶ Sharing remotely

▶ Changing your password

*H*ave you ever wanted to grab a file from your Mac while you were half-way around the world or even around the corner or in the next room? If so, I have good news for you: It's not difficult with OS X (believe it or not) even though computer networking in general has a well-deserved reputation for being complicated and nerve-wracking. The truth is that you won't encounter anything scary or complicated about sharing files, folders, and disks (and printers, for that matter) among comput-ers as long as the computers are Macs. And even if some of the computers are running Windows, OS X El Capitan even makes that (almost) painless.

Your Macintosh includes everything that you need to share files and printers, except the printers and the cables (and maybe a router). So here's the deal: You supply the hardware, and this chapter supplies the rest. And when you're done hooking it all up, you can take a rest.

The first sections of this chapter provide an overview and tell you everything that you need to know to set up new user accounts and share files successfully. I don't show you how to actually share a file, folder, or disk until the "Connecting to a Shared Disk or Folder on a Remote Mac" sec-tion, later in this chapter. Trust me, there's a method to my madness. If you try to share files without doing all the required prep work, the whole mess becomes confusing and complicated pretty fast — kind of like networking PCs.

One last thing: If you're the only one who uses your Mac, you don't intend to share it or its files with anyone else, and you never intend to access your Mac from another computer in a different location, you can safely skip this whole chapter.

Introducing Networks and File Sharing

El Capitan's file sharing enables you to use files, folders, and disks from other Macs on a network — including the Internet — as easily as though they were on your own local hard drive. If you have more than one computer, file sharing is a blessing.

Before diving in and actually sharing, allow me to introduce a few necessary terms:

- **Network:** For the purposes of this chapter, a *network* is two or more Macs connected by Ethernet cables, wireless networking (Apple refers to this as AirPort or Wi-Fi), or FireWire cables (rarely seen anymore).

- **Ethernet:** This network protocol and cabling scheme lets you connect two or more computers so they can share files, disks, printers, or whatever.

- **Ethernet ports:** This is where you plug an Ethernet cable into your Mac. Be careful to match the cable to its specific jack. On your Mac and printer, the Ethernet ports look a lot like phone jacks, and the connectors on each end of an Ethernet cable look a lot like phone cable connectors — but they aren't the same. Ethernet cables are typically thicker, and the connectors (RJ-45 connectors) are a bit larger than the RJ-11 connectors that you use with telephones. (See examples of both types of ports in the margin.) Standard phone cables fit (very loosely) into Ethernet ports, but you shouldn't try that, either; they'll probably fall out with the slightest vibration. It's unlikely that such a mistake will cause damage, but it won't work and will be frustrating.

  If your Mac didn't include an Ethernet port but you'd like one, you can find Thunderbolt and USB adapters that will let you have your cake (and Ethernet port) and eat it too (plug it into a Thunderbolt or USB port).

- **Local devices:** Such devices are connected directly to your computers, such as hard or optical drives. Your internal hard drive, for example, is a local device.

- **Remote devices:** These devices you access (share) over the network. The hard drive of a computer in the next room, for example, is a remote device.

- **Protocols:** These are the languages that networks speak. When you read or hear about networks, you're likely to hear the words *Bonjour,*

Ethernet, SMB, and *TCP/IP* bandied about with great regularity. These are all *protocols.* Macs can speak several different protocols, but every device (Mac or printer) on a network needs to speak the same protocol at the same time to communicate.

Support for the TCP/IP protocol is built into every Mac, and OS X El Capitan includes all the software you need to set up a TCP/IP network; the hardware you provide consists of Ethernet cables and a hub (if you have more than two computers) or an AirPort or other Wi-Fi base station. Here, I'm using *hub* generically; its more powerful networking cousins, switches and routers, also work for this purpose.

By the way, in addition to providing wireless networking, the AirPort Extreme wireless Base Stations — as well as the Time Capsule device — are all members of the router class of devices. Time Capsule is a pretty cool deal: It combines a wireless Base Station, three-port Ethernet router, and a big hard disk that can be shared by all computers on the network and also used as a Time Machine backup disk.

Portrait of home office networking

A typical Mac home office network consists of two Macintoshes, an AirPort Extreme wireless Base Station (or other type of Ethernet hub, switch, or router), and a network printer. Check out Figure 12-1 to see the configuration of a simple network. In the figure, the black lines between the devices are Ethernet cables; the rectangular device with those cables going into it is an Ethernet hub, router, AirPort Extreme Base Station, or Time Capsule. (I tell you more about cables and such devices in the section "Three ways to build a network," later in this chapter.) You need enough Ethernet cable to run among all your devices.

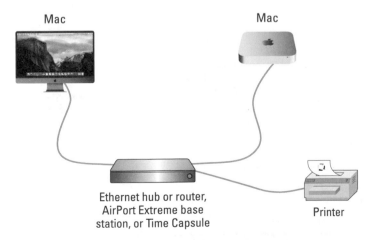

Figure 12-1: Two Macs and a printer make up a simple Mac network.

File sharing made easy with AirDrop

Perhaps all you want to do is share an occasional file (not necessarily a printer or a home Internet connection or a folder of music files or pictures). In that case, check out AirDrop on Macs built in the past few years, which uses Apple's proprietary zero-configuration network protocol, known as Bonjour. It's a big part of the secret sauce in OS X that makes Mac networking so simple.

Here's how it works: If two devices (and this includes all Macs running OS X Jaguar or later) speak Bonjour, you don't have to do *any* configuration other than, possibly, turning on the sharing capability, as I explain in "Setting Up File Sharing," later in this chapter. Bonjour queries the other available networked devices to see what services they support and then configures the connections for you automatically. Sweet!

It gets even better if you're using Lion, Mountain Lion, Mavericks, Yosemite, or El Capitan 'cause you can use the nifty sharing feature called AirDrop. It appears in your Finder window Sidebar and locates all other AirDrop-capable Macs on your local wireless network.

In Yosemite and El Capitan, AirDrop can also locate and share files with AirDrop-capable iPhones, iPads, and iPod touches.

The only caveats are that AirDrop is Wi-Fi only, and users must enable AirDrop from the Control Center on iDevices or by selecting it in the Sidebar on a Mac's Finder window. On a Mac, you see AirDrop in the Finder window, as shown in the figure here.

To send a file (or multiple files and/or folders) to the other Mac or iDevice, just drag it onto the other Mac's or iDevice's icon as shown. AirDrop displays a dialog on the other Mac asking whether the user wants to accept delivery; if so, the items are transferred immediately to the Downloads folder on the Mac. If you're sending to an iDevice, its user gets an alert asking whether to accept the file, and then is asked what app to open it in using a familiar Share sheet-like interface.

When you close the AirDrop window, you are no longer visible to other AirDrop users.

Drag

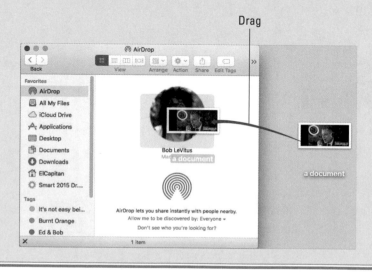

With the setup shown in Figure 12-1, either Mac can use the other Mac's files, and both Macs can print to the same printer. If you have a broadband Internet connection, you can also connect the cable or DSL modem to the hub/switch/router so all Mac users on the network can share the Internet connection.

A network can — and often does — have dozens or hundreds of users. Whether your network has two nodes (machines) or 2,000, the principles and techniques in this chapter apply.

Three ways to build a network

In this chapter, I assume you're working on a small network, the kind typically found in a home or small business. If you're part of a megamonstrous corporate network, and you have questions about your particular network, talk to the PIC (*person in charge,* also known as your *network administrator*). In other words, if you're trying to build a meganetwork, you're going to need a book a lot thicker and harder to understand than this one.

The following list gives you three common ways to build a modern small home or office network:

- ✔ **Wi-Fi:** All Macs come equipped with Wi-Fi; if you have an AirPort or AirPort Extreme Base Station, a Time Capsule, or any other Wi-Fi router, you don't need cables at all.

  For what it's worth, you could also use most third-party Wi-Fi routers, but if you go that route, you're on your own.

  Just plug in the Base Station, and Macs can communicate with one another. If you use an Ethernet printer (connected to your Mac by Ethernet cable), you have to connect it to the Base Station before you can print from your wireless Macs. Both the Base Station and printer have Ethernet ports, so you can use a crossover cable (more about that in a minute) to make the connection.

  Recent vintage AirPort Extreme and Time Capsule devices from Apple include a USB port so you can connect any printer via USB and share it wirelessly (rather than having to use a more expensive Ethernet-equipped networkable printer).

  Although this setup is more expensive than connecting everything with Ethernet cables and a cheap hub or router, it's also more flexible because you can move your devices anywhere. (Well, almost anywhere; you're limited to a maximum of 150 to 200 feet from each Base Station, and that's assuming that there's absolutely nothing in the way to block your signal. Your mileage may vary.) That said, Ethernet is usually significantly faster than Wi-Fi.

I've been using wireless printers for years. If you have a Wi-Fi network available, many inexpensive printers (and expensive ones, too) now offer wireless printing, which means you can stash your printer in a closet or another room if you care to.

✓ **Traditional Ethernet:** Most modern Macs have an Ethernet port, with the exception of the MacBook, MacBook Air, and Retina Display MacBook Pro. To connect Ethernet-equipped Macs to a wired network, you need Ethernet cables for each Mac and a little device called a *hub, switch,* or *router.* This device is like the center of a wheel; the wires coming out of it are the spokes.

A typical Ethernet router includes two to eight Ethernet ports. You plug the router into an electrical outlet and then connect Ethernet cables from each of your Macs and printers (from their Ethernet ports) to the router. *Voilà* — instant network. These gadgets are pretty cheap, starting at around $30; cables start at a few bucks, increasing in price with the length and quality.

✓ **Small Ethernet:** If you have only two devices to network (two Macs, or a Mac and an Ethernet printer, in most cases), you can use an Ethernet cable to connect them directly to each other via the Ethernet ports. You can purchase an Ethernet cable at your local electronics store. Plug one end of the Ethernet cable into one device and the other end into the other device.

If you use an Apple AirPort Extreme Base Station or Time Capsule, you may not need a hub, switch, or router at all because these devices incorporate small routers with three Ethernet ports. Either one is all you need unless you have more than three Ethernet devices to connect. If that's the case, you'll need to add a hub, switch, or router with additional Ethernet ports to accommodate them all (in addition to your AirPort or Time Capsule).

If you have a cable modem or digital subscriber line (DSL) as your Internet connection, you might need a router or switch instead of a (cheaper-but-going-out-of-fashion) hub. Routers and switches are similar to hubs but cost more and have additional features that you may or may not need. Your ISP can tell you whether you're going to need one.

Setting Up File Sharing

Before you get into the nitty-gritty of sharing files, you must complete a few housekeeping tasks, such as enabling the appropriate type of file sharing. Follow these steps to do so:

1. **Choose ⇨ System Preferences and then click the Sharing icon.**

   The Sharing System Preferences pane appears. The first word of the long username of the first admin account created on this computer appears in the Computer Name field by default, followed by the type of Mac (for example, Robert LeVitus' MacBook Pro).

2. **If you want to change the name of your computer from whatever El Capitan decided to call it to something more personal, do that now in the Computer Name text field at the top of the Sharing pane.**

   In Figure 12-2, you can see that I renamed mine Doctor El Capitan. You can name yours anything you like.

3. **Select the File Sharing check box, as shown in Figure 12-2.**

   Now other users on your network can access files and folders on your computer, as you see later in this chapter.

   By default, only one folder in your Home folder is shared, and that folder is your Public folder. If you want to access files or folders on this computer while you're using another computer on the network, you can so long as you first provide your username and password. Everyone else on the network can see only your Public folder.

   These are the safest settings. Unless you have good reason to tinker with them, you should probably not change anything here. That said, if you feel you must change these settings, you find out how to do so in the next section of this chapter.

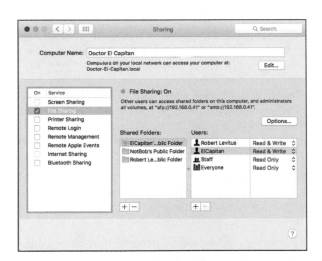

Figure 12-2: Turning file sharing on and off.

4. **(Optional) If you want remote users to upload and download files to and from this computer, click the Options button and then select either or both of the Share Files and Folders Using AFP or SMB check boxes.**

Doing so gives users on the Internet but not on your local area network (LAN) some alternatives to file sharing: an Apple File Protocol (AFP) or a client program that uses Server Message Block (Samba, or SMB).

If you want to enable Windows or Linux users — or users of other operating systems — to share files with you, the SMB check box must be selected.

Select the On check box (in the leftmost column) for each account you want to enable to use these protocols to access your Mac, providing the password when prompted.

5. **Click the Done button when you're done, and then proceed to the following section to continue setting up your network.**

Access and Permissions: Who Can Do What

After you set up file sharing (as I explain in the preceding section), your next step on the path to sharing files on a network is telling your Mac who is allowed to see and access specific folders. Fortunately, this happens to be what I cover in the following sections.

Users and groups and guests

Macintosh file sharing (and indeed, OS X as well) is based on the concept of users. You can share items — such as drives or folders — with no users, one user, or many users, depending on your needs.

✓ **Users:** People who share folders and drives (or your Mac) are *users*. A user's access to items on your local hard drive is entirely at your discretion. You can configure your Mac so only you can access its folders and drives, or so only one other person or group — or everyone — can share its folders and drives.

When you first set up your Mac, you created your first user. This user automatically has administrative powers, such as adding more users, changing preferences, and having the clearance to see all folders on the hard drive.

For the purposes of this book, I assume that some users for whom you create identities won't be folks who actually sit at your Mac but those who connect to it only from remote locations when they need to give or get files. But you could allow such a user to use the same name and password to log in while sitting at your desk.

For most intents and purposes, a remote user and a local user are the same. Here's why: After you create an account for a user, that user can log in to your Mac while sitting in your chair in your office, from anywhere on your local area network via Ethernet, or anywhere in the world via the Internet if you give him an Administrator, Standard, or Managed account.

✏ **Administrative users:** Although a complete discussion of the special permissions that a user with administrator permissions has on a Mac running OS X is far beyond the scope of this book, note two important things:

- The first user created (usually when you install OS X for the first time) is automatically granted administrator (admin) powers.

- Only an administrator account can create new users, delete some (but not all) files from folders that aren't in his or her Home folder, lock and unlock System Preferences panes, and a bunch of other stuff. If you try something and it doesn't work, make sure you're logged in as an administrator or can provide an administrator user-name and password when prompted.

You can give any user administrator permissions by selecting that user's account in the Users & Groups System Preferences pane and selecting the Allow User to Administer This Computer check box. You can select this check box when you're creating the user account or anytime thereafter.

✏ **Groups:** *Groups* are Unix-level designations for privilege consolida-tion. For example, there are groups named Staff and Everyone (as well as a bunch of others). A user can be a member of multiple groups. For example, your main account is in the Staff, Admin, and Everyone groups (and others, too). Don't worry — you find out more about groups shortly.

✏ **Guests:** Two kinds of guests exist. The first kind lets your friends log into your Mac while sitting at your desk without user accounts or pass-words. But they have no access to your data. When they log out, all information and files in the guest account's Home folder are deleted automatically.

If you want this kind of guest account, you need to enable the Guest Account in the Users & Groups System Preferences pane. To do so, click the Guest Account in the list of accounts on the left and select the Allow Guests to Log In to This Computer check box.

The second kind of guest is people who access Public folders on your Mac via file sharing over your LAN or the Internet. They don't need usernames or passwords. If they're on your LAN, they can see and use your Public folder(s), unless you or the Public folder's owner has altered the permissions. If they're on the Internet and know your IP address, they can see and use your Public folder(s) if you don't have a firewall blocking such access. Public folders are all that guests can access, luckily. You don't have to do anything to enable this type of guest account.

Creating users

Before users can share folders and drives (or have their own accounts on your computer, for that matter), they must have an account on your Mac. You can create two different kinds of accounts for them — a User account or a Sharing Only account.

- ✔ **When you create a User account** for a person (I call that person and account *User 1*), the account has its own Home folder (called — what else? — User 1), which is filled with User 1's files. Nobody but User 1 can access files in this Home folder unless, of course, User 1 has provided someone the account name and password.

- ✔ **When you create a Sharing Only account** for a person (I call that person and account *Sharing 1*), the person using that account doesn't have a Home folder and can't access other users' Home folders. Sharing 1 can access only the Public folders inside all the Home folders on that Mac.

You can create a new *User* account only in the Users & Groups System Preferences pane. You can create a new *Sharing* account in either the Users & Groups or Sharing System Preferences panes.

Anyone can remotely access files or folders in your Public folder(s) over a LAN or the Internet. But if you want them to be able to access folders or files other than those in the Public folder(s) on your Mac, they need either a User account or a Sharing account.

When you add (create) a user, you need to tell your Mac who this person is. This is also the time to set passwords and administrative powers for this new user. Here's the drill:

1. **Choose ⇨ System Preferences (or click the System Preferences icon on the Dock), click the Users & Groups icon, and then make sure that the Password tab is selected.**

   The Users & Groups System Preferences pane appears. In this pane (shown in Figure 12-3), you can see the name of the first user (ElCapitan) and the administrative control that this user is allowed. (Note that the Allow User to Administer This Computer check box is selected.)

   The first user created (usually at the same time you installed OS X or turned on a brand-new Mac) always has administrator permissions.

2. **Click the + button beneath the list of users.**

   A sheet appears in which you enter the new user's information.

   If the + button is dimmed, here's how you get it functioning: First click the lock (at bottom left), supply an administrator name and password in the resulting dialog, and then click OK.

Figure 12-3: The Users & Groups System Preferences pane is where you manage user accounts on this Mac.

3. **Choose Standard from the New Account menu.**

4. **In the Full Name text box, type the full name of a user you want to add.**

   In the Account Name text box, your Mac inserts a suggested abbreviated name (formerly known as the *short name*). Check out Figure 12-4 to see both.

Figure 12-4: Name the new user, and your Mac suggests a shortened name and password.

In Figure 12-4, I added Steve Wozniak as a user, typing his full name in the Full Name field. You don't really need to type the user's full name, but I do so in this example to show you the difference between a Full Name and an Account Name.

5. **Press the Tab key to move to the next field.**

   OS X suggests an abbreviated version of the name in the Account Name field (as shown in Figure 12-4).

   Because he's the only Steve who matters around here, I change the Account Name suggested by OS X (stevewozniak) to just plain Woz, which is shorter. (In other words, I typed **Woz** in the Account Name field, replacing the suggested stevewozniak.) The name of each user's folder (in the Users folder) is taken from the Account Name that you enter when you create a user.

   Users can connect to your Mac (or log in from their own Macs, for that matter) by using the Account Name, rather than having to type their full names. The Account Name is also used in environments in which user-names can't have spaces and are limited to eight or fewer characters. Although OS X El Capitan allows longer usernames (but no spaces), you might be better off keeping your Account Name shorter than eight characters, just in case.

6. **Select either Use iCloud Password (for this user's iCloud account) or Use Separate Password.**

   If you select Use iCloud Password, merely type the user's Apple ID (such as Woz@mac.com), click Create User, and skip Steps 7–12.

   If you choose Use Separate Password, please continue with Steps 7–12.

7. **Tab to the Password field and enter an initial password for this user.**

   The small, square button with the key to the right of the Password field, when clicked, displays the Password Assistant. You can use the Password Assistant, as seen at lower left in Figure 12-4, to help generate a password that should be fairly easy for the user to remember (choose Memorable from the Password Assistant's Type pop-up menu) but hard for a cracking program to guess (or meet other requirements).

   To make your password even harder to guess or crack, choose Random or FIPS-181–compliant from the Password Assistant's Type pop-up menu. It will also make it harder for you to remember, so make sure you either memorize it or store it in a safe place.

8. **Press the Tab key to move your pointer to the Verify text field.**

9. **In the Verify text box, type the password again to verify it.**

10. **(Optional) To help remember a password, type something in the Password Hint text box to jog the user's memory.**

    If a user forgets her password and asks for a hint, the text that you type in the Password Hint field pops up, ideally causing the user to exclaim, "Oh, yeah . . . *now* I remember!" A password hint should be something simple enough to jog the user's memory but not so simple that an unauthorized person can guess. Perhaps something like "Your first teddy bear's name backward" would be a good hint.

11. **Click the Create User button to create the account.**

    The sheet disappears, and the new user now appears in the Users & Groups System Preferences pane's Users list.

12. **(Optional) Click the account picture and choose a different one.**

    OS X suggests a picture from its default collection for each account, but you can select a different one from the sheet that appears when you click the account picture. Or, choose Camera in the sheet and take a photo with an attached or built-in camera (such as an iSight).

Changing a user

Circumstances might dictate that you need to change a user's identity, password, or accessibility, or perhaps delete a user. Follow these steps to change a user's name, password, or account type:

1. **Choose ⚫⇨ System Preferences (or click the System Preferences icon on the Dock or Launchpad).**

   The System Preferences window appears.

2. **In the System Preferences window, click the Users & Groups icon.**

   The Users & Groups System Preferences pane appears.

   If the lock icon at the bottom of the window is locked, you have to click it and provide an administrator password before you can proceed.

3. **Select the user's name in the accounts list.**

   The information for that person appears.

4. **Make your changes by selecting the existing username and replacing the old with new text or a different setting.**

   - *If you want to change the password,* click the Reset Password button and make your changes in the sheet that appears.

   - *To change the picture or other capabilities,* click the Picture, Login Options, Allow User to Administer This Computer (to enable or disable administrator privileges), or Enable Parental Control check box (more on this in a moment) and make the appropriate changes.

   To change a user, you must be logged in using an account that has administrator powers.

5. **Quit the System Preferences application or choose a different System Preferences pane.**

   Your changes are saved when you leave the Users & Groups pane.

Removing a user

To delete a user — in effect, to deny that user access to your Mac — select the user you want to delete in the list of accounts and click the – (minus sign) button. A sheet appears, offering three choices:

- ✔ **Save the Home Folder in a Disk Image** saves a disk image of the user's Home folder in a folder named Deleted Users (which it creates inside the Users folder).

- ✔ **Don't Change the Home Folder** removes the user from the Users & Groups System Preferences pane and login screen but leaves that user's Home folder in the Users folder. *(Deleted)* is appended to the folder's name, so if I had selected this option in the previous example, Steve Wozniak's Home folder would be renamed *Steve (Deleted)*.

- ✔ **Delete the Home Folder** does what it says. You have the option of a secure erase (the contents get overwritten multiple times) if you select this option.

  Be certain you really want to kiss that Home folder goodbye, because after you delete it there's no way to get it back.

To remove a user from your Mac, you must be logged in using an account that has administrator permissions. And you can't remove the first user ever created on this Mac.

Limiting a user's capabilities

Sometimes — especially with younger children, computerphobic family members, or employees in a small business — you want to limit what users can access. For example, you might want to make certain programs off-limits. You do this by clicking the Parental Controls button in the Users & Groups System Preferences pane.

1. **Choose ⚙ System Preferences (or click the System Preferences icon on the Dock).**

   The System Preferences window appears.

2. **In the System Preferences window, click the Users & Groups icon.**

   The Users & Groups Preferences pane appears.

3. **Click the user's name to select it, select the Enable Parental Controls check box, and then click the Open Parental Controls button.**

   Note that clicking the Open Parental Controls button without first selecting the Enable Parental Controls check box puts you in the Parental Controls System Preferences pane with a button front and center for you to click to turn on Parental Controls. So either select the check box as instructed or click the Enable Parental Controls button here.

To change any of these items, you must be logged in using an account that has administrator powers, and the account you're modifying *can't* have administrator powers.

The Parental Controls System Preferences pane for that person appears with six tabs: Apps, Web, Stores, Time (shown in Figure 12-5), Privacy, and Other.

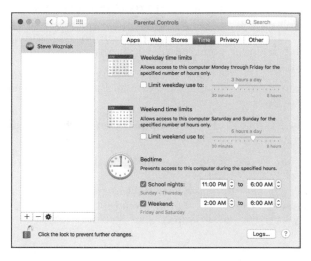

Figure 12-5: You can control an account's access in six categories (the Time tab is shown here).

4. **Set the controls in each of the six tabs.**

   - *Apps:* Determine whether the user is restricted to a very limited and simplified Finder interface and which applications the user may access. Also set whether the user can modify the Dock and whether Mail communicants are limited to a specified list. This option also lets you notify someone (usually yourself) by email if the user tries to exchange email with a contact who is not in the approved list. You can also disallow joining Game Center multi-player games or adding Game Center friends.

   - *Web:* Control access to websites.

   - *Stores:* Control access to iTunes and iBooks Stores, including age-based restrictions for movies, TV shows, and apps.

   The Web and People controls do not affect non-Apple apps like Chrome or Firefox, only the OS X provided apps like Mail and Safari. So remove or disable third-party apps if you want these controls to work as intended.

- *Time:* Set time limits for weekdays and weekends and prevent access to this computer during specified hours on school nights and weekends.

  School nights doesn't account for holidays or vacations and such.

- *Privacy:* Determine whether third-party apps can access Contacts, Calendar, Reminder, and other data.

- *Other:* Determine whether profanity is hidden during Dictionary access, control whether the user can add or remove printers or modify printer settings, prevent (or allow) burning CDs and DVDs in the Finder, and control whether the user is allowed to change his password.

  You can also disable Dictation and prevent the user from modifying the Dock.

5. **Quit the System Preferences application or choose a different System Preferences pane.**

   Your changes are saved when you leave the Parental Controls pane.

A quicker way to set or change Parental Controls for an already-existing account is to click the Parental Controls icon in the System Preferences application (instead of Users & Groups).

Last but not least, you can apply Parental Controls to the Guest Account, but you can't apply them to any account that has administrator permissions.

To turn off Parental Controls for a Managed account, navigate to the Parental Controls System Preferences pane, select the account in the list on the left, click the Action menu at the bottom of the list (the one that looks like a gear), and choose Turn off Parental Controls for *<username>*.

If you want to apply the same Parental Controls settings to more than one user, set them as just described for the first user and then select that account in the Accounts list in Parental Controls, click the Action menu, and choose Copy Settings. Then select the user you want to have the same settings, click the Action menu, and choose Paste Settings.

And one last thing: Although they're called Parental Controls, you can use them with adults, too. For example, it's often useful to restrict access to certain features on your Guest account. Just a thought.

OS X knows best: Folders shared by default

When you add users in the Users & Groups System Preferences pane as I describe earlier, OS X automatically does two things behind the scenes to facilitate file sharing: It creates a set of folders, and it makes some of them available for sharing.

Each time you add a Managed, Standard, or Administrator user, OS X creates a Home folder hierarchy for that user on the Mac. The user can create more folders (if necessary) and also add, remove, or move anything inside these folders. Even if you create a user account solely to allow him or her to exchange files with you, your Mac automatically creates a Home folder for that user. Unless you, as the owner of your Mac, give permission, the user can't see inside or use folders outside the Home folder (which has the user's name), with only three exceptions: the Shared folder in the Users folder, the top level of other user account folders, and the Public folders in every other user's folder, as well as the Shared folder within the Users folder. A description of the latter follows:

- ✒ **Public:** A Public folder is located inside each user's folder. That folder is set up to be accessible (shared) by any user who can log in to the Mac. Furthermore, any user can log in (as a guest) and copy things out of this folder as long as she knows your Mac's IP address, even if she doesn't have an account on this Mac at all. Files put into the Public folder can be opened or copied freely.

  It's not hard for someone to obtain your IP address. For example, when you visit most web pages, your IP address is saved to that site's log file. So be careful what you put in your Public folder. This is also an excellent reason to employ a firewall. El Capitan has an excellent software implementation available via the Firewall tab in Security & Privacy System Preferences (see Chapter 18), and most routers (for example, AirPort Extreme) include a hardware firewall.

  Inside each user's Public folder is a Drop Box folder. As the name implies, this folder is where others can drop a file or folder for you. Only the owner can open the Drop Box to see what's inside — or to move or copy the files that are in it. Imagine a street-corner mailbox: After you drop your letter in, it's gone, and you can't get it back out.

  Be aware that there is a popular cloud-based storage service called Dropbox. The Drop Box folder in your Public folder has nothing to do with that Dropbox service beyond having a similar name.

- ✒ **Shared:** In addition to a Public folder for each user, OS X creates one Shared folder on every Mac for all users of this Mac. The Shared folder *isn't* available to guests, but it's available to all users who have an account on this Mac. You find the Shared folder within the Users folder (the same folder where you find folders for each user). The Shared folder is the right place to put stuff that everyone with an account on this Mac might want to use. (Check out my introduction to the Mac OS El Capitan folder structure in Chapter 6.)

Sharing a folder or disk by setting permissions

As you might expect, permissions control who can use a given folder or any disk (or partition) other than the startup disk.

Why can't you share the startup disk? Because OS X won't let you. Why not? Because the startup disk contains the operating system and other stuff that nobody else should have access to.

Throughout the rest of this chapter, whenever I talk about *sharing a folder,* I also mean *sharing disks and disk partitions other than your startup disk* (which, when you think of it, are nothing more than big folders anyway). Why am I telling you this? Because it's awkward to keep typing *a folder or any disk (or partition) other than your startup disk.* So anything that I say about sharing a folder also applies to sharing any disk (or partition) other than your startup disk. Got it?

You can set permissions for

- ✔ The folder's owner
- ✔ A subset of all the people who have accounts on the Mac (a group)
- ✔ Everyone who has the Mac's address, whether they have an account or not (guests)

To help you get a better handle on these relationships, a closer look at permissions, owners, and groups is coming right up.

Contemplating permissions

When you consider who can use which folders, three distinct kinds of users exist on the network. I describe each of them in this section. Then, in the "Useful settings for permissions" section, later in this chapter, I show you how to share folders with each type of user. Here's a quick introduction to the different user types:

- ✔ **Owner:** The *owner* of a folder or disk can change the permissions to that folder or disk at any time. The name you enter when you log in to your Mac — or the name of your Home folder — is the default owner of Shared folders and drives on that machine. Ownership can be given away (more on that in the "Useful settings for permissions" section, later in this chapter). Even if you own the Mac, you can't change permissions for a folder on it that belongs to another user (unless you get Unix-y and do so as root). The owner must be logged in to change permissions on his folders.

    OS X is the owner of many folders outside the Users folder. If OS X owns it, you can see that system is its owner if you select the folder and choose File➪Get Info (or press ⌘+I).

Folders that aren't in the User directories generally belong to system; it's almost always a bad idea to change the permissions on any folder owned by system.

If you *must* change permissions on a file or folder, select its icon and choose File➪Get Info (⌘+I) and then change the settings in the Sharing & Permissions section at the bottom of the resulting Get Info window. I urge you not to change permission settings if you're not absolutely sure of what you're doing and why. And by all means think twice before deciding to apply changes to all the items in a folder or disk; change permissions on the contents of the wrong folder and you could end up with a mess.

✔ **Group:** In Unix systems, all users belong to one or more *groups.* The group that includes everyone who has an account with administrator permissions on your Mac is called Admin. Everyone in the Admin group has access to Shared and Public folders over the network, as well as to any folder that the Admin group has been granted access to by the folder's owner.

For the purpose of assigning permissions, you can create your own groups the same way you create a user account: Open the Users & Groups System Preferences pane, click the little plus sign, choose Group from the New Account pop-up menu, type the name of the group, and then click the Create Group button.

The group appears in the list of users on the left, and eligible accounts appear with check boxes on the right, as shown in Figure 12-6.

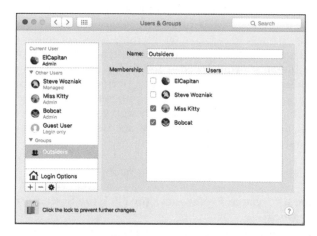

Figure 12-6: This group, The Outsiders, contains the Bobcat and Miss Kitty accounts.

✔ **Everyone:** This category is an easy way to set permissions for everyone with an account on your Mac at the same time. Unlike the Admin group, which includes only users with administrative permissions, this one includes, well, everyone (everyone with an account on this Mac, that is).

If you want people without an account on this Mac to have access to a file or folder, that file or folder needs to go in your Public folder, where the people you want to see it can log in as guests.

Sharing a folder

Suppose you have a folder you want to share, but it has slightly different rules than those set up for the Public folder, for the Drop Box folder within the Public folder, or for your personal folders. These rules are *permissions,* and they tell you how much access someone has to your stuff.

Actually, the rules governing Shared and Public folders are permissions, too, but they're set up for you when OS X is installed.

I suggest that you share only those folders located in your Home folder (or a folder within it). Because of the way Unix works, the Unix permissions of the enclosing folder can prevent access to a folder for which you *do* have permissions. Trust me, if you share only the folders in your Home folder, you'll never go wrong. If you don't take this advice, you could wind up having folders that other users can't access, even though you gave them the appropriate permissions.

By the way, you can set permissions for folders within your Public folder (like the Drop Box folder) that are different from those for the rest of the parent folder.

I said this before, but it bears repeating: Whenever I talk about *sharing a folder,* I also mean sharing disks — and disk partitions other than your startup disk (which you just can't share, period). So don't forget that anything I say about sharing a folder also applies to sharing any disk (or partition) other than your startup disk. Although you can't explicitly share your startup disk, anyone with administrator access can mount it for sharing from across the network (or Internet).

To share a folder with another user, follow these steps:

1. **Choose ➪ System Preferences (or click the System Preferences icon on the Dock).**

   The System Preferences window appears.

2. **In the System Preferences window, click the Sharing icon.**

   The Sharing System Preferences pane appears.

3. **Click File Sharing in the list of services on the left.**

   The lists of shared folders and their users appear on the right, as shown in Figure 12-7.

   If an entry in, for example, the Shared Folders list is too long for you to make out the folder name, hover your pointer over it, and a tooltip will appear, giving you the full name as shown in Figure 12-7.

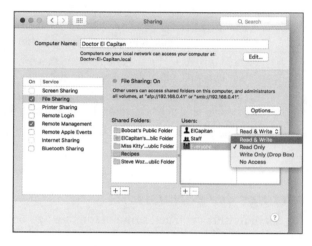

Figure 12-7: Changing the privileges of the Recipes folder for the group Everyone.

4. **Click the + (plus) button under the Shared Folders list or drag the folder from the Finder onto the Shared Folders list to add the folder you want to share (Recipes in Figure 12-7).**

   If you select the Shared Folder check box in a folder's Get Info window, that folder already appears in the list of Shared Folders, so you won't have to bother with Step 4.

   Alas, although selecting the Shared Folder check box in a folder's Get Info window causes it to appear in the Sharing System Preferences pane's Shared Folders list, you still have to complete the steps that follow to assign that folder's users and privileges.

5. **Click the + (plus) button under the Users column to add a user or group if the user or group you want isn't already showing in the Users column.**

6. **Click the double-headed arrow to the right of a user or group name and change its privileges.**

   I'm changing the permission for Everyone from Read Only (checked in Figure 12-7) to Read & Write (selected in Figure 12-7). You can choose among three types of access (in addition to no access) for each user or group, as shown in Table 12-1. If you're the folder's owner (or have administrator access), you can click the padlock icon and change the owner and/or group for the file or folder.

Table 12-1	Privileges
Permission	*What It Allows*
Read & Write	A user with Read & Write access can see, add, delete, move, and edit files just as though they were stored on her own computer.
Read Only	A Read Only user can see and use files that are stored in a Shared folder but can't add, delete, move, or edit them.
Write Only (Drop Box)	Users can add files to this folder but can't see what's in it. The user must have read access to the folder containing a Write Only folder.
No Access	With no permissions, a user can neither see nor use your Shared folders or drives.

Useful settings for permissions

The following sections show you just some of the most common ways that you can combine permissions for a folder. You'll probably find one option that fits the way you work and the people you want to share with.

Owner permissions — in this case, single silhouette; ElCapitan (Me) in Figure 12-8 — must be at least as expansive as Group permissions (double silhouette; Staff in Figure 12-8), and Group permissions must be at least as expansive as Everyone's permissions (triple silhouette; Everyone in Figure 12-8). So to set the Everyone privilege to Read & Write, the Group and Owner privileges must also be set to Read & Write.

In the following examples, I show how to set permissions in the Sharing System Preferences pane. Another way to set permissions is by selecting an icon in the Finder and choosing File⇨Get Info (⌘+I) and then changing the settings in the Sharing & Permissions section at the bottom of the resulting Get Info window. The two methods are pretty much interchangeable, so you can use whichever is more convenient.

- **Allow everyone access:** In Figure 12-8, I configure settings that allow everyone on a network to access the Bob's Downloads folder. Everyone can open, read, and change the contents of this Shared folder. Do this by choosing Read & Write for Others from the pop-up menu to the right of the user's name in the Sharing System Preferences pane or the folder's Get Info window.

✔ **Allow nobody but yourself access:** The settings shown in Figure 12-9 reflect appropriate settings that allow owner-only access to the Bob's Downloads folder. No one but me can see or use the contents of this folder. Members of the Staff group can drop files and folders into this folder (see the later bullet "Allow others to deposit files and folders without giving them access: A drop box"). Use the pop-up menus to choose Write Only (Drop Box) as the Staff privilege and No Access as the Everyone privilege.

Figure 12-8: Allow everyone access, if you want.

Figure 12-9: Allow access for no one but the folder's owner.

✔ **Allow all administrative users of this Mac access:** Check out Figure 12-10 to see settings that allow the group Staff (in addition to the owner, ElCapitan) access to see, use, or change the contents of the Bob's Downloads folder. Use the pop-up menu to choose Read & Write for the Staff privilege.

Figure 12-10: Allow access for the Staff group and the folder's owner.

✔ **Allow others to deposit files and folders without giving them access: A drop box:** The settings in Figure 12-11 enable everyone to drop their own files or folders in the Bob's Downloads folder without being able to see or use the contents of the Shared folder. After a file or folder is deposited in a drop folder, the dropper can't retrieve it because she doesn't have permission to see the items in the drop folder.

✔ **Read-only bulletin boards:** If you want everyone to be able to open and read the files and folders in this Shared folder — but not to modify them — choose Read Only from the pop-up menus for Group and Others. If you do this, however, only the owner can make changes to files in this folder.

✔ **One more privilege:** The Apply to Enclosed Items button (click the gear at the bottom of the Sharing and Permissions section of Get Info windows in the Finder) does exactly what its name implies. This feature (which is only available in Get Info windows and doesn't appear in the Sharing System Preferences pane) is a fast way to assign the same permissions to many subfolders at the same time. After you set permissions for the enclosing folder the way you like them, click this button to give these same permissions to all folders inside it.

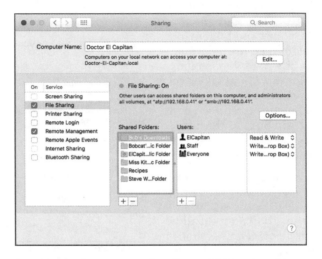

Figure 12-11: Everyone can drop files and folders into this folder.

What is true of Get Info windows is also true of their Inspector window variant. Show Inspector replaces Get Info on the File menu when the Option key is pressed (also Option+⌘+I).

Be careful — there is no Undo for this action.

Unsharing a folder

To unshare a folder that you own, change the permissions for every other user and/or group to No Access. When you do, nobody but you has access to that folder. If you're not sure how to do this, see the "Sharing a folder" and "Useful settings for permissions" sections, earlier in this chapter.

Connecting to a Shared Disk or Folder on a Remote Mac

After you set up sharing and assign permissions, you can access folders remotely from another computer. (Just make sure first that you have the correct administrative permissions to it.)

File sharing must be activated on the Mac where the shared files/folders reside; it doesn't have to be activated on the Mac that's accessing the files/folders. When file sharing is turned off, you can still use that Mac to access a remote Shared folder on another machine as long as its owner has granted you enough permissions and has file sharing enabled. If file sharing is turned off on your Mac, others won't be able to access your folders, even if you've assigned permissions to them previously.

If you're going to share files, and you leave your Mac on and unattended for a long time, logging out before you leave it is a very good idea. This prevents anyone who just walks up to your Mac from seeing your files, email, applications, or anything else that's yours — unless you've given that person a user account that has permissions for your files. If you don't want to log out, at least consider requiring that your password be entered when waking from sleep or dismissing the screen saver (General tab of Security & Privacy System Preferences).

Move along now and see how to access your Home folder from a remote Mac — a supercool feature that's only bound to get more popular as the Internet continues to mature.

The following steps assume that you have an account on the remote Mac, which means you have your own Home folder on that Mac.

To connect to a Shared folder on a Mac other than the one you're currently on, follow these steps:

1. **Make sure that you're already set up as a user on the computer that you want to log in to (LisaMBP in Figure 12-12).**

   If you need to know how to create a new user, see the "Creating users" section, earlier in the chapter.

Figure 12-12: I am connected to LisaMBP as a guest.

2. **On the computer that you're logging in from (my MacBook Pro in this example), click the Show button to show the Shared section in the Sidebar if it's not already showing.**

   The button says Hide in Figure 12-12 because the shared section is showing.

   All available shared servers appear. (Two are visible in the Sidebar in Figure 12-12 — MacBook The Knife XIII and LisaMBP.)

   Note that you might also see shared resources like wireless printers or network storage devices (such as Apple's Time Capsule), and other networked devices in the Shared section of the Sidebar.

3. **Click the name of the remote Mac (LisaMBP) you want to access in the Sidebar.**

   At this point, you're connected to the remote Mac as a guest, as shown in Figure 12-12.

4. **Click the Connect As button.**

   The Connect dialog appears. The name of the person logged in and using this Mac automatically appears in the Name field (my account name, bobl, in Figure 12-13).

   If that's not your username on the Mac you're trying to access, type that username in the Name field.

   If you select the Remember This Password in My Keychain check box in the Connect dialog, OS X remembers your password for you the next time you connect to this server. Sweet!

Figure 12-13: The Connect dialog needs my password.

5. **Select the Guest radio button if you don't have an account on the remote computer and then click Connect; if you're logging in as a user, skip to Step 6.**

   Pressing ⌘+G is the same as selecting the Guest radio button, and pressing ⌘+R is the same as selecting the Registered User radio button.

   As a guest user, you see Public Folders for users who have accounts on LisaMBP (Lisa LeVitus, Bob LeVitus, and Jacob in Figure 12-12) but nothing else.

6. **Type your password and click the Connect button.**

   After you connect as a registered user, you see your Home folder (bobl in Figure 12-14) and everyone else's Public folders.

File sharing must be active on LisaMBP (the Mac I'm accessing remotely in the example). If file sharing weren't active on LisaMBP, its name wouldn't appear in the Shared section of the Sidebar, and I wouldn't be able to connect to it. But file sharing doesn't have to be active on the computer *you're* using (my MacBook Pro in this example) to give you access to the remote computer and make this trick work.

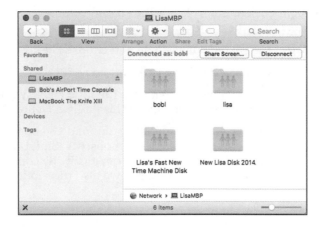

Figure 12-14: Connecting to LisaMBP as Bob LeVitus (bobl).

When you access your Home folder on a remote Mac as I did in this example, you see an icon with the short name of your Home folder on that Mac (bobl in Figure 12-15) on the Desktop of the Mac you're using (unless you've deselected Connected Servers in the Finder's General Preferences pane, under Show These Items on the Desktop).

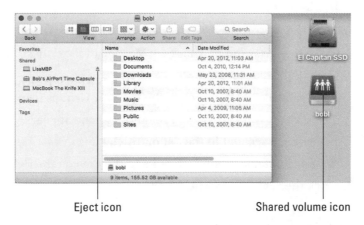

Eject icon   Shared volume icon

Figure 12-15: Accessing my Home folder on LisaMBP remotely.

7. **When you finish using the remote Mac, disconnect by using one of these methods:**

   - Drag the shared-volume icon (bobl in Figure 12-15) to the Eject icon on the Dock.

     When a disk or volume is selected (highlighted), the Trash icon turns into a little arrow, which represents *eject.* Nice touch, eh?

   - Right-click or Control-click the shared volume icon and choose Eject from the contextual menu that appears.

   - Select the shared volume icon and choose File➪Eject.

   - Select the shared volume icon and press ⌘+E.

   - In a Finder window Sidebar, click the little Eject symbol to the right of the remote computer's name (LisaMBP in Figure 12-15).

   - If you've finished working for the day, and you don't leave your Mac on 24/7 (as most folks do), choose ➪Shut Down or Log Out. Shutting down or logging out automatically disconnects you from shared disks or folders. (Shut Down also turns off your Mac.)

Changing Your Password

You can change your password at any time. Changing your password is a good idea if you're concerned about security — for example, if there's a chance your password has been discovered by someone else.

You can change the password for your account on your own Mac, or you can change the password you use to connect to your account on a remote Mac. I show you how to do both in the following sections.

Changing your account password on your Mac

To change the password on your own Mac, just follow these steps:

1. **Choose ➪System Preferences, or double-click its icon in your Applications folder and click the Users & Groups icon.**

   The Users & Groups System Preferences pane appears.

2. **Select your account in the list on the left.**

   Your account information appears in the area on the right.

3. **Click the Change Password button.**

   If you aren't using your iCloud password, a dialog appears and asks:

   Would you like to change the password for "ElCapitan," or begin using your iCloud password to log in and unlock this Mac? You will only need to remember one password if you use your iCloud password to log in to this Mac.

Your choices are Use iCloud Password, Cancel, or Change Password.

4. **Click Change Password.**

   A sheet drops down.

5. **Type your current password in the Old Password field.**

   This demonstrates that you are who you're supposed to be, not someone who just walked up to your unattended Mac.

6. **Type your new password in the New Password field.**

7. **Retype your new password in the Verify field.**

8. **(Optional but recommended) Type a hint in the Password Hint field.**

9. **Click the Change Password button.**

   Assuming that you entered your old password correctly, the sheet disappears.

10. **Close the System Preferences window.**

Changing the password of any account but your own on your Mac

To change a password on your own Mac, just follow these steps:

1. **Choose System Preferences or double-click its icon in your Applications folder and click the Users & Groups icon.**

   The Users & Groups System Preferences pane appears.

   You may have to click the lock (at bottom left), supply an administrator name and password in the resulting dialog, and then click OK before you can proceed.

2. **Select the account you want to change the password for in the list on the left.**

   The account information appears in the area on the right.

3. **Click the Reset Password button.**

   A sheet drops down.

4. **Type the new password in the New Password field.**

5. **Retype the new password in the Verify field.**

6. **(Optional but recommended) Type a hint in the Password Hint field.**

7. **Click the Reset Password button.**

8. **Close the System Preferences window.**

Changing the password for your account on someone else's Mac

When you log in to a remote Mac, you can change your own password if you like. Follow these steps to do so:

1. **Log in to the remote computer on which you want to change your password.**

   See the "Connecting to a Shared Disk or Folder on a Remote Mac" section, earlier in this chapter, if you don't know how to log in to a remote computer.

   The Connect dialog appears.

2. **Type your username in the Connect dialog, if it's not already there.**

3. **Click the Change Password button in the bottom-left corner of the dialog.**

   A sheet for changing your password appears.

4. **Type your current password in the Old Password field.**

5. **Type your new password in the New Password and Verify fields.**

   You can use the Password Assistant (the little key to the right of the New Password text box) to help you generate a secure password.

6. **Click the Change Password button.**

   Your password is changed, and you return to the Connect dialog.

7. **(Optional) Type your new password and click Connect to log in to the other Mac.**

   You can skip this step by clicking the Cancel button in the Connect dialog if you don't need to use anything on the remote Mac at this time. Your password is still changed, and you need to use the new password the next time you log in to this Mac.

   Select the Add Password to Keychain check box in the Connect dialog to store your passwords in a single place on the Mac; this way you don't have to retype them each time you access a Mac or other remote resource. (Read more about the Keychain in Chapter 19.)

More Types of Sharing

Several more types of sharing exist, and I'd like to at least mention a few in passing. All are found in (where else?) the Sharing System Preferences pane, which you can find by launching the System Preferences application (from the Applications folder, menu, or Dock) and clicking the Sharing icon.

Screen Sharing

Here's the sharing that I consider the coolest. Screen Sharing lets you control another Mac on your network from your Mac. In essence, you see the other Mac's screen on *your* Mac — and control it using *your* mouse and keyboard.

To set up Screen Sharing on the Mac you want to control remotely, follow these steps:

1. **Open the Sharing System Preferences pane by launching the System Preferences application (from the Applications folder, , Launchpad, or Dock) and clicking the Sharing icon.**

2. **Select the check box for Screen Sharing in the list of services on the left.**

3. **Select either the All Users or Only These Users radio button.**

   If you opt for Only These Users, click the + (plus sign) button and add the user or users you want to allow to control this Mac remotely. Notice that the Staff group is included by default.

To take control of your Mac from another Mac, follow these steps:

1. **Click the now-you-see-it-now-you-don't Show tag to the right of Shared to open the Shared section in the Sidebar, if it's not already open.**

   All available servers appear.

2. **Click the name of the remote Mac you want to control.**

3. **Click the Share Screen button.**

   Depending on whether you selected the All Users or Only These Users radio button, you may have to enter your name and password, and then click the Connect button.

   A window with the name of the remote Mac in its title bar appears. In it, you see the screen of the Mac you're looking to control remotely.

4. **Go ahead and click something.**

   Pull down a menu or open a folder. Isn't that cool? You're controlling a Mac across the room or in another room with your mouse and keyboard!

Internet Sharing

If your Mac has an Internet connection and another Mac nearby doesn't, you can enable Internet Sharing, and the other Mac can share your Internet connection. The following steps show you how:

1. **Open the Sharing System Preferences pane by launching the System Preferences application (from the Applications folder, menu, Launchpad, or Dock) and clicking the Sharing icon.**

2. **Select the Internet Sharing check box in the list of services on the left.**

3. **Choose the connection you want to share — Wi-Fi, Bluetooth, FireWire, Ethernet, or Thunderbolt — from the Share Your Connection From pop-up menu.**

4. **Select the check boxes next to connections other computers will use: Wi-Fi, Ethernet, or Built-In FireWire.**

   Figure 12-16 shows Internet Sharing configured to share my Ethernet Internet connection with other Macs and iDevices over Wi-Fi.

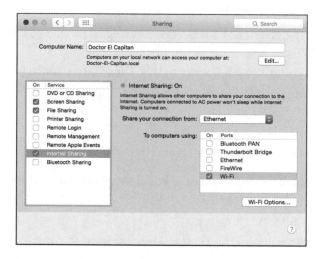

Figure 12-16: Sharing my wired (Ethernet) Internet connection with other Macs and iDevices over Wi-Fi.

5. **(Optional) Click the Wi-Fi Options button to name, select a wireless channel for, enable encryption for, and/or set a password for your shared network.**

   That's all there is to it.

And yet more ways to share

A few more cool ways to share your Mac include

- ✔ **DVD or CD Sharing:** When you select this one, remote users can access CDs and DVDs in your Mac's optical drive(s). You can select to have El Capitan notify you and request permission when a remote user makes such a request. This feature is especially handy if you have two or more Macs, and one doesn't have an optical drive.

✔ **Printer Sharing:** If you turn on Printer Sharing in the Sharing System Preferences pane, other people on your LAN can use any printer connected to your computer.

✔ **Scanner Sharing:** Analogous to Printer Sharing, Scanner Sharing allows others on your local network to use scanners connected to your Mac.

✔ **Bluetooth Sharing:** If you have a Bluetooth mobile phone or PDA and your Mac has Bluetooth, you can configure many of the default behaviors for transferring files to and from your Mac. A picture is worth a thousand words, so Figure 12-17 shows all the things Bluetooth Sharing lets you configure.

Figure 12-17: Configure items for Bluetooth file transfers between your phone and Mac.

One last thing: If you have an iPhone 4 or later, you can use its cellular connection for Internet access on your Mac. For details on this and other Continuity features for iDevices (Handoff, SMS, and Instant Hot Spot), see the book's cheat sheet at www.dummies.com/cheatsheet/osxelcapitan.

Part IV
Getting Creative in El Capitan

Check out www.dummies.com/extras/osxelcapitan for more on watching movies with DVD Player.

IMG_4619 IMG_4618 IMG_4617 IMG_4616

IMG_4611 4608

In this part . . .

- Music and your Mac: Introducing iTunes
- Read any good iBooks lately?
- Working with photos
- Importing and exporting media
- Enough information about fonts and typefaces to impress your friends and family
- Setting up a printer without tearing out your hair
- Making sense of the myriad Print options

IMG_4603 IMG_4602 IMG_4601 IMG_4600

Desktop

1 of 74 selected

13

The Musical Mac

A long time ago, before the iPod and the iTunes Store were even born, iTunes was a program that stored, managed, and played your MP3 music files. Over the ensuing years, it has grown into much more. In fact, many feel it has grown into a bloated monstrosity barely resembling the iTunes we knew and loved.

In El Capitan, iTunes manages more than music. And if you use devices such as an iPod, Apple TV, iPad, or iPhone, iTunes is also the application you use to manage (sync) your music, as well as videos, TV shows, podcasts, iOS apps, and more.

In other words, the anachronistically named iTunes is what you use to manage audio, video, and iOS app files on your hard drive. If you have an iDevice or Apple TV, it's what you use to sync files. Oh yeah, and it is still a music player.

Entire books have been dedicated to iTunes. (I wrote one called *The Little iTunes Book,* which is now out of print.) The best I can do in this chapter is show you the handful of things you really need to know.

Before you can look at iTunes, you need to know a few things about the new Apple Music and not-so-new iTunes Match subscription services, since what you'll see in iTunes is different for those who subscribe to one or both.

Apple Music and iTunes Match Rock!

iTunes Match and Apple Music are a pair of subscription music services offered by Apple.

iTunes Match is the older of the two, designed to let you store all your music in iCloud so you can stream all your songs to any Mac, PC, or iDevice. iTunes Match performs its magic by first determining which songs in your iTunes Library are already available in iCloud. Because Apple's vast iCloud repository contains tens of millions of songs, chances are that most of your music is already there. Then iTunes proceeds to upload a copy of every song it *can't* match (which is much faster than uploading your entire music library). The result is that you can stream any song in your iTunes Library on any of your Macs, PCs, or iDevices, regardless of whether the song file is available on the device. As a bonus, all the music iTunes matches plays back from iCloud at 256Kbps AAC DRM-free quality even if your original copy was lower quality. (You can even download higher quality versions of those songs to replace your lower bit-rate copies.)

Subscribers can store up to 25,000 songs in iCloud, and songs you purchased from the iTunes Store don't count. Only tracks or albums you specify are stored locally on your devices, saving tons of precious storage space.

At just $24.99 a year, iTunes Match is a bargain. But Apple Music, introduced in early 2015, may be a better (albeit more expensive) option. For $9.99 a month (or $14.99 a month for you and up to five family members), your subscription provides instant access to more than 30 million songs. Whatever you want to hear, it's probably not more than a few clicks away. And if you have an iPhone or other iDevice, you can ask Siri to play just about anything.

It would behoove you to make a complete backup of your iTunes library before enabling either iTunes Match or Apple Music, just in case. There were reports early in their existence that enabling one or both scrambled the data in some users' iTunes libraries.

Both subscription services require Internet access (of course), but as long as you're connected you can have your entire music library (iTunes Match) or access to a library of over 30 million songs (Apple Music) on your Mac, iPhone, or other device. You'll never have to worry about filling up your device's storage space with your music.

And here's a tip for subscribers to either service (one I learned the hard way): Before you travel on a plane or ship, remember to tap the iCloud download button next to any songs, albums, and playlists you want to listen to when Internet access isn't available.

You're entirely welcome.

Introducing iTunes

iTunes is the Swiss Army knife of multimedia software. After all, what other program lets you play audio CDs; create (burn) your own audio or MP3 CDs; listen to MP3, AIFF, AAC, WAV, Audible.com, and several other types of audio files; view album cover art; enjoy pretty visual displays in time to the music; view and manage TV shows, movies, and other video files; manage media for iPods (or other MP3 players), Apple TVs, iPads, and/or iPhones; listen to iTunes radio or Apple Music. And (deep breath) on top of all that, it's your interface to the iTunes Store, the world's leading (legitimate) source of down-loadable music and video content. (Whew!)

To open iTunes, click its icon on the Dock or double-click its icon in the Applications folder. The iTunes window opens (see Figure 13-1). The important items are labeled, but I encourage you to click anything and everything you see on the screen — you won't break anything.

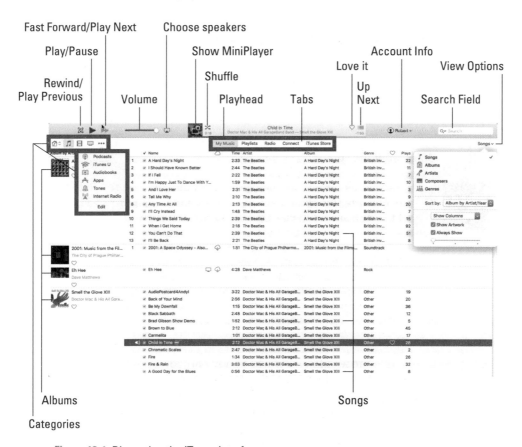

Figure 13-1: Dissecting the iTunes interface.

Perhaps the most important thing on the screen are the category buttons near the upper-left corner — Home, Music, Movies, and TV in Figure 13-1. These act as filters for the various types of media in your iTunes Media Library.

The rest of your media — your Podcasts, iTunes U courses, Audiobooks, Apps, Tones, and Internet Radio stations — are hidden beneath the . . . button. Click that button to reveal them, as shown in Figure 13-1.

To add a button for a hidden category, click Edit, select the check box for that category, and then click Done.

To the right of the category buttons are tabs for the selected category (Music in Figure 13-1): My Music, Playlists, Radio, Connect, and iTunes Store. (Apple Music subscribers have two additional tabs: For You and New.) Click a tab to see its contents. To play a song (or other media such as a movie, TV show, or podcasts) in any tab, double-click it or single-click (to select it) and then press Return or the spacebar.

Spacebar is the Play/Pause shortcut for all media in iTunes.

Things work pretty much the same for the other categories. Double-click movies, TV shows, podcasts, or whatever to watch or listen to them; use the Fast Forward/Next Item, Play/Pause, and Rewind/Previous Item controls to manage playback.

I'd like you to take note of a few other interface items before we move on to doing stuff in iTunes:

✔ You can use the more manageable MiniPlayer (on the left in Figure 13-2) by clicking the MiniPlayer button (labeled in Figure 13-1), choosing Window➪MiniPlayer, or pressing ⌘+Option+M.

The main window remains onscreen along with the MiniPlayer. You can close it if you like and leave only the MiniPlayer onscreen, or keep 'em both on your screen if you prefer.

To close the MiniPlayer, click the little X in its upper-left corner.

Finally, you can toggle between the main window and the MiniPlayer by choosing Window➪Switch To/From MiniPlayer, or use the shortcut ⌘+Shift+M.

While the MiniPlayer works in any category, it's most useful for listening to audio — music, podcasts, and audiobooks.

✔ iTunes offers a ten-band graphic equalizer that can make your music (or video) sound significantly better. Just choose Window➪Equalizer or use the shortcut ⌘+Option+E to invoke it onscreen. You can see the equalizer on the right in Figure 13-2.

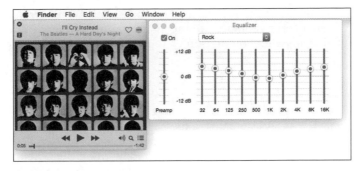

Figure 13-2: The iTunes MiniPlayer window (left) and equalizer (right).

➤ Don't miss the iTunes Visualizer, which offers a groovy light show that dances in time to the music, as shown in Figure 13-3. You turn it on by choosing View➪Show Visualizer or pressing ⌘+T. If you like the default Visualizer, check out some of iTunes's other built-in Visualizers such as Lathe, Jelly, or Stix, which are available in the Visualizer submenu. Search the web for *iTunes Visualizer* to find even more.

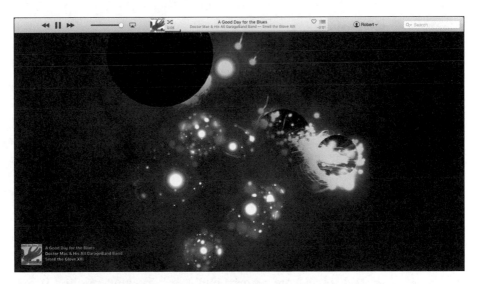

Figure 13-3: The iTunes psychedelic light show that is the iTunes Visualizer.

When you get sick of the Visualizer (as you surely will), just choose View➪Hide Visualizer or press ⌘+T again to make it disappear.

Try this: Choose View➪Full Screen or press ⌘+Control+F while the Visualizer is running, and the Visualizer takes over your entire screen. Click anywhere on the screen to bring the iTunes window back.

Working with Media

iTunes is, first and foremost, a media manager and player, so the next thing I examine is how to get your favorite media *into* iTunes. Of course, you can acquire media a number of ways, depending upon the type of media and where the files reside. For example, you can add song or video files you download from websites or receive as enclosures in email messages. Or you can add songs by ripping audio CDs. You can buy music, movies, TV shows, audiobooks, and apps for your iDevice at the iTunes Store (and, to be fair, from many other online vendors, including www.amazon.com and www.audible.com). You can subscribe to free podcasts at the iTunes Store (and from most podcasts' websites as well). And you can listen to all sorts of music on the Internet radio stations included with iTunes. Finally, Apple Music subscribers can listen to pretty much any song they can think of.

To use the iTunes Store, Internet radio, or Apple Music, you must be connected to the Internet.

In the following sections, you discover the various ways to add media — songs, movies, videos, and podcasts — to your iTunes Library, followed by a quick course in listening to iTunes Internet radio stations.

Adding songs

You can add songs from pretty much any source, and how you add a song to iTunes depends on where that song comes from. Here are the most common ways people add their songs:

- **Add a song file (such as an MP3 or AAC file) from your hard drive.** Drag the document into the iTunes window, as shown in Figure 13-4, drag the document onto the iTunes Dock icon, or choose File➪Add to Library (⌘+O) and choose the file in the Open File dialog. In all three cases, the file is added to your iTunes Music library.

- **Add songs from a store-bought or homemade audio CD.** Insert the CD, and iTunes will launch itself and offer a dialog asking whether you want to import the CD into your iTunes Library. Click the Yes button, and the songs on that CD are added to your iTunes Music library. If you don't see a dialog when you insert an audio CD, you can import the songs on that CD, anyway. Just select the CD by clicking the CD button that appears on the right of the Apps category button when a CD is mounted and then clicking the Import CD button right below the Search Field.

Drag to here

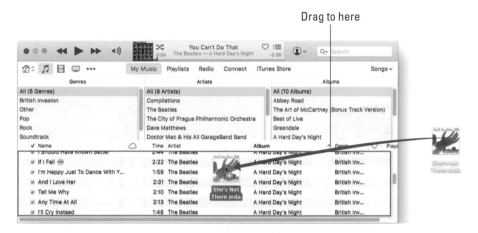

Figure 13-4: Drag and drop songs to the iTunes content pane or Library to add them to your Music library.

If your computer is connected to the Internet, iTunes magically looks up the song title, artist name, album name, song length, and genre for every song on the CD. Note that this works only for store-bought CDs containing somewhat popular music — and that iTunes might not be able to find information about a very obscure CD by an even more obscure band, even if the disc is store-bought. And in most cases it can't look up information for homemade (home-burned) audio CDs. Finally, it sometimes gets things wrong.

✔ **Buy your songs from the iTunes Store.** Click the iTunes Store tab to visit the iTunes Store. From the home page, you can either click a link or type the song title, album title, artist name, keyword, or phrase in the Search field, and then press Return to start the search. When you find an item that interests you, you can double-click any song to listen to a 30-second preview of it (or the whole thing if you're an Apple Music subscriber) or click the Buy Song or Buy Album button to purchase the song or album, as shown in Figure 13-5.

✔ **Buy your songs from other online vendors, such as Amazon.** Amazon (www.amazon.com) has a huge downloadable music store on the web. Its MP3 Downloads section has more than a million songs, with more being added every day. The prices at Amazon are often lower than the prices for the same music at the iTunes Store.

The first time you make a purchase from the iTunes Store, you have to create an Apple account, if you don't already have one. To do so, just click the Account button, and then click the Create New Account button in the Sign In dialog. After your account is established, future purchases require just one or two clicks.

Figure 13-5: At the iTunes Store, buying music is as easy as clicking the Buy Song or Buy Album button.

Adding movies and TV shows

To add a video file (such as an MOV or MP4) from your hard drive, drag the file to the iTunes window (as shown in Figure 13-4, earlier in this chapter), drag the file to the iTunes Dock icon, or choose File➪Add to Library (⌘+O) and choose the file in the Open File dialog. In all cases, the file is added to your iTunes Movie library.

You can also buy movies, TV shows, and other video content from the iTunes Store. Shopping for video is almost the same as shopping for music. Here are the steps:

1. **Click the Movie or TV category button and then click the iTunes Store tab.**

2. **Either click a link or type a movie title, music-video name, actor or director name, or other keyword or phrase in the Search field; then press Return to start the search.**

3. **When you find a video item that interests you, double-click it to see a preview or click the Buy button to purchase the episode or video.**

Adding podcasts

Podcasts are like radio or television shows, except that when you subscribe to them, you can listen to or watch them (using iTunes or your iPod, iPad, or iPhone) at any time you like. Thousands of podcasts are available, and many (or most) are free. To find podcasts, follow these steps:

1. **Click the Podcasts category button (or select it from the . . . button) and then click the iTunes Store tab.**

2. **Click the Podcasts link on the store's home page.**

3. **Click a link on the content pane or type a keyword or phrase in the Search field.**

4. **When you find a podcast that appeals to you, double-click it to listen to a preview, click the Get Episode button to download the current episode of that podcast, or click the Subscribe button to receive all future episodes of that podcast automatically.**

   Figure 13-6 shows all these things for the Mac Geek Gab audio podcast from The Mac Observer.

Subscribe   Get Episodes

Get Info

Figure 13-6: The Mac Geek Gab podcast from The Mac Observer.

For more information on most podcasts, just click the little *i* button on the right side of the description field, as shown in Figure 13-6.

Subscribing to a podcast is a cool deal. You can configure how often iTunes checks for new episodes (hourly, daily, weekly, or manually) and what to do when new episodes become available (download the most recent one, download all episodes, or do nothing) and how many episodes to keep in your iTunes Library (all, all unplayed, or a specific number between 2 and 10). To specify these settings, click the My Podcasts tab, right-click (or Control-click) the podcast in the list on the left, and then choose Podcast Settings from the shortcut menu.

When you start listening to a subscribed podcast on your Mac in iTunes and switch to an iDevice, the podcast will pick up where it left off on your Mac. Or at least that's what's supposed to happen — and it usually does.

Learning from iTunes U

Want to learn something for free? Click the iTunes U tab in the iTunes Store, and you can choose from tens of thousands of free audio and video courses, including a good number produced by colleges and universities that include Harvard, Oxford, Stanford, and hundreds more.

You download or subscribe to a course the same way you download or subscribe to a podcast. Check it out the next time you're in the iTunes Store. It's a great way to learn something new for free.

Listening to iTunes Radio

Streaming audio is delivered over the Internet in real time. Think of streaming audio as being just like radio but using the Internet rather than the airwaves as its delivery medium.

To listen to iTunes Radio, with dozens of stations curated by Apple's music experts, click the Music category button and then click the Radio tab. The first thing you see, at the top of the screen, is Beats 1. This new live radio station from Apple is on the air worldwide 24 hours a day, 7 days a week and offers world-class programming, interviews, and music. To listen to Beats 1, click the Listen Now button.

If Beats 1 isn't your cup of tea, scroll down the page for additional radio stations organized by

- **Recently Played:** These are stations that — you guessed it — you've played recently. Tap one to listen to it now.

- **Featured Stations:** This handful of stations was handpicked for your enjoyment by the nice folks at Apple. Tap one to listen to it.

- **Genres:** These stations are organized by genre, with stations as subgenres. Tap a subgenre to listen to it.

Did I mention that iTunes Radio is available on your iPhone, iPad, iPod touch, Mac, PC, and Apple TV for free? Sure, you'll hear the occasional ad, but you can listen to iTunes Radio without ads if you subscribe to iTunes Match.

iTunes also offers more than 100 Internet radio stations that aren't curated by Apple. To see and listen to these stations, click the . . . button near the top-left and choose Internet Radio.

And that, friends, is pretty much all you need to know to use and enjoy radio stations in iTunes.

All About Playlists

Playlists are a big deal in iTunes; they let you manage otherwise-unmanageable amounts of media, such as the 16,000+ songs in my iTunes Library. Playlists let you create subsets of a large collection, so it's easier to enjoy exactly the kind of music you want in iTunes or on your iDevices.

To play with your playlists, click the Music icon near the top left and then click the Playlists tab near the top center.

iTunes offers two types of playlists:

- **Regular playlists,** which contain the songs (or videos, podcasts, or radio stations) that you specify by dragging them to the playlist.
- **Smart playlists,** which select songs from your library based on criteria you specify. Furthermore, smart playlists are updated automatically if you add new items to your library that meet the criteria.

All playlists appear in the Sidebar on the left side of the iTunes window.

Creating a regular playlist

To create a regular playlist, follow these steps:

1. **Click the Music category button and then click the Playlists tab, as shown in Figure 13-7.**

   Your playlists appear in the Sidebar, as shown in Figure 13-7.

2. **Click the + button in the bottom-left corner of the iTunes window and choose New Playlist from its drop-down menu, or choose File⇨New Playlist, or press ⌘+N.**

   A new playlist named Playlist appears in the Sidebar.

Figure 13-7: Playlists appear in this Sidebar when you click the Playlists tab.

3. **(Optional) As long as the playlist's name, Playlist, is selected and ready to be edited, you probably want to rename it something meaningful by typing a new name for it.**

   If you decide not to name it now, you can double-click it and type a new name anytime.

4. **To add a song or songs to a playlist:**

   a. *Click the Edit Playlist button.*

      A list of all your songs appears on the left.

   b. *Drag the song or songs to the playlist on the right.*

      The faint blue line shown on the playlist (see Figure 13-8) indicates where the song or songs will appear when you release the mouse button.

   The song is added to that playlist. Note that adding a song to a playlist doesn't remove it from the library. And if you delete a song from a playlist, the song isn't deleted from your library. And if you delete a playlist from the Sidebar, the songs it contains aren't deleted from your library. In other words, think of songs in playlists as being aliases of songs in your library.

5. **Click the Done button when you're finished adding songs.**

6. **Click the playlist in the Sidebar to select it, and then click Play to listen to the songs it contains.**

Drag to here

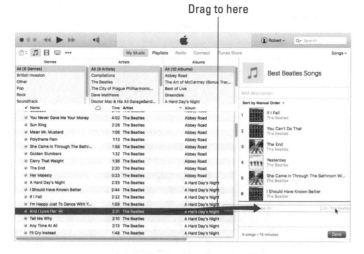

Figure 13-8: Adding songs to a playlist is as easy as dragging them onto the playlist.

If you don't want to drag songs to your playlist one by one, there are two easy ways to do it in one fell swoop. Create a regular playlist that includes songs you've selected from your music library: First, ⌘-click all the songs you want to include in the playlist. Then, either choose File➪New Playlist from Selection or click the + button and choose New Playlist from Selection in the pop-up menu.

Both ways can be seen in Figure 13-9.

You could also use the keyboard shortcut, ⌘+Shift+N, which is visible next to the New Playlist from Selection submenu item near the top of Figure 13-9.

You can also use that ⌘-click multiple songs technique to select and then drag a batch of songs onto an existing playlist.

The three columns above the list of songs in Figures 13-8 and 13-9 (6 Genres, 9 Artists, and 10 Albums) are the Column Browser, which is hidden by default in El Capitan. If you're not seeing the Column Browser but would like to, choose View➪Column Browser or use the shortcut ⌘+B. The Column Browser menu item also allows you to choose the columns that appear; the shortcut, alas, merely shows or hides the Column Browser.

Figure 13-9: Create a playlist from songs you select in your Music library.

Working with smart playlists

To create a *smart playlist* that builds a list based on criteria and updates itself automatically, follow these steps:

1. **Either click the + button in the bottom-left corner of the iTunes window or choose File⇨New Smart Playlist (⌘+Option+N).**

   The Smart Playlist dialog appears, as shown in Figure 13-10.

2. **Use the pop-up menus to select the criteria that will build your smart playlist and click the + button(s) (far right) to add more criteria.**

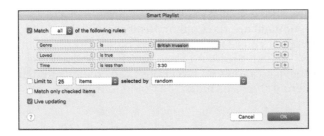

Figure 13-10: Specify the criteria for your smart playlist.

3. **Click OK when you're done.**

   The playlist appears alongside your other playlists in the Sidebar. You can tell it's a smart playlist by the gear on its icon. To modify the criteria of a smart playlist after it's been created, right-click (or Control-click) the smart playlist and choose Edit Smart Playlist to reopen the dialog.

I use Smart Playlists for many things. I have one that gathers Beatles songs and songs by individual Beatles; another for songs in my library that have never been played; and one that gathers all Doctor Mac & His All GarageBand Band's hits in one playlist. Try 'em — you'll like 'em.

Burning a playlist to CD

Another use for playlists is for burning audio CDs you can listen to on almost any audio CD player. The only trick is to make sure the total playing time of the songs in the playlist is less than the capacity of the blank CD you're using, which is usually 74 to 80 minutes. Don't forget to account for the gap between tracks, which is two seconds by default. When you have all the songs you want on your CD on the playlist, choose File⇨Burn Playlist to Disc. The Burn Settings dialog appears.

Note that although the default type of disc iTunes burns is an audio CD, it can also burn two other types — MP3 CDs or data CDs (and DVDs):

- **MP3 CD** is a special format that can be played in many CD audio players and set-top DVD players. The cool thing about an MP3 CD is that rather than holding a mere 74 to 80 minutes of music, it can hold more than 100 songs! The uncool thing about MP3 CDs is that many older audio CD players won't play them.

- **A data CD or DVD** is nothing more than a disc formatted to be read and mounted by any computer, Mac or Windows.

If you click the Burn button now, you'll get an audio CD. To burn an MP3 CD or Data CD or DVD, select the appropriate radio button in the Burn Settings dialog.

When you're satisfied, click the Burn button. In a few minutes, you have an audio CD that contains all the songs on the playlist — and plays the songs in the order in which they appeared on the playlist (unless, of course, you elected to burn a data CD or DVD).

Looking at the Genius playlist

I'd like to draw your attention to one more relatively new playlist: the Genius.

Who is the Genius?

The Genius is actually more of a "what": an iTunes feature that lets you find new music — in your iTunes Library or the iTunes Store — that's related to a song of your choosing. Or, as the Genius splash screen you see when you turn the Genius on puts it: "Genius makes playlists and mixes from songs in your library that go great together. And the Genius selects music from the iTunes Store that you don't already have." To get started, choose Account ⇨ Turn On Genius, if you haven't done so already. When you finish reading, the Genius splash screen appears; click the Turn On Genius button in the bottom-right corner.

Turning Genius on sends information about your iTunes Library to Apple. There's a Learn More button on the What Is Genius screen if you want to (d'oh!) learn more about it.

To use Genius, you must (for some unknown reason) have an iTunes Store account, even though the information the Genius sends to Apple about your iTunes Library is stored anonymously. And even though no purchase is required, I think it's a dumb requirement — but that's the way it works, so take it or leave it.

Assuming you take it, sign in to your iTunes Store account if you have one (or create one if you don't). After agreeing to the Genius Terms of Service, the Genius gathers info about your iTunes Library, sends the info to Apple, and then (finally) delivers your results. When all this is done, you can create Genius playlists and peruse Genius suggestions.

How? Glad you asked! Click the . . . next to any song in your Library and choose either Create Genius Playlist or Genius Suggestions. After a bit of cogitation, iTunes presents you with a Genius playlist based on the song you clicked. A Genius Playlist and Genius Suggestions are shown in Figure 13-11.

If you're not a fan of The Beatles and British rock music, let me assure you that most of the songs in the Genius playlist pretty much do "go great together."

That being said, the tech editor of previous editions of this book, the late Dennis R. Cohen, said Genius was not so hot with classical music or comedy. And I've noticed that it works better with big names than lesser-known indie artists.

Genius icon

Genius playlist   ...   Genius suggestions

Figure 13-11: The Genius suggests songs that go nicely with the song the suggestions are based on.

Even so, it's free. So if you don't have issues with all the legal mumbo jumbo, the iTunes Store account, or sending information about your iTunes Library to Apple, give Genius a try.

One last thing: If you're new to iTunes, may I suggest exploring the excellent iTunes Tutorials, which you'll find in the Help menu along with other excellent Help resources.

14

The Multimedia Mac

edia content is more than just music (the topic of Chapter 13), and your Mac is ready, willing, and able to handle almost any type of media (with any type of content) you can throw at it. Which is why, in addition to the aforementioned iTunes, OS X El Capitan includes applications for viewing and working with media (such as DVD movie discs and QuickTime movie files) as well as graphics in a variety of file formats (including PDF, TIFF, and JPEG).

In this chapter, you look at some bundled applications you can use to work with such media — namely QuickTime Player, iBooks, Photo Booth, and Preview — followed by a brief section about importing your own media (photos and videos) into your Mac and the Image Capture app.

Playing Movies and Music in QuickTime Player

QuickTime is Apple's technology for digital media creation, delivery, and playback. It's used in a myriad of ways by programs such as Apple's iMovie, by websites such as YouTube (www. youtube.com), and in training videos delivered on CD or DVD.

QuickTime Player is the OS X application that lets you view QuickTime movies as well as streaming audio and video, QuickTime VR (Virtual Reality), and many types of audio files as well. The quickest way to launch it is by double-clicking its icon in the Applications folder. It is also the default application for most QuickTime movie document files.

I say most QuickTime movies because some will open QuickTime Player, and others will open iTunes. To change the app that opens for a particular movie, right-click or Control-click its icon in the Finder and choose the application you prefer from the Open With submenu. This opens the file with that program this one time only. To make the change permanent, press Option, and the Open With command becomes the Always Open With command.

To play a QuickTime movie, merely double-click its icon, and QuickTime Player (or iTunes) launches itself.

Using QuickTime Player couldn't be easier. All its important controls are available right in the player window, as shown in Figure 14-1.

Figure 14-1: QuickTime Player is simple to use.

Here are a few more QuickTime Player features you might find useful:

- **The Movie Inspector window** (Window⇨Show/Hide Movie Inspector or ⌘+I) provides a lot of useful information about the current movie, such as its location on your hard drive, file format, frames per second, file size, and duration.

- **The Trim control** (Edit⇨Trim or ⌘+T) lets you delete frames from the beginning and/or end of a movie.

- **The Share Menu** lets you send your movies to others via the Mail or Messages apps or via AirDrop, or upload them to YouTube, Vimeo, Flickr, or Facebook, and other similar sites.

See Chapter 17 for details about El Capitan's cool AirPlay Mirroring option, which lets you mirror what's on your Mac screen and view it on an HDTV wirelessly. The only thing you need is an Apple TV (from $69) connected to your HDTV.

One last thing: If you want to know about watching movies with the OS X DVD Player, it's covered in an online article at www.dummies.com/extras/elcapitan.

iBooks on the Mac

Don't be surprised if you have to answer this question from an inquisitive child someday: "Is it true, Grandpa, that people once read books on paper?"

 Don't get me wrong; I still love physical books as much as anyone and think they'll be around a lot longer than you or I. But I also recognize the real-world benefits that e-books have over paper ones including (but not limited to) the following:

- **Lose some weight.** You can cart around a whole bunch of e-books when you travel on your MacBook Air or MacBook Pro, iPad, or iPhone without breaking your back. To the avid bookworm, this potentially changes the whole dynamic in the way you read. Because you can carry so many books wherever you go, you can read whatever type of book strikes your fancy at the moment, kind of like listening to a song that fits your current mood. You have no obligation to read a book from start to finish before opening a new bestseller just because that happens to be the one book in your bag. In other words, weight constraints are out the window.

- **Feel like reading a trashy novel?** Go for it. Rather immerse yourself in classic literature? Go for that. You might read a textbook, cookbook, or biography. Or gaze in wonder at an illustrated beauty. What's more, you can switch among the various titles and styles of books at will before finishing any single title.

- **Enjoy flexible fonts and type sizes.** With e-books — or as Apple calls 'em, *iBooks* — you can change the text size and fonts on the fly, which is quite useful for people with less than 20/20 vision.

- **Get the meaning of a word on the spot.** No more searching for a physical dictionary. You can look up an unfamiliar word on the spot.

- **Search with ease.** Need to do research on a particular subject? Enter a search term to find each and every mention of the subject in the book you're reading.

- **Read in the dark.** Your Mac has a high-resolution backlit display so that you can read without a lamp nearby, which is useful in bed when your partner is trying to sleep.

✒ **See all the artwork in color.** Indeed, you're making no real visual sacri-
fices anymore, as unlike early releases of iBooks, this one lets you experience (within certain limits of your hardware) stunning artwork that
was once the exclusive province of big, expensive coffee table books.
(It's also awesome for reading colorful children's books and comics.)

Everything that follows will make more sense if you have at least one iBook
in your library. So the first thing to do is stock your virtual library with an
iBook from the app's built-in iBooks Store. Don't worry. This won't cost you a
penny unless you want it to — the store is chock-full of free books! (For more
on creating an Apple account, turn to Chapter 13.)

So without further ado, here's how to acquire some iBooks.

Buying iBooks

First things first. The iBooks app needs to be running, so launch it by one of
these routes:

✒ Single-clicking its Dock icon

✒ Double-clicking its icon in the Applications folder

✒ Single-clicking its icon in LaunchPad

If this is your first time launching iBooks, click the Get Started button. Next,
click the iBooks Store button in the upper-left corner of the iBooks window,
which is the Library button in Figure 14-2 (because I already clicked it).

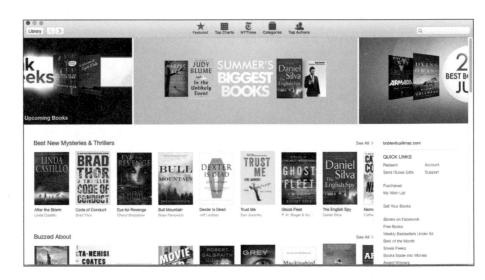

Figure 14-2: The iBooks Store's Featured tab.

If you think the iBooks Store looks suspiciously like the iTunes Store (see Chapter 13), you're right. Until Mavericks (OS X 10.9) was released, Mac users had to shop for iBooks in the iTunes Store using iTunes but couldn't read an iBook on their Mac with iTunes (or anything else for that matter).

If you have purchased iBooks with iTunes, they should automatically appear in your iBooks Library. If you don't see them in iBooks, choose File➪Move Books From iTunes, and in a minute or two you will (see them).

There are many ways to look for iBooks. At the top of the iBooks window are five tabs that represent different ways of browsing for iBooks. Click a tab — Featured, Top Charts, NY (New York) Times, Categories, or Top Authors — to browse its iBooks.

Of course, you can also search for a book or author; just type a word or two into the search field near the upper-right corner of the iBooks window and press Return.

When you see a book or ad that interests you, click it, and details will fill the screen, as shown in Figure 14-3 for the previous edition of this book,

Click the Buy Book button to buy a book or click the Get button to "buy" a free book.

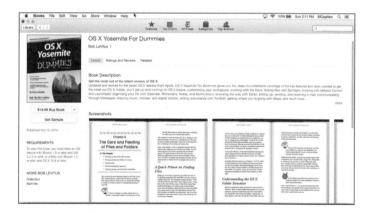

Figure 14-3: Buy books from the iBooks Store and add them to your iBooks Library.

Most books offer a free sample, or a chapter/chapters you can download for free. Click the Get Sample button, and a sample will appear in your iBooks Library within a few minutes.

One last thing: The little arrows to the right of the Library button are for-ward and Back buttons (⌘+[and ⌘+], respectively), which work just like the Forward and Back buttons in the Finder and Safari. Click the one on the left to return to the previous screen; click the one on the right to move to the next screen (just like the iTunes Store).

When you finish shopping, click the Library button in the upper-left corner of the iBooks window to return to your iBooks Library.

Shopping for books without Apple

iBooks can also handle books you acquire elsewhere, and it supports a technical standard called *ePub,* which is a format that offers hundreds of thousands of free and public domain books on the web. You can import such files into iBooks, so you don't really ever have to shop (or only shop) in the iBooks Store. The only possible gotcha is that the ePub titles must be *DRM-free,* which means free of any digital rights restrictions.

You can find ePub titles at numerous cyberspace destinations:

- **Feedbooks:** www.feedbooks.com
- **Google Play:** Not all the books here are free, and Google has a down-loadable app. http://play.google.com/store/books
- **Project Gutenberg:** www.gutenberg.us
- **Smashwords:** www.smashwords.com
- **Baen:** www.baen.com

To import an ePub title, download the file to your Mac, fire up iBooks, and then do one of the following:

- Choose File⇨Add to Library and then select the ePub file and click Add.
- Drag the ePub file onto your iBooks Library.

Before I move on to reading iBooks, I feel obliged to mention that between the free books in the iBooks Store and ePub books available from the sites in the preceding list and elsewhere, there are tons of great books out there that are free as well as tons more that are good, pretty good, or okay (and free). The point is that you can read a lot without spending a dime.

You can't add books made for the Amazon Kindle to iBooks, not even ones that are DRM-free. You have to download the free Kindle app from the Mac App Store to read them.

You can add PDF files to iBooks; it works the same as adding an ePub title. Once imported, they appear in the PDF section of your iBooks library.

Reading iBooks

To start reading a book, double-click it, and it leaps off the shelf. At the same time, it opens to either the beginning of the book or the place where you left off, even if you left off reading on another device — an iPhone, iPod touch, iPad, or another Mac. iBooks uses your Apple ID to save your virtual place in your virtual book and syncs it among your devices (as long as the devices have Internet access).

Figure 14-4 shows two pages of text from a typical iBook.

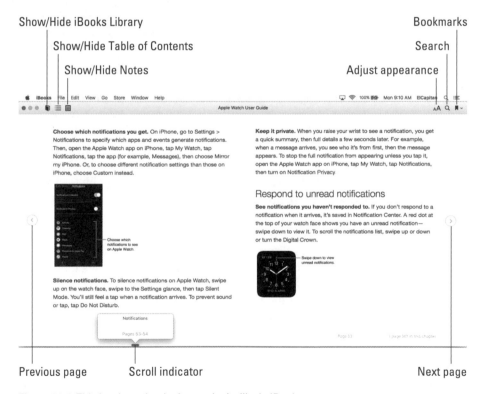

Figure 14-4: This is what a book chapter looks like in iBooks.

You have to move your cursor to the top of the window before the buttons will appear.

Now, here's how to actually read an iBook:

- **To go to the next page:** Click in the right margin or press the right arrow (→) key.

- **To go to the previous page:** Click in the left margin or press the left arrow (←) key.

- **To jump to a specific chapter:** Click the Table of Contents button.

- **To jump to a specific page:** Move the cursor to the bottom of the iBooks window to make the scroll bar appear; then drag the scroll indicator left or right to move forward or back in your book. The current page number appears in a balloon above the scroll bar, as shown at the bottom of Figure 14-4.

- **To make/delete a bookmark:** Although iBooks kindly returns you to the last page you were reading when you closed a book (on any device), you may want to bookmark a specific page so you can easily return to it. To do so, just click the Bookmarks button near the upper-right corner of the iBooks window. A red ribbon appears, signifying that a bookmark is in place. Click the red ribbon to remove the bookmark.

- **To return to a bookmark:** After setting a bookmark, you can return to it later by clicking the little chevron next to the Bookmarks button and selecting the desired bookmark from the drop-down menu.

- **To make the text bigger or smaller:** Click the Adjust Appearance button near the upper-right corner of the screen, and then click the uppercase *A* to make the type larger or the lowercase *a* to make it smaller.

- **To change the font typeface:** Click the Adjust Appearance button and select the font style you want to switch to.

  Your choices at this time are Original (the default), Athelas, Charter, Georgia, Iowan, Palatino, San Francisco, Seravek, and Times New Roman. I don't necessarily expect you to know what these look like just by the font names. Fortunately, you get to examine the change right before your eyes. A check mark indicates the currently selected font style.

- **To change the page color:** Click White (the default; shown in Figure 14-4), Sepia, or Night.

- **To have the book read to you aloud:** Use your Mac's VoiceOver feature. It may not be quite like having Mom or Dad read you to sleep, but it can be a potential godsend for people with impaired vision. To listen instead of reading,

  - *Click at the spot you want to begin from or select the text you want to hear.*

  - *Choose Edit ⇨ Speech ⇨ Start Speaking.*

    In a few seconds, a robotic voice will begin reading you the story.

  - *To stop, simply choose Edit ⇨ Speech ⇨ Stop Speaking.*

You're the Star with Photo Booth

 The Photo Booth application provides all the fun of an old-time (or new-time) photo booth like the ones you sometimes see in malls or stores. It lets you shoot one photo, shoot a burst of four photos in a row, or shoot a movie using your Mac's built-in camera. If yours is one of the rare Macs with no built-in camera (such as the Mac mini) or you own a USB or FireWire webcam better than the built-in model, you'll be pleased to hear that most USB and FireWire webcams work with Photo Booth right out of the box with no drivers or other software necessary. Just launch Photo Booth and look in the Camera menu, where all compatible cameras appear.

 If you have only one camera available — mine is called FaceTime HD Camera (Built-in) — it's selected automatically, so you shouldn't have to even bother with the Camera menu.

Photo Booth couldn't be easier to use. Start by clicking one of the three buttons in the lower-left corner of the Photo Booth window — Burst (of four photos), Single Photo (selected in Figure 14-5), or Movie — and then click the big, red camera button to take a picture, as shown in Figure 14-5.

Figure 14-5: Photo Booth about to take a picture of yours truly.

Before you shoot, you may want to explore the five pages of special effects — Sepia Tone, Color Pencil, Pop Art, and dozens more — by clicking the Effects button (lower right) and then clicking the particular effect you want to try. If you like it, click the big, red camera button and shoot a picture, pictures, or video; if you don't, click the Effects button again and click another effect. Or, if you prefer to shoot with no effects, click the Normal effect in the center of all the Effects pages.

Photo Booth includes a feature called Screen Flash, which uses your computer display as a camera flash by turning the screen all-white as it shoots the photo. If *your* screen isn't flashing when you shoot, look in the Camera menu for the Enable Screen Flash command. If there's not a check mark before its name, select Enable Screen Flash, and there will be. Finally, Screen Flash is (understandably) disabled when you're shooting movies.

After you shoot, your pictures or movies drop into the tray at the bottom of the window (there's one in Figure 14-5). You can then select one or more photos in the tray and then do any of the following:

- **Delete them** by pressing the Delete or Backspace key.

- **Share them** by clicking the Share button, which replaces the Effects button when one or more photos are selected in the tray.

- **Export them as JPEG files** by choosing File⇨Export.

- **Print them** by choosing File⇨Print or pressing ⌘+P.

- **Drag them from the tray** to the Desktop, a folder, an email, or iMessage, where they appear as JPEG files; or drag them onto the icon (Dock or Applications folder) of an image editor, such as Photos.

So that's the scoop on Photo Booth. It's fun and easy, and if you have a camera (as most of you do), you should definitely launch Photo Booth and give it a try.

If you have kids who are old enough to trust with a Mac, Photo Booth and its effects will entertain them for hours (or, more likely, for a few minutes). It's guaranteed to entertain and delight kids of all ages the first time they play with it.

Viewing and Converting Images and PDFs in Preview

You use Preview to open, view, and print PDFs as well as most graphics files (TIFF, JPEG, PICT, and so on). *PDF files* are formatted documents that can include text and images. User manuals, books, and the like are often distributed as PDF files. You can't edit the existing text in a PDF file with Preview, but you can leaf through its pages, annotate and mark it up, and print it. You can often select text and graphics in a PDF file, copy them to the Clipboard (⌘+C), and paste (⌘+V) them into documents in other applications. It's also the application that pops open when you click the Preview button in the Print dialog, as I describe in Chapter 16.

Actually, that's not entirely true. You can edit one certain type of PDF file: a form that has blank fields. Preview allows you to fill in the blanks and then resave the document. And although it's technically not editing, you can annotate a PDF document by using the Annotate tools on the toolbar.

One of the most useful things Preview can do is change a graphic file in one file format into one with a different file format. For example, say you're signing up for a website and want to add a picture to your profile. The website requires pictures in the JPEG file format, but the picture file on your hard drive that you'd like to use is in the TIFF file format. Preview can handle the conversion for you:

1. **Open the TIFF file with Preview by double-clicking the file.**

   If another program (such as Adobe Photoshop) opens instead of Preview, drag the TIFF document onto the Preview icon or launch Preview and choose File⇨Open (⌘+O) to open the TIFF file.

2. **Choose File⇨Export.**

3. **Choose the appropriate file format — such as JPEG — from the Format pop-up menu, as shown in Figure 14-6.**

Figure 14-6: Preview makes it easy to convert a TIFF graphic file into a JPEG graphic file.

4. **(Optional) If you want to make sure you don't confuse your original image with the one in the new format, change the name of your file in the Export As field, too.**

5. **(Optional) Add a tag or tags if you like.**

6. **Click Save.**

As you can see in Figure 14-6, Preview lets you convert any file it can open to any of the following file formats: JPEG, JPEG-2000, OpenEXR, PDF, PNG, and TIFF.

Chances are good that you'll never need to convert a file to most of these formats, but it's nice to know that you can if you need to.

Almost every OS X program with a Print command allows you to save your document as a PDF file. Just click and hold down the PDF button (found in all Print dialogs) and choose Save As PDF. Then, should you ever need to convert that PDF file to a different file format, you can do so by using the preceding steps.

Importing Media

Chances are good that you'll want to import pictures or video from your digital camera or DV camcorder someday. It's a piece of cake. So in the following sections, I show you how easy it is to get your digital photos into your Mac and help you get started with digital video (which is a bit more complex).

In the sections that follow, I focus on applications that are a part of OS X.

Downloading photos from a camera

This is the Mac I'm talking about, so of course, getting pictures from your digital camera onto your hard drive is a pretty simple task. Here's how to do it step by step using Image Capture:

1. **Turn on your digital camera, and set it to review or playback mode.**

   This step may not be necessary for some cameras. It was for my old Olympus, but isn't for my Nikon Coolpix P1.

2. **Connect the camera to your Mac with its USB cable or insert its SD card into a USB or the built-in SD card reader on some Mac models.**

   At this point, Image Capture may launch automatically. If you have iPhoto or Photos, it may launch instead.

If the wrong one opens when you connect your camera, you can change that behavior in Image Capture's Device Settings pane. How do you know which is the right one? Well, Image Capture does only one thing — import photos from an external device to a folder on your Mac. The Photos app is a full-service photography studio in a single app. It not only imports photos to its own library but also offers myriad features for managing, organizing, and editing your images. For simplicity's sake, I use Image Capture in this example; the process is similar for Photos.

Launch Image Capture (in your Applications folder) if it didn't launch when you connected your camera. Now choose the application you prefer for photo management from the Connecting This Camera Opens pop-up menu. (It says Image Capture in Figure 14-7; other options could include iPhoto, Aperture, Photoshop, Photoshop Elements, Adobe Bridge, or whatever photo-management app you happen to have installed on your hard disk.)

If your camera isn't selected in the Devices section of the sidebar, select it now.

Eject disk

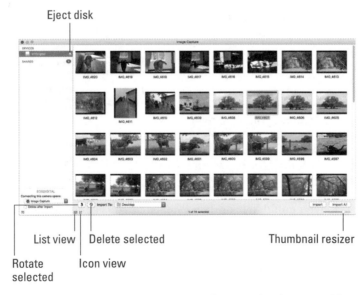

List view | Delete selected   Thumbnail resizer

Rotate   Icon view
selected

Figure 14-7: I told my Mac to open Image Capture when I connect this camera.

3. **From the Image Capture window, you can either click Import All to download all the photos in your camera or click Import to import only the selected photos.**

   • *To choose contiguous photos,* click the first photo you want to download, press Shift, and then click the last photo you want to download.

   • *To choose noncontiguous photos,* press ⌘ and click each photo you want to download. Either way, the names of selected files are highlighted to indicate which photos will be downloaded when you click the Import button (such as the first, third, fourth, and sixth photos in Figure 14-7).

In Figure 14-7, the Import To pop-up menu is set to the Desktop folder (the default is your Pictures folder). If you were to click the Import or Import All button now, Image Capture would download the photos in your camera to your Desktop.

If you want to delete selected photos from your camera after they're downloaded to your hard drive, select the photos you want to delete, and click the Delete Selected button (a red circle with a slash through it). To delete all photos after you import them, select the Delete After Import check box.

If a disk icon (EOS_DIGITAL in Figure 14-7, but frequently named NO NAME) appears in the Devices section of the Sidebar when you plug in your camera, you have to eject that disk by clicking the Eject Disk icon next to its name in the Image Capture window (or by ejecting it in the Finder in the usual way) before you disconnect your camera; oth-

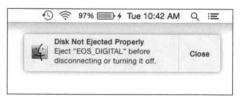

Figure 14-8: This warning means you forgot to eject your camera's disk.

erwise, you could lose or damage files in your camera. So try to remember. If you don't, Image Capture scolds you with the scary warning notification shown in Figure 14-8.

When you connect a camera or an iDevice to your Mac, it appears in the Devices section of Image Capture, just like a camera or camcorder. Which makes total sense if you think about it, since they are (among other things) cameras and camcorders.

And before we leave Image Capture, I'd be remiss not to mention that you can use it also to control many third-party scanners and multifunction printer scanners. If they're available in the Printers & Scanners System Preferences pane and you've enabled Printer Sharing in the Sharing System Preferences pane, they'll appear in the Shared section of Image Capture's sidebar.

If you want a different app (or no app at all) to launch when you connect this camera or iDevice to your Mac, check out the tip in Step 2.

Downloading DV video from a camcorder

Getting video from a DV camcorder to your hard drive is almost as easy as importing photos from your digital camera. It's beyond the scope of this book to explain how to download video, considering the myriad of video-recording devices available, but here are a few general tips to get you started.

iMovie works well for downloading video from miniDV and HD camcorders that include output via FireWire or USB2 or USB3.

If you do plan to use iMovie, don't forget about the built-in Help system (⌘+Shift+/). Here, you find extensive assistance, as shown in Figure 14-9, which is the main Help page for iMovie.

Never insert a mini-DVD into a slot-loading optical drive like the ones in many Macs shipped before 2013. If your camcorder records on mini-DVDs, you'll need to spring for a tray-loading external optical drive.

One last thing: Some video cameras may require you to install driver software before your Mac can "see" them. Check your camera's manual for details.

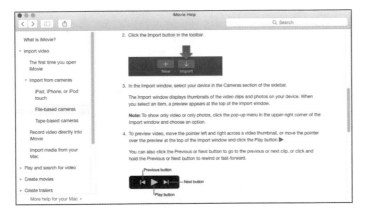

Figure 14-9: Don't forget that help is just a click (or a keystroke) away.

Living the iLife

In previous editions of this book, I called iLife "one of the fantastic bargains in software" and said, "If you had to buy all these programs from other vendors (or for a Windows PC), you'd pay a whole lot more." And that was when the only way to get iLife was on a DVD for $79.

iMovie, Photos, and GarageBand are bundled with every Mac sold these days, but that only started in 2013, so if you don't have copies in your Applications folder and you want them, visit the Mac App Store and buy iMovie or GarageBand *à la carte* for $14.99 each. (The Photos app is included in every OS X El Capitan installation.)

As for iWeb and iDVD, they're no longer supported. Even if you find the suite on a DVD, there's no guarantee that they will still work properly, so caveat emptor.

Finally, don't forget that iPhoto and Aperture were discontinued in 2015 and replaced by the (free) Photos app bundled with El Capitan.

15

Words and Letters

In This Chapter

▶ Processing words with TextEdit
▶ Finding out all about OS X fonts
▶ Managing fonts with Font Book

A s I discuss in previous chapters, your Mac is well equipped for creating and managing media — music, movies, and photos — but your Mac is also ready to handle more common tasks, such as typing a letter or writing an essay.

I think it's fair to say that the TextEdit application is all that many users will ever need for writing letters or essays.

If you need more control over your pages, try Pages from Apple, which is a free Mac App Store download for Macs sold since late 2013, or it is available in the Mac App Store for $19.99.

Furthermore, OS X comes with a wide variety of fonts (sometimes called *typefaces*) plus a handy little app called Font Book for managing those fonts. Fonts allow you to change how text looks on the screen and the printed page.

In this chapter, you look at the OS X text composition and editing program — TextEdit — and then explore fonts and how to manage them.

Processing Words with TextEdit

TextEdit is a word processor and text editor that you can use to write letters, scribble notes, or open Read Me files. It's not as sophisticated as Microsoft Word (or Apple's Pages for that matter), but you can definitely use it for light word processing and text editing. TextEdit is capable of performing a respectable amount of text formatting, and it can even check your spelling and read text to you in a natural-sounding (if somewhat creepy) voice.

TextEdit supports images, too. Just copy an image from another program and paste it into a TextEdit document. Or just drag and drop an image into a TextEdit document from many applications or the Finder.

TextEdit can even open Microsoft Word documents (.doc and .docx files), which is fabulous if you don't happen to have a copy of Microsoft Word on your hard drive. It can also open .rtf, .odt, .htm and .html, and .txt files, should you need to view a document saved in any of these popular file formats.

Like all apps included with El Capitan, you find TextEdit in the Applications folder at root level on your hard disk.

The Dock doesn't have a TextEdit icon preinstalled, but if you like it, use it regularly, or would just like to have it on your Dock, either drag its icon from the Applications folder to anyplace on the left side of the Dock or launch it, right- or Control-click its Dock icon, and then choose Options ➪ Keep in Dock.

Creating and composing a document

You'll get the most from the rest of this chapter if you have TextEdit open. So . . . if it's not already open, open TextEdit now.

When you launch TextEdit, it presents an Open File dialog (see Chapter 6). So, if you're following along at home, you should now have an Open File dialog on your screen. Click the New Document button in the lower-left corner, and an Untitled document appears. Let its default (and ambiguous) name — *Untitled* — be a message to you that before you begin working on this document you should probably give it a name and save it to your hard drive or iCloud Drive. To do so now, choose File ➪ Save or press ⌘+S. (If you're new to Mac OS X Save sheets, flip to Chapter 6 for details.)

As you work with the document, it's a good idea to save it every few minutes, just in case. After you name a file, all you need to do to save its current state is choose File ➪ Save or press ⌘+S.

TextEdit uses the new-style version support and auto-save features, so your work is saved automatically on the fly. However, don't be lulled into a false sense of security; many third-party apps that come from sources other than the Mac App Store don't support this feature. (Chapter 6 has the lowdown on versions and saving.)

It's a good idea to choose File⇨Save or use its shortcut, ⌘+S, every so often regardless of whether the app supports versions and auto-save. Better safe than sorry.

Now begin typing your text. When you type text in a word processor, you should know a few handy things:

- ✓ **Press the Return key only when you want to start a new paragraph.** You don't need to press Return at the end of a line of text; the program automatically wraps your text to the next line, keeping things neat and tidy.

- ✓ **Type a single space after the punctuation mark at the end of a sentence, regardless of what your typing teacher might have told you.** Word processors and typewriters aren't the same. With a typewriter, you want two spaces at the end of a sentence; with a word processor, you don't. (Typewriters use *fixed-width* fonts; computers mostly use fonts with variable widths. If you put two spaces at the end of a sentence in a computer-generated document, the gap looks too wide.) Trust me on this one.

- ✓ **Limit most documents to a maximum of two different fonts.** OS X offers you a wide selection of fonts, but that doesn't mean you have to use them all in one document.

To put special characters in your TextEdit document, choose Edit⇨Emoji & Symbols (⌘+Control+Spacebar). This command opens the Character palette, from which you can choose characters such as mathematical symbols, arrows, ornaments, stars, accented Latin characters, Emoji (such as smiley faces), and so on. To insert a character, make sure your cursor is in the document where you want (the insertion point), and then click the character in the palette.

Working with text

TextEdit operates on the "select, then operate" principle, as do most Mac programs, including the Finder. Before you can affect (style, or format) text in your document — that is, change font face, style, size, margins, and so on — you need to select the text you want formatted.

You can use several methods to select text in a document:

- ✓ **Select a word.** Double-click the word.

- ✓ **Select a paragraph.** Triple-click a word in that paragraph.

- ✓ **Select a chunk.** Click anywhere in the document, hold down the Shift key, and then click again somewhere else in the document. Everything between the two clicks will be selected.

✔ **Extend the selection.** Click anywhere in the document, hold down the Shift key, and use the keyboard arrow keys to extend the selection. You can also click, hold the mouse button down, and drag to select text; release the mouse button when done selecting.

✔ **Select all text in the document.** Choose Edit ➪ Select All or use the shortcut ⌘+A.

Figure 15-1 shows some selected text. You can tell that it's selected because it is highlighted.

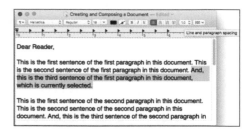

Give all these methods of selecting text a try, decide which ones feel most comfortable, and then memorize them for future use.

Rather than bore you with a rundown of what the buttons on the

Figure 15-1: This sentence is selected.

TextEdit toolbar do, just hover the cursor over any item to display its tooltip, as I've done for the Line and Paragraph Spacing drop-down menu in Figure 15-1.

After your text is selected, you can format it. For example, you can use the Format menu's Font submenu to choose Bold, Italic, Outline, or Underline (among others), as shown in Figure 15-2. I opted for bold in Figure 15-2, and you can see in the figure how the selected sentence is now bold.

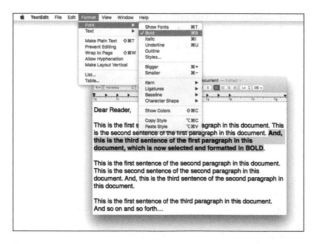

Figure 15-2: Only the selected text is affected by these formatting commands.

Another way to apply the Bold style to the text in Figure 15-2 is by clicking the B (for Bold) button on the toolbar. Note that the toolbar and ruler won't be visible if you're working on a plain text (.txt) document, or choose Format ➪ Make Plain Text (⌘+Shift+T) while working on any document, and the toolbar and ruler disappear.

The same idea applies to tabs and margins. In Figure 15-3, I dragged the left and right margin markers in one inch. Notice that the selected text is now indented by one inch from the left and right margins.

Select some text in your document, and try all the items in the Format menu's Font and Text submenus. As you see, you have a great deal of control over the way your words appear on the screen. And because TextEdit, like most Macintosh software, is WYSIWYG (What You See Is What You Get), when you print the document (by choosing File ➪ Print), the printed version should look exactly like the version you see on the screen. For help with printing, see Chapter 16.

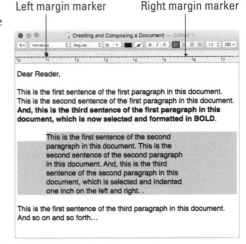

Figure 15-3: The selected paragraph is now indented.

The View menu is your friend. Choose View ➪ Actual Size or use its shortcut (⌘+0) to see your document just as it will print. Use the View menu Zoom In and Zoom Out commands or their shortcuts — ⌘+Shift+. (period) and ⌘+Shift+, (comma) — to make everything larger or smaller.

Before you print your masterpiece, however, you may want to check your spelling and grammar — something that TextEdit makes extremely simple. Merely choose Edit ➪ Spelling and Grammar ➪ Check Document Now or press ⌘+; (semicolon). TextEdit highlights and underlines what it perceives to be mistakes in your document. Right-click (or Control-click) to bring up a menu with correction choices, as shown in Figure 15-4.

Don't put too much faith in the El Capitan spelling and grammar checker. It's good, but not perfect and no substitute for a good proofreading.

Figure 15-4: Right- or Control-click to correct a spelling or grammar error.

Adding graphics to documents

Last but not least, you have a couple of ways to add pictures to a TextEdit document. The first works as follows:

1. **Copy an image in another program — Preview, Safari, or whatever.**

2. **Put the pointer where you want the picture to appear in your TextEdit document.**

3. **Choose Edit⇨Paste.**

   The image magically appears on the page.

Or you can drag an image from the Finder (or another application such as Safari or Mail) to a TextEdit document, as I did in Figure 15-5.

Note that you can't wrap text around images in TextEdit. So if you drag an image to the middle of a sentence by accident, you'll have text before and after the image but a huge gap on either side. To fix it, click and drag the image between paragraphs. (You may find it necessary to add an extra Return between paragraphs to get the image where you want it.)

Drag file to here
(the TextEdit
document window)

Drag file from here
(the Desktop, a folder,
or another application)

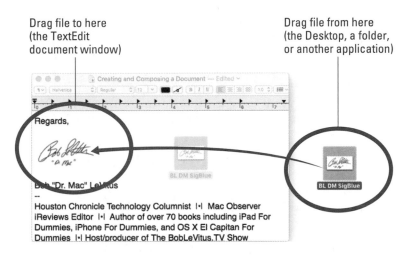

Figure 15-5: Drag an image into a TextEdit document.

Font Mania

You can jazz up your documents — or make them a little more serious — with different fonts. To a computer user, *font* means *typeface* — what the text characters look like. Although professional typographers will scream at my generalization, I'll go with that definition for now.

Tens of thousands of different fonts are available for the Macintosh. You don't want to use the same font for both a garage-sale flyer and a résumé, right? Luckily for you, OS X comes with hundreds of fonts. Some are pretty predictable, such as Times New Roman, but OS X gives you some artsy ones, too, such as Brush Script.

If you *really* get into fonts, you can buy single fonts and font collections anywhere you can buy software. Plenty of shareware and public domain fonts are also available from online services and user groups. Some people have thousands of fonts. (Maybe they need to get out more.) To see how to manage extra fonts you collect, check out the upcoming section, "Managing your fonts with Font Book."

The preinstalled fonts live in two different folders, both called Fonts. One is in the Library folder at root level on your hard drive; the other is in the Library subfolder within the System folder.

OS X actually has four Font folders. A third one, also called Fonts, is in the (hidden) Library folder in your Home directory. The upcoming section explains the subtle distinctions among those three locations.

The fourth one is in the Network/Library folder, and you see it only when you're connected to a NetBoot network server.

Types of fonts

You can find many font formats with names like OpenType, Mac TrueType, Windows TrueType, PostScript Type 1, bitmap, and dfont. No problem — OS X supports them all.

The only font format I know that OS X *doesn't* support is PostScript Type 3.

All you really need to know is that pretty much any font you buy or download will probably work with El Capitan.

Managing your fonts with Font Book

Font Book lets you view your installed fonts, install new fonts, group your fonts into collections, and enable and disable installed fonts. As usual, you find the Font Book application in the Applications folder at root level on your hard disk.

The easiest way to install a new font is to double-click it in the Finder. Font Book opens and displays the font. Click the Install Font button to install the font.

Other ways you can install new fonts are to choose File ➪ Add Fonts or press ⌘+O. A standard Open dialog allows you to select a font or fonts to be installed.

Note that, by default, new fonts are installed in your Home folder's Fonts folder, which is inside your invisible Library folder (Users/Home/Library/Fonts). You can change the default installation location in Font Book's Preferences (Font Book ➪ Preferences or ⌘+, [comma]).

To view a font or font family, click its name in the Font list. Click the disclosure triangle before the name of a font to see all the variants that are installed.

To change the size of the viewed font, click the triangle next to the font size (40, in Figure 15-6) in the top-right corner of the Font Book window and choose a new size from the drop-down list that appears, or type a different number where the number 40 appears in Figure 15-6, or move the size slider — the white dot with a blue line below it near the right edge of the window — up or down.

To disable a font so it no longer appears on any applications' Font menus, choose Edit ➪ Disable or click the Disable button (the check mark in a square on the toolbar).

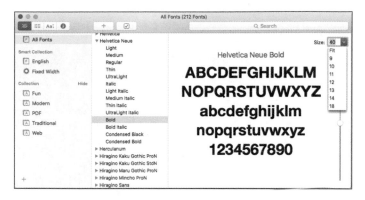

Figure 15-6: Click a font in the Font list to display its characters in the right pane.

To enable a previously disabled font, choose Edit ⇨ Enable or click the Enable button (same as the Disable button).

Font Book looks out for your best interests; it won't allow you to disable or delete any fonts required by El Capitan — including (but not limited to) Lucida Grande, Helvetica, and Helvetica Neue.

Installing fonts manually

To install a new font manually, drag its icon into one of the two Fonts folders that you have access to. Why might you want to install them manually? If you install a font via the double-click-and-use-Font Book method, the font will be installed in your Home/Library/Fonts folder, and available only to you.

If you want other users to be able to access the new font, drag the font's icon to the Fonts subfolder inside the Library folder, which is at the root level of your hard drive. This Fonts folder offers universal access. Or, if you usually want to install fonts for everyone, change the Default Install Location in Font Book Preferences (Font Book ⇨ Preferences or ⌘+, [comma]).

The Fonts folder in the Library inside the System folder is reserved for OS X and can't be modified easily. If you try to remove a font from it — or add one, for that matter — you first have to authenticate yourself as an administrator. Do yourself a favor and never remove fonts from /System/Library/Fonts. You can really screw up your El Capitan operating system if you remove the wrong font, so don't go messing with the fonts in folders unless you know what you're doing. Your best bet is to always use Font Book, which prevents you from doing anything bad to fonts.

16

Publish or Perish: The Fail-Safe Guide to Printing

In This Chapter

▶ Connecting a printer

▶ Using Page Setup to prepare your document for printing

▶ Printing to most printers

▶ Mastering the printing process

*W*hen you want to get what's on your screen onto paper, printing under OS X should be as simple as pressing the keyboard shortcut ⌘+P and pressing Return. Happily, that's usually just how easy printing something is. Unfortunately, when it isn't just that easy, printing can turn into a raging nightmare. If you configure your printer and printing software properly, however, printing is generally a simple affair forever more.

In this chapter, I scare away the bogeymen to help you avoid any printing nightmares. I walk you through the entire process as though you just unpacked a new printer and plugged it in.

Before Diving In . . .

Before I even start talking about hooking up printers, you need to know a few essential things. So here's a little list that tells you just what those things are:

✒ **Read the documentation that came with your printer.**
Hundreds of different printer makes and models are available for the Mac, so if I contradict something in your printer manual, follow your manual's instructions first. If that effort doesn't work, try the techniques in this chapter.

✔ **The Print and Page Setup sheets differ slightly (or even greatly) from program to program and from printer to printer.** Although the examples I show you in this chapter are representative of what you'll *probably* encounter, you might come across sheets that look a bit different. For example, the Print and Page Setup sheets for Microsoft Word include choices that I don't cover in this chapter (such as Even or Odd Pages Only, Print Hidden Text, and Print Selection Only). If you see commands in your Print or Page Setup sheet that I don't explain here, they're specific to that application; look within its documentation for an explanation. Similarly, many graphics-related apps — such as Adobe Illustrator and Photoshop — have added their own Print dialog, which appears before the El Capitan print sheet with list boxes, radio buttons, and other controls, to the point where you might not even recognize them as Print dialogs.

✔ **Don't forget about the Help.** Of course, it's built into El Capitan and better than ever, but many third-party programs support this excellent Apple technology, which can be the fastest way to figure out a feature that has you stumped. So don't forget to check out the Help menu before you panic. (I cover the Help menu in Chapter 1.)

Ready: Connecting and Adding Your Printer

Before you can even think about printing something, you have to connect a printer to your Mac and tell OS X that the printer exists.

If you have a printer and are able to print documents already, you can skip ahead to the "Set: Setting Up Your Document with Page Setup" section. The info between here and there pertains only to setting up a *brand-new* printer — one that still has its manual.

Connecting your printer

Once again, I must remind you that you *could* connect your Mac to thousands of printer models, and each one is a little different from the next. In other words, if what you're about to read doesn't work with the printer you're trying to connect, RTFM (Read the Fine Manual). It should tell you how to load your ink or toner cartridges, and anything else you might need to know to set up your printer successfully.

That said, here are some very general steps to connect a printer to your Mac:

1. **Connect the printer to your Mac with the cable snugly attached at both ends (printer and Mac).**

   For your printer to work, you have to somehow connect it to a data source. (Think of your phone — you can't receive calls without some sort of connector between callers.)

Ignore this step if your printer supports wireless printing and you intend to only print wirelessly.

2. **Plug the printer's AC power cord into a power outlet.**

   Yup, I mean the regular kind of outlet in the wall; on a power strip; or, best of all, on a UPS (uninterruptible power supply). Some printers require you to plug one end of the AC power cord into the printer; others have the AC power cord attached permanently. The point is that your printer won't work if it's not connected to a power source.

3. **Turn on your printer.**

   Look in the manual if you can't find the power switch.

Setting up a printer for the first time

After you connect your computer and printer, provide a power source for your printer, and install the software for your printer, you're ready . . . to configure your Mac. You have to do that so your Mac and your printer can talk to each other.

Many, if not all, of the steps involving the Printers & Scanners System Preferences pane require that your printer be turned on and warmed up (that is, already run through its diagnostics and startup cycle) beforehand. So before doing anything else, make sure your printer is turned on, warmed up, and connected to your Mac.

The first time you connect your printer, you may see an alert asking whether you want to download and install software for your printer. The new printer I'm setting up is an HP Officejet Pro 8620, as shown in Figure 16-1.

You do, so click the Install button. At this point, you may see a License Agreement window. If so, click the Agree button to proceed. (You may click Disagree if you wish, but that halts the installation process.)

After clicking the Install and Agree buttons, a Software Update window may appear and tell you it's finding software. If it does, just leave it alone; it disappears after a minute or two. Don't click the Stop button unless you want to abort the installation.

If you connect a new printer and *don't* see an alert like the one shown in Figure 16-1, it's not an issue; just follow the upcoming instructions.

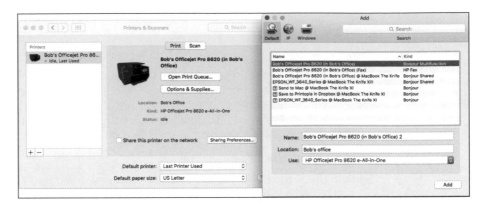

Figure 16-1: The printer that El Capitan recognizes — Bob's Officejet Pro 8620 (in Bob's Office) — is on the left side of the System Preferences window.

Here are the steps to set up a printer for the first time:

1. **Launch System Preferences, click the Printers & Scanners icon, and then click your printer's name in the Printers list on the left side of the window.**

   You can open System Preferences from the menu, or launch it from the Applications folder, Dock, or Launchpad.

   El Capitan is a pretty smart cat; it should have already recognized your printer at this point. If so, your printer's name appears in the Printers list of the Printers & Scanners System Preferences pane, as shown on the left in Figure 16-1.

   The reason it's named Bob's Officejet Pro is that I set up this printer for my other Macs previously. Had it been fresh out of the box, it would have borne a generic name such as Officejet Pro 8620 and not Bob's Officejet Pro 8620 (in Bob's Office), which is what I named it when I set it up initially.

   • *If your printer isn't in the list at this point:* Click the + button at the bottom of the Printers list, and then select it from the list in the Add dialog that appears (the right image in Figure 16-1), and then click the Add button.

   If you see a dialog that says something about installing developer tools, click Not Now unless you're a developer who uses Xcode.

- *If you still can't see your printer in the Add dialog:* You probably need to install (or reinstall) its driver software manually, either from the CD or DVD that came with the printer or by downloading the latest driver software from your printer manufacturer's website. See the nearby sidebar "Go for a driver" for more on drivers.

    You can't proceed until the Printers & Scanners System Preferences pane recognizes your printer. So install that driver if necessary and then proceed onward.

2. **Choose the printer you want selected by default when you print documents from the Default Printer pop-up menu (Last Printer Used is selected in Figure 16-1).**

3. **Select the default paper size you want to use with this printer from the Default Paper Size menu (usually US Letter, if you live in the United States).**

    That's all there is to it. Close System Preferences, and you're ready to print your first document! Before you do, however, make sure you have the document set up to look just the way you want it to look printed. Read through "Set: Setting Up Your Document with Page Setup" later in this chapter for more info.

One last thing: Printer sharing

If you want to share a printer that's connected directly to your Mac (with others on your local area wired or wireless network), select it in the Printers list on the left side of the Printers & Scanners System Preferences pane, and then select the Share This Printer on the Network check box.

Go for a driver

Many printer manufacturers periodically introduce new drivers with enhanced functionality. So, the driver software on the CD in the box with your printer is probably out of date when you buy that printer. Check whether the CD contains the latest version of the printer driver on the manufacturer's website, and download a more recent version of the driver if necessary.

Apple includes a library of printer drivers with El Capitan, which covers most popular printer brands and models. These drivers are installed by default. El Capitan also checks to see whether a newer driver is available — for every driver in its library — and if it finds one, offers to download and install the new driver (refer to Figure 16-1).

If OS X El Capitan can't find a driver for your printer, you need to manually install the appropriate printer drivers before your printer will appear in the Printers & Scanners System Preferences pane's Printers list. So download the driver from the manufacturer's website, install it, and get ready to print.

To fine-tune your shared printer, click the Sharing Preferences button on the right, and the Sharing System Preferences pane (which I discuss in much detail in Chapter 12) replaces the Printers & Scanners pane. Make sure the check box next to Printer Sharing is enabled.

By default, printer sharing is available to everyone. If you want to limit it to specific users, click the + button beneath the Users section of the Sharing System Preferences pane and add them by user name.

Set: Setting Up Your Document with Page Setup

After you set up your printer, the hard part is over. You should be able to print a document quickly and easily — right? Not so fast, bucko. Read here how the features in the Page Setup sheet can help you solve most basic printing problems.

Many programs have a Page Setup command on their File menu. Note that some programs use the name *Page Setup,* and others use *Print Setup.* (Print Setup is the quaint, old term, more popular in the 1980s' System 6 era and in today's Windows than on today's Macs.) Either way, this is the sheet where you can choose your target printer, paper size, page orientation, and scale (as shown in Figure 16-2).

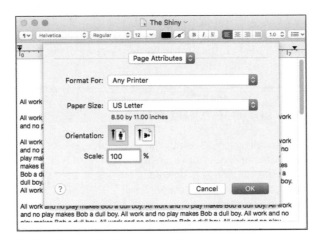

Figure 16-2: The Page Setup sheet in the TextEdit application.

Become familiar with Page Setup. You might not need to use it right this second, but it's a good friend to know. Even though some apps offer some of these Page Setup settings in their Print sheets, Page Setup is the only place you find these options in many programs.

Users of network printers might see slightly different versions of the Print and Page Setup sheets. The differences should be minor enough not to matter.

Click the little question mark in the bottom-left corner of the Page Setup or Print sheets at any time for additional help. If you do, Page Setup or Printing help opens immediately in the Help Center. (Okay, maybe not *immediately,* but Help Center in El Capitan is faster than the Help Viewer in, say OS X Mountain Lion or Mavericks.)

The options within the Page Setup sheet are as follows:

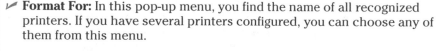

- **Format For:** In this pop-up menu, you find the name of all recognized printers. If you have several printers configured, you can choose any of them from this menu.

  This menu usually defaults to Any Printer, which is the least-effective setting. Unless the printer you want to use appears here, you may not get full functionality when you print.

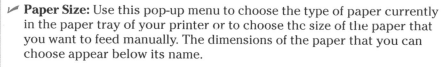

- **Paper Size:** Use this pop-up menu to choose the type of paper currently in the paper tray of your printer or to choose the size of the paper that you want to feed manually. The dimensions of the paper that you can choose appear below its name.

  Page Setup sheet settings (including Paper Size) remain in effect until you change them. For example, when you print an envelope, don't forget to change back to Letter before trying to print on letter-size paper again.

- **Orientation:** Choose among options here to tell your printer whether the page you want to print should be *portrait-oriented* (like a letter, longer than it is wide) or *landscape-oriented* (sideways, wider than it is long).

- **Scale:** To print your page at a larger or smaller size, change this option to a larger or smaller percentage.

Some programs offer additional Page Setup choices. If your program offers them, they usually appear in the Settings pop-up menu in the Page Setup sheet. (Adobe Photoshop and Microsoft Word have them; TextEdit doesn't.)

Print: Printing with the Print Sheet

After you connect and configure your printer and set up how you want your document to print, you come to the final steps before that joyous moment when your printed page pops out of the printer. Navigating the Print sheet is the last thing standing between you and your output.

Although most Print sheets that you see look like the figures I show here, others may differ slightly (or, occasionally, greatly). The features in the Print sheet are a function of the program with which you're printing. Many programs choose to use the standard-issue Apple sheet, but not all do. If I don't explain a certain feature in this chapter, chances are good that the feature is specific to the application or printer you're using (in which case, the documentation for that program or printer should offer an explanation).

Printing a document

If everything has gone well so far, the actual act of printing a document is pretty simple. Just follow the steps here, and in a few minutes, pages should start popping out of your printer like magic. (In the sections that follow, I talk about some print options that you'll probably need someday.)

1. **Open a document that you want to print.**

2. **Choose File ⇨ Print (or press ⌘+P).**

   You see the basic Print sheet, as shown in Figure 16-3.

3. **Click Print.**

   Wait a few minutes for the network to tell the printer what to do, and then walk over to your printer to get your document.

Choosing File ⇨ Print (⌘+P) *won't* work for you if any one of the following is true for the software you're using:

- ✏ The Print command is on a different menu.
- ✏ There *is* no Print command. (Hey, it could happen! For example, the Finder has no Print command.)
- ✏ The Print keyboard shortcut is something other than ⌘+P.

If any of the preceding is true for a program you're using, you just have to wing it. Look in all the menus and check out the product's documentation to try to get a handle on the Print command for that pesky program.

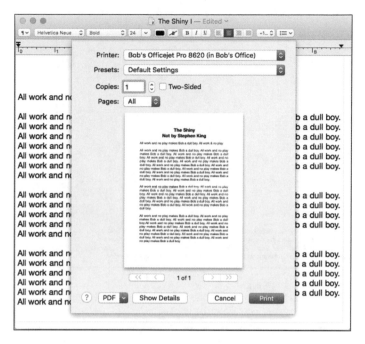

Figure 16-3: Your basic Print sheet.

Choosing among different printers

Just as you can in the Page Setup sheet, you can choose which printer you want to use from the Printer pop-up menu of the Print sheet.

You can choose only among the printers you added via the Printers & Scanners System Preferences pane, as I describe earlier in this chapter in the section I lovingly call "Setting up a printer for the first time." This includes printers connected to wireless base stations and routers, as well as Wi-Fi–enabled printers. After they're set up, Macs (and other devices) within range can print to these printers wirelessly.

Choosing custom settings

By default, the Print sheet is displayed with its details hidden. As such, just four menus are available: Printer, Presets, Pages, and PDF. To reveal the rest of the Print options, click the Show Details button near the bottom of the Print sheet. An expanded Print sheet with all the details you're likely to need, as shown in Figure 16-4, replaces the more streamlined version shown earlier in Figure 16-3.

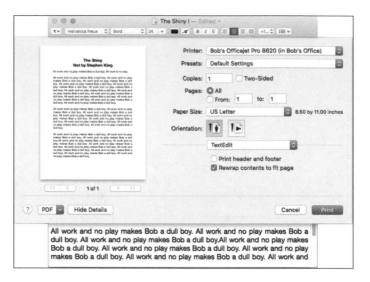

Figure 16-4: Your expanded Print sheet.

Click in any of the fields and press the Tab key. Your cursor jumps to the next text field; likewise, press Shift+Tab to jump to the previous field. By the way, this shortcut works in almost any program, window, dialog, or web page that has text fields.

In addition to the drop-down Printer menu, your expanded Print sheet offers the following options:

✔ **Presets:** This menu lets you manage and save print settings, as described in the "Saving custom settings" section later in this chapter.

✔ **Copies:** In this text field, set how many copies you want to print. The Print sheet defaults to one copy (1) in most applications, so you probably see the numeral 1 in the Copies field when the Print sheet appears. Assuming that's the case, don't do anything if you want to print only one copy. If you want to print more than one copy of your document, highlight the 1 that appears in the Copies field and replace it, typing the number of copies you want.

✔ **Pages:** Here, you find two radio buttons: All and From. The default behavior is to print your entire document, so the All option is prese-lected. But if you want to print only a specific page or range of pages, select the From radio button and type the desired page numbers in the From and To text fields.

Suppose that you print a 10-page document and only then notice a typo on Page 2. After you correct your error, you don't have to reprint the whole document — only the page with the correction. Reprint only Page 2 by typing **2** in both the From and To fields. You can type any valid range of pages (um, you can't print page 20 if your document is only 15 pages long) in the From and To fields.

✒ **Paper Size:** Use options in this pop-up menu to choose the type of paper currently in your printer's paper tray, or to choose the size of the paper that you want to feed manually. The dimensions of the paper appear below its name.

Yeah, this setting is also in Page Setup. The difference is that the settings here (in the Print sheet) apply only *to this document,* whereas the settings in Page Setup are the default *for all documents* and remain in effect until you change them in Page Setup. This can be very handy when, for example, you print an envelope. If you change the paper size setting for the envelope document, you don't have to remember to change it back to Letter in Page Setup.

✒ **Orientation:** Yeah (again), this setting is also in Page Setup. And once again, the choice you make in Page Setup is the default for all pages you print. Keep in mind that the setting you choose here (in the Print sheet) applies only to this document. Choose among options here to tell your printer whether the page you want to print should be portrait or landscape oriented.

The following list describes the features you can find in the unlabeled menu found in the expanded Print sheet (the one that says *TextEdit* in Figure 16-4). In addition to the TextEdit, Layout, and other options I cover in a moment, your pop-up menu may offer options such as Media & Quality, Color Options, Special Effects, Borderless Printing, and so on. (Whether you have these options depends on your printer model and its driver as well as the application from which you're printing.) Check out these options if you have 'em; they usually offer useful features:

✒ **TextEdit:** The only TextEdit-specific options, as shown in Figure 16-4, are two check boxes. One governs whether to print a header and footer for this document; the other lets you choose to rewrap the contents of the document to fit the page.

You can see the results of clicking these check boxes in the proxy image of your document on the left half of the sheet.

✒ **Layout:** Choose Layout to set the number of pages per printed sheet, the layout direction, and whether you prefer a border. Here are your options for Layout:

• *Pages per Sheet:* Choose preset numbers from this pop-up menu to set the number of pages that you want to print on each sheet.

Pages appear onscreen smaller than full size if you use this option.

• *Layout Direction:* Choose one of the four buttons that govern the way pages are laid out on the printed page.

- *Border:* Your choices from this pop-up menu are None, Single Hairline, Single Thin Line, Double Hairline, and Double Thin Line.

- *Two-Sided:* If your printer supports two-sided (known as *duplex*) printing, the three radio buttons allow you to specify whether you're going to use two-sided printing — and if so, whether you'll be binding (or stapling) along the long or short edge of the paper or creating a booklet.

Two check boxes — Reverse Page Orientation and Flip Horizontally — do just what they say if you enable them.

- **Paper Handling:** Choose Paper Handling if you want to reverse the order in which your pages print or to print only the odd- or even-numbered pages. You can also specify whether the document's paper size is to be used (in which case, you might have lines that break across pages) or whether the output should be scaled to fit the chosen paper size.

- **Cover Page:** Choose Cover Page to add a cover page.

- **Paper Type/Quality:** Choose Paper Type/Quality to specify the type of paper in your printer and the print quality you desire. The choices are Draft, Normal, or Best when you print from TextEdit; other apps may offer other options.

- **Supply Levels:** Choose Supply Levels to see the current ink levels for your printer.

Saving custom settings

After you finalize printer settings, you can save them for future use. Just click the Presets pop-up menu, choose Save Current Settings as Preset, and then provide a name for this preset. From then on, the preset name appears as an option in the Presets pop-up menu. Just choose your saved preset before you print any document, and all the individual settings associated with that preset are restored.

To manage your custom settings, known in El Capitan-speak as *presets,* choose Show Presets from the Print sheet's Presets pop-up menu. This nifty feature displays a list of your presets and their settings and allows you to delete, duplicate, or rename (by double-clicking their current name) your presets.

Preview and PDF Options

To see a preview of what your printed page will look like, choose Open PDF in Preview from the PDF pop-up menu in the bottom-left corner of the expanded Print sheet. When you do so, you see the page or pages that you're about to print displayed by the Preview application, as shown in Figure 16-5.

Edit toolbar

Show/Hide
Edit toolbar

Figure 16-5: A preview of a TextEdit document.

As you probably know, OS X can save any printable document as a PDF file. To do so, choose Save As PDF in the PDF pop-up menu in every print dialog or sheet.

If you have any doubt about the way a document will look when you print it, check out Preview first. When you're happy with the document preview, just choose File➪Print, press ⌘+P, or click the Print button at the bottom of the Preview window. Or click the Cancel button to return to your application and make changes to the document.

Preview works with the Preview application. With the Preview feature, you can do cool things like these:

- See all the pages in your document the way they'll be printed, one by one.

- Zoom in or out to get a different perspective on what you're about to send to the printer (pretty cool!).

- Rotate the picture 90 degrees to the left or right.

- Insert (via drag and drop), delete, or reorder pages in Preview's sidebar.

- Spot errors before you print something. A little up-front inspection can save you paper, ink/toner, and frustration.

Click the Show/Hide Edit Toolbar button (shown in the margin) to reveal a small toolbar with several useful tools, as shown in Figure 16-5.

Check out the Preview program's View menu, where you'll find (among other things), four useful views: Content Only, Thumbnails (shown in Figure 16-5), Table of Contents, and Contact Sheet, as well as the zoom commands and more.

Also check out Preview's toolbar, which you can add or delete buttons from by choosing View⇨Customize Toolbar.

And speaking of tools, don't miss the selections in the Tools menu, which let you rotate pages, move forward or backward (through multipage documents), and unleash the awesomeness of the Magnifier, shown in Figure 16-6.

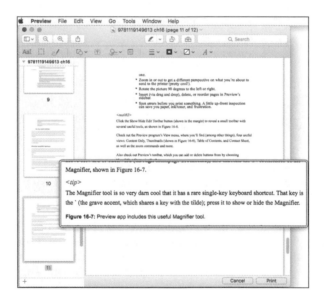

Figure 16-6: Preview app includes this useful Magnifier tool.

 The Magnifier tool is so very darn cool that it has a rare single-key keyboard shortcut. That key is the ` (the grave accent, which shares a key with the tilde); press it to show or hide the Magnifier.

One last thing: OS X El Capitan includes the capability to fax a document right from the Print sheet, but it requires a compatible device with compatible fax modem drivers. To find out whether *your* device is compatible, connect the device to your Mac and attempt to add it as a fax modem in the Printers & Scanners System Preferences pane.

Part V
The Care and Feeding of El Capitan

Read the article on installing and reinstalling OS X El Capitan at www.dummies.com/extras/osxelcapitan.

In this part . . .

- ✓ Protecting your valuable data by backing it up

- ✓ The little bit you need to know about Macintosh security

- ✓ Utilities you might or might not find useful (but ones you should know about just the same)

- ✓ Dr. Mac's prescription: What to do when things go wonky (which also, thankfully, doesn't happen very much)

- ✓ The doctor's top troubleshooting tips for a good El Capitan gone bad

17

Features for the Way You Work

In This Chapter

▶ Talking to your Mac

▶ Listening to your Mac

▶ Enhancing productivity by using automation

▶ Trying out more useful technologies and techniques

▶ Running Microsoft Windows on your Mac (really!)

▶ Mirroring your Mac screen to your HDTV screen wirelessly

*T*his chapter delves into some OS X El Capitan features that might very well improve the ways you interact with your computer. Unlike the more mainstream applications, System Preferences panes, and utilities that I discuss in Part I — Desktop, Finder, Screen Saver, Appearance, Keyboard, Trackpad, Mouse, and such — the items in this chapter are a little more esoteric. In other words, you don't *have* to use any of the technologies I'm about to show you. That said, many of these items can make you more productive and can make using your Mac even better. So I'd like to believe that at least some of you will *want* to use at least some of the cool features I'm about to introduce.

Talking and Listening to Your Mac

Your primary methods for interacting with your Mac are typing and reading text. But there's another way you can commune with your faithful computer: voice.

Whether you know it or not, your Mac has a lot of speech savvy up its sleeve (er . . . up its processors?) and can talk to you as well as listen. Believe it or not, it can type the words you speak and obey your spoken commands. And most of you already have a microphone built into your Mac unless your Mac happens to be a Mac Mini or a Mac Pro, which require an external microphone to hear you speak.

In the following sections, you discover how to make your Mac do that and more.

Dictation & Speech System Preferences pane: You talk and your Mac types

Many users don't realize that dictation is available in Mac OS X and has been for years. In this section, you find out how to harness its power.

First, make sure Dictation is enabled in the Dictation & Speech System Preferences pane's Dictation tab; if it's set to Off, click the On button.

Dictation requires an Internet connection unless you enable the Use Enhanced Dictation check box in the Dictation & Speech System Preferences pane. Otherwise, when you dictate text, what you say is sent to Apple's servers to convert it to text. If you enable Use Enhanced Dictation, you can use Dictation without an Internet connection after your Mac downloads the necessary files to your Mac. That's the good news. The bad news is that the necessary files are pretty big — it's 1.2GB and could take an hour or more to download depending on the speed of your network connection.

Other information, such as your contacts, may also be sent to Apple over the Internet to help your Mac understand what you're saying. If that makes you uncomfortable, you probably shouldn't use the Dictation feature without first selecting the Use Enhanced Dictation check box.

After it's enabled, with or without the Enhanced option, Dictation couldn't be easier to use. First, click where you want your words to appear in a document, dialog, web form, or whatever, and then choose Edit⇨Start Dictation, or press the Fn key twice in rapid succession.

If your keyboard doesn't have an Fn key, click the Shortcut pop-up menu in the Dictation & Speech System Preferences pane to change the shortcut to one that works with your keyboard.

When you start Dictation, a little microphone icon appears. The white filling indicates the level (relative loudness) of your voice. Try to keep the white near the middle — not too high and not too low, as shown in Figure 17-1.

Figure 17-1: Volume levels for dictation (left to right): Too soft, just right, and too loud.

When you see the microphone icon, start speaking. After you dictate a few sentences, click Done and let your Mac catch up. When the words appear, you can start Dictation again. Repeat as necessary.

It might not be a bad idea to save your document after you speak a few sentences or paragraphs; if you don't, the words you dictated since your last Save will be lost if the app or your Mac crashes.

You can insert punctuation by speaking its name, such as "period" or "comma." You can also perform simple formatting by saying "new line" or "new paragraph" to add space between lines.

Here are a few more tips to help you get the best results when you dictate:

- ✏ **Speak in a normal voice at a moderate volume level.** Try to keep the white in the microphone icon about half-full (or half-empty if you're a pessimist).

- ✏ **Avoid background noise.** If you expect to use dictation in a noisy environment or a room with a lot of ambient echo, you should consider using a headset microphone.

    The headset that comes with iPhones and iPod touches is compatible with many Mac models.

- ✏ **Be sure the microphone is not obstructed.** Check your Mac's User Guide for the location of your built-in microphone (if you have one).

- ✏ **Be sure the input volume of an external microphone is sufficient.** If you're using an external microphone and the white meter doesn't respond to your voice, select the microphone in the drop-down menu beneath the microphone in the Dictation tab of the Dictation & Speech System Preferences pane.

Commanding your Mac by voice

Speech Recognition enables your Mac to recognize and respond to human speech. The only thing you need to use it is a microphone, which most of you have built right into your Mac (unless it's a Mac Mini or Mac Pro as noted previously).

Speech Recognition lets you issue verbal commands such as "Get my mail!" to your Mac and have it actually get your email. You can also create AppleScripts and trigger them by voice.

An *AppleScript* is a series of commands, using the AppleScript language, that tells the computer (and some applications) what to do. You find out a bit more about AppleScript later in this chapter.

In versions of OS X before Yosemite, you had to explicitly turn on Speech Recognition; in El Capitan, if you've enabled Dictation, you can use speech commands to instruct your Mac.

To see a list of commands your Mac will understand if you speak them, open the Accessibility System Preferences pane, click Dictation in the list on the left, and then click the Dictation Commands button. A sheet appears, in which you can enable or disable the available dictation commands, as shown in Figure 17-2.

Figure 17-2: The Accessibility System Preferences pane's Dictation Commands sheet displaying a few of the things your Mac will understand if you say them (properly). Usually.

If you have a laptop or an iMac, you may get better results from just about any third-party microphone or headset with a microphone. The mic built into your Mac works okay, but it's not great. To select a third-party microphone, first connect the mic to your Mac. Then open the Sound System Preferences pane and select it from the list of sound input devices in the Input tab. Below the list is an input volume control (not available with some third-party mics) and a level meter, as shown in Figure 17-3. Adjust the Input Volume so that most of the dots in the Input Level meter darken (11 of 15 in Figure 17-3).

Speech Recognition is the same as Dictation; enable Dictation as I show you earlier in this section, and you're good to go. To give it a try, press Fn twice (or whatever shortcut you set earlier) and speak one of the items from

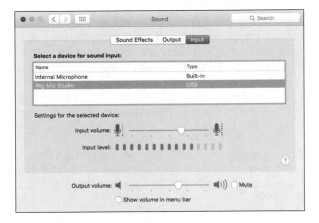

Figure 17-3: This is a good level for Speech Recognition.

the list of Dictation Commands, such as "Open TextEdit." If the command is recognized, it will appear in text above the microphone icon, as shown in Figure 17-4.

This technology is clever and kind of fun, but it can also be somewhat frustrating when it doesn't recognize what you say, which is far too often, if you ask me. And it requires a decent microphone even though the mic built into most Macs sometimes works okay. The bottom line is that I've never been able to get Speech Recognition to work well enough to continue using it beyond a few minutes at best. Still, it's kind of cool (and it's a freebie), and I've heard more than one user profess love for it. Which is why it's included here.

Figure 17-4: *Open TextEdit* above the mic icon means your command was recognized.

Listening to your Mac read for you

The camera pans back. A voice tells you what you've just seen. And suddenly it all makes sense. Return with me now to those thrilling days of the off-camera narrator.... Wouldn't it be nice if your Mac had a narrator to provide a blow-by-blow account of what's happening on your screen?

Or, your eyes are tired from a long day staring at the monitor, but you still have a lengthy document to read. Wouldn't it be sweet if you could sit back, close your eyes, and let your Mac read the document to you in a (somewhat) natural voice? The good news is that both are possible with OS X El Capitan: the first scenario with VoiceOver, and the second with Text to Speech.

VoiceOver

El Capitan's VoiceOver technology is designed primarily for the visually impaired, but you might find it useful even if your vision is 20/20. VoiceOver not only reads what's on the screen to you but also integrates with your keyboard so you can navigate around the screen until you *hear* the item you're looking for. When you're there, you can use Keyboard Access to select list items, select check boxes and radio buttons, move scroll bars and sliders, resize windows, and so on — all with just a simple key press or two.

To check it out, launch the System Preferences application (from Launchpad, the Applications folder, 🍎 menu, or Dock), click the Accessibility icon and then click VoiceOver or press ⌘+Fn+F5 on MacBook models and most Apple keyboards (or try ⌘+F5).

After VoiceOver is enabled, you can turn it on and off in the Accessibility System Preferences pane or by pressing ⌘+Fn+F5 or ⌘+F5.

While VoiceOver is on, your Mac talks to you about what is on your screen. For example, if you click the Desktop, your Mac might say something along the lines of "Application, Finder; Column View; selected folder, Desktop, contains 8 items." It's quite slick. Here's another example: When you click a menu or item on a menu, you hear its name spoken at once, and when you close a menu, you hear the words "Closing menu." You even hear the spoken feedback in the Print, Open, and Save (and other) dialogs.

VoiceOver is kind of cool (talking alerts are fun), but having dialogs actually produce spoken text becomes annoying really fast for most folks who aren't visually impaired. (Those who are visually impaired, however, rave about VoiceOver and say it lets them do things they couldn't easily do in the past.) In any case, I urge you to check it out. You might like it and find times when you want your Mac to narrate the action on-screen for you.

The VoiceOver Utility

The VoiceOver Utility lets you specify almost every possible option the VoiceOver technology uses. You can adjust its verbosity; specify how it deals with your mouse and keyboard; change its voice, rate, pitch, and/or volume; and more.

You can open the VoiceOver Utility by clicking the Open VoiceOver Utility button in the Accessibility System Preferences pane or in the usual way: by double-clicking its icon (which you find in your Utilities folder).

Of course, you might get the machines-are-taking-over willies when your Mac starts to talk to you or make sounds — but if you give it a try, it could change your mind.

I wish I had the space to explain further, but I don't. That's the bad news. The good news is that VoiceOver Help is extensive and clear, and it helps you harness all the power of VoiceOver and the VoiceOver Utility.

Text to Speech

The second way your Mac can speak to you is via Text to Speech, which converts onscreen text to spoken words. If you've used Text to Speech in earlier versions of OS X, you'll find that it's pretty much unchanged.

Why might you need Text to Speech? Because sometimes hearing is better than reading. For example, I sometimes use Text to Speech to read aloud to me a column or page I've written before I submit it. If something doesn't sound quite right, I give it another polish before sending it off to my editor.

You can configure this feature in the Dictation & Speech System Preferences pane:

1. **Open System Preferences (from Launchpad, the Applications folder, Dock, or menu), click the Dictation & Speech icon, and then click the Text to Speech tab.**

2. **Choose one of the voices in the System Voice pop-up menu to set the voice your Mac uses when it reads to you.**

3. **Click the Play button to hear a sample of the voice you selected.**

4. **Use the Speaking Rate slider to speed up or slow down the voice.**

5. **Click the Play button to hear the voice at its new speed.**

   I really like Alex, who says, "Most people recognize me by my voice." My second favorite is Fred, who sounds like the Talking Moose and says, "I sure like being inside this fancy computer."

6. **(Optional) Select the Announce When Alerts Are Displayed check box if you want to make your Mac speak the text in alert boxes and dialogs.**

   You might hear such alerts as "The application Microsoft Word has quit unexpectedly" or "Paper out or not loaded correctly."

7. **(Optional) Click the Set Alert Options button to choose the voice and phrase used to announce your alerts — "Alert," "Attention," "Yo, dude," and the like — when alerting you.**

   You can also set the delay between the time the alert appears and when it's spoken to you.

8. **(Optional) Select the Speak Selected Text When the Key Is Pressed check box to create a hot key to speak selected text.**

   The default keyboard shortcut is Option+Esc, but you can assign any key combo you like by clicking the Change Key button.

9. **(Optional) If you want to have the clock announce the time, click the Open Date & Time Preferences button, and you're whisked to that System Preferences pane; then click the Clock tab and select the Announce the Time check box.**

Now, to use Text to Speech to read text to you, copy the text to the Clipboard, launch any app that supports it (I usually choose TextEdit), paste the text into the empty untitled document, click where you want your Mac to begin reading to you, and then choose Edit ⇨ Speech ⇨ Start Speaking. To make it stop, choose Edit ⇨ Speech ⇨ Stop Speaking.

Another great place Text to Speech is available is in the Safari web browser. It works the same as TextEdit but you don't have to paste — just select the text you want to hear and choose Edit ⇨ Speech ⇨ Start Speaking.

Automatic Automation

OS X El Capitan offers a pair of technologies — AppleScript and Automator — that makes it easy to automate repetitive actions on your Mac.

AppleScript is "programming for the rest of us." It can record and play back things that you do (if the application was written to allow the recording, such as the Finder), such as opening an application or clicking a button. You can use it to record a script for tasks that you often perform, and then have your Mac perform those tasks for you later. You can write your own AppleScripts, use those that come with your Mac, or download still others from the web.

Automator is "programming without writing code." With Automator, you string together prefabricated activities *(actions)* to automate repetitive or scheduled tasks. How cool is that?

Automation isn't for everyone. Some users can't live without it; others could go their whole lives without ever automating anything. So the following sections are designed to help you figure out how much — or how little — you care about AppleScript and Automator.

Script Editor app: Write and edit AppleScripts

Describing AppleScript to a Mac beginner is a bit like three blind men describing an elephant. One man might describe it as the Macintosh's built-in automation tool. Another might describe it as an interesting but often-overlooked piece of enabling technology. The third might liken it to a cassette recorder, recording and playing back your actions at the keyboard. A fourth (if there were a fourth in the story) would assure you that it looked like computer code written in a high-level language.

They would all be correct. AppleScript, a built-in Mac automation tool, is a little-known (at least until recently) enabling technology that works like a cassette recorder for programs that support AppleScript recording. And scripts do look like computer programs. (Could that be because they *are* computer programs? Hmm. . . .)

If you're the kind of person who likes to automate as many things as possible, you might just love AppleScript because it's a simple programming language you can use to create programs that give instructions to your Mac and the applications running on your Mac. For example, you can create an AppleScript that launches Mail, checks for new messages, and then quits Mail. The script could even transfer your mail to a folder of your choice. Then there's Automator, which includes a whole lot of preprogrammed actions that make a task like the one just described even easier.

I call AppleScript a time-and-effort enhancer. If you just spend the time and effort it takes to understand it, using AppleScript can save you oodles of time and effort down the road. Therein lies the rub. This stuff is far from simple; entire books have been written on the subject. So it's far beyond the purview of *OS X El Capitan For Dummies*. Still, it's worth finding out about if you'd like to script repetitive actions for future use. To get you started, here are a few quick tips:

- ✔ **Script Editor (in the Utilities folder inside the Applications folder) is the application you use to view and edit AppleScripts.** Although more information on Script Editor is beyond the scope of this book, it's a lot of fun. And the cool thing is that you can create many AppleScripts without knowing a thing about programming. Just record a series of actions you want to repeat and use Script Editor to save what you recorded as a script. If you save your script as an application (by choosing Format ⇨ Application in the Save sheet), you can run that script by double-clicking its icon.

- ✔ **You can put frequently used AppleScripts in the Dock or on your Desktop for easy access.**

- Many AppleScripts are designed for use in the toolbar of Finder windows, where you can drag and drop items onto them quickly and easily.

- Scripts can enhance your use of many apps including iTunes, iPhoto, and the Finder, to name a few.

- Apple provides a script menu extra that you can install on your menu bar in the Script Editor's Preferences window, along with a number of free scripts to automate common tasks (in the Scripts folder in the root-level Library, or choose Open Example Scripts Folder from the Script Editor's Help menu). Finally, you can download additional example scripts from www.apple.com/applescript.

- If the concept of scripting intrigues you, I suggest that you explore the examples in the Scripts folder (in the root-level Library or choose Open Example Scripts from the Script Editor's Help menu). Rummage through this folder and when you find a script that looks interesting, double-click it to launch the Script Editor program, where you can examine it more closely.

Automator app: Automate almost anything

Automator does just what you'd expect: It enables you to automate many common tasks on your Mac. If it sounds a little like AppleScript to you (which I discuss in the preceding section), you're not mistaken; the two have a common goal. But this tool is a lot simpler to use, albeit somewhat less flexible, than AppleScript.

For example, in AppleScript, you can have *conditionals* ("if *this* is true, do *that;* otherwise do something else"), but Automator is purely *sequential* ("take *this,* do *that,* then do the next thing, and then . . ."").

The big difference is that conditionals allow AppleScripts to take actions involving *decision-making* and *iteration* ("while *this* is true, do *these* things"); Automator workflows can't make decisions or iterate.

The upsides to Automator are that you don't have to know anything about programming, and you don't have to type any archaic code. Instead, if you understand the process you want to automate, you can just drag and drop Automator's prefab actions into place and build a *workflow* (Automator's name for a series of actions).

You do need to know one thing about programming (or computers), though: *Computers are stupid!* You heard me right — even my top-of-the-line MacBook Pro is dumb as a post. Computers do only what you tell them to do even though they can do it faster and more precisely than you can. But all computers run on the GIGO principle (Garbage In, Garbage Out), so if your instructions are flawed, you're almost certain to get flawed results.

When you launch the Automator application, click the New Document button and the window and sheet shown in Figure 17-5 appear. Choose one of the starting points if you want Automator to assist you in constructing a new workflow; or, choose Workflow to start building a workflow from scratch.

Figure 17-5: Choose Workflow to start a workflow from scratch.

I'm going to choose Service for the sake of this demonstration (you'll see why in a second). When I select Service and click the Choose button, I see the window shown in Figure 17-6.

Actions Library   Actions   Drag actions here

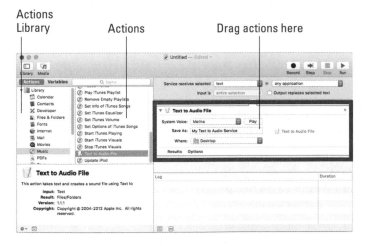

Figure 17-6: This converts text that I select to an audio file.

The Library pane on the left contains all the applications Automator knows about that have Actions defined for them. Select an application in the top part of the Library window, and its related actions appear below it. When you select an action, the pane at the bottom of the Library window (Text to Audio File in Figure 17-6) explains what that Action does, what input it expects, and what result it produces. Just drag Actions from the Action list into the window on the right to build your workflow.

This particular Service, which took me less than five minutes of trial and error to perfect, is quite useful. First, I select text from any source — a web page, Microsoft Word document, email message, or whatever. Then I choose Services from the Application menu or right- or Control-click and select my newly created Text to Audio Service from the Services menu. My Automator workflow then converts the selected text into an audio file and saves it to the Desktop. Then, I can have it read to me in iTunes at home or on my iPhone or iPad in the car, on a plane, or just about anywhere. Sweet!

Automator is a very useful addition to OS X; it's deep, powerful, and expandable, yet relatively easy to use and master. Do yourself a favor, and spend some time experimenting with ways Automator can save you time and keystrokes. You won't regret it.

For additional information about AppleScript, Automator, Services, and much more, visit `www.macosxautomation.com`.

A Few More Useful Goodies

Even more neat and useful technologies are built into El Capitan, but I'm running out of space. So here are, at least in my humble opinion, the best of the rest.

App Store app: The place to buy Mac apps

The App Store app is the OS X software version of the iTunes Store for media and iOS apps. Here, you'll find applications of all types — Business, Entertainment, Graphics, Productivity, Social Networking, and more — at prices that start at zero (free).

Just about everything I tell you in Chapter 13 about the iTunes Store could be said for the App Store. It looks and works the same, and it uses the same credit card you have on file at the iTunes Store.

If you see a little number on the App Store icon in your Dock, it means that a number of your apps have updates available. Launch the App Store app and click the Updates tab to see the apps with updates awaiting them. Even if you don't see a little number in the App Store's Dock icon, it wouldn't hurt to launch the App Store every once in a while to check for updates manually, as the little number sometimes fails to appear in the App Store Dock icon.

Accessibility System Preferences pane: Make your Mac more accessible

If you've read the chapter to this point, you got a brief glimpse of the Accessibility System Preferences pane when I discussed commanding your Mac by voice. But this System Preferences pane is mostly designed for users with disabilities or who have difficulty handling the keyboard, mouse, or trackpad.

Select the Show Accessibility Status in Menu Bar check box at the bottom of the window on the left to see the status of all Accessibility Preferences in your menu bar.

The pane has four sections — Vision, Media, Hearing, and Interacting — each of which has one or more subsections.

The Vision section's Display subsection lets you alter the behavior of the screen display. Select the Use Grayscale check box to desaturate your screen into a *grayscale display* (so it looks kind of like a black-and-white TV). Enable the Invert Colors option to reverse what you'd see onscreen. For example in the real world you know what the Accessibility System Preferences pane looks like; Figure 17-7 is what it looks like onscreen with Invert Colors enabled.

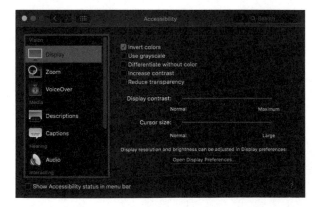

Figure 17-7: A note with inverted colors.

The Vision section's Zoom subsection is where you can turn on a terrific feature called *hardware zoom,* which lets you make things on your screen bigger by zooming in on them. To control it by keyboard, select the Use Keyboard Shortcuts to Zoom check box. Then you can toggle it on and off with the shortcut ⌘+Option+8 and zoom in and out using the shortcuts ⌘+Option+= (equal sign) and ⌘+Option+– (hyphen), respectively. Finally, the More Options button lets you specify minimum and maximum zoom levels, display a preview rectangle when zoomed out, and toggle image smoothing on or off.

Try this feature even if you're not disabled or challenged in any way; it's actually a great feature for everyone.

You looked at the Vision section's VoiceOver subsection earlier in the chapter.

I leave it to you, gentle reader, to explore the remaining sections and subsections of the Accessibility System Preferences pane at your leisure. Until then, you might find the following useful:

- ✔ **If you want the screen to flash whenever an alert sound occurs, choose Audio.**

- ✔ **To treat a *sequence* of modifier keys as a key combination, choose Keyboard and then enable Sticky Keys.**

    In other words, you don't have to simultaneously hold down ⌘ while pressing another key. For example, with Sticky Keys enabled, you can do a standard keyboard shortcut by pressing ⌘, releasing it, and then pressing the other key. You can select check boxes to tell you (with a beep and/or an onscreen display) what modifier keys have been pressed.

    As useful as Sticky Keys can be, they're really awkward in applications like Adobe Photoshop, Adobe Illustrator, and other applications that toggle a tool's state when you press a modifier key. So if you're a big Photoshop user, you probably don't want Sticky Keys enabled.

- ✔ **To adjust the delay between a keypress and its activation, choose Keyboard and then enable Slow Keys.**

Energy Saver System Preferences Pane: For energy conservation and sleep

All Macs are Energy Star–compliant (and have been for years), allowing you to preset your machine to turn itself off at a specific time or after a specified idle period. To manage your Mac's energy-saving features, open the Energy Saver System Preferences pane by choosing ⌘ ⇨ System Preferences and clicking the Energy Saver icon.

If you have a notebook computer, you have two mostly identical tabs —
Battery and Power Adapter — in your Energy Saver System Preferences pane.
The Battery tab controls your notebook Mac's behavior when it's running on
battery power (not plugged in); the Power Adapter tab controls its behavior
when it *is* plugged in.

If you have a desktop Mac, you won't have tabs, but you do have most of the
same controls, including a pair of sliders that control sleep times for your
computer and display. To enable Computer or Display sleep, move the appropriate slider to the desired amount of time. You can choose any number
between 1 minute and 3 hours or turn off either type of sleep entirely by
moving its slider all the way to the right, to Never.

Setting the display to sleep is handy if you want your Mac to keep doing what
it's doing but you don't need to use the monitor. And if you're a notebook
user, display sleep will save you battery power.

To wake up your Mac from its sleep, merely move your mouse or press any
key. Sometimes moving the mouse or a finger on the trackpad won't wake a
sleeping Mac, but a keystroke will. So try both (or all three) before you give up.

Below the Sleep sliders are some check boxes for other useful energy settings, such as the following:

- **Put the Hard Disk(s) to Sleep When Possible:** Enabling this option
  forces your hard drive to sleep after a few minutes of inactivity. It's not
  a particularly useful feature on a desktop Mac, but if you have a laptop,
  letting your hard drive sleep when it's idle will save you some battery
  power.

- **Wake for Wi-Fi Network Access:** Enable this option if you want your
  Mac to wake up automatically for Wi-Fi network access.

If you have a laptop, you'll have some additional options, including

- **Slightly Dim the Display While on Battery Power (Battery tab):** The
  display dims slightly and uses less power when running on the battery.

- **Enable Power Nap while on Battery Power (Battery tab):** This option
  allows your Mac to check for new email, calendar, and other iCloud
  updates while it's sleeping.

- **Enable Power Nap while Plugged into a Power Adapter (Power
  Adapter tab):** This option allows your Mac to back up to Time Machine
  as well as check for new email, calendar, and other iCloud updates while
  it's sleeping.

  ✔ **Prevent Computer from Sleeping Automatically When the Display is Off (Power Adapter tab):** Prevents sleep when the lid is closed and the display is off.

  ✔ **Show Battery Status in the Menu Bar:** This option adds a little battery-status indicator icon and menu.

Finally, to start up, shut down, or put your Mac to sleep at a predetermined time, click the Schedule button and then select the appropriate check box and choose the appropriate options from the pop-up menus.

Bluetooth System Preferences pane: Where Bluetooth lives

Bluetooth is wireless networking for low-bandwidth peripherals, including mice, keyboards, and mobile phones. If your Mac has Bluetooth built in or is equipped with a USB Bluetooth adapter, you can synchronize wirelessly with phones and Palm devices, print wirelessly to Bluetooth printers, and use Bluetooth headsets, mice, and keyboards.

To manage your Mac's Bluetooth features, open the Bluetooth System Preferences pane by choosing System Preferences and clicking the Bluetooth icon.

Ink System Preferences pane: Visible to pen-input tablet users only

Ink is the OS X built-in handwriting-recognition engine. Sadly, it works only if a third-party drawing tablet with a stylus is connected. Even more sadly, "tablet" in this sense doesn't include your iPad (at least not so far . . .).

To write instead of typing, enable Ink in this pane and you'll be able to hand-write anywhere your Mac accepts typing with the keyboard.

To manage your Mac's Ink features, open the Ink System Preferences pane by choosing System Preferences and clicking the Ink icon.

The Ink pane is one you see only if you have one of the pen-input drawing tablets that Ink supports connected to your Mac. Most of the supported drawing tablets come from Wacom (www.wacom.com), with prices starting under $100 for a small wireless stylus and drawing tablet.

Automatic Login in the Users & Groups System Preferences pane: Don't bother with the login screen

Some users don't care for the fact that OS X El Capitan is a multiuser operating system and dislike having to log in when they start up their Mac. For those users, here's a way to disable the login screen:

1. **Open the Users & Groups System Preferences pane, select yourself in the list of users, and click the Login Options button below the list.**

   Click the lock and provide your password first, if necessary.

2. **Choose the account you want to be logged in to automatically from the Automatic Login pop-up menu.**

   To disable the logging-in requirement, you have to be an administrator, and you may need to unlock the Users & Groups System Preferences pane.

When you disable logging in, you also affect all the preferences set by anyone else who uses your Mac unless they log out of your account and log into theirs. (Yikes.) So if your Desktop pattern, keyboard settings, and so forth are different from those of someone else who uses your Mac, those preferences won't be properly reflected unless each of you has a separate, individual login account. Even if you're not worried about security, consider keeping logging in enabled if any other users have accounts on your machine, or if you don't want just anyone to be able to turn on your Mac and see your personal stuff.

Note that only one account is allowed to use auto-login. If another user wants to use this Mac, you need to choose ⇨ Log Out, press ⌘+Shift+Q, or have Fast User Switching enabled. And if you've disabled automatic login in the Security System Preferences pane, you can't enable it here.

Boot Camp Assistant app: Run Windows on your Mac . . . really

Boot Camp is El Capitan's built-in technology that allows you to run Microsoft Windows 10 and (on some Mac models) Windows 7 or 8 on El Capitan-capable Macs. If your Mac meets the following requirements, you can run Windows on your Mac (if you so desire):

✔ An El Capitan-capable Mac (of course)

✔ A hard drive that isn't already partitioned

✔ (Optional) A printer (for printing the instructions)

   It's optional 'cause you could just email them to yourself. . .

✔ A full install copy of Microsoft Windows 7 or newer (Windows 8 Home Premium, Professional, or Ultimate edition)

You really do need a *full retail* copy of Windows: one that was purchased in a retail box. If your copy of Windows came with your PC, you probably can't install it in Boot Camp.

To install Windows on your Mac, here are the basic steps:

1. **Launch the Boot Camp Assistant application, which is in your Utilities folder.**

   This step creates a partition on your hard drive for your Windows installation.

2. **Install Windows on the new partition.**

   From now on, you can hold down Option during startup and choose to start up from either the OS X El Capitan disk partition or the new Windows partition.

If running Windows on your Mac appeals to you, you may want to check out Parallels Desktop or VMware Fusion (around $80 each) or VirtualBox (free). All three programs allow you to run Windows — even older versions like XP and Vista — as well as Linux on your Mac without partitioning your hard drive or restarting every time you want to use Windows. In fact, you can run Mac and Windows programs simultaneously with all three of these products.

One last thing: Apple has a special Boot Camp support page on the web at `http://www.apple.com/support/bootcamp/`.

AirPlay mirroring

I would be remiss if I didn't mention the AirPlay Mirroring feature, even though most of you won't be able to use it without first buying an Apple TV.

With AirPlay Mirroring, you can stream whatever is on your Mac (or iOS device) screen wirelessly to your HDTV with a connected Apple TV.

Apple TV couldn't be easier to use. If it's on the same network as your Mac, an option for AirPlay Mirroring will appear in the Displays System Preferences pane. Just enable AirPlay Mirroring, and what is on your Mac screen will appear on your HDTV screen almost instantaneously.

Enable Show Mirroring Options in the Menu Bar When Available in the Displays System Preferences pane, and a handy menu, shown in Figure 17-8, lets you switch AirPlay Mirroring on and off without the bother of first opening the Displays System Preferences pane.

The bad news is that many older Macs — including my wife's six-year-old MacBook Pro — don't support mirroring to an Apple TV.

Figure 17-8: The AirPlay menu makes life much easier for AirPlay users like me.

Handoff

I'd be remiss if I didn't at least mention the Handoff feature, which lets you start working on a document, an email, or a message on any Apple device and pick up where you left off on another device. Handoff works with Apple apps including Mail, Safari, Maps, Messages, Reminders, Calendar, Contacts, Pages, Numbers, and Keynote as well as a handful of third-party apps.

Handoff is useful only if you own other Apple devices. For details on it and other Continuity features for iDevices, including SMS and Instant Hot Spot, see the book's cheat sheet at `www.dummies.com/cheatsheet/osxelcapitan`.

18

Safety First: Backups and Other Security Issues

In This Chapter

▶ Backing up . . . it's easy

▶ Discovering why you should back up

▶ Finding out what happens to you if you don't back up

▶ Keeping your Mac safe from rogue viruses and malicious attacks

▶ Protecting your data from prying eyes

lthough Macs are generally reliable beasts (especially Macs running OS X), someday your hard drive (or SSD) will die. I promise. They *all* do someday. And if you don't back up your drive (or at least back up any files that you can't afford to lose) before that day comes, chances are good those files are gone forever.

If you turn on FileVault (described later in this chapter) and forget both your login password and your master password, you can't log in to your account — and your data is lost forever. Really. Not even DriveSavers or Apple can recover it, so don't forget both passwords, okay?

Time Machine Backup D

941 GB of 1.4 TB available

Oldest backup: Today, 4:3

Latest backup: Today, 6:20

Next backup: Today, 6:33

Select Disk...

Time Machine keeps:

• Local snapshots as space permits

• Hourly backups for the past 24 hours

ly backups for the past month

kups for all previous months

s are deleted when vou

In other words, you absolutely, positively, without question *must back up* your files if you don't want to risk losing them. Just as you adopt the Shut Down command and make it a habit before turning off your machine, you must remember to back up important files on your hard drive to another disk or device — and back them up often.

D'oh!

And if you do see them again, my friend, it will be only after paying someone like DriveSavers Data Recovery Service. And even if you pay, there's no guarantee of success.

DriveSavers is the premier recoverer of lost data on hard drives. The people there understand Mac hard drives quite well, do excellent work, and can often recover stuff that nobody else could. (Ask the producers of *The Simpsons* about the almost-lost episodes.) Understandably, DriveSavers charges accordingly.

If you aren't going to back up your data, here are the phone numbers for DriveSavers: 800-440-1904 toll-free and 415-382-2000. You'll probably need them someday (along with a bucketful of cash) if you refuse to believe that you *must* back up and back up often.

How often is often? That depends on you. How much work can you afford to lose? If your answer is that losing everything you did yesterday would put you out of business, you need to back up hourly or perhaps even continuously. If you would lose only a few unimportant documents if your hard disk died today, you can probably back up less frequently.

Following the comprehensive coverage of backup options, I explain the possible threat to your data from viruses and other icky things, as well as how you can protect against them.

Finally, I cover what you can do to keep other people from looking at your stuff.

Backing Up Is (Not) Hard to Do

You can back up your hard drive in basically three ways: the super-painless way with El Capitan's excellent Time Machine, the ugly way using the brute-force method, or the comprehensive way with specialized third-party backup and disk-cloning software. Read on and find out more about all three.

Backing up with El Capitan's excellent Time Machine

Time Machine is a most excellent backup system that was introduced with OS X Leopard — and it's gotten better. I say it's a system because it consists of two parts: the Time Machine System Preferences pane, shown in Figure 18-1, and the Time Machine application, shown in Figure 18-2.

Figure 18-1: The Time Machine System Preferences pane and menu.

Figure 18-2: The Time Machine application is ready to restore a folder in the Finder.

To use Time Machine to back up your data automatically, the first thing you need is another hard drive that's the same size as or larger than your startup disk. It can be an external FireWire, USB2 or USB3, or Thunderbolt hard drive, an SSD (if you can afford to use a solid-state drive for backups), or even another internal hard drive, if your Mac is a Mac Mini or an older Mac Pro.

Another option is an *Apple Time Capsule,* which is a device that combines an AirPort Extreme wireless base station with a large hard drive so you can automatically back up one or more Macs over a wired or wireless network.

Moving right along, the first time a new disk suitable for use with Time Machine is connected to your Mac, a dialog pops up and asks whether you want to use that disk to back up with Time Machine. If you say yes, the Time Machine System Preferences pane opens automatically, showing the new disk already chosen as the backup disk.

If that doesn't happen or you want to use an already connected hard drive with Time Machine, open the Time Machine System Preferences pane and click the big On/Off switch to On. Now click the Select Disk button and select the hard drive you want to use for your backups. Mine is called emiTenihcaM daoRnoitidE (Time Machine Road Edition, backward, which is what I named this backup disk) in Figure 18-1.

The only other consideration is this: If you have other hard disks connected to your Mac, you should click the Options button to reveal the Exclude These Items from backups list, which tells Time Machine which volumes (disks) or folders *not* to back up. To add a volume or folder to this exclusion list, click the little + button; to remove a volume from the list, select the volume and then click the – button.

The Options sheet also has a check box for notifying you when old backups are deleted; check it if you want to be notified. And if your Mac is a laptop, a second check box governs whether Time Machine backs up your Mac when it's on battery power.

For the record, Time Machine stores your backups for the following lengths of time:

- Hourly backups for the past 24 hours
- Daily backups for the past month
- Weekly backups until your backup disk is full

When your backup disk gets full, the oldest backups on it are deleted and replaced by the newest.

That's why you should always buy the biggest drive you can afford to use as your backup disk; otherwise Time Machine will be deleting backups all the time rather than archiving them for future use.

When does it run? Glad you asked! It runs approximately once per hour.

If you enable and set up Time Machine as I just described, you'll never forget to back up your stuff, so just do it.

What does Time Machine back up?

Time Machine backs up your whole hard disk the first time it runs and then backs up files and folders that have been modified since your last backup. That's what backup systems do. But Time Machine does more — it also backs up things like contacts in your Contacts, pictures in your Photos Library, events in your calendars, and emails in your Mail, not to mention its support of versions and locking. About the only thing Time Machine doesn't back up is the contents of Home folders other than your own.

Those features — sweet ones, indeed — make Time Machine unlike any other backup system.

How do I restore a file (or a contact, a photo, an event, and so on)?

To restore a file or any other information, follow these steps:

1. **Launch the appropriate program — the one that contains the information you want to restore.**

   If what you want to restore happens to be a file, that program is the Finder, which (as you know) is always running. So to restore an individual file, you don't actually need to launch anything, just switch to the Finder if it's not the active application. But to restore a contact, a photo, an email message, or an event, for example, you need to launch Contacts, Photos, Mail, or Calendar, respectively.

2. **With the appropriate application running (or the appropriate Finder window open), launch the Time Machine application, as shown in Figure 18-2.**

   If you selected the Show Time Machine in Menu Bar check box in the Time Machine System Preferences pane, you can choose Enter Time Machine from the Time Machine menu, as shown in Figure 18-1.

   It will be easier to restore a file in the Finder if the folder the file is in (or was in) is the *active* folder (that is, open and frontmost) when you launch the Time Machine application. If not, you have to navigate to the appropriate folder before you can perform Step 3.

3. **Click one of the bars with dates near the lower-right corner of the screen *or* click the big Forward and Back arrows on the right of the Documents window in Figure 18-2 to choose the backup you want to restore from (Saturday, July 26 at 4:13PM in Figure 18-2).**

4. **Select the file, folder, Contacts contact, Photos photo, email message, or Calendar event you want to restore.**

5. **Click the Restore button below the window.**

If the file, folder, Contacts contact, Photos photo, email message, or Calendar event exists in the same location today, Time Machine politely inquires as to your wishes, as shown in Figure 18-3.

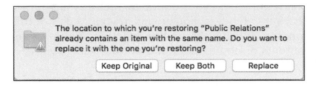

The location to which you're restoring "Public Relations" already contains an item with the same name. Do you want to replace it with the one you're restoring?

Keep Original   Keep Both   Replace

Figure 18-3: Time Machine asks what to do with the file you're restoring.

Don't forget that you can use the Search field, shown in Figure 18-2, to find files or folders in Time Machine.

Backing up by using the manual, brute-force method

If you're too cheap to buy a second hard drive, the most rudimentary way to back up is to do it manually. You accomplish this by dragging said files a few at a time to another volume — usually a DVD-R, DVD-RW, or USB flash drive. (If you use an optical disc, don't forget to actually *burn the disc;* merely dragging those files onto the optical disc icon won't do the trick.)

By using this method, you're making a copy of each file that you want to protect. (See www.dummies.com/extras/osxelcapitan for more info on removable storage.)

Yuck! If doing a manual backup sounds pretty awful, trust me — it is. This method can take a long, long time, you can't really tell whether you copied every file that needs to be backed up, and you can't really copy only the files that have been modified since your last backup. Almost nobody in his right mind sticks with this method for long.

Note that optical media is slow and costly and USB flash drives are not much better. It would behoove you to spend a few more dollars and purchase a higher capacity device such as an external hard drive. But if you do, why wouldn't you use it with Time Machine and forget about the inefficient brute-force method?

Of course, if you're careful to save files only in your Documents folder, as I suggest several times in this book, you can probably get away with backing up only that. Or if you save files in other folders within your Home folder or have any files in your Movies, Music, Pictures, or Sites folders (which often contain files you didn't specifically save in those folders, such as your Photos photos and iTunes songs), you should probably consider backing up your entire Home folder.

As you read in the following section, backing up your Home folder is even easier if you use special backup software.

Backing up by using commercial backup software

Another way to back up your files is with a third-party backup program. Backup software automates the task of backing up, remembering what's on each backup disc (if your backup uses more than one disc), and backing up only files that have been modified since your last backup.

Furthermore, you can instruct your backup software to back up only a certain folder (Home or Documents) and to ignore the hundreds of megabytes of stuff that make up OS X, all of which you can easily reinstall from your recovery disk or the Mac App Store.

Your first backup with commercial software might take anywhere from a few minutes to several hours and use one or more optical discs (CD-R, CD-RW, DVD-R, DVD-RW, magneto-optical disc) or non-optical media (such as another hard drive or any kind of tape). Subsequent backups, *incremental backups* in backup-software parlance, should take only a few minutes.

If you do incremental backups with optical discs, be sure to label and number all the discs you use during that operation. Your backup software may prompt you with a message such as *Please insert backup disk 7.* If you haven't labeled your media clearly, you could have a problem figuring out which disc *is* disc 7 or which disc 7 belongs to that particular backup set.

One of the best things about good backup software is that you can set it up to automate your backups and perform them even if you forget. And although Time Machine is a step in the right direction and might be sufficient for your needs, it's not good enough for me. I use a total of nine hard drives for backups.

Why You Need Two Sets of Backups

You're a good soldier. You listened to Dr. Mac and you back up regularly. You think you're immune to file loss or damage.

Now picture yourself in the following scenario:

> You leave the office one day for lunch. When you return, you discover that your office has been burglarized, struck by lightning, flooded, burned to the ground, or buried in earthquake rubble — take your pick.

Alas, although you did have a backup, the backup disk was right next to your Mac, which means it was either stolen or destroyed along with your Mac and everything else.

This scenario is totally unlikely — but it *could* happen, and it does demonstrate why you need multiple backups. If you have several sets of backup disks, and don't keep them all in the same room as your Mac, chances are pretty good that one of the sets will work even if the others are lost, stolen, or destroyed.

Non-Backup Security Concerns

As you probably surmised by now, backing up your files is critical unless you won't mind losing all your data someday. And although backing up is by far your most important security concern, several other things could imperil your data — things like viruses or other types of malware, including worms, spyware, and intruder attacks. That's the bad news. The good news is that all those things are far more likely to affect Windows users than Mac users. In fact, I'd venture to say that viruses, worms, malware, spyware, and intruder attacks are rarer than hens' teeth for Mac users.

That said, here are a few precautions Mac users should consider, just in case.

About viruses and other malware

A computer *virus,* in case you missed it in *Time* magazine and the rest of the news media, is a nasty little piece of computer code that replicates and spreads from disk to disk. A virus could cause your Mac to misbehave; some viruses can destroy files or erase disks with no warning.

Malware (short for *malicious software*) is software that's hostile, intrusive, annoying, or disruptive. Malware is often designed to gain unauthorized access to your computer and/or collect personal data (including passwords) without your knowledge.

The difference between a virus and other types of malware is that malware doesn't spread by itself. It relies upon trickery, mimicry, and social engineering to induce unsuspecting users to open a malicious file or install a malicious program. So a virus is a type of malware, but not all malware is viral.

You don't hear much about viruses on the Mac because there have been few (if any) since the dawn of the modern OS X era (so many big cats and California landmarks ago). Almost all viruses are specific to an operating system — Mac viruses won't affect Windows users, Windows viruses won't affect Mac users, and so forth. And the vast majority of known viruses affect only (you guessed it) Windows.

The one real exception here is a "gift" from the wonderful world of Microsoft Office (Word and Excel, for example) users: the dreaded *macro viruses* that are spread with Word and Excel documents containing macros written in the Microsoft VBA (Visual Basic for Applications) language. But you're safe even from those if you practice safe computing as I describe (although you can unknowingly pass them along to Windows users).

As it happens, so far, much of the viral activity affecting OS X involved various Windows macro viruses. Sadly, a very real threat known as Flashback appeared in early 2012. It exploited a security flaw in Java and stealthily installed itself on Macs. Soon after its discovery, Apple issued software updates for OS X that removed the malware and corrected the security flaw. There have been numerous similar instances since then, but in every case Apple has patched OS X before many (or any) users were affected (or infected).

By default, your Mac automatically checks for software updates every week, but you can change that setting in the Software Update System Preferences Pane. Click the Check Now button to run Software Update manually and check for the latest updates. The moral of the story is that it's usually a good idea to install Apple updates sooner rather than later.

Although few truly viral Mac OS X threats have been spotted in the wild so far, most malware is spread via social engineering, which is easy to protect yourself against; here's how:

✔ In Safari Preferences, Disable Open Safe Files after Downloading.

✔ If a suspicious alert or window appears on your screen, Force Quit your web browser (⌘⇨ Force Quit or ⌘+Option+Esc) immediately.

✔ If the OS X Installer launches for no apparent reason, *do not click Continue!* Don't install the software, and for heaven's sake, don't type your administrator password.

✔ And by all means read the section on El Capitan's Gatekeeper later in this chapter for details on the three different levels of protection it can offer.

✔ Don't run *any* installer — the kind built into OS X or the third-party kind — unless you're absolutely certain that it came from a trusted source.

✔ Don't use credit or debit cards with unfamiliar vendors and/or nonsecure websites (for example, if you don't see http*s* instead of http, or see a little lock icon in the address field of your browser, the site may not be secure).

If you use disks that have been inserted into other computers, you need some form of virus-detection software. If you download and use files from web and File Transfer Protocol (FTP) sites on the Internet, you need some form of virus detection as well.

You don't have too much to worry about if

- You download files only from commercial online services, such as AOL, CNET, or MacUpdate, which are all very conscientious about malware.

- You buy software only from the Apple Mac App store.

- You use only commercial software, and never download files from websites with strange names.

You should definitely worry about malicious infection if

- An unsavory friend told you about a website called Dan'sDenOfPiratedIllegalStolenBootlegSoftware.com, and you actually visited it.

- You swap disks or USB thumb drives with friends regularly.

- You shuttle disks or USB thumb drives back and forth to other Macs.

- You use your disks or USB thumb drives at public computers, photo-printing machines, or other computers likely to have had exposure to many disks.

- You download files from various and sundry places on the Internet, even ones that don't sound as slimy as Dan'sDenOfPiratedIllegalStolenBootleg Software.com.

- You receive email with attachments (and open them). Note that you can receive malicious software in messages that look like they're from people you know and trust. It's called *spoofing* and it's easily accomplished, so think carefully before opening an attachment and contact the sender if you have any doubt about the message's authenticity.

If you're at risk, do yourself a favor, and buy a commercial antivirus program. I'm not quite ready to install antivirus software myself; I find that they're obtrusive and slow my Mac. If you think you need protection, consider Mac Internet Security X8 ($49.99; www.intego.com), MacScan ($39.99; http://macscan.securemac.com), or ClamXav 2 ($29.95; www.clamxav.com).

If you decide to do as I do and not as I just suggested, I urge you to visit some of or all the websites in Chapter 22 regularly. If nothing else, you'll get advance warning the next time a particularly heinous piece of Mac malware is on the loose. I don't know about you, but I'll wait until then to reassess my position on this antivirus conundrum.

Firewall: Yea or nay?

According to the OS X built-in Oxford American Dictionary, a firewall is

> *Part of a computer system or network that is designed to block unauthorized access while permitting outward communication.*

Using a firewall protects your computer from malicious users on other networks or the Internet and keeps them from gaining access to your Mac.

Unlike older versions of Windows, OS X is quite difficult to crack. There have been few (if any) reports of outsiders gaining access to Macintosh computers running OS X. One reason might be that OS X has a built-in firewall. That's the good news. The bad news is that the firewall is disabled by default, so you'll need to activate it if you want to be protected against unauthorized network access to your computer.

If you use a router with its own firewall (and the router's firewall is enabled), *do not also activate the El Capitan firewall.* Running multiple firewalls can cause serious network issues.

To activate OS X's firewall, follow these steps:

1. **Open the System Preferences application (from the Applications folder, menu, Launchpad, or Dock).**

2. **Click the Security & Privacy icon and click the Firewall tab.**

   If the lock in the bottom-left corner of the Security & Privacy pane is locked (as it should be), click it, and provide your administrator account name and password.

   The default setting is Allow All Incoming Connections, which is the least-secure option.

3. **Click the Turn On Firewall button to turn the firewall on, if it's not already running.**

4. **Click the Firewall Options button to configure your firewall's settings.**

5. **For the highest level of protection, select the Block All Incoming Connections check box.**

6. **Click OK.**

Alas, you probably won't want to keep this setting for long because you won't be able to use awesome OS X features such as Messages and file, screen, printer, and music sharing, to name a few. If (or when) it becomes desirable to allow certain incoming connections from outside computers, enable them in the Sharing System Preferences pane.

The only other issue you're likely to face is when a particular application needs you to allow outside connections to it in order to function. How would you know? Check the user manual, Read Me file, or application Help. Or you might see an error message that the program can't connect to the Internet. Don't worry — if a program requires you to open your firewall, you can almost certainly find some information in one (or more) of these places.

The solution is to click the little + button on the left below the list of rules in the Firewall Options window. A standard Open File sheet drops down over the window; select the appropriate program and click the Add button. Your firewall will then allow incoming connections to that particular application evermore.

Selecting the Automatically Allow Signed Software to Receive Incoming Connections check box will solve some, albeit not all, incoming connection problems by allowing any program that has a trusted certificate filed with Apple to receive incoming connections without a trip to the Sharing System Preferences pane.

Install recommended software updates

I mention this earlier in a short tip, but it bears repeating: By default, your Mac checks with the mothership (Apple) once per week to look for any new or updated software for your Mac. If there is, your Mac informs you that a new Software Update is available and asks whether you'd like to install it. In almost all cases, you do. Apple issues Software Updates to fix newly discovered security concerns, to fix serious bugs in OS X, or to fix bugs in or add functionality to Apple applications.

You can perform this check manually by choosing Software Update from the menu, which will open the App Store and display its Updates tab. If any updates are available, you'll see them here.

Use the App Store System Preferences pane to disable automatic checking completely, and/or instruct your Mac to automatically download and install updates.

Once in a blue moon, one of these Software Updates has an unintended side effect; while fixing one problem, it introduces a different problem. Apple is generally pretty careful, and this doesn't happen very often, but if you want to be safe, don't install a Software Update until you visit Macworld (www.macworld.com), The Mac Observer (www.macobserver.com), or other authoritative site and look at what they have to say about the update you have in mind. If there are widespread issues with a particular Software Update, sites like these will have the most comprehensive coverage (and possible workarounds).

Apps need updates, too. So make a habit of launching the Mac App Store application now and then, clicking the Updates tab, and then updating any apps that require it.

Many third-party programs, including Microsoft Office and most Adobe products, use their own update-checking mechanism. Check and make sure that you have yours enabled. Many third-party apps offer a Check for Updates option in the Help (or other) menu or as a preference in their Preferences window.

One last thing: If you see a little number on the App Store icon in the Dock, you have that many updates waiting. Launch the Mac App Store, and click the Updates tab.

Protecting Your Data from Prying Eyes

The last kind of security I look at in this chapter is protecting your files from other users on your local area network (LAN) and users with physical access to your Mac. If you don't want anyone messing with your files, check out the security measures in the following sections.

Blocking or limiting connections

The first thing you may want to do is open the Sharing System Preferences pane by launching the System Preferences application (from the Applications folder, ® menu, or Dock) and clicking the Sharing icon. Nobody can access your Mac over the network if all the services in the Sharing pane are disabled and your firewall is set to Block All Incoming Connections. See the section "Firewall: Yea or nay?" earlier in this chapter for details on these settings.

Locking down files with FileVault

If you absolutely, positively don't ever want anyone to be able to access the files in your Home folder, FileVault allows you to encrypt your entire disk and protect it with the latest government-approved encryption standard: Advanced Encryption Standard with 128-bit keys (AES-128).

When you turn on FileVault, you're asked to set a master password for the computer. After you do, you or any other administrator can use that master password if you forget your regular account login password.

I said it at the beginning of the chapter but it bears repeating: If you turn on FileVault and forget both your login password and your master password, you can't log in to your account — and your data is lost forever. Really. Not even DriveSavers has a hope of recovering it. So don't forget both passwords, okay?

FileVault is useful primarily if you store sensitive information on your Mac. If you're logged out of your user account and someone gets access to your Mac, there is no way they can access your data. Period.

Because FileVault encrypts your entire hard drive, some tasks that normally access your disk might be prevented. For one thing, some backup programs (not Time Machine, of course) choke if FileVault is enabled. Also, if you're not logged in to your user account, other users can't access your Shared folder(s).

Because FileVault is always encrypting and decrypting files, it can slow older Macs a tiny bit when you add or save new files, and it can take extra time before it lets you log out, restart, or shut down. If your Mac is less than three years old, you'll probably notice little or no delay from enabling FileVault.

To turn on FileVault, follow these steps:

1. **Open the Security & Privacy System Preferences pane.**

2. **Click the FileVault tab.**

3. **Click the Turn on FileVault button to enable FileVault.**

To turn off FileVault, click the Turn Off FileVault button.

One last thing: You have the option of encrypting Time Machine backups as well as iTunes backups of your iDevices. Just enable the appropriate check box in the Time Machine System Preferences pane or iTunes Summary pane for your iDevice.

Setting other options for security

The General tab of the Security & Privacy System Preferences pane offers several more options that can help keep your data safe. They are

- ✔ **Change Password:** Click this button to change the password for your user account.

- ✔ **Require Password after Sleep or Screen Saver Begins:** Enable this option if you want your Mac to lock itself up and require a password after the screen saver kicks in or it goes to sleep. It can become a pain in the butt, having to type your password all the time. But if you have nosy co-workers, family members, or other individuals you'd like to keep from rooting around in your stuff, you should probably enable this option.

When enabled, this option offers a pop-up menu that lets you specify how long after sleep or screen saver this password protection should kick in. The options range from immediately to four hours.

✔ **Show a Message When the Screen Is Locked:** Type the message you want on your screen when it's locked in this text entry box.

✔ **Allow Apps Downloaded from:**

Last, but certainly not least (at least with regard to the General tab), are three options that can help protect you from downloading and running malicious software by limiting the applications your Mac can run.

In case you were wondering, Apple calls this feature *Gatekeeper,* though that name doesn't appear in the System Preferences pane.

You have three mutually exclusive options — Mac App Store, Mac App Store and Identified Developers, or Anywhere. Select the radio button next to the level of protection you desire, and the other two options are automatically deselected.

Here's what they do:

- *Mac App Store:* This option allows you to run only apps you download from the Mac App Store. It's the safest and most restrictive setting.

- *Mac App Store and Identified Developers:* Apple offers a Developer ID program to certified members of the Mac Developers Program. Apple gives them a unique Developer ID, which allows Gatekeeper to verify that their app is not known malware and that it hasn't been tampered with. If an app doesn't have a Developer ID associated with it, Gatekeeper can let you know before you install it.

  This choice is probably the best for most users. It allows third-party apps from Apple-vetted vendors, such as Microsoft, Adobe, and thousands more. It's a lot less restrictive than the Mac App Store option and a lot safer than choosing Anywhere.

- *Anywhere:* What its name suggests; this option lets you run any app, no matter where it came from.

Finally, the Privacy tab of the Security & Privacy System Preferences pane has several potentially useful options:

✔ **To Enable or Disable Location Services:** Click Location Services on the left, and you'll see a list of apps that are allowed to use your computer's current location. Check or uncheck these apps to enable/disable their use of Location Services.

✓ **To Enable or Disable Other Apps Access to your Contacts, Calendars, and Reminders:** Click Contacts, Calendars, or Reminders in the list on the left and apps with access to their contents will appear on the right. Check or uncheck the check box for each app to enable/disable its permission to access Contacts, Calendars, or Reminders.

✓ **To Enable or Disable Apps Allowed to Control Your Computer:** Click Accessibility in the list on the left, and apps allowed to control your computer appear on the right. Check or uncheck the check box for each app to enable/disable its permission to control your computer.

✓ **To Automatically Send Anonymous Diagnostic & Usage Data to Apple:** Click Diagnostics and Usage in the list on the left and then select the Send Diagnostic & Usage Data to Apple check box. This sends details of system crashes, apps that quit unexpectedly, freezes, or kernel panics (anonymously) to the mothership in Cupertino (Apple's world HQ), where engineers pore over the data and issue software updates to eliminate the bugs. For bonus points, send crash reports to app developers, too, by enabling the Share Crash Data with App Developers check box as well.

And that's all you really need to know about security and privacy (or at least enough to make you dangerous).

19

Utility Chest

In This Chapter

▶ Crunching numbers with the Calculator

▶ Plumbing El Capitan's innards

▶ And much, much more . . .

O S X El Capitan comes with a plethora of useful utilities that make using your computer more pleasant and/or make you more productive when you use your computer. In this chapter, I give you a glimpse of the ones that aren't covered elsewhere in this book.

The first item, Calculator, is in your Applications folder; all the other items in this chapter are in your Utilities folder, *inside* your Applications folder (or use the Utilities folder's keyboard shortcut, ⌘+Shift+U).

	% CPU ∨	CPU
	10.1	16:51.90
	6.0	17:51.52
...s Agent	3.4	13:12.83
...otolibraryd	2.3	13:57.72
Activity Monitor	0.7	13.45
mdworker	0.3	0.14
UserEventAgent	0.2	16.24
com.apple.photomoments	0.1	2:49.32
akd	0.1	28.72
ScreensharingAgent	0.1	9.34
mdworker	0.1	2.57
mdworker	0.1	0.20
mdflagwriter	0.1	6.69
Finder	0.1	42.47
SafariCloudHistoryPushAgent	0.1	5.27

		CPU LOAD
System:	6.53%	
User:	4.52%	
Idle:	88.94%	

Calculator

Need to do some quick math? The Calculator application gives you a simple calculator with all the basic number-crunching functions that your pocket calculator has. To use it, you can either click the keys with the mouse or type numbers and operators (math symbols such as +, −, and =) using the number keys on your keyboard (or numeric keypad, if you have one). Calculator also offers a paper tape (Window⇨Show Paper Tape) to track your computations — and, if you want, provide a printed record. It can even speak numbers aloud (Speech⇨Speak Button Pressed and Speech⇨Speak).

Check out the Calculator in Figure 19-1.

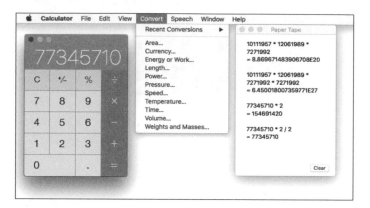

Figure 19-1: The Calculator (left), Convert menu (middle), and Paper Tape (right).

In my humble opinion, the most useful feature in the Calculator (after the Paper Tape) is the Convert menu — more specifically, the currency-conversion feature. It actually checks the Internet for the exchange rate before calculating the conversion for you. That's very cool.

Beyond that, Calculator has three modes: Basic, Scientific, and Programmer. Basic is the default, and you access the other two modes as follows:

- Pressing ⌘+2 (View➪Scientific) turns the formerly anemic calculator into a powerful scientific calculator.

- Choosing View➪Programmer (⌘+3) turns it into the programmer's friend, letting you display your data in binary, octal, hexadecimal, ASCII, and Unicode. It also performs programming operations, such as shifts and byte swaps. (If you're a programmer, you know what all that means; if you aren't, it really doesn't matter.)

Activity Monitor

In Unix, the underlying operating system that powers OS X, applications and other things going on behind the scenes are called *processes*. Each application and the operating system itself can run a number of processes at the same time.

In Figure 19-2, you see 288 different processes running, most of them behind the scenes. Note that when this screen shot was taken, I had half a dozen or more programs running, including the Finder, Photos Agent, and Activity Monitor itself.

Activity Monitor window   CPU Monitor windows

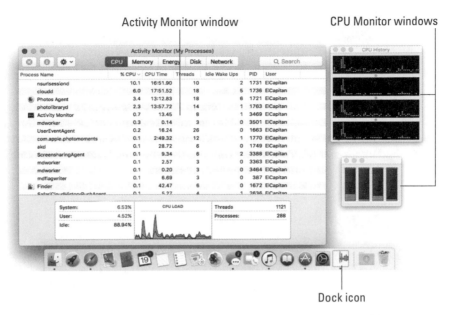

Dock icon

Figure 19-2: The Activity Monitor window, two little CPU monitors, and the Dock icon.

To display the two CPU monitor windows on the right side of the Activity Monitor window as shown in Figure 19-2, choose Window➪CPU Usage (⌘+2) and CPU History (⌘+3).

You also select what appears in the Activity Monitor's Dock icon — CPU Usage, CPU History, Network Usage (shown in Figure 19-2), Disk Activity, or the Activity Monitor icon — by choosing View➪Dock Icon. All but the Activity Monitor icon appear *live,* meaning that they update every few seconds to reflect the current state of affairs.

To choose how often these updates occur, choose View➪Update Frequency.

Setting Activity Monitor to update more frequently causes it to use more CPU cycles, which can decrease overall performance slightly.

Finally, the bottom portion of the Activity Monitor window displays information for the active tab. Select the CPU, Memory, Energy, Disk, or Network, and the middle and bottom portions of the Activity Monitor window change to reflect that selection.

Because all Macs that can run El Capitan have at least a dual-core processor, you'll see at least two, and possibly four or more, CPUs displayed in Activity Monitor: one for each core.

Geeks and troubleshooters (and even you) can use Activity Monitor to iden-tify what processes are running, which user owns the process, and how much CPU capacity and memory the process is using. You can even use this feature to quit or force-quit a process that you think might be causing problems for you.

Messing around in Activity Monitor isn't a good idea for most users. If you're having problems with an application or with OS X, try quitting open applica-tions, force-quitting applications (press ⌘+Option+Esc — the Mac three-finger salute), or logging out and then logging back in again before you start mucking around with killing processes.

Disk Utility

If you're having problems with your hard drive or need to make changes to it, Disk Utility is a good place to start. Start by clicking a disk or volume in the column on the left and then click one of the buttons on the toolbar as described in the following sections.

First Aid button

If you suspect that something's not quite right with your Mac, the First Aid button in Disk Utility should be among your first stops. Use First Aid to verify and (if necessary) repair an ailing drive. To use it, select a volume icon in the list on the left and then click the First Aid button in the upper-left corner of the Disk Utility window. A sheet asks if you'd like to run First Aid on the selected disk; click Run to do it or Cancel to dismiss the sheet. When it's fin-ished, you'll get information about any problems that the software finds. If First Aid doesn't find any problems, you can go on your merry way, secure in the knowledge that your Mac is A-okay. If First Aid turns up a problem that it can't fix, it will advise you what to do next.

You can't use Disk Utility First Aid to fix a CD or DVD, nor can you use it to fix most disk image files. These types of disks are read-only and can't be altered.

Partition button

Use this button to create disk partitions (multiple volumes on a single disk). OS X treats each partition as a separate disk. The Partition button is enabled only when an eligible item is selected in the column on the left.

Of partitions and volumes

Partitioning a drive lets you create multiple volumes. A *volume* is a storage space that (from the Mac's point of view) looks and acts just like a hard drive; a *partition* is simply a designated volume on a drive, completely separate from all other partitions (volumes). You can create any number of partitions, but it's a good idea to limit yourself to no more than a small handful.

By the same token, it's absolutely not necessary to use partitions unless you're running Boot Camp (see Chapter 17). Many users never partition a hard drive and get along just fine. If you do choose to partition, you should probably limit the number of partitions you create. An iMac with a 1TB drive will do just fine with one partition; there's no need to create more.

Be careful here. Although some adjustments can be made to partitions without loss of data, not all adjustments can. You'll be warned if what you're about to do will permanently erase your data, but I thought I'd give you fair warning first.

Erase button

Use Erase to format (completely erase) any disk except the current startup disk.

When you format a disk, you erase all information on it permanently. Formatting can't be undone — so unless you're *absolutely sure* this is what you want, don't do it. Unless you have no use for whatever's currently on the disk, make a complete backup of the disk before you format it. If the data is critical, you should have at least two (or even three) known-to-be-valid backup copies of that disk before you reformat.

Mount/Unmount button

A drive can be connected but not available to your Mac. For example, when you eject a hard disk or SSD, it's still connected to the computer but doesn't appear in the Finder. This is called an *unmounted disk*.

The Mount/Unmount button lets you dismount (eject) or mount a connected disk or partition on a disk. For reasons that should be obvious, you can't eject the disk from which you booted.

Info button

Click the Info button to see myriad technical details about the selected disk including its size, capacity, and free and used space.

One last thing: You'll find out more about Disk Utility (mostly how to use it for troubleshooting) in Chapter 20.

Grab

Want to take a picture of your screen? You can use Grab to take a picture of all or part of the screen and save that file for printing or sending around (say, to all your screaming fans who want to see your Desktop pattern or how you've organized your windows).

And guess what? There are universal keyboard shortcuts that let you create a picture of your entire screen (⌘+Shift+3) or just a portion of it (⌘+Shift+4) even when Grab isn't running.

Grab's best feature is its capability to do a timed screen capture. Like those cameras that let you start the timer and then run to get into the shot, Grab gives you ten seconds to bring the window you want to the front, pull down a menu, and get the cursor out of the way or whatever you need to do to get the screen just right.

Grab's default behavior is to not display a cursor. If you want to show a cursor in your screen shots, choose Grab➪Preferences and then select a pointer from the ten choices in the Preferences window. To have no cursor, click the topmost, leftmost item, which is an empty box that indicates *no cursor*.

Grapher

Grapher is a venerable piece of eye candy that shows off your CPU's computational power. A quick, visual math instructor, Grapher can graph equations in two or three dimensions and speaks hexadecimal, octal, base ten (decimal), and binary to boot. You can even graph curves, surfaces, inequalities, differential equations, discrete series, and vector and scalar fields . . . whatever that means. (I found all that information in Apple Help.)

Keychain Access

A *keychain* is a way to consolidate your passwords — the one you use to log in to your Mac, your email password, and passwords required by any websites. Here's how it works: You use a single password to unlock your keychain (which holds your various passwords), and then you don't have to remember all your other passwords. Rest assured that your passwords are secure because only a user who has your keychain password can reach the other password-protected applications.

The Keychain Access utility is particularly cool if you have multiple email accounts and each one has a different password. Just add them all to your keychain, and you can get all your mail at the same time with one password.

A special master keychain called the Login Keychain is created automatically for every OS X El Capitan user.

Here's how to add passwords to your login keychain:

✔ **To add passwords for applications,** just open Mail or another application that supports the keychain. When the program asks for your password, supply it and choose Yes to add the password to the keychain.

How do you know which programs support the Keychain Access utility? You don't, until you're prompted to save your password in a keychain in that Open dialog, connect window, or so forth. If a program supports Keychain Access, it offers a check box for it in the user ID/password dialog or window.

✔ **To add a website password to a keychain,** open the Keychain Access application and click the Password button. In the New Password Item window that opens, type the URL of the page (or copy and paste it) in the Keychain Item Name text field, type your username in the Account Name field, and then type your password in the Password text field, as shown in Figure 19-3.

Click the little key to the right of the password field to use the Password Assistant window, which can help you select a memorable high-quality password.

To use the new URL password, use Safari to open the URL. If the account name and password aren't filled in for you automatically, choose Edit➪AutoFill Form (⌘+Shift+A) and they will be.

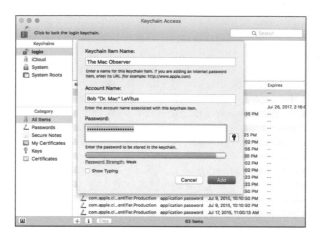

Figure 19-3: Add a URL to the keychain manually by using Keychain Access.

If you select the User Names and Passwords check box on the AutoFill tab of Safari's Preferences window (Safari⇨Preferences or ⌘+, [comma]), you don't have to add sites, accounts, or passwords manually. Instead, the first time you visit a site that requires an account name and a password, Safari asks whether you would like to save your password, and then it does so.

iCloud Keychain syncing is a great feature that makes keychains even better. Turn it on (System Preferences⇨iCloud), and your Safari passwords will be securely synced to (and from) all of your Apple devices including iPhones and iPads.

Migration Assistant

Migration Assistant is pretty much a one-trick pony, but that pony is a prize-winner. You use the Migration Assistant to transfer your account and other user information from another Mac, another volume on the current Mac, or a Time Machine backup. You need to authenticate as an administrator to use it, but it's a pretty handy way to transfer an entire account without having to re-create all the preferences and other settings. When you first installed El Capitan (or when you booted your nice, new El Capitan-based Mac for the first time), the setup utility asked you whether you wanted to transfer your information from another Mac. If you answered in the affirmative, it ran the Migration Assistant.

It's not just for new El Capitan installs. You can launch this one-trick-pony anytime to transfer all or some user accounts, applications, settings, and files from another Mac, PC, or Time Machine backup to this one. You can use it also after replacing a hard drive or reinstalling OS X. Check out the article on installing and reinstalling OS X at www.dummies.com/extras/osxelcapitan. Last but not least, Migration Assistant can import user accounts, applications, settings, and files from Windows PCs as well as from Macs.

System Information

System Information (the App Formerly Known as System Profiler) is a little program that is launched when you click the System Report button in the About This Mac window (⇨ About This Mac). It provides information about your Mac. (What a concept!) If you're curious about arcane questions such as what processor your Mac has or what devices are stashed inside it or are connected to it, give this baby a try. Click various items in the Contents list on the left side of the window, and information about the item appears on the right side of the window. Feel free to poke around this little puppy as much as you like; it's benign and can't hurt anything.

If you ever have occasion to call for technical support for your Mac, software, or peripherals, you're probably going to be asked to provide information from System Information, so don't get rid of it just because you don't care about this kind of stuff.

Terminal

OS X is based on Unix. If you need proof — or if you actually want to operate your Mac as the Unix machine that it is — Terminal is the place to start.

Because Unix is a command line–based operating system, you use Terminal to type your commands. You can issue commands that show a directory listing, copy and move files, search for filenames or contents, or establish or change passwords. In short, if you know what you're doing, you can do everything on the command line that you can do in OS X. For most folks, that's not a desirable alternative to the windows and icons of the Finder window. But take my word for it; true geeks who are also Mac lovers get all misty-eyed about the combination of a command line *and* a graphical user interface.

You can wreak havoc upon your poor operating system with Terminal. You can harm your El Capitan in many ways that just aren't possible using mere windows and icons and clicks. *Before you type a single command in Terminal, think seriously about what I just said.* And if you're not 100 percent certain about the command you just typed, don't even think about pressing Return.

20

Troubleshooting OS X

In This Chapter

▶ Facing the ol' "My Mac Won't Boot" blues

▶ Dealing with the prohibitory sign

▶ Recovering from startup crashes

*A*s a bleeding-edge Mac enthusiast and consultant with more than a quarter century of Mac experience, I've seen more than my share of Mac troubles. Over those years, I've developed an arsenal of mostly surefire tips and tricks that I believe can resolve more than 90 percent of Mac issues without a trip to the repair shop.

Alas, if your hardware is dead, then, sadly, neither you nor I can do anything about it because it is now a job for your friendly Mac repairman — and your fat checkbook or high-limit credit card. But if your hardware is okay, you have a fighting chance of using the suggestions in this chapter to get your machine up and running.

About Startup Disks and Booting

Although you usually see a stylish Apple logo when you turn on your computer, once in a blue moon, you may not. You may instead see a solid blue screen, a solid gray screen, a solid black screen, or something else entirely, as described in the next section.

The point is that your Mac isn't starting up as it should. When this happens, it usually indicates that something bad has happened to your Mac. Sometimes, a hardware component has bitten the dust; other times, OS X itself has somehow been damaged.

Rest assured that these occurrences are rather uncommon — many Macs and Mac users go an entire lifetime without ever having an issue. But if you ever have a Mac that won't boot, don't despair. Before you declare your Mac terminally ill or worse, try out the advice in this chapter.

Finally, I use the term *hard disk* generically throughout the chapter to refer to hard or solid-state disks.

Finding or creating a startup disk

First things first: When I talk about *booting,* I mean using a particular disk or disk partition as your startup disk.

Because El Capitan (like Yosemite and Mavericks before it) doesn't come on a (bootable) DVD, the OS X Installer creates a bootable partition named Recovery HD when you first install El Capitan on a disk.

I recommend that you also make a bootable Recovery disk (in addition to the one El Capitan should have created) or a clone of your Mac startup disk. If not, it's something you may wish you had done when your Mac starts acting wonky.

Explaining how to create a bootable recovery disk or clone is beyond the purview of this book, but I hope you'll take it upon yourself to figure it out and make one. The Recovery HD partition is a good concept, but if your hard disk dies, the Recovery HD partition generally dies with it — which is why *I strongly recommend making a bootable clone of your startup disk as soon as possible,* just in case.

Apple offers a free program called Recovery Disk Assistant (`http://support.apple.com/kb/DL1433`), which can create a bootable El Capitan installer disk for you. Another option is Carbon Copy Cloner (`www.bombich.com`), a donation-ware app that lets you create a clone of your boot disk with a minimum of fuss. Or try my favorite, SuperDuper! (shareware from `www.shirt-pocket.com`); just add a hard disk as large as or larger than your boot disk, and you'll be good to go with any of these options.

They call it a prohibitory sign for a reason

When you turn on your Mac, the first thing it does (after the hardware tests) is check for a startup disk that has a viable copy of OS X on it. If your system doesn't find such a disk on your internal hard drive, it begins looking elsewhere — on a FireWire, Thunderbolt, Universal Serial Bus (USB) disk, a thumb drive, or a DVD.

At this point, your Mac usually finds your internal hard drive (or SSD), which contains your operating system, and the startup process continues on its merry way with the subtle Apple logo and all the rest. If your Mac can't find your hard drive (or doesn't find on it what it needs to boot OS X), you encounter the dreaded prohibitory sign. Think of the prohibitory sign as your Mac's way of saying, "Please provide me a startup disk."

If you have more than one startup disk attached to your Mac, as many users do, you can choose which one your Mac boots from in the Startup Disk System Preferences pane or by pressing and holding down the Option key when you start up your Mac.

If Apple can figure out a way to put a prohibitory sign on the screen, why the heck can't the software engineers find a way to put the words *I need a startup disk* on the screen as well? The curtness of these icons is one of my pet peeves about the Macintosh. I know — you're clever and smart (because, of course, you're smart enough to be reading *OS X El Capitan For Dummies*), so *you* know that a prohibitory sign means you should insert a startup disk. But what about everyone else?

If you encounter any of these warning icons, shown in Figure 20-1, go through the steps I outline later in this chapter. You can try different options, such as using Disk Utility's First Aid, zapping the parameter RAM (PRAM), and performing a Safe Boot. Try them in the order listed, starting with Step 1. Then, if one doesn't work, move on to the next.

You need to restart your computer. Hold down the Power button for several seconds or press the Restart button.

Veuillez redémarrer votre ordinateur. Maintenez la touche de démarrage enfoncée pendant plusieurs secondes ou bien appuyez sur le bouton de réinitialisation.

Sie müssen Ihren Computer neu starten. Halten Sie dazu die Einschalttaste einige Sekunden gedrückt oder drücken Sie die Neustart-Taste.

コンピュータを再起動する必要があります。パワーボタンを数秒間押し続けるか、リセットボタンを押してください。

Figure 20-1: Any of these means it's troubleshooting time.

Recovering with Recovery HD

If you see a prohibitory sign (top left in Figure 20-1), spinning-disc cursor (top right), or kernel panic alert (the text in six languages that appears below the other two images) that doesn't go away when you start up your Mac, the first thing to do is attempt to repair hidden damage to your hard drive with the Disk Utility program's First Aid feature. And to do that, you'll have to boot from the Recovery HD partition. That's because you can't run Disk Utility's First Aid feature on the current startup disk.

To start up from this magical disk (actually, a disk partition), here's what to do:

1. **Restart your Mac.**

2. **Press and hold down ⌘+R until you see the Apple logo.**

If your Mac doesn't boot from the Recovery HD after Step 2, hold down the Option key while booting to display the built-in Startup Manager (see Figure 20-2).

If you press Option after the startup chime instead of ⌘+R, the built-in Startup Manager appears. From this screen, you can click the Recovery HD icon (see Figure 20-2), and then click

Figure 20-2: The built-in Startup Manager appears in the middle of your Mac screen.

the arrow below it or press Return to boot from it. Or, if you're going to boot from a disk other than the Recovery HD, you can select it here.

Pressing Option during startup displays icons for all bootable volumes it sees and allows you to select one (including the Recovery HD partition).

Click the disk you want to start up from (Macintosh HD in Figure 20-2), and then click the arrow below it or press Return to start up your Mac from it.

This technique is quite useful if your usual startup disk is damaged or having an identity crisis during startup and the ⌘+R trick isn't working to boot from the Recovery HD partition.

If you can boot from the Recovery HD partition: If you see the OS X Utilities window after booting from the Recovery HD partition, hope flickers for your Mac. The fact that you can boot from another volume indicates that the problem lies in one of two places: your startup volume and/or the OS X installation on that volume.

Regardless of what the cause is, your Mac will probably respond to one of the techniques I discuss throughout the rest of this chapter.

So if you can boot from the Recovery HD partition, proceed to section "Step 1: Run First Aid" now.

If you can't boot from the Recovery HD partition (or an external startup drive, clone, DVD-ROM, or other disk):

Skip directly to section "Step 5: Things to try before taking your Mac in for repair."

Step 1: Run First Aid

In most cases, after you've booted successfully from the Recovery HD or another bootable disk, the first logical troubleshooting step is to use the First Aid option in the Disk Utility application.

Every drive has several strangely named components, such as B-trees, extent files, catalog files, and other creatively named invisible files. They're all involved in managing the data on your drives. Disk Utility's First Aid feature checks all those files and repairs the damaged ones.

One last thing: If you booted from a disk other than the Recovery HD partition, you'll have to find and launch Disk Utility on that disk before you can follow these instructions.

1. **Boot from the Recovery HD volume by restarting your Mac while pressing the ⌘ and R keys.**

   The OS X Utilities window appears.

2. **Select Disk Utility and click Continue.**

3. **When the Disk Utility window appears, click the icon for your boot hard drive, to the left of the Disk Utility window.**

   Your boot drive is the one with OS X and your Home folder on it; mine is called *Macintosh HD*.

4. **Click the First Aid button in the toolbar.**

   A sheet drops down asking if you'd like to run First Aid on that disk.

5. **Click the Run button.**

   Your Mac whirs and hums for a few minutes, and a sheet eventually drops down.

6. **(Optional): Click Details to see (mostly unintelligible) details of what First Aid has done to your disk.**

7. **Click the Done button.**

8. **Quit Disk Utility.**

   Choose Disk Utility ➪ Quit Disk Utility, press ⌘+Q, or click the red Close Window gumdrop.

9. **Quit OS X Utilities.**

   Choose OS X Utilities ➪ Quit OS X Utilities, press ⌘+Q, or click the red Close Window gumdrop. A sheet drops down and asks if you're sure. Click Restart (don't hold down any keys).

If First Aid finds damage that it can't fix, a commercial disk-recovery tool, such as Prosoft's excellent Drive Genius 3 or Alsoft's also excellent DiskWarrior may be able to repair the damage. And even if First Aid gave you a clean bill of health, you may want to run a third-party utility anyway, just to have a second opinion.

Make sure you're running a current version; older versions may not be compatible with OS X El Capitan and could make things worse.

If everything checks out with First Aid but you still get the prohibitory sign after you restart, proceed to the next section to try a dance called booting into Safe Mode.

Step 2: Safe Boot into Safe Mode

Booting your Mac in Safe Mode may help you resolve your startup issue by not loading nonessential (and non–OS X) software at boot time. You do it by holding down the Shift key during startup.

If your Mac is set up so you don't have to log in, keep pressing the Shift key during startup until the Finder loads completely. If you do log in to your Mac, type your password as usual — but before clicking the Log In button, press the Shift key again and hold it down until the Finder loads completely.

You know you held the Shift key long enough if your Login Items don't load (assuming that you have Login Items; you can designate them in the Users & Groups System Preferences pane, although some programs create them for you).

Booting in Safe Mode does three things to help you with troubleshooting:

✓ It forces a directory check of the startup (boot) volume.

✓ It loads only required kernel extensions (some of the items in /System/Library/Extensions).

✓ It runs only Apple-installed essential startup items (some of the items in /Library/StartupItems and /System/Library/StartupItems). Note that the Startup Items in the Library folders are different from the Login Items in the Users & Groups System Preferences pane. Startup Items run at boot time before the login window even appears; Login Items don't run until after you log into your user account.

Taken together, these changes often work around issues caused by software or directory damage on the startup volume.

Some features may not work in Safe Mode. Among them are DVD Player, capturing video (in iMovie or other video-editing software), using AirPort, and using some audio input or output devices. Use Safe Mode only when you need to troubleshoot a startup issue.

If your Mac boots in Safe Mode, you may be able to determine what's causing the issue by moving the contents of your Preferences folder (in Home/Library, which you can make visible by pressing the Option key when opening the Go menu) to the Desktop temporarily or by disabling Login Items (in the Users & Groups System Preferences pane). If either of these things resolves the issue, you can put preferences files back in Home/Library/Preferences a few at a time, or you can re-enable login items one at a time until you figure out which preferences file or login item is causing your problems. If your Mac still has problems, see the following section.

Step 3: Zapping the PRAM/NVRAM

Sometimes your parameter RAM (PRAM) or non-volatile RAM (NVRAM) becomes scrambled and needs to be reset. Both of these are small pieces of memory that aren't erased or forgotten when you shut down. They keep track of things such as

✓ Time zone setting

✓ Startup volume choice

✓ Speaker volume

✓ Any recent kernel-panic information

✓ DVD region setting

To reset (a process often called *zapping)* your PRAM/NVRAM, restart your Mac and press ⌘+Option+P+R (that's four keys — good luck; it's okay to use your nose) until your Mac restarts itself. It's kind of like a hiccup. You might see the spinning-disc pointer for a minute or two while your Mac thinks about it . . . then the icon disappears, and your Mac chimes again and restarts. Most power users believe you should zap it more than once, letting it chime two, three, or even four times before releasing the keys and allowing the startup process to proceed.

Now restart your Mac without holding down any keys. If the PRAM/NVRAM zap didn't fix your Mac, move on to the section "Step 4: Reinstalling OS X."

Your chosen startup disk, time zone, and sound volume are reset to their default values when you zap your PRAM. So after zapping, open the System Preferences application to reselect your usual startup disk and time zone, and set the sound volume the way you like it.

Step 4: Reinstalling OS X

I present the procedure to reinstall the system software as a second-to-last resort when your Mac won't boot correctly because it takes the longest and is the biggest hassle. I detail this reinstallation procedure at length in an article at www.dummies.com/extras/elcapitan.

Read the article, and follow the instructions. If you're still unsuccessful after that point, you have no choice but to consider the last step. Keep reading.

Step 5: Things to try before taking your Mac in for repair

To get your Mac up and running again, you can try any of the following:

- **Call the tech-support hotline.** Before you drag it down to the shop, try calling 1-800-SOS-APPL, the Apple Tech Support hotline. The service representatives there may be able to suggest something else that you can try. If your Mac is still under warranty, it's even free.

- **Ask a local user group for help.** Another thing you might consider is contacting your local Macintosh user group. You can find a group of Mac users near you by visiting Apple's User Group web pages at www.apple.com/usergroups.

✔ **Try Dr. Mac Direct.** Doctor Mac Direct is (in all due modesty) the troubleshooting, training, and technical support site I started over a decade ago. I'm no longer affiliated, but my former Senior Agent in Charge, Pat Fauquet, has taken over and is easily a better and more patient troubleshooter than I ever was.

Her only goal is to help you with whatever is ailing your Mac (or iPhone or iPad or other Apple device) at a price you can afford. You can reach her at www.doctormacdirect.com or 408-627-7577.

✔ **Check whether you have RAM issues.** Here's a common problem: If you have problems immediately after installing RAM — or any new hardware, for that matter — double-check that the RAM chips are properly seated in their sockets.

Don't forget to shut down your Mac first. *With the power off and your Mac unplugged,* remove and reinsert the RAM chips to make sure they're seated properly.

If you still have problems, remove the RAM chips temporarily and see whether the problem still exists.

Follow the installation instructions that came with the RAM chips or the ones in the booklet that came with your Mac.

First discharge any static spark, either by using an antistatic strap (available from most RAM sellers) or by touching an appropriate surface (such as the power-supply case inside your Mac) *before you handle RAM chips.*

Some new Macs, notably some MacBook and MacBook Air models, don't have upgradeable RAM. So before you open your Mac, check online to see whether its RAM is upgradeable.

If none of my suggestions works for you, and you're still seeing anything you shouldn't when you start up your Mac, you have big trouble. You could have any one of the following problems:

✔ Your hard drive is dead.

✔ You have some other type of hardware failure.

✔ All your startup disks are defective (unlikely).

The bottom line: If you still can't start up normally after trying all the cures I list in this chapter, you almost certainly need to have your Mac serviced by a qualified technician.

If Your Mac Crashes at Startup

Startup crashes are another bad thing that can happen to your Mac. These crashes can be more of a hassle to resolve than prohibitory sign problems, but they are rarely fatal.

You know that a *crash* has happened when you see a Quit Unexpectedly dialog, a frozen cursor, a frozen screen, or any other disabling event. A *startup crash* happens when your system shows a crash symptom any time between the moment you flick the power key or switch (or restarting) and the moment you have full use of the Desktop.

Try all the steps in the previous sections *before* you panic. The easiest way to fix startup crashes (in most cases) is to just reinstall OS X from the Recovery HD partition. I detail this procedure at great length online, at www.dummies.com/extras/osxelcapitan. If you're still unsuccessful after that point, read the "Step 5: Things to try before taking your Mac in for repair" section.

21

Almost Ten Ways to Speed Up Your Mac Experience

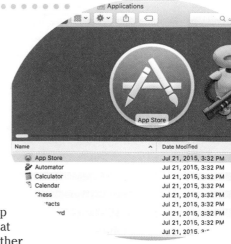

This chapter is for speed demons only. At some time in their Mac lives, most users have wished that their machines would work faster — even if their Macs have multiple cores or processors. I can't help you make your processors any faster, but here's where I cover some ways to make your Mac at least *seem* faster. Better still, at least some of these tips won't cost you one red cent.

Because this is a chapter in the infamous Part of Tens, the powers that be require the word *ten* in the chapter title. But try as I might, I couldn't come up with ten ways to speed up your Mac. The nine tips that follow were the best I could do. So if you think of another great way (or two) to speed up your Mac, please send it to me at ElCapitan4Dummies@boblevitus.com. If your suggestion is really good, I'll include it in the next edition and give you full credit for thinking of it!

Use Those Keyboard Shortcuts

Keyboard shortcuts (see Table 21-1 for a nice little list of the most useful ones) can make navigating your Mac a much faster experience compared with constantly using the mouse, offering these benefits:

Table 21-1		Great Keyboard Shortcuts
Keyboard Shortcut	*Name*	*What It Does*
⌘+O	Open	Opens the selected item.
⌘+. (period)	Cancel	Cancels the current operation in many programs, including the Finder. The Esc key often does the same thing as Cancel.
⌘+P	Print	Brings up a dialog that enables you to print the active window's contents. (See Chapter 16 for info on printing.)
⌘+X	Cut	Cuts whatever you select and places it on the Clipboard. (I cover the Clipboard in Chapter 6.)
⌘+C	Copy	Copies whatever you select and places it on the Clipboard.
⌘+V	Paste	Pastes the contents of the Clipboard at the spot where your cursor is.
⌘+F	Find	Brings up a Find window in the Finder; brings up a Find dialog in most programs.
⌘+A	Select All	Selects the entire contents of the active window in many programs, including the Finder.
⌘+Z	Undo	Undoes the last thing you did in many programs, including the Finder.
⌘+Shift+?	Help	Brings up the Mac Help window in the Finder; usually the shortcut to summon Help in other programs.
⌘+Q	Quit	Perhaps the most useful keyboard shortcut of all. Quits the current application (but not the Finder because the Finder is always running).
⌘+Shift+Q	Log Out	Logs out the current user. The login window appears onscreen until a user logs in.
⌘+Delete	Move to Trash	Moves the selected item to the Trash.
⌘+Shift+Delete	Empty Trash	Empties the Trash.

Part VI
The Part of Tens

Enjoy another Part of Tens list at www.dummies.com/extras/osxelcapitan.

In this part . . .

- Ways to speed up a pokey Mac
- Awesome Mac websites worthy of your attention

✔ If you use keyboard shortcuts, your hands stay focused on the keyboard, reducing the amount of time that you remove your hand from the keyboard to fiddle with the mouse or trackpad.

✔ If you memorize keyboard shortcuts with your head, your fingers will memorize them, too.

✔ The more keyboard shortcuts you use, the faster you can do what you're doing.

Trust me when I say that using the keyboard shortcuts for commands you use often can save you a ton of effort and hours upon hours of time.

Make a list of keyboard shortcuts you want to memorize, and tape it to your monitor or where you'll see it all the time when using your Mac. (Heck, make a photocopy of Table 21-1!)

Improve Your Typing Skills

One way to make your Mac seem faster is to make your fingers move faster. The quicker you finish a task, the quicker you're on to something else. Keyboard shortcuts are nifty tools, and improving your typing speed and accuracy *will* save you time, plus you'll get stuff done faster if you're not always looking down at the keys when you type. As your typing skills improve, you also spend less time correcting errors or editing your work.

The speed and accuracy that you gain have an added bonus: When you're a decent touch typist, your fingers fly even faster when you use those nifty keyboard shortcuts. (I list a gaggle of these in the preceding section, in Table 21-1.)

An easy way to improve your keyboarding skills is by using a typing tutor program such as Ten Thumbs Typing Tutor ($25.95 at www.tenthumbstypingtutor.com) or any of the myriad of typing-instruction apps you'll find in the Mac App Store (search for *typing*).

Resolution: It's Not Just for New Year's Day Anymore

A setting that you can change to potentially improve your Mac's performance is the resolution of your monitor. Most modern monitors and video cards (or onboard video circuitry, depending on which Mac model you use) can display multiple degrees of screen resolution. You change your monitor's display resolution in the Displays System Preferences pane. First, click the Display tab and then click the Scaled button, which makes a list of resolutions appear, as shown in Figure 21-1. Select the resolution you want to try from the list below the Scaled button.

Display tab

Scaled button

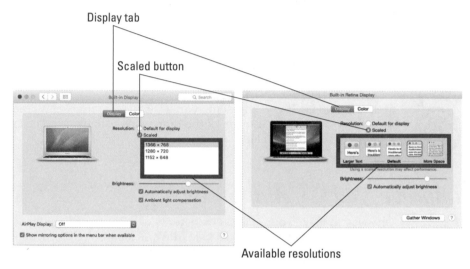

Available resolutions

Macs with Non-Retina Displays   Macs with Retina Displays

Figure 21-1: Lower resolutions make things larger onscreen.

You see much more at native resolution, but everything is much bigger at lower resolutions, as shown in Figure 21-2.

Figure 21-2: My MacBook Air at its highest resolution, 1366 x 768 (left), and its lowest, 1152 x 648 (right).

Here's the deal on display resolution: The first number is the number of pixels (color dots) that run horizontally, and the second number is the number of lines running vertically. It used to be that fewer pixels refreshed faster. But with LCD and LED (flat-panel) monitors and notebooks, this usually isn't true — or if it *is* true, it's almost unnoticeable. Furthermore, because you can see more onscreen at higher resolutions, a higher resolution reduces the amount of scrolling that you have to do and lets you have more open windows on the screen. Finally, the highest resolution is almost always the native resolution of that display, which means it will usually look the sharpest. So you could just as easily say that higher resolutions can speed up your Mac experience as well.

On the other hand, if you can't discern icons in toolbars and other program components, using a lower resolution may actually enhance your work speed.

Choose a resolution based on what looks best and works best for you. That said, if your Mac seems slow at its current resolution, try a lower resolution, and see whether it feels faster.

A Mac with a View — and Preferences, Too

The type of icon display and the Desktop background that you choose affect how quickly your screen updates in the Finder. You can set and change these choices in the View Options window. From the Finder, choose View➪Show View Options (or use the keyboard shortcut ⌘+J).

The View Options window, like your old friend the contextual menu, is . . . well, contextual: Depending on what's active when you choose it from the View menu, you see one of five similar versions (shown in Figure 21-3). Clockwise from upper-left, the figure shows the options for the active window (Applications) in Icon view, List view, Column view, Cover Flow view, and the view options for the Desktop.

A handful of settings can affect the speed of your Mac or your ability to see what you want quickly:

- **Icon Size:** The smaller the icon, the faster the screen updates, especially if the folder has many graphic files with *thumbnails* (those little icon pictures that represent the big picture the file contains).

  In the Icon view of the View Options window, moving the Icon Size slider to the left makes icons smaller and faster; moving it to the right makes them bigger and slower. In List view, select one of the two Icon Size radio buttons to choose smaller (faster) or larger (slower) icons. The difference is greater if you have a slower Mac.

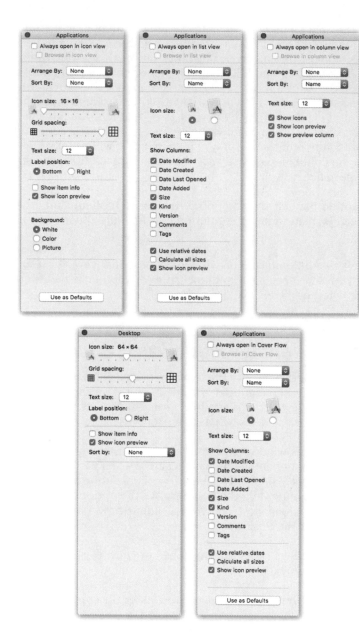

Figure 21-3: Your choices in the View Options windows.

▸ **Calculate All Sizes:** If windows in List view take a little while to populate after you open them, try deselecting the Calculate All Sizes check box in the View Options window for List view. If you activate this option, the Finder calculates the size of every folder of every open window in List view and displays that number in the Size column. At least to me, the screen feels as though it redraws faster with this feature turned off.

If you want to know how big a folder is, you can always just click it and choose File⇨Get Info (or use the keyboard shortcut, ⌘+I).

▸ **Show Columns:** When it comes to speed, don't worry about the Show Columns check boxes in the View Options window for List view — Date Modified, Date Created, Size, Kind, Version, and Comments. The effect of these items on screen updating is small these days, so your choice should be made according to the specific information you want to see in Finder windows, not on whether choosing them slows your Mac.

The Use as Defaults buttons at the bottom of the Icon, List, and Cover Flow View Options windows set the default appearance for *all* Finder windows of that type. If you don't click the Use as Defaults button, any changes you make apply only to the active window (Applications in Figure 21-3). Note that Column view windows and the Desktop don't have a Use as Defaults button; in both cases, any changes you make automatically become the defaults.

Get a New, Faster Model

Apple keeps putting out faster and faster Macs at lower and lower prices, and all Macs now ship with at least 4GB of RAM. And even though 4GB is officially enough RAM to run El Capitan, if you like to keep a few apps running all the time, it's not enough to run it at its best.

Check out the latest iMacs and Mac minis — they're excellent values. Or if you crave portability, MacBook Air and MacBook Pro models are rocking good computers and have never been less expensive. You might even consider a used Mac that's faster than yours. eBay (www.ebay.com) has hundreds of used Macs up for auction at any given time. Shopping on eBay might just get you a better Mac at an outstanding price. Or try Craigslist (www.craigslist.org) if you prefer to see and touch the Mac before you commit. Give it a try! Another excellent option is to visit the Apple website's refurbished and clearance section (http://store.apple.com/us/browse/home/specialdeals).

You can frequently save hundreds of dollars by purchasing a slightly used Mac that has been refurbished to factory specifications by Apple. Another advantage to Apple refurbs is that they come with an Apple warranty. If you're on a tight budget, definitely check it out.

You Can Never Have Too Much RAM!

You get a lot of bang for your buck when you upgrade your Mac's RAM. Get an additional 2GB, 4GB, or even 8GB; you can never have too much. Your Mac will run better with at least 8GB of RAM, which will cost you less than $100 in most cases and can be installed by anyone. Yes, anyone — the instructions are right there in your User Guide booklet, or you can find them at the Apple Technical Support pages (www.apple.com/support; search for *RAM upgrade* and your Mac model).

Unless, that is, you own a certain late-model MacBook, MacBook Air, or iMac. These models are exceedingly difficult to open, and Apple frowns upon users opening the MacBook Air. Plus, some of these models have RAM soldered to the motherboard and can't be upgraded. You might want to opt for the services of an authorized, certified Mac cracker-opener to perform your MacBook Air or iMac RAM upgrade (if yours is upgradeable). The bottom line is that it's best to order your Mac with as much RAM as you can in the first place.

Get an Accelerated Graphics Card

An accelerated graphics card is designed to speed up one thing: the screen-update rate. They're extremely popular with graphic arts professionals and with gamers. Accelerated graphics cards blast pixels onto your screen at amazing speeds. And because the OS X Quartz Extreme imaging architecture hands off part of its load to the processor on an accelerated graphics card, it might make your Mac's other tasks faster because it does some of the work that your Mac's main processor (CPU) used to do. That's the good news.

The bad news is that you can use a graphics accelerator only if your Mac has an accelerated PCI slot or Thunderbolt connection for it, which is where you install these suckers. Only the previous generation Mac Pro models are equipped with accelerated PCI slots. And although the current Mac Pro includes a pair of powerful GPUs (graphics processing units), they aren't upgradeable. There are no Macs in production as of this writing with internal PCI slots, but you'll still be able to add an accelerated graphics or other PCI cards to most Mac models using external devices connected via Thunderbolt.

I've included this topic to get you to at least consider ordering your next Mac with an upgraded video subsystem. Most Macs today are available with at least two levels of video subsystem; consider ordering the higher-performance model. Put it this way — if you're thinking about upgrading the video in your current Mac, you'll probably be happier if your next one has the fastest video you can afford.

Visit www.macworld.com for information on the various graphics cards available and how they compare with one another. Cards start at around $100 and go up from there. And remember, the older your Mac, the greater the performance boost you'll see.

Get a Solid-State Drive (SSD)

The latest and greatest storage device is a solid-state drive (SSD). It uses flash memory in place of a mechanical hard drive's spinning platters, which means, among other things, that it has no moving parts. Another benefit is that an SSD performs most operations at up to twice the speed of mechanical drives.

The bad news is that an SSD is somewhat more expensive — two or three times the price per gigabyte — of a mechanical hard drive with the same capacity. That said, most users report that it's the best money they ever spent on an upgrade. I put the biggest one I could afford (960GB) in my MacBook Pro and I'll never go back to booting from a hard disk.

Honestly, folks, if you're only going to do one thing to make your old Mac faster, this is what you should do: Replace your hard drive with an SSD. Your old Mac will do everything faster.

Get a New Hard Drive

Depending on how old your Mac is, a faster hard drive could provide a substantial speedup. Because you have a Mac with an Intel processor ('cause Macs with older PowerPC processors can't run El Capitan), the internal hard drive that came with your Mac is probably pretty fast already. Unless you also need more storage space, a new hard drive is probably not the best way to spend your bucks.

On the other hand, if you have an older model, a faster (and larger) hard drive — whether FireWire, USB, or Thunderbolt — could be just the ticket. USB 3 and Thunderbolt are the fastest *busses* (data pathways) you can use for external devices on most Macs.

FireWire and Thunderbolt are the state of the art in connecting devices that need fast transfer speeds. Both connect devices that require high-speed communication with your Mac — hard drives, CD burners, scanners, camcorders, and such. FireWire is often the fastest bus that an older Mac will support natively.

The most recent Mac models that had FireWire used the type called FireWire 800, which has a different type of connector than does FireWire 400, which was available on older Macs. If you get a device that has only FireWire 400, and your Mac has only FireWire 800 (or vice versa), everything will work as long as you get a FireWire 400–to–FireWire 800 adapter cable, available at the Apple Store and many other places.

Thunderbolt, which is available on Mac models introduced since 2012, is the fastest bus around by far. That said, there are still relatively few Thunderbolt peripherals at this writing. Furthermore, the Thunderbolt devices that are already out there are significantly more expensive than their FireWire or USB counterparts. So although Thunderbolt shows tons of promise for the future, at present, Thunderbolt hard drives are currently more expensive than either FireWire or USB drives.

And just to confuse things, all new Macs since 2014 use USB 3 (Universal Serial Bus 3), which is many times faster than the previous generations of USB (and FireWire).

If you're buying an external USB drive, get one with USB 3. It isn't much more expensive than a USB 2 drive these days and is speedy on Macs with USB 3. If your Mac doesn't have USB 3, you should get a USB 3 drive anyway. It'll run at the same speed as a USB 2 drive on your current Mac — and will run a lot faster on your new Mac when you upgrade.

If you're not sure what generation of USB your Mac has, choose About This Mac, click the System Report button to launch the System Information application, and then click USB in the hardware list on the left.

The good news is that whatever you choose — USB 2, USB 3, Thunderbolt, FireWire 400 or 800, or a hard or solid-state drive — you can usually just plug it in and start using it. Most of the time, there's nothing more to it!

One last thing: The new MacBook (not the MacBook Pro or MacBook Air; this is the newest model, which is just a MacBook) has USB 3, but also has a new port for it known as a USB-C port. The USB-C port is the MacBook's only port and is used for recharging as well as connecting peripherals. Because the port is incompatible with any other type of USB cable ever made, if you have a new MacBook, you'll need a USB-C adapter for every device you want to use with a new MacBook.

22

Ten Great Websites
for Mac Freaks

In This Chapter

▶ The Mac Observer

▶ Macworld

▶ AppleWorld.Today

▶ TidBITS

▶ Download.com

▶ Alltop

▶ Apple Support

▶ Other World Computing

▶ EveryMac.com

▶ dealmac

As much as I would love to think that this book tells you everything you need to know about using your Mac, I know better. You have a lot more to discover about using your Mac, and new tools and products come out every single day.

The best way to gather more information than you could ever possibly soak up about all things Macintosh is to hop onto the web. There you can find news, *freeware* and *shareware* (try-before-you-buy software) to download, troubleshooting sites, tons of news and information about your new favorite OS, and lots of places to shop.

The sites in this chapter are the best, most chock-full-o'-stuff places on the web for Mac users. By the time you finish checking out these websites, you'll know so much about your Mac and OS X El Capitan that you'll feel like your brain is in danger of exploding. On the other hand, you might just feel a whole lot smarter. Happy surfing!

The Mac Observer

www.macobserver.com

The Mac Observer gives you Apple news, views, reviews, and much more.

Disclosure: I write columns and reviews for The Mac Observer regularly. But I loved The Mac Observer long before I wrote a word for it. Its best feature is that it offers insightful opinion pieces in addition to the usual Apple news and product reviews. The quality and depth of the writing by the TMO staff is superior to most other sites covering the Apple beat.

Macworld

www.macworld.com

Although the print publication ceased to exist last year, this site still describes itself as: "Your best source for all things Apple." And it's still true. Macworld is perhaps the best and most comprehensive source of product information for Apple products. It's especially strong for reviews of Mac and iPhone/iPad products. For example, when you want to know which inkjet printer or digital camera is the best in its price class, Macworld can almost certainly offer guidance, feature comparison charts, and real-world test results. And you won't merely find product information here — you'll find it accompanied by expert opinions and professional editing and fact checking.

Put another way, I trust the writers and editors at Macworld more than I trust the writers and editors of many other Mac-oriented websites. Any other Mac-oriented sites, that is, except the others in this chapter.

AppleWorld.Today

http://www.appleworld.today

For the latest in Mac news, updated every single day, check out AppleWorld. Today, which arose from the ashes of The Unofficial Apple Weblog (TUAW) after its untimely demise. With an excellent staff of Apple newshounds, this site keeps you on the bleeding edge of Mac news — including software updates, virus alerts, and Apple happenings. It also offers extensive and unbiased reviews of many products soon after their release.

I consider AppleWorld.Today essential for keeping up with what's new and cool for your Mac — and I have since its inception in 2014.

TidBITS

http://tidbits.com

TidBITS is an online newsletter and website with the motto: "Apple News for the Rest of Us since 1990." With some of the most insightful and detailed writing on the web, TidBITS is another must-read for me. I always look forward to reading the latest issue (which comes out every Monday) as well as articles posted regularly throughout the week.

Disclosure: I have known the proprietors of TidBITS, Adam and Tonya Engst, since the 1980s and consider them friends. That said, they've prospered and grown for nearly 25 years (check out TidBITS's inexpensive and excellent Take Control series of e-books) because Adam, Tonya, and all TidBITS contributors are still as passionate about sharing information about Apple products and services as they were in 1990.

I recommend subscribing to the email newsletter so that you get a new issue every Monday, like I do. But even if you don't choose to subscribe, you should check out the site; TidBITS is one of my all-time faves.

Download.com

http://download.cnet.com/mac

For free software or shareware, check out the CNET Download site's Mac Downloads section. It's one of the best sites in the world for software to use with El Capitan (or any version of OS X, for that matter). It's also terrific for getting the latest version of any kind of software: commercial, shareware, and/or freeware. Download.com is a virtual treasure trove of software and updates, and it's worth visiting even when you aren't looking for anything in particular.

I love this site and try to visit it several times a week. (I know — I should get a life.)

Alltop

http://mac.alltop.com

Alltop aggregates news from a variety of websites and serves them up in an appealing format that allows you to scan a large number of headlines and summaries from a wide variety of sources in a very short time. This is a case where a picture is worth 1,000 words, as shown in Figure 22-1.

Figure 22-1 shows the custom Alltop page I created at http://my.alltop.com/levitus so I could scan the headlines of my favorite websites quickly and easily. My cursor is hovering over a story I wrote for The Mac Observer.

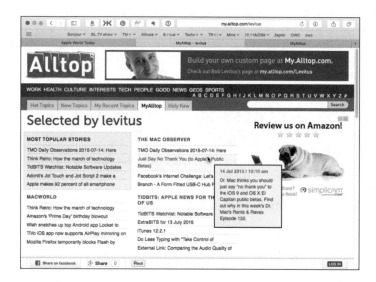

Figure 22-1: Hover the pointer over any headline, and Alltop provides a concise summary of the story.

Note the little summary, which appears only when you hover the cursor over that story. That's Alltop's killer feature, at least in my humble opinion.

You can build your own customized Alltop page at http://my.alltop.com.

Alltop isn't just for Mac news. There are Alltop pages for a plethora of subjects, including

Marketing: http://marketing.alltop.com

Science: http://science.alltop.com

Gadgets: http://gadgets.alltop.com

Filmmaking: http://filmmaking.alltop.com

And literally hundreds more. Alltop has become one of my favorite places to keep track of what's going on in technology today.

Apple Support

www.apple.com/support

Do you have a technical question about any version of Mac OS or any Apple product — including OS X El Capitan? March your question right over to the Apple Support page, where you can find searchable archives of tech notes, software update information, and documentation. The Support pages are especially useful if you need info about your old Mac; Apple archives all its info here. Choose among a preset list of topics or products, and type a keyword to research. You're rewarded with a list of helpful documents. Clicking any one of these entries (they're all links) takes you right to the info you seek. The site even has tools that can help narrow your search.

Doctor Mac Direct

I already had ten sites in this chapter but there's one more site I'd like you to know about (in all due modesty), so consider this sidebar a bonus. Doctor Mac Direct (www.doctormacdirect.com) is the troubleshooting, training, and technical-support site I started over a decade ago. I'm no longer affiliated, but my former Senior Agent in Charge, Pat Fauquet, has taken over and has become a better troubleshooter than I ever was.

Her only goal is to help you with whatever is ailing your Mac (or iPhone or iPad or other Apple device). With expert technicians on staff, Doctor Mac Direct provides jargon-free expert technical help at a fair price, regardless of your physical location — and usually on the same day. Let one of Pat's experts provide high-quality Macintosh troubleshooting, technical support, software or system training, prepurchase advice, and more! It's all accomplished via phone, email, Messages, or custom web-enabled and remote-control software (or El

Capitan Screen Sharing), which lets your agents fix many common Mac ailments in less than an hour, controlling your mouse and keyboard remotely as they explain to you on the phone everything they're doing. Best of all, if they don't fix it, you don't pay!

The next time you need help, and none of the aforementioned sites does the trick, why not let Doctor Mac Direct make the mouse call? (So to squeak.)

Note: This crass commercial message is one of two places in the entire book where I blather on about the service I founded many years ago (and retired from last year). The bottom line is that if there's something you want to know about your Mac, or something you would like examined or fixed, they can probably help you in less than an hour. I hope you'll give them a try.

And that, as they say in baseball, retires the side!

The site also offers a section with user discussions of Apple-related topics. Although not officially sanctioned or monitored by Apple, it's often the best place to gain insights, especially on slightly esoteric or obscure issues not covered in other sections of the site.

Other World Computing

www.macsales.com

Other World Computing has become the go to place for Mac peripherals. Whether you need RAM, hard drives, SSDs, optical drives, video cards, processor upgrades, cables, discs, or anything else you can think of, Other World Computing probably has it at a reasonable price. And, if it's memory or internal storage, it probably comes with a pretty good illustrated installation manual.

Because of its inexpensive and reliable delivery and a solid guarantee of every item, you can't go wrong buying from OWC. I'd say I buy at least half my storage devices and most of my RAM from these guys, and I trust them more than most of the others.

EveryMac.com

www.everymac.com

The author of this site claims that it's "the complete guide to every Mac, iPod, iPhone, iPad, and Mac clone in the world, with technical, configuration, and pricing info."

You can't argue with that (unless you've done a staggering amount of research). Check out the Forum and Q&A sections (recently updated for El Capitan) for answers to Mac-related questions.

dealmac

www.dealmac.com

Shopping for Mac stuff? Go to dealmac (see Figure 22-2) first to find out about sale prices, rebates, and other bargain opportunities on upgrades, software, peripherals, and more.

Figure 22-2: If I didn't still have a drawer full of USB 2 flash drives, I'd be all over this deal.

"How to go broke saving money," this site boasts, and if you're a bargain hunter, it's not far from the truth. Check out the deal in Figure 22-2 and tell me you wouldn't consider a 128GB USB 3.0 flash drive for $30 with free shipping?

Index

About the Author

Bob LeVitus, often referred to as "Dr. Mac," has written or cowritten more than 70 popular computer books, including *iPhone For Dummies, iPad For Dummies,* and versions of *OS X For Dummies* for every cat and California locale Apple has thought up so far, all for John Wiley & Sons, Inc. His books have sold millions of copies worldwide.

Bob has penned the popular Dr. Mac column for the *Houston Chronicle* since 1996 and has been published in dozens of newspapers and computer magazines over the past 25 years. His achievements have been documented in major media around the world and yes, that was him juggling a keyboard in *USA Today* many years ago!

Bob is known for his Apple expertise, trademark humorous style, and ability to translate techie jargon into usable and fun advice for regular folks. Bob is also a prolific public speaker, presenting more than 100 Macworld Expo training sessions in the United States and abroad, Macworld keynote addresses in three countries, and Macintosh training seminars in many U.S. cities. (He also won the Macworld Expo MacJeopardy World Championship three times before retiring his crown.)

From 1986 to 1989 Bob served as Editor-in-Chief of the first desktop-published Mac magazine, *The MACazine*; from 1989 to 1997, he was a contributing editor/columnist for *MacUser* magazine, writing the Help Folder, Beating the System, Personal Best, and Game Room columns at various times.

In his copious spare time, Bob's been working on a pilot for a TV show about — you guessed it — Apple technology. Check it out at www.boblevitus.tv.

Prior to giving his life over to computers, Bob worked in advertising at Kresser/Craig/D.I.K., a Los Angeles advertising agency and marketing consultancy and its subsidiary, L & J Research. He holds a B.S. in marketing from California State University.

Dedication

For the seventy-something-th time (I've lost count), this book is dedicated to the love of my life, my wife and best friend, Lisa, who has pretty much taught me everything I know about pretty much everything I know except technology. You still rock, honey!

And, again for the umpteenth time, this book is also dedicated to my adults (they're not kids anymore), Allison and Jacob, who love Apple gadgets almost as much as I love them (my adults, of course, not my gadgets).

Author's Acknowledgments

A tip of the hat to super-agent, Carole "Swifty" Jelen, who has represented me for as long as I've been writing books — almost 25 years — and is still the world's greatest literary agent if you ask me.

Special thanks to everyone at Apple who helped me turn this book around in record time: Keri Walker, Monica Sarkar, Janette Barrios, Greg (Joz) Joswiak, Teresa Brewer, and others too numerous to mention. I couldn't have done it without you.

Big-time thanks to the gang at Wiley: Steve "Firefighter" Hayes, Andy "Big Boss Man" Cummings, tech editor Ryan Williams, and everyone else at Wiley who put their heart and soul into getting this book to you. And a special double thank you to my long-time editor, Susan Pink, thank you and thank you again.

Thanks also to my family and friends for putting up with my cranky demeanor during my all-too-lengthy hibernation sessions during this book's gestation.

Super-special thanks to Saccone's Pizza, Sodastream, Diet Coke, The Garden Spot Café & Catering, The Noble Sandwich, J. Mueller Meat Company, Hops & Grain's *The One They Call Zoe*, Black's Barbecue, and Torchy's Tacos, for sustenance during the writing process.

And last but certainly not least, thanks to you, gentle reader, for buying this book.

Publisher's Acknowledgments

Executive Editor: Steve Hayes

Project Editor: Susan Pink

Copy Editor: Susan Pink

Technical Editor: Ryan Williams

Editorial Assistant: Claire Johnson

Sr. Editorial Assistant: Cherie Case

Production Editor: Kinson Raja

Cover Image: Front Cover image: Sahani Photography/Shutterstock